The History of
St. Philip's Episcopal Church
1878–1994

Dear Jack,
Thought you might be interested.
The book has been brewing for
twenty-one years and represents
several layers of concern.
Harold

The History of
St. Philip's Episcopal Church
1878–1994

Harold T. Parker

with Judith Hobart Pearson, Sibyl Powe,
Louise Newton, George Pyne, and Betty Hodges

ST. PHILIP'S EPISCOPAL CHURCH, DURHAM, NORTH CAROLINA

Contents

APPENDIXES

Illustrations

Preface

Families have their stories of difficulties surmounted, victories achieved, serious stories and funny stories, of life together and life continuing.

Peoples have their stories. Think of the Hebrews, and their story of crossing the Red Sea and the destruction of the Egyptian host, a story that they told over and over.

The Christians, too, have their story, of the birth, life, sacrifice, and resurrection of Jesus Christ, a story that is remembered in the seasons of the liturgical year and reenacted nearly every Sunday in Holy Communion.

The congregation of St. Philip's Church has its story, which started with the Walk. On Sunday, May 26, 1878 Deacon Joseph Blount Cheshire, Jr., walked the twelve miles from Chapel Hill to Durham and conducted morning and evening prayer for ten or so Episcopal communicants. They met in a second-floor upper room of a store on a dusty main street of a struggling tobacco manufacturing village of two thousand persons, just emerging from Reconstruction and depression. Neither Cheshire nor the congregation knew what, if anything, would come of their meeting, but the communicants hungered for regular worship, and they stepped out in faith.

This book attempts to tell what happened next and next and next . . . , as the history of St. Philip's unrolled in all its complexity until January 30, 1994, when its fifteenth Rector took his leave.

The book, we think, achieves more than one purpose. As a memorial it reminds us of those parishioners who served St. Philip's and have passed on. As an invitation to the living to reflect on their church's past it will enable us to rediscover and to reaffirm its mission in the past, present, and future. In this way a sense of history will serve as ballast, as a steadying force amid eddying winds of doctrine and storms of controversy. More professionally, since the story of St. Philip's was intertwined with municipal, diocesan, and national social trends, this book can be viewed as a contribution to the social history of Durham, the state of North Carolina, and the United States. It can also be regarded as institutional history, as a study of how a religious/ecclesiastical institution evolved in a tumultuous century.

Or, quite simply, the history can be read for fun, as a story filled with suspense.

Acknowledgments

An attempt to mention all the fine people who contributed to the making of this book risks overlooking someone. Yet, even so, the attempt must be made.

The Parish History Committee, formed in 1976 and still in existence, comes to mind first. Four of its members, Gert Embree, Harold Parker, George Pyne, and Richard Watson, served from its inception to the present. Phyllis Bowman, Priscilla McBryde, and Ethel Reade were very active in its early years; Fran Dilts and the Reverend Thomas Rightmyer as well as de facto members Betty Hodges and Dorothy Manning have rendered eminent service recently. The Rectors, the Reverends Thomas Eugene Bollinger, C. Thomas Midyette III, and Scott Benhase, as members ex officio, were continuously supportive. A talented and cooperative group, the committee helped the author in many ways, notably by applauding and correcting successive drafts and by early establishing the principle of Truth above all, even when Truth is unpleasant and may hurt or offend some people. Only a history that is honest and complete will prepare a congregation for actuality, for living in the present and the future.

The co-authors next come to mind. Judith Hobart Pearson extensively researched and wrote Chapter III, "Mission to the Deaf." Sibyl Powe and Louise Newton contributed their inimitable pen portrait of the saint of St. Philip's, the Reverend David Yates. George Pyne assembled the illustrations, and Betty Hodges wrote their captions.

The source base of Vestry minutes and of annual reports delivered to the yearly parish meeting was greatly enlarged in several ways. Early interviews of parishioners were conducted in 1976 by Phyllis Bowman and Harold Parker. The spirit of the early church (1878–98) could not have been caught without those conversations. Later interviews, conducted by Parker and Betty Hodges from 1992 to 1994, focused on specific points of crisis and controversy that needed further illumination. Interestingly, when the interviews were dovetailed and checked with the manuscript evidence, they turned out to be one hundred percent accurate.

However, rarely could interviewees remember what the Rectors and Assistant Rectors said in their sermons. That gap in the evidence was filled by the sermons themselves. The Reverends L. Bartine Sherman and C. Thomas Midyette III deposited a typed copy of nearly all their sermons in the archives of St. Philip's. Also in the archives are copies of sermons by the Reverends Sidney Stuart Bost, David Yates, Tom Turney Edwards, Robert Watson, John Denham, Thomas Eugene Bollinger, Edward F. Glusman, Victoria Jamieson-Drake, and Joanne Stearns. Both thoughtful and inspirational in nature, the sermons greatly contributed to the solidity and reality of our account. The History Committee is planning to publish a collection of them in a supplementary volume entitled *Sermons from St. Philip's.*

Elizabeth (Libby) Roberts discovered in the basement of her house a complete file of the *Epistle to the Philippians*, from its first issue in 1952 through the rectorships of Edwards, Sherman, and Bollinger. Without these Epistles the chapters on those Rectors could not have been composed in their present form. Ben Roberts contributed a photocopy of the chapter of Betsy Holloway's *Unfinished Heaven. Durham, North Carolina: A Story of Two Schools* that describes the remarkable musical careers of the William Twaddells at St. Philip's and elsewhere.

As research associate for this history, David Ross, who was reared in St. Philip's, ransacked the voluminous correspondence of Keith Plummer Lewis that is stored in the North Carolina Collection at Chapel Hill. Lewis was a top executive and eventually president of Erwin Cotton Mills as well as treasurer, vestryman, and senior warden at St. Philip's. His letters clarify several dubious points during the 1920s when the Vestry minutes are absent. Ross also read the *Durham Morning Herald* for the Bost years (1898–1935), the crisis decade of the 1960s, and the achievements of the Midyette tenure (1978–94). In addition, Ross read *The Churchman*, 1963–69, and discovered there Bollinger's article on vestries that formed the basis of my interpretation of his rectorship.

At the next to last minute in the preparation of the index it was discovered that following the sources we had the names of the husbands of the two hundred married women mentioned in the history but we lacked the first names of the women themselves. In response to our appeal, Gert Embree, Betty Hodges, Priscilla McBryde, Dorothy Manning, Nancy Mason, Irene Nashold, Claudia Powe Watkins, Ruth Watson, and Matt West pitched in and identified them. Irene Nashold also located the names of the presidents of the St. Philip's chapter of Episcopal Church Women from 1978 to 1994. These willing, cooperative actions were typical of the aid I have received from many parishioners on many occasions throughout the investigation.

In addition to the existing Parish History Committee, the first draft of the manuscript was read by several "outside" readers: Henry S. Lewis and Lawrence Foushee London, of Chapel Hill, who perused the Prologue and Chapter I; three former Rectors, Tom Turney Edwards, L. Bartine Sherman, and C. Thomas Midyette III, who read the entire volume; as did my neighbor, the Right Reverend Gray Temple, who had served three parishes in North Carolina before moving to South Carolina. The valuable observations of these readers have been incorporated in the text.

Laura Oaks was more than an outside reader. As consultant and creative copyeditor of the first draft of the history, she was an essential participant in its creation. She also recruited Katie Haywood, Stevie Champion, and Shelley Gruendler to prepare the final draft for publication. For their indispensable and invaluable aid we are deeply grateful.

However, since the Parish History Committee accorded me the freedom to accept or reject any suggestion, I am alone responsible for what is said in this history.

July 1, 1996

Harold T. Parker
Parish Historian

The History of
St. Philip's Episcopal Church
1878–1994

Prologue — The Walk

Legend has it that the congregation of St. Philip's took its start when Deacon Joseph Blount Cheshire, Jr., walked on Sunday, May 26, 1878 from Chapel Hill to Durham and conducted morning and evening prayer for ten or so Episcopal communicants in a hall over Duke's store.

Contemporary accounts confirm the legend.[1] Yet the same accounts reveal that there was much more to the story than that. How did it happen that the young deacon had conducted his celebrated walk? The Episcopal Church in North Carolina was largely a missionary church. In North Carolina nearly a million people were dispersed across a rural countryside. There were in the entire state only sixty Episcopal clergymen. Sixty counties were without any Episcopal church. Here and there a few manufacturing villages of two to three thousand people were sprouting, stimulated by the fabrication of tobacco products and textiles. Winston, Company Shops (later Burlington), and Durham were among them. They, a novel sight on the vast rural landscape, and their unchurched Episcopalians caught the eye of the itinerant Bishop Thomas Atkinson and his Assistant Bishop Theodore Lyman as they journeyed across the Diocese of North Carolina, which then covered the entire state.[2]

Sporadically Atkinson and Lyman visited Durham until in 1878 the latter could report: "1st Sunday after the Epiphany, January 13th, in a public hall in Durham, I conducted the service and preached both morning and evening. I was glad to find a considerable addition to the number of our church people, several having gone to Durham since my last visit there. The place is growing quite rapidly, and I felt anxious to do what I could to awaken an increased interest in the church. I promised to make every effort to provide monthly services for them. . . . After the evening service, I baptized an infant at a private house."[3]

The promise of regular monthly services was soon kept. On April 21, 1878 Atkinson received to the Order of Deacons a vigorous young lawyer, Cheshire, Jr., in Calvary Church, Tarboro, the church of Cheshire's father.[4] Soon after, Atkinson informed the younger Cheshire "that he was to serve his diaconate at the Chapel of the Holy Cross in Chapel Hill under the direction of Rev. Robert B. Sutton."[5] The Bishop instructed Cheshire to conduct services once a month in Durham.[6] The young deacon lost no time. He conducted his first service at Chapel Hill on Sunday, May 19, and then on the following Sunday, May 26, made his celebrated walk to Durham. "After spending one Sunday in Chapel Hill," he wrote, "I proceeded to Durham, and on Sunday, May 26, 1878, being 5th Sunday after Easter, I read services and preached morning and afternoon in an upper room known as Duke's Hall." Attending this first of a series of regular monthly services were, to quote Cheshire, "Robert F. Webb and wife, Wm. L. Wall and wife, Spencer W. Chamberlain and wife, Chas. M. Herndon, Henry M. Rosemond, Mrs. M. P. Raiford, Mrs. C. A. W. Barham, Mrs. Claude B. Hooker, Miss Maggie Palmer, besides several others." These had all become members of the Church before their removal to Durham. "Mr. Jack Gammon, Jr., not member of the Church, but desirous of enjoying its regular services," was also present.[7]

So three elements entered into the inauguration of regular Episcopal services in Durham: the missionary concern of two bishops for their flock and for their church ("I felt anxious to do what I could to awaken an increased interest in the church"); the desire of a small group of Episcopal communicants for the comfort of regular worship according to the familiar rites ("I promised to make every effort to provide monthly services for them"); and an active young minister. Yet the event, the Cheshire action, the Walk deserves its place in legend. It was significant: it brought the three elements together; it started a process by which a group of Christians working together under God with a minister and within an Episcopal organization could come to form a continuing institution conscious of its identity.

The sources enable us to see yet a fourth element in the situation: the Book of Common Prayer, which was used in every service throughout the Episcopal Church. As we have seen in his autobiographical remarks, Cheshire very carefully notes that "he read service" and that May 26, 1878 was the Fifth Sunday after Easter. With this in mind we pick up the edition of the Book of Common Prayer he was using, that of 1854.[8] As a deacon, Cheshire could not celebrate Holy Communion; hence, in the morning he led the congregation through the printed Order of Morning Prayer. Imaginatively, we are now with Cheshire and the small group of communicants in the public hall above the store. We read the words along with them. "*The minister shall begin the Morning Prayer, by reading one or more of the following sentences of Scripture.*" Perhaps Cheshire chose "The Lord is in his holy temple; let all the earth keep silence before him. *Heb.* 11:30" or "Let the words of my mouth, and the meditation of my heart be always acceptable in thy sight, O Lord, my strength and my redeemer. *Psalm* xix. 14, 15." There followed the long invitation to confession, said by Cheshire, "Dearly beloved brethren, the Scripture moveth us, in sundry places, to acknowledge and confess our manifold sins and wickedness . . . ," the General Confession said by the entire congregation after the minister, all kneeling, "Almighty and most merciful Father; we have erred, and strayed from the ways like lost sheep. . . ." The Lord's Prayer, said by the minister and people, kneeling, followed.

Anthems and canticles, sung or chanted by the congregation, then alternated with the reading by the minister of a Psalm, a passage from the Old Testament, and a passage from the New Testament according to a prescribed calendar of readings. The congregation then affirmed its faith by reciting together the Apostles Creed or the Nicene Creed. There followed, said by the minister, the Collect for the Day, which for the Fifth Sunday after Easter was, "O Lord, from whom all good things do come: Grant us thy humble servants, that by thy holy inspiration we may think those things that are good, and by thy merciful guiding may perform the same, through our Lord Jesus Christ,"[9] other set Collects including a "Prayer for the President of the United States and All Those in Civil Authority," a General Thanksgiving, a Prayer of St. Chrysostom, and the conclusion: "The grace of our Lord Jesus Christ, and the love of God, and the fellowship of the Holy Ghost, be with us all evermore." When Holy Communion was first administered to the Durham congregation by Assistant Bishop Lyman on Sexagesima Sunday, February 1, 1880, "in a hall,"[10] we can follow in the old Prayer Book the communion rite with them, including the Collect for that day: "O Lord God, who seest that we put not our trust in anything that we do; mercifully grant that by thy power we may be defended against all adversity; through Jesus Christ our Lord."[11] To our knowledge only one thing is lacking: we do not know the sermons Lyman preached in the morning and evening of that day, nor do we have those Cheshire gave at his monthly services.

The Durham group was thus incorporated into the long tradition of Anglican worship: a worship service that was biblical in its reading ("the Anglican Church reads more of the Bible to its faithful than any other group of Christians"), liturgical in its settled and lovely ritual, and sober and restrained in the quality of its devotion. The Book of Common Prayer gave structure and continuity to the worship of every church in the Anglican Communion. In Durham Rectors might come and go; sermons, good, bad, and indifferent, might be given, but the worship services in the cadences of Elizabethan prose went on. Great, shattering events might occur outside the Church. War might be declared in Europe during the last week in July 1914: the Order for Morning Prayer and the Collect for the adjacent Sixth Sunday after Trinity was still said. The stock market might crash on Tuesday, October 29, 1929: the Order for Morning Prayer and the Collect for the Nineteenth Sunday after Trinity were still offered the following Sunday. The Japanese might bomb Pearl Harbor on Sunday, December 7: the Collect for the Second Sunday in Advent was still the order of the day. Throughout the history of St. Philip's this continuity of a prescribed liturgical worship service was always there. It is rarely mentioned, but it flows on, affording to successive generations of communicants consolation, support, and spiritual sustenance.[12]

I

In Search of a Rector
Who Would Stay
1878–1898

Every new congregation has many problems. A chief problem of the Durham group was simply to find a clergyman who would stay for more than a year or two. Each new minister upon his arrival was a hope; and upon his resignation, a disappointment. The Durham congregation could attract able clergymen, but it could not hold them. It is a tribute to the dedication and devotion of the early group of laity that despite the transiency of the clerical leadership the congregation took root and survived.

Part of the problem may have been fiscal. Durham, thanks to the tobacco industry, had grown from a hamlet of approximately 100 persons in 1860 to in 1880 a town of 2,041 people, of whom an estimated 1,347 were white and 694 were black. But it was still only a village, of a few stores, a few factories, a few residences, and dusty or muddy unpaved streets. Ready cash was scarce. In the tobacco-buying season even the Dukes, who were just starting, had to borrow from their mule drivers. The Durham Episcopal congregation paid their ministers $700 annually, which was $100 to $400 less than the Baptist, Methodist, and Presbyterian pastors were receiving and possibly less than Episcopal clergymen were being paid in other cities.[1]

Whatever the reason, the story of the first twenty years is monotonous in its repetition. A new minister arrives; the Bishop reports that he is welcomed by the congregation; he takes hold, attendance is affirmed, he initiates (sometimes) new programs, everything (according to the record) seems to be going well, and he leaves; a new minister arrives; the Bishop reports that he is welcomed by the congregation; he takes hold. . . .

The "Cheshire years" (1878–81) were among the best, and the Durham congregation was off to a good start. For nearly three years Cheshire, who was now Rector at the Chapel of the Cross, came over from Chapel Hill to Durham on the first Sunday of every month (it is not recorded whether he walked!). In three years the number of communicants increased from ten or twelve in 1878–79 to twenty in 1880 and to thirty-five in 1881. On January 4, 1880, the second Sunday after Christmas, after Evening Prayer and a sermon in Duke's Hall, a meeting was held to organize the congregation as an independent Mission Station. Cheshire presided, and he suggested that until the Bishop could be heard from Col. Robert Webb should act as clerk of the congregation, William Wall as treasurer, and Charles Herndon as warden. Upon application from the congregation Bishop Atkinson on February 25 authorized the organization of the Mission Station in Durham, with the officers Cheshire had named. The congregation had been meeting hither and yon—in the schoolhouse, in the mayor's office, in Duke's Hall on Main Street. It was realized that the mission would lack stability and real influence in the community until it had a building of its own. A lot (the present site) was secured on the very edge of town, too distant, it was thought, from the center of commercial activity ever to be desirable for business purposes. Under the supervision of Cheshire and the officers of the mission a pleasing frame church was erected. The lot and the building together cost $2,500. Cheshire, his family, and his friends in Calvary Church, Tarboro, contributed one-fourth of the cost, Cheshire himself giving his savings from his lawyer days.[2] Cheshire named the church after St. Philip, the deacon, "feeling it to be the 'fruit' of his work as deacon."[3] The building was first used for worship on March 27, 1881 and four months later was consecrated by Bishop Lyman on July 24. The ceremony was a fitting climax to the intelligent and dedicated work of Cheshire and his lay associates in the congregation.[4]

No sooner was the church consecrated than the congregation had to look for a minister. Cheshire was reluctant to leave Chapel Hill and Durham, but the Bishop ordered him to St. Peter's in Charlotte and Cheshire conducted his last regular monthly service at St. Philip's in September 1881. It seemed natural for the congregation to call the Reverend Charles J. Curtis. As late as January 1880, as Rector of St. Matthews, Hillsborough, he had ministered when he could to people of the Durham area. He was now in 1881 editor of an Episcopal weekly journal, *The Church Messenger*, with headquarters in Winston. Curtis responded to the Durham appeal and in January 1882 brought the editorship with him. He was not in charge of St. Philip's, but as a missionary he conducted the services and preached there regularly for a year. But a rolling stone often keeps on rolling. By February 1883 he had accepted appointment as traveling missionary evangelist for the Convocation of Charlotte and had transferred his residence to Charlotte. Meanwhile, the number of communicants at St. Philip's had dropped from thirty-five to twenty, so important is vigorous clerical leadership in an Episcopal parish.[5]

Curtis's successor, the Reverend John Huske, came with a good record of developing a young church in Hickory.[6] At first he had the double charge of St. Philip's and the Chapel of the Cross, but in July 1884 he relinquished the latter to devote his entire attention to St. Philip's. During his able ministry the number of communicants rose from twenty (1882) to eighty (1885), and in 1884 St. Philip's achieved the legal status of an independent, self-supporting parish. However, when Bishop Lyman paid his annual visit to St. Philip's on the third Sunday in Lent, March 28, 1886, he was saddened "to learn that Mr. Huske has resigned the charge of the Parish, and had accepted a position in Buffalo, New York." The Bishop added in his annual report, "The Parish is in a very prosperous and encouraging condition, and I trust may speedily be supplied with a faithful and zealous Rector."[7]

The Reverend T. M. N. George, Huske's successor, seemed an answer to the Bishop's prayer. When Bishop Lyman visited Durham on Friday, April 29, 1887 and in St. Philip's Church "preached, confirmed fifteen persons, and addressed them," he could note that the number of communicants had now risen from 80 to 101. Indeed, Lyman was much gratified to observe "the harmonious and prosperous condition of this Parish, and the cordial co-operation, on every side, with their faithful and energetic Rector."[8] Sunday services, as was then customary in all Durham denominations, were three. At St. Philip's, Sunday School was at 9:30 A.M., Mr. William L. Wall, Superintendent; Morning Prayer or Holy Communion with sermon at eleven o'clock; and Evening Prayer at 7:30 or 8:15 P.M., the earlier hour during the winter and the later one during the summer.[9] Regular attendance at all three events was expected of every church member as a matter of course. If communicants were absent, we are told, they were visited that afternoon, on the only possible assumption that they were sick and needed

Christian care. The spirit of closeness and cooperation among members of the congregation was manifested in many acts of dedication. The Vestry placed a furnace in the cellar of the church, "adding greatly to the comfort of the congregation." The interior of the church was improved by recoloring the walls and adding racks to the pews. The Ladies Aid Society bought a new cabinet organ and new white hangings for the chancel. The Children's Sewing Society furnished the chancel with cushions and kneeling stools. The gift of a flagon, by a communicant, completed the communion service. Two alms basins were presented as an Easter offering. The Rector's salary was raised from $700 to $1,000, and in 1889 a rectory was purchased for him.[10]

George led the parish to reach out to meet the spiritual needs of the black people of Durham. The needs of this segment of the population in the Diocese of North Carolina had long been on the consciences of Bishops Atkinson and Lyman. In his report to the General Convention of 1882 Lyman expressed his concern. "Millions of this race are around us," he said, "and a heavy responsibility rests upon us to do what we can to guide their steps aright."[11] The Anglican way, he thought, was especially suitable for them: "I am more and more convinced every day of the special fitness of our Church services for the colored people, and I have no doubt that, before many years we shall have a large ingathering from the ranks of those who now are carried away with the idea that an emotional religion is the only true and acceptable form of Christianity." What was required was "careful instruction, and an intelligent apprehension of the Christian scheme." He was certain that once "these people" were "under proper guidance, the prejudices and errors which now prevail so widely among them, will give place to better and more enlightened ideas."[12] In accord with the spirit of Lyman's observations, the Diocesan Convention of the following year (1883) adopted two resolutions announcing what became diocesan policy for decades to come. The first resolution stated the basic assumption: "That the Church in North Carolina is persuaded that one branch of the One, Catholic and Apostolic Church, of which she is a part, is capable of best ministering to the intellectual, moral and spiritual needs not only of the other races and classes of men in the Southern States, but also of the vast colored population." The second resolution gave the recommended implementing action: "That, in the judgment of this Convention, the Church can best promote the Christian elevation of the colored people, not by giving to them an ecclesiastical organization autonomous and independent of our own, but by fostering colored congregations under the care and supervision of our Bishops, to be represented in our Conventions, and to be ministered to by our own rectors and missionaries, until they can be supplied with duly educated colored Clergymen; and further by establishing and maintaining institutions of Christian learning for their special benefit, and theological seminaries for the training of colored candidates for the ministry."[13]

So it was in harmony with diocesan policy and the best contemporary diocesan thought that George in 1887 "secured the use on Sunday's of a public schoolhouse in 'Haiti,' a colored quarter in Durham," and began "work among the colored people. A colored student from St. Augustine's Normal School came up every week to assist George in the work." St. Philip's paid his expenses. "Regular services were held, and a Sunday School numbering 25 scholars was gathered." In his annual report George commented that "thus far the work is something of an experiment," a journey outward, a venture for Christ into the unknown. "But," he continued, "I hope much from it. We need help to build a chapel and to push on the venture to success."[14]

The next year George expanded the work. With the consent of a Miss Ledgers, the teacher, who was a communicant of St. Philip's, and with the approval of the trustees, all black men, George took over a flourishing Negro school. On weekdays the entire school of thirty to sixty pupils was taught the Church catechism and the use of the Prayer Book. Then, by paying the tuition of sixteen pupils, George obligated these to attend the Negro Sunday School, which he conducted on Sunday afternoons. He expressed the hope that erelong he would have the aid of a black deacon, "to assist in this important work."[15]

However, George did not stay at St. Philip's long enough to bring his labors to fruition. In 1890 Bishop Lyman had to report George's departure from St. Philip's, where he had "endeared himself to the whole congregation and was carrying on so excellent a work." But, the Bishop continued, "It has afforded me much satisfaction to learn that the new Rector, Rev. Mr. Charles Wingate, has been very cordially received and proves a most faithful and acceptable worker."[16]

But Wingate, a seasoned priest from the Diocese of Kentucky, had scarcely time to report that he found St. Philip's "in a most gratifying condition," when he left for St. Timothy's at Wilson, on May 15, 1891.[17] For over a year St. Philip's was without a Rector, until the Reverend Stewart McQueen, of Georgetown, South Carolina, took charge on June 1, 1892. Yet, though the Bishop reported in 1893 that he "was pleased to find that the new Rector had been most cordially received and that everything was going on pleasantly and encouragingly in the Parish," McQueen transferred to the Diocese of East Carolina on October 1, 1894.[18] During another interim year when St. Philip's was without a Rector, the Reverend George Zellers officiated from December 16, 1894 to November 16, 1895, when the Reverend Alfred A. Pruden arrived to give the parish once again vigorous leadership.[19] Through these six interim years from George to Pruden, the number of communicants at St. Philip's slipped. Numbers, especially in an enterprise that is holy, are not everything, of course, but they are sometimes symptomatic of the vigor of a church. Under Huske the number of communicants rose dramatically from 20 (1882) to 80 (1885) and under George from 79 (1886) to 127 (1889). But during the next six years the number dropped and fluctuated: 111 (1890), 97 (1891), 100 (1892), 112 (1893), 95 (1894), and 103 (1895).[20]

Through the six years, however, St. Philip's, in cooperation with the Diocese, maintained the mission to the black people that George had founded. Over the years the mission had eight to twelve communicants, and it steadily maintained a day school for twenty to twenty-five scholars and a Sunday School of the same number. By 1893, although still termed "St. Philip's Mission (Colored)," it had obtained in the *Diocesan Journal* the status of an independent report and had a separate minister-in-charge, the Reverend Franklin L. Bush. The Diocese had appointed Bush to perform the Durham work along with serving the St. James Negro Mission in Pittsboro on alternate weekends. "A native of Boston and graduate of Harvard, he had studied at Berkeley Divinity School in Middletown, Connecticut, and after considerable parochial experience on both sides of the Mason-Dixon line, had resolved to devote himself entirely to a ministry to Negroes."[21] Twice a month Bush officiated on Sunday, "holding service in the small room rented for a day-school. The Rector of St. Philip's Church held a Sunday-school or service on the alternate Sunday evenings in the same place."[22] On his annual visits to Durham Bishop Lyman not infrequently confirmed Negro candidates at the mission. Unfortunately Bush and Lyman died in 1894. The chapel that the Reverend Mr. George had prospected for the mission was never built. On the ground that meeting in a poorly furnished hall rendered the future of the mission precarious, Rev. William Walker, the archdeacon in charge of colored work in the Diocese, transferred the mission schoolteacher to Pittsboro, where there was a chapel, and withdrew diocesan support from the Durham Negro mission. St. Philip's at the moment was without a Rector, and although its officiating minister, probably Zellers, tried to keep the mission going by himself, his efforts came to nothing. It soon closed, presumably in 1895, a casualty, finally, to the incessant turnover of clergy at St. Philip's.[23]

Yet in 1895, a low point in our history, St. Philip's was on the eve of a remarkable expansion that lasted until 1922, as its congregation responded to new challenges and opportunities in Durham and the Diocese. Several factors help explain this expansion. One factor, of course, and an indispensable one, was the growing core of families that stayed with St. Philip's through years of difficulty and of prosperity. All the witnesses—the Bishops, the successive Rectors, the oral testimony of survivors and eyewitnesses—concord in praising the closeness, the harmony, and the Christian dedication of this early and continuing group. It included Mr. and Mrs. Robert F. Webb, Mr. and Mrs. William L. Wall, Mr. Charles M. Herndon and his family, Mrs. Henry M. Rosemond, and Mrs. C. A. W. Barham, who were with the congregation at the start, in 1878. To them were added in 1880, Mr. Abbott E. Lloyd and Mr. and Mrs. DeWitt C. Mangum; in 1881, Mrs. Eliza Jane Burcham and Mr. and Mrs. John T. Mallory; in 1882–85, Mr. and Mrs. Charles P. McGary and Mr. and Mrs. William Bell McGary; in 1886, Mr. and Mrs. R. W. B. Happer and Mr. and Mrs. Reuben Hibberd; in 1887, Mr. and Mrs. Herbert J. Bass, Mr. and Mrs. William A. Guthrie, Mr. and Mrs. Abraham B. Sites, and Mr. and Mrs. John W. Webb; in 1888, Mr. and Mrs. William J. Griswold, Mr. and Mrs. Charles Jetton, Mr. and Mrs. James S. Manning; and Colonel and Mrs. Richard B. Sauders; in 1889, Dr. and Mrs. John M. Manning and Mr. and Mrs. A. H. Michaels; in 1892, Mr. and Mrs. William A. Erwin and Mr. E. K. Powe, and shortly after Mr. and Mrs. J. H. Erwin.[24] Others, to be mentioned in due course, joined in the early twentieth century. They lived, for the most part, near the church on Dillard, Ramseur, Queen, and adjacent streets; St. Philip's was their neighborhood parish. In 1890 the Reverend Mr. Wingate, one of the Rectors-in-passage, went out of his way to testify to their spirit. "He desires to put on record the fact that he found the Parish in a most gratifying condition, thoroughly organized for its work, and the people very zealous and ready to co-operate with him in every enterprise for its welfare."[25] They were serving the Lord together, in and through His Church, with joy.

A second factor was Durham, the growth of its population and the enterprising spirit of its leading businessmen. Durham was then an up-and-coming, self-confident, proud manufacturing community. Its innovative businessmen were doing innovative things, in tobacco manufacturing and textiles, to make money and, as it turned out, to build enterprises renowned throughout the world. They were doing something new in the South. They were using local resources in raw materials, capital, and labor to develop more resources, new wealth. From 1880 to 1900 the population of Durham and the adjacent urban areas septupled, from 2,041 to 14,100, and then went on increasing, at a somewhat slower rate, to 28,300 in 1920 and 52,037 in 1930.[26] Here in the new migrants, and especially in the factory operatives, was an opportunity and a challenge to the Durham churches. The congregations were aware of this. During the summer of 1895 the Durham Sunday School Association canvassed the inhabitants of Durham Township with respect to church membership. The devastating results were published in the *Durham Daily Sun*:[27]

	White	Colored
No. of church members	3,244	1,489
No. not church members	4,290	2,706
No. attending Sunday School	3,086	1,341
No. not attending Sunday School	4,457	2,854
No. promised to attend	381	261
No. persons over 21 years of age	3,487	1,999
No. persons under 21 and over 4	3,207	1,710
No. persons under 4	849	477
No. printed invitations given	1,348	778
No. visits made	1,517	1,003

The response of the Durham congregations, as announced in the *Daily Sun*, was interesting. "A Union Meeting," the article said, "of all the churches will be held on next Sunday night, August 4th, at 8 o'clock, at the First Baptist Church, to perfect or adopt some plan to overtake the religious destitution and neglect in the County and town of Durham as indicated by the Statistics of the Colporteur's report gathered by a careful canvass recently made. Addresses will be made by prominent representative laymen from the different congregations. E. J. Parrish will preside. Everyone in the town ought to attend this meeting."

The Durham spirit of enterprise—the faculty for seeing opportunities, for seizing opportunities, and for getting things done—was carried from business into the field of education and, as we shall see again and again in this history, into religious affairs. In education, Washington Duke gave $100,000 and Julian Shakespeare Carr donated the land to bring Trinity College from western North Carolina to Durham in 1892. Under the college presidencies of John Crowell and John Kilgo there was always an air of fame about early Trinity and insistence on the attainment in freedom of the highest standards of academic performance and Christian conduct. By 1900 the Carnegie Endowment could find only two colleges in the entire South that met its standards for reception of pensions for retired professors. One of these was Trinity and the other Vanderbilt in Nashville, Tennessee. Through participation of its faculty and its graduates in the life of the community, Trinity exercised a pervasive influence upon the main-line Durham congregations. "Through the medium of its school of religion, especially, Trinity was to have a broadening and liberalizing effect on the local theological climate of opinion."[28]

A third factor in the growth of St. Philip's and the expansion of its influence in the Diocese of North Carolina was the leadership of two Rectors, Alfred A. Pruden (1895–98) and Sidney Stuart Bost (1898–1935), and of a Bishop, our old friend Joseph Blount Cheshire (1894–1933). Pruden followed the early pattern of not staying long, but while he was at St. Philip's he was very effective. He did things, and he made sure that what he did was suitably recounted in the *Durham Daily Sun*. Episcopal churches do not generally hold revivals, but in November 1896, a year after Pruden's arrival, St. Philip's sponsored a "preaching mission" by a visiting clergyman, a Reverend Mr. Winecoff. Under the column head

BUSTLING DURHAM
The News of a Day to be Read Today

the *Daily Sun* for Thursday, November 12, told what went on:

> The mission now being held at St. Philip's church, is growing in interest. The people are becoming deeply interested in spiritual matters.

A large congregation was out last night, and Mr. Winecoff preached from Matt. 6–12: "Forgive us our debts as we forgive our debtors." God does not deal in shams. Everything is reality with Him. He wants everyone to open the way for forgiveness of sin so that He may do his perfect work. He does not forgive unless we forgive those who trespass against us. God unites with man in sending away sin, but He will not do it unless man is willing. Man must make the effort and fight against his own sin — then God comes in and helps him. It was a plain sermon, but very pointed and practical.

A growing number of petitions were sent up by persons who desired prayers for themselves, their friends, and the sick and afflicted.

Services again this evening at 7:30. The public is cordially invited.

This little article appeared on page one, column one, where in the 1890s the *Daily Sun* printed the news of the churches. Also, at the bottom of column one (and we quote just to give atmosphere) appeared a two-line advertisement: "Others have found health, vigor and vitality in Hood's Sarsaparilla, and it surely has power to help you. Why not try it."

When Lent came in 1898 Pruden did not hesitate to advertise the services at St. Philip's in the *Daily Sun*. Over his name, A. A. PRUDEN, on page one, column one, of Saturday, February 26, appeared an article explicating the Episcopal philosophy of Lenten observance:

FIRST SUNDAY IN LENT

The services that will be held at St. Philip's Church Tomorrow will be the first Sunday in Lent, and the services at St. Philip's church will be as follows:

9:30 A.M., Sunday School

11 A.M., Morning Prayer, Litany, Altar Service and sermon.

5 P.M., Evening Prayer.

Although the Sundays in Lent are not to be observed as Fast days (being weekly commemorations of the resurrection of our blessed Lord and are, therefore, always Feast days) yet the devotional tone given to them in Lessons, Litany, Epistles, and Gospels, is carefully assimilated to that of the season, and a constant memorial of it is kept up by the use of Ash Wednesday's Collect, after that of the week, on Sundays as well as week days.

It is said by some, your church enjoins fasting during Lent, is not this Romish? We answer, no. We read in the Bible that Christ fasted, but nowhere can we find that Christ lived, taught or practiced the teachings of the Roman Catholic Church. Our Lenten fast is neither a gift nor an offspring of the Roman Catholic Church; nor is it a co-incident of any of the special seasons of the religious bodies around us, call them revivals, or whatever name you choose, for Lent is not a time for excitement, but rather for quiet; it is a going apart into the wilderness, quiet, solitude; the beginning of self, face to face with self, so to speak. It is the time, as another has so beautifully said, "to get rid of vice and substitute virtue, to get rid of sin and substitute the Christian graces," to drive from the soul earth-born baseness and fill the soul with pure, bright light. The world cannot see this, the world sees only the other side.

May God grant we may see what the world cannot see, and if our Lent be real, our spiritual life strengthened, what difference if the world see it not. A. A. Pruden.

Also, on page two of the *Daily Sun* (once we start quoting the newspapers we just can't stop):

Mules for Sale

Duke and Durham have a lot of fine mules for sale, which can be seen at McGown's stable. If you want a good team here is your chance. See them.

And on the last page, another nostalgic item:

Original Observation

It takes thirteen minutes to load an elephant on a train, while it takes twenty for a woman to kiss her friends good-bye and lose the check of her trunk. — Orange (Va.) Observer

But on page four, something more serious, as the Spanish-American War looms:

Situation Graver
Accident Theory of Maine Disaster Almost Abandoned

And on Monday, February 28, appeared a story about a St. Philippian:

WEST DURHAM NEWS IN A SPICY WAY

Caught Up and Served up by H. A. Riggs, Reporter and Agent. Last Saturday afternoon C. M. Herndon sent several bunches of fresh fish up here to those who were sick and needed them. This was a very kind and Christian act on the part of Mr. Herndon. W. G. Lasaster very kindly distributed them for him, and he comes in for his part of the praise.

Meanwhile, on Wednesday, March 2, Pruden announced in the *Sun* a series of mid-week Lenten lectures on the Book of Common Prayer, and each week thereafter he published a précis of the lecture to come. His course "set forth the Anglican concept of the Church as an organic body, an interpretation quite at variance with individualistic sectarianism encouraged by the doctrine of the so-called 'free' churches."[29] He taught his parishioners and anyone else in town who read the *Daily Sun*:

Christ did not write a book. He gathered a few persons around him and formed a society, trained them, sent them out. Christianity is a living organism, an institution, not merely a philosophy or scheme of doctrine.[30]

Under Pruden St. Philip's was obtaining such excellent coverage of its programs that in the Methodist and Baptist town of Durham it provoked critical comment. The editor of the *Daily Sun* felt called upon to explain:

We have several times asked why we publish so much about the services of St. Philip's Church. That is easily answered. It is because that church pays for the space occupied by these notices — something that no other church has done in Durham, that we know of, and consequently it has access to our column; in other words, it is a business transaction, based on dollars and cents.[31]

Truly Pruden had his own style. And it was effective. "In Pruden's first year, he baptized more people and presented more candidates" for confirmation to the Bishop "than had been seen in many a year; and similar gains were registered in the succeeding years of his pastorate."[32]

In twenty-eight months the number of communicants increased from 103 to 183![33]

At the same time Pruden was bringing the West Durham and East Durham missions within the orbit of St. Philip's jurisdiction and activity. The Sunday School in West Durham had been pioneered by William A. Erwin, secretary-treasurer and general manager of Erwin Cotton Mills, a Duke enterprise. When in 1892 the Dukes decided to invest in cotton textiles, they sought out the best manager in North Carolina, and found him in Erwin, then thirty-six years old. A native of Burke County in western North Carolina, Erwin was a member of the Holt family, which had for many years been prominent in textile manufacturing and in the Episcopal Church. He was "a grand-nephew of Edwin M. Holt, founder of an important antebellum textile enterprise, and for a decade or so prior to moving to Durham he had served as the treasurer and general manager of the famous E. M. Holt Plaid Mills in Burlington, North Carolina."[34] A big man physically, a leader wherever he went, Erwin had also been the main force in establishing in Burlington an Episcopal Sunday School and St. Athanasius's Church.[35] He was already a great giver of his time, energy, and money to the Church.

When he came to Durham in 1892, Erwin repeated the career he had already achieved in Burlington. He brought with him as manager of production in his plant a fellow Episcopalian, E. K. Powe. Several years later he added to his enterprises his brother, J. Harper Erwin. The three men joined St. Philip's. Though a newcomer, Erwin was soon a member of the Vestry; in 1895 he and Powe were elected lay delegates of St. Philip's to the Diocesan Convention.[36] In business Erwin borrowed from New England textile capitalists the concept of the mill village, which they in turn had borrowed from great Britain, where the idea had originated with Robert Owen's father-in-law. It was a concept that harmonized with many psychologies of paternalism, from the philanthropic socialism of an Owen to the Christian paternalism of an Erwin. In the mill village the company benevolently took care of its employees by building and then leasing them houses, providing a company store, and, in Erwin's case, maintaining an Episcopal Sunday School. "Each Sunday, with the assistance of W. B. LaFar, Erwin instructed some 75 of his employees, assembled in the second-story hall of the combination store–post office owned by the mill, in the Scriptures and Prayer Book catechism." When Pruden arrived, he "began to visit West Durham on Friday nights to conduct services for the mill-hands, while Erwin and LaFar continued the Sunday classes." [37] At the other end of town, Pruden also worked with Mrs. Eliza Jane Burcham and her family to establish a Sunday School in East Durham.

Everything seemed to be going along fine, everything seemed in control, when in mid-Lent 1898, before Pruden had completed his Lenten series of lectures, he resigned. Appropriately, the news of his resignation reached the town and indeed most of his parishioners on page one, column one, of the *Daily Sun*. On Tuesday, March 22, 1898, the lead article read:

THE RECTOR RESIGNS
Called Meeting of the Vestry Last Night
Mr. Pruden is an Earnest Worker and the Public
Regrets to Hear of This

There was a called meeting of the Vestry of St. Philip's Church last evening, at which the Rector, Rev. A. A. Pruden, tendered his resignation, to take effect on the 16th of May.

This is a surprise to the people of Durham, and many of the churchmen, as Mr. Pruden has been an earnest and enthusiastic worker, and is highly esteemed in this community, where he has been doing a good work during his Rectorship, covering a period of twenty-eight months.

The causes leading up to this action are a matter with which the SUN has nothing to do, and takes no part in, but as our readers will be curious to know, we will state that it grew out of matters pertaining to the affairs of the Church, and like all such things in a church family, there are two sides, and it is not the desire of this paper to go into details. Mr. Pruden had his reasons for tendering his resignation, and he acted upon them. The Vestry, as well as his Parish, regret the matter has taken such a turn, and hope that the spirit of brotherly love will prevail in the end.

Mr. Pruden has done a very aggressive work here during his Rectorship, and the register shows nearly as many confirmations in that time as during the former sixteen years. The actual number, heretofore being 90; and during the past twenty-eight months, 70.

At present Mr. Pruden has no definite plans for the future, and will continue his relations with this Parish until his resignation takes effect. He has made warm friends here who will sincerely regret his determination to sever his connection with this Parish, and his work and influence will be held in lasting remembrance by our progressive city.

2

The Bost Years: Expansion, Consolidation, and Hesitation 1898–1935

Perhaps with Alfred A. Pruden and certainly with his successor, Sidney Stuart Bost, St. Philip's entered a new phase in its history. Prior to Pruden a core of dedicated families kept St. Philip's alive. Rectors came and went, but the families stayed and kept the church on course. With Pruden and Bost the core of dedicated and influential families continued as a stabilizing force, but the Rector became the central figure in the congregation's life and history. He was the shepherd of his flock—the focus of regard, the authority to whom people turned, and the trusted counselor and friend. In technical ecclesiastical terms St. Philip's was becoming a pastoral church.

THE SETTING

Bost's official title was Rector of the Parish of St. Philip's, which then included the mother church of St. Philip's and its two parochial missions in West Durham and East Durham. Bost thus related to three neighborhoods: the cluster of original families that still lived within five minutes' walking distance from the church and from each other on Dillard, Holloway, Queen, Mangum, and Ramseur Streets; the textile manufacturers, William A. Erwin and E. K. Powe, and their textile mill employees who lived a mile distant in West Durham, which was not legally incorporated into the city until 1925; and a small group of Episcopal families that resided in East Durham. At first on Sunday Bost conducted services for all three congregations.

The Durham that Bost entered was a rather small town of nearly 7,000 people, with about twice as many whites as blacks. The majority of the black community lived across the railroad tracks from St. Philip's in an area that came to be known as Hayti. There were in Durham separate black and white churches, public schools, colleges, hospitals, restaurants, and even fire-hose companies. Notably in contrast to the several black Baptist and Methodist churches, there was no black Episcopal church in Durham until 1909, when St. Titus was founded as a diocesan mission. At the turn of the century the division of the population into two separate racial groups was being formalized in law. As a result of the "white supremacy" elections of 1898 and 1900 most blacks in North Carolina were disfranchised. And as late as 1928 in Durham only fifty black citizens were registered voters. A series of Jim Crow laws was segregating access to public accommodations. By 1920 "the separation of the races had become so complete that everywhere in the south duplication of public accommodations was provided: black and white restrooms, drinking fountains, railroad cars, waiting rooms, hotels, and restaurants. Blacks were confined to balconies in theaters and to the back seats of city buses."[1]

In Durham, however, it was segregation with a difference: both white and black sectors were up-and-coming communities. In the white community industrialists of drive and ingenuity were building immensely profitable tobacco and textile enterprises. By their multiple charities they were supporting their churches, Watts Hospital, and an aspiring and struggling Trinity College. It was very important to the destiny of St. Philip's and its Rectors that the founders of Erwin Cotton Mills, William A. Erwin, J. Harper Erwin, and E. K. Powe, its later executives, Kemp P. Lewis, William H. Ruffin, and Nat Gregory, and their descendants were members of the parish.

Meanwhile, in the black community business and educational leaders of like drive and ingenuity were founding similar enterprises: John Merrick and Charles Clinton Spaulding (North Carolina Mutual and Provident Association in 1898), Richard Burton Fitzgerald (the Mechanics and Farmers Bank in 1908), and James Edward Shepard (an educational facility in 1910 that eventually grew into North Carolina Central University). When Booker T. Washington visited Durham in 1910 he wrote enthusiastically about "black Durham's progress," attributing it not only to "the ambition and thriftiness of the Negro" but also to the tolerant attitude and generosity of the leading whites, such as Washington Duke.[2] W. E. B. Dubois after a visit in 1912 identified what made Durham different from other places in the South: "I consider the greatest factor in Durham's development to have been the disposition to say 'Hands off—give them a chance—don't interfere.' "[3] During the first three decades of Bost's rectorship, from 1898 to 1928, Durham was thus in all sectors an active, thriving, self-confident, wide-awake town that was expanding in substantial wealth and increasing in population (from 6,679 in 1900 to 52,037 in 1930).

Yet in this wide-awake, up-and-coming town there were still interrelated tensions between white and black, employer and employee, capital and labor. Such tensions would later explode in violent action and impinge on the history of St. Philip's; hence, their existence should be noticed now. They appear, for example, in the papers of Kemp P. Lewis, which are in the North Carolina Collection at Chapel Hill. Lewis was a leader in every field of endeavor: in business he was an executive of Erwin Mills and eventually became its president; as a devoted church worker he was Treasurer of St. Philip's and at one time an active member of the Diocesan Executive Council; as a civic leader he was a member of the Durham Board of Education and deeply concerned about the quality of instruction in the public schools. In his papers there is a letter, dated October 26, 1925, from the Board of Directors of the Interracial Committee for the County of Durham, requesting a contribution of ten dollars. The board was composed of eight white and six "colored" business, educational, and civic leaders. Names such as Dr. J. E. Shepard, Dr. S. L. Warren, W. G. Pearson, J. M. Avery, C. C. Spaulding, and W. Gomez among the black community still command recognition. Among the whites was Burke Hobgood, an eminent St. Philippian. The letter said that "the relation between the two races here in Durham has always been good; we believe at the present time it is fine." Nevertheless, the board "attempts to iron out in its incipiency any instances and causes for friction between the races before such instances or causes can, by running along unnoticed, develop into something of a serious nature." Lewis shared their sentiments and said so with his pocketbook. At the same time it was part of his complex of attitudes that he was concerned when northern representatives of the American Federation of Labor invaded Durham and by their agitation stirred "negro helpers" to demand a raise in daily pay from $1.65 to $3.00. He hoped the City Council would deny use of the municipal auditorium by the AFL to show a pro-labor movie and would thus help to keep things quiet.[4]

St. Philip's was a member not only of the Durham community but also of the Episcopal Diocese of North Carolina, whose Bishops, diocesan institutions, and diocesan policies affected the parish's history in many ways. During its formative years St. Philip's, by great good fortune, worked with two outstanding Bishops, Joseph Blount Cheshire (1893–1932) and Edwin Anderson Penick (Bishop Coadjutor 1922–32, Diocesan 1932–59). They belonged to different generations (Cheshire was born in 1850, Penick in 1887), they encountered in the Diocese different conditions, and they had very different personalities and styles of action; but they were alike in their ability to focus on the central problems of their times.

To members of his flock, young and old, Cheshire was an unforgettable figure. Lawrence London, his biographer, wrote: "As very young boys, my brothers and I were fond of looking at him for with his flowing white beard and rather stocky figure, he appeared the very embodiment of Santa Claus!" Priscilla McBryde was likewise impressed: "To me, as a little girl, looking up at him standing beside the high altar in St. Philip's Church, in his voluminous bishop's robes (I never saw him that I remember with staff or mitre), he was so impressive that I thought he must look like God!" [5]

Cheshire was blunt and forthright: he was known to stop an organist and choir in the middle of an anthem or a hymn if the tempo was too difficult or the harmony too flowery. He loved hunting and fishing, and he enjoyed a reputation as a raconteur of rare charm. But his main passion was to extend the work of God's Kingdom by bringing the Episcopal Church to the unchurched in the Diocese and by developing diocesan institutions. By 1898 the Diocese of North Carolina had long since relinquished (in 1883) the eastern counties of the state to the Diocese of East Carolina and was in the process of severing its connection with the western counties, which were to form the Missionary District of Asheville under Bishop Junius M. Horner. This left the Diocese of North Carolina with the central counties and the most populous towns, Raleigh, Durham, Greensboro, Winston-Salem, and Charlotte. In those towns there were organized Episcopal congregations. But in between them "many communities in the Diocese with from one to eight Episcopal families were without the services of the Church. There were some communities, and in a few cases entire counties, where 'the teachings of the Episcopal Church were unknown.'" Among them, the

Executive Missionary Committee reported, there were "over 100,000 persons living in the cotton mill villages in much spiritual destitution who needed the sympathy and aid of the Church."[6]

As Bishop Cheshire responded to that need and opportunity, he remembered the happy days when as rector at the Chapel of the Cross (Chapel Hill) and St. Peter's (Charlotte) he was establishing mission churches: "I believed I worked harder and with more enthusiasm in my mission of St. Philip's, Durham, and afterwards in establishing St. Mark's, Mecklenburg . . . than in any other work I ever undertook." He continued as Bishop to treat the Diocese as his personal parish. He was tireless in his visitation of existing churches, tireless in writing to them—more than 66,000 letters longhand (he did not have a secretary until late in his tenure)—and tireless in recruiting missionary clergy and parishes to undertake the foundation of mission churches. In 1901–2, to supervise the missionary endeavor, he persuaded the Diocesan Convention to establish three convocations: the Convocation for Work among Colored People, and (for white congregations) the Convocation of Raleigh and the Convocation of Charlotte, each with an archdeacon to direct missionary work within his jurisdiction. The effort paid off. By 1912, for example, sixteen missions had been established in industrial towns.

Bishop Cheshire and the clergy were not alone. Working with them was "a core of helpers comprising the Woman's Auxiliary, the Brotherhood of St. Andrew, and the Daughters of the King, all of whom helped to widen the influence of the Church in North Carolina."[7] At this point the Woman's Auxiliary especially deserves attention. First organized in the Diocese of North Carolina in 1872 under the title of Woman's Auxiliary to the Board of Missions, it had by 1900 "a total of 596 members in 36 branches. St. Peter's, Charlotte, had the largest number (48), followed by St. Philip's, Durham (34); Holy Innocents, Henderson (34); Christ Church, Raleigh (30); and St. Luke's, Salisbury (30)."[8] It played so important a part in "the growth of mission work inside and outside the Diocese" that Bishop Cheshire in 1901 was moved to exclaim, "to the Women of the Auxiliary I can only say what I have so often said before—that their assistance has been so effective in the missionary work that no Bishop can now understand how the Church ever could have gotten on without it."[9]

In a male-dominated society, however, participation in the government of the Church came late to its women, who did much of its work.

As late as 1900 the president of each parish chapter of the Woman's Auxiliary was the rector, who appointed its officers; the president of its diocesan organization was the Bishop. Nor, by diocesan canon, were women permitted to vote in a congregational meeting for members of the Vestry, to serve on the Vestry, or to be delegates to the Diocesan and National Conventions of the Episcopal Church. Bishop Cheshire's attitude toward the question of woman suffrage illuminates the sentiment then prevailing among many people. His biographer, Lawrence London, writes:

> He made no reference to the subject in any of his addresses to the annual Diocesan Conventions. He evidently did not wish to exert his influence either for or against the proposed amendments, although he privately expressed his opposition. On the place of women in parochial and diocesan work and on woman suffrage, the bishop made his position quite clear in response to an inquiry from a layman in another diocese. He replied that women had no part in the legislative work of his Diocese. Their field of endeavor was in the Woman's Auxiliary and other voluntary organizations which he thought were "important and effective." The bishop continued: "As to my personal view on the subject I am strongly opposed in sentiment and judgment to women suffrage in both civil and ecclesiastical matters. It seems to me opposed to the fundamental conception of the very important and sacred function of women in the scheme of human life." Moreover, he said, "I do not observe, so far as I have opportunity of observing, that where women have been admitted to the suffrage any special good results have come from it." Although these views seem strange today, they were not uncommon at that time.[10]

The legislature of North Carolina refused to ratify the Nineteenth Amendment, which accorded the suffrage to women and came into effect in 1921. Nor were Cheshire's views held only by men. As late as 1913 the Woman's Auxiliary of the Diocese in its Annual Convention disapproved, by a vote of twenty-five chapters against to four in favor, the proposal to grant women the suffrage in congregational meetings.

Nevertheless, gradually, very gradually, legal discriminations were removed. In 1904 women in each parish or mission chapter were granted the power to elect their own president and officers, while their delegates to their own Auxiliary Diocesan Convention could choose its officers. In 1918 and 1919 two successive Diocesan Conventions, composed of male delegates elected by male Vestries, enacted a cautiously worded amendment to the canons: "any parish may by vote of the majority of the voters at present qualified permit all members of the Parish of the age of twenty-one years" to vote in a parish election. St. Philip's was one of the first churches in the Diocese to avail itself of this option, when in 1919 its qualified male voters admitted qualified women to vote for the Vestry. The diocesan canon restricting service on the Vestry to men remained in force until the 1960s.

BOST THE BUILDER

Sidney Stuart Bost was fitted by his education and personality for effective work in Durham and the Diocese of North Carolina. At that time not all pre-ministerial students attended a seminary; they could instead "read" theology and liturgy with a practicing rector, just as law students used to read law with an attorney. By good fortune Bost was born on February 12, 1871 in Rowan County near Salisbury, and thus had the opportunity to read theology with Dr. Francis J. Murdoch, rector of St. Luke's, Salisbury, and the most eminent educator of pre-ministerial candidates in the Diocese of North Carolina. Murdoch taught not simply by words but by example. He stayed at the same parish for thirty-eight years, from 1872 until his death in 1910. He founded mission churches, twelve in all, both inside and outside Rowan County. One of these was a mission church in the cotton mill town of Cooleemee, built in 1899 with the assistance of William A. Erwin of Durham. Murdoch was, in the words of Bishop Cheshire, "a pioneer in parochial missions." And he involved himself in community affairs. When a visiting evangelist observed in 1883 that what Salisbury "needed most besides religion was a good cotton mill, Murdoch took the lead in organizing the Salisbury Cotton Mills and became its secretary-treasurer." Bishop Cheshire, always understanding, stated in a memorial address on Murdoch that "this secular side of his interests grew out of a high and unselfish desire and effort for the good of others." [11] In all this—length of tenure at a single church, institution of missions, easy cooperative working relationship with leading industrialists, and involvement in secular affairs to do good—Bost resembled his mentor.

By all reports Bost was gentle by nature, modest in manner, a friend to all, a good shepherd to his flock, quietly firm and persevering in his action. He entered into the lives of his parishioners. Kate Herndon, who was born in 1882 as the daughter of St. Philip's first senior warden and lived to celebrate in 1978 the centennial of the congregation's first meeting, told many stories of Bost and the early congregation that reveal its spirit and closeness. Her favorite was the tale of the Old Man, the Old Horse, and the Rector, which should enter some collection of North Carolina folklore. The Herndons lived on Ramseur Street, a few blocks from the church. Bost often dropped in for a visit and sometimes a meal. During the last years of his life Kate's father, Charles Herndon, became blind from glaucoma. When the family horse became so enfeebled by age that he lay on his side in the backyard and would not get up, the blind old man strained to lift his old companion to his feet, until the family feared for their father's life. To save him they mixed in the horse's mash a large dose of strychnine, sufficient to kill any ordinary horse. The poison served as a tonic, and the old horse pranced around the yard, good as new. The family turned to Bost, their counselor and friend. He got out a long-barreled revolver, aimed it between the horse's eyes, and fired. The horse merely looked at Bost, shook his head, saying in effect, "you do not do that to me," and walked toward him. It took a second shot to bring the horse down.

St. Philip's was Bost's first parish and his last. Ordained deacon by Bishop Lyman in 1892 and priest by Bishop Cheshire on May 31, 1896, he accepted the offer of St. Philip's on May 20, 1898 at an annual salary of one thousand dollars.

From the start he was an innovator and a builder. Because the extant Vestry minutes do not begin until 1914, we cannot discern at first the process by which he worked, but from his annual reports to the Diocesan Convention we can record the results. In St. Philip's alone he found, on his arrival, 64 families, 305 baptized persons, and 183 communicants. In addition to these, Bost wrote, "services are held every Sunday afternoon in a hall in West Durham. This service is in connection with the Mission Sunday School which is under the efficient superintendency of Mr. W. A. Erwin and enrolls about 100 pupils. Everything considered, this is the most flourishing Sunday-school this writer has ever seen. The pupils from eldest to youngest are thoroughly drilled in the Church catechism. This mission work in the hands of

7 devout men and women cannot but bear precious fruit for the Church." [12] His remarks are confirmed by the record of an interview with Erwin's nephew, J. Harper Erwin, Jr., who remembered his Uncle Will as a big man physically, tall and broad-shouldered, who towered over every group he was in: "a hard worker, an exacting man who did not spare either himself or others in business or in the work of extending God's kingdom, he made sure that Sunday School students were *drummed* in the Ten Commandments," including the catechetical injunction against "picking and stealing."

Since Erwin is a major figure in this history, these passages are interesting both in themselves and for what lay behind them. The Sunday School met Sunday afternoon so that Erwin's Baptist, Methodist, and Presbyterian textile mill employees could attend the services at their own churches in the morning. Erwin contributed financially to the support of their churches as well as his own, but he taught in the West Durham Episcopal Sunday School. The Sunday School taught a strong ethical stance in which Erwin firmly believed as a Christian but which was also advantageous to him as an employer and a well-to-do member of society. It is to his credit that he was aware of the problem of reconciling his Christian duties of paternalistically caring for the spiritual, ethical, and material welfare of his employees with the necessity of making a profit. Caring for his employees in a mill village, he thought, was both Christianity in action and good business, by assuring a stable workforce. But he also recognized that if, hypothetically, there was a conflict between Christian benevolence and the necessity to pay dividends to the principal stockholders, the Dukes, the latter option must take precedence. Erwin's honesty, his realism, and his lack of self-deception mark him as a superior person, a big man not only in physique but in character as well. In a complex, rapidly changing industrializing society which posed multiple ethical choices that were novel and not always as simple and clear as they once had been, he labored indefatigably to do what was right.[13] It was also to his credit that, as Bost predicted, Erwin's Sunday School bore fruit in a full-fledged Episcopal mission, where Bishop Cheshire confirmed as many as five persons annually in the West Durham meeting hall.

By 1900 Bost could report to the Diocese that he hoped to found a mission in East Durham. A. E. Burcham, the historian of the mission, tells how this came about in a story that recapitulated the formation of St. Philip's more than twenty years before:

It was about the year 1900, on a hot Sunday afternoon, when a group of interested members from St. Philip's Church came down to East Durham. They met in a hall over a Drug Store at the southern end of Driver Avenue.

Among those who came to that first meeting were our beloved Rector, the Rev. Sidney S. Bost, Mr. William L. Wall, Col. J. Harper Erwin, Mr. and Mrs. Charles M. Herndon, Sr., Mrs. R. W. Winston, Miss Laura B. Saunders. There were others whose names I do not recall at this time.

There to meet the above mentioned group was the Burcham family, the only Episcopalian family in East Durham at that time. Also a good number of children, who were affiliated with the Methodist or Baptist churches, and probably some that were not connected with any church.

During the early months of the school, we moved to the East Durham school building and met there for a short while. In about 1901, Col. J. Harper Erwin bought a lot on Hart Street and gave it to the parish on which to build a chapel. Members of the Brotherhood of St. Andrew provided the money for the building. It is obvious from this why the name St. Andrew's was chosen.[14]

As a parochial mission of St. Philip's it was to play an important role in our history, its congregation distinguished by dedication and zeal.

Bost then turned to another problem that could no longer be ignored. Attendance at St. Philip's itself was increasing so rapidly that the old frame church, built for two hundred people in 1880, was bursting at the seams. Soon after the turn of the century tentative plans were made to raise money for a new building. The services of Ralph Adams Cram, of Boston, the foremost ecclesiastical architect of his time, were secured, probably through Bishop Cheshire's New England connections. The first service in the handsome brownstone structure was held on the first Sunday of Advent in 1907. Bost had already persuaded the Vestry in 1905 to grant him an Assistant Rector, Deacon Thomas Lee Trott, who had "read" for the ministry with Bost's mentor, the Reverend Francis J. Murdoch. So, it was appropriate that at this glorious inaugural service Murdoch should be the main speaker and Bost should present Trott to Bishop Cheshire for ordination to the priesthood. The *Durham Morning Herald* gave the occasion a front-page spread. The building, it said, was "one of the most beautiful [churches] in this section of the state." It stood "as a monument to the work of the Rev. S. S. Bost, the rector," "through whose efforts the new church was built," and to the officials who worked with him. The service, the article added, included the installation of a vested choir and recognition of recently elected vestrymen. Their names testify to Bost's ability to hold representatives of the older families, such as William A. Erwin, A. E. Lloyd, John M. Manning, James S. Manning, and William Wall, while attracting new parishioners, such as George Carr and Kemp Lewis, who would be among the leaders of the future.

After the bills were paid and the new church was consecrated in 1912, St. Philip's hosted the annual Diocesan Convention. Bishop Cheshire, once the deacon who had walked from Chapel Hill to Durham on May 26, 1878 to hold the congregation's first service, singled out St. Philip's for praise in his annual address:

> How changed is the outward aspect of St. Philip's! The small frame building, which the few, who can remember it thirty-one years ago, regarded as a great achievement for our little band, has given place to this beautiful stone structure; and even this is hardly adequate to the needs of the growing congregation. This change indicates a wonderful increase in numbers and in material resources, and a corresponding increase in the power and opportunity of extended service. I am happy in the belief that this congregation is not wholly unresponsive to its increasing responsibilities, but that rector and people are endeavoring to bear their share in the work of extending God's kingdom, both at home and abroad.[15]

Actually, Bost and the congregation of St. Philip's were living up to Bishop Cheshire's vision for them. Trott, as assistant in charge of the West Durham mission, was proving to be an ideal choice. Before coming to Durham he had already served as deacon in the Cooleemee textile mission founded by Murdoch and Will Erwin. He and Erwin continued to work well together, and the West Durham mission flourished. In 1908 Erwin gave it a handsome stone church of Rowan County granite, as a memorial to his parents Joseph J. and Elvira J. Erwin. The mission itself was designated St. Joseph's.

Bost was now free to turn his attention to a special mission, ministry to the deaf, previously a neglected unchurched group:

He was influenced to take on this unusual ministry by Miss Robina Tillinghast, who had come to Durham to teach the deaf. Bost threw himself wholeheartedly into the work and even learned to "sign." In May 1906 the missionary to the deaf from Baltimore, the Reverend Mr. Oliver J. Whildin, was able to present seventeen deaf people for confirmation. The work was supported in part by funds contributed by Bishop Cheshire. A Sunday school session was held at St. Philip's every Sunday afternoon, and usually the group stayed on for the remainder of the afternoon, regarding this relaxed social encounter as the highlight of their week. Miss Tillinghast started a week-day kindergarten for deaf children in 1915 "in the mute room of the Parish House," but this was allowed to lapse when she had to resign in January 1915 to return to her parents in South Carolina. Bost then recommended Roma Coxey Fortune, who had been a member of the first deaf confirmation class, as leader of the group. He thus launched Mr. Fortune's career, which was to bring him to the priesthood and to national prominence as a leader of work for the deaf, both in the Church and in legislatures and law courts. For his own work and for his sponsorship of Fortune's work Bost was granted the Cross of the Order of the Sangreal in 1931.[16]

In answering a particular need—the silence in which the deaf lived—with a particular measure, the mission to the deaf, St. Philip's under Bost's leadership had persuaded the larger diocesan community to be of service. Bost's work was such a significant example of St. Philip's outreach that a separate chapter of this history (Chapter III, by Judith Hobart Pearson) is devoted to it.

Like his bishop Joseph Blount Cheshire, his mentor Dr. Francis J. Murdoch, and his St. Philip's colleague William A. Erwin, Bost was animated by zeal to extend the work of God's Kingdom. In 1912 he even started traveling once a month to conduct services at "an unorganized but encouraging mission at Holly Springs." Bost continued there for three years, until 1915, when the mission could be organized.

On December 4, 1916 at the annual congregational meeting of St. Philip's Parish, which included St. Philip's Church and its missions St. Joseph's and St. Andrew's in West Durham and East Durham, Bost summarized the growth of the Parish during his rectorship. The official figures show that the number of families had increased from 64 in

1898 to 183 in 1916, the number of baptized persons from 305 to 902, and the number of communicants from 185 to 614. Aggregate annual offerings had risen from $1,596.69 to $5,315.03 plus a $2,000 payment on the rectory debt, and the value of church property from $6,100 to $51,000 minus a debt of $6,000. The minutes continued: "The growth was alluded to by the Rector as being very satisfactory, and his remarks were very gratifying to the congregation."[17]

CONSOLIDATION

By 1916 the Episcopal ecclesiastical landscape in Durham had assumed the shape it was to retain for a generation: in the white community, a mother church, St. Philip's, and its two parochial missions, St. Joseph's and St. Andrew's; in the black community, St. Titus, a diocesan mission. There was close contact between St. Philip's Church and its two missions, but very little between St. Philip's and St. Titus.

The favorable situation of St. Philip's Parish in 1916 gave Bost and his close associates the opportunity to take stock, to work at problems that had risen during a period of uninterrupted expansion, and to consolidate the gains already achieved. A run-through of the Vestry minutes from 1914 to 1921 and of the minutes of the meetings of the Brotherhood of St. Andrew from 1916 to 1923 enables us to look at the institutions and operations of an Episcopal parish at the opening of the twentieth century, before and during World War I. We also have records from interviews, conducted by Phyllis Bowman and Harold Parker in 1976, with surviving parishioners for whom the Bost years were a significant experience: Lester C. Butler, Sarah Lindsey Boettke, Amy Burcham, J. Harper Erwin, Jr., Nat Gregory, Kate Herndon, Richard and Kitty Leigh, Angus and Priscilla McBryde, Nelson McGary, Kitty Nelson, Claudia Powe Watkins, and Hugh White. Their memories encourage the historian to attempt the impossible: to recapture and to convey the spirit of St. Philip's Church as its congregation entered, without expecting it, a second period of transforming alteration.

St. Philip's Church in 1916 was a congregation of Christian families who worshiped God together by the Episcopal Prayer Book of 1892. Nearly everyone still lived within a few blocks of the church. At the Sunday morning service at eleven o'clock each family by immemorial custom sat in its own pew. On the Epistle side of the church, for example, the first pew was occupied by the Burchams, Mr. and Mrs. A. E. Burcham and Mr. and Mrs. C. H. Burcham, who came over from their homes in East Durham. Along with Mr. and Mrs. J. E. Abernethy they were the founders and mainstays of St. Andrew's Chapel, and on Sunday evenings they attended another service there, also conducted by Bost. The Herndons, Mr. and Mrs. Charles M. Herndon, now an elderly couple, and their grown son, Charlie, Jr., sat in the second pew; their three daughters had probably moved away, though Kate would return. In back of the Herndons were the Erwins, who came over from West Durham for the service: in the third pew, William A. Erwin, president of Erwin Cotton Mills, and his family; in the fourth pew, E. K. Powe, his general manager who had married Erwin's sister Claudia, and their children; and in the sixth pew William Erwin's brother, J. Harper Erwin, and his family. To the children of E. K. Powe and of J. Harper Erwin, William Erwin was Uncle Will. The Gregorys, Mr. and Mrs. J. M. M. Gregory and their five children, Mary, John, Priscilla, Nathaniel (Nat), and Claiborne, sat in the fifth pew. Until recently they had lived in a house beside the church on Queen Street, which was now the rectory. When Nat grew up, he too would become an executive in Erwin Mills. Throughout the congregation there were similar family and business relationships.

The service—Holy Communion and a sermon on the first Sunday of each month, Morning Prayer and a sermon on the other Sundays—was "very, very low church": no candles in the chancel, no genuflections, a rudimentary choir singing hymns, no chanting, no dramatics, no innovations; just the simple, profound, powerful, and familiar phrases and action of the Anglican liturgy and the cadenced passages from the King James version of the Bible. When in 1919 the Misses Cowan offered to give St. Philip's eucharistic lights as a memorial to their mother, the Vestry thanked them warmly but declined the gift and gave its reason for doing so: "The Vestry has reason to believe that the introduction of Eucharistic Lights as the *First Offering* of lights in our chancel would be regarded (at least, by some persons) as a departure from the moderate and conservative type of churchmanship which has prevailed in this parish, and might tend to mar the harmonious spirit that has kept us a happy and united congregation."[18] Bost's sermons, likewise, were "low-key": he just talked, slowly, deliberately, earnestly, the fundamental theology and ethics of the Apostles Creed and the Ten Commandments, which he read each Communion

Sunday. Everyone agreed that Bost was a wonderful man, a true friend and counselor, and a "regular guy": everyone also agreed that his sermons were interminable. The communion service and sermon lasted sometimes two hours, even in the heat of a Southern summer, the children growing restless or, perhaps best of all, falling asleep.[19] Yet in these years everyone, it appeared, accepted the service and its implicit theology without discussion, skepticism, or controversy. This was the faith in which they had been baptized, confirmed, and married; it was the faith by which they would be buried.

It was expressed concretely in the eulogy Bost delivered at the memorial service held at St. Philip's in honor of General Julian S. Carr, an eminent Durham citizen. When people said, "Isn't it a pity that General Carr cannot know today how much he was appreciated," Bost responded: "I would have to subtract much from my faith if I thought that the thing which we call death means the loss of apprehension, the loss of the intelligent, the sensory and the vital touch. He does know. Jesus said, I am the Resurrection, and the Life. He that liveth and believeth in Me shall never die."[20] The faith was also expressed by Mrs. A. E. Burcham, a founder of St. Andrew's, when she was interviewed for this history in 1976. Now a widow, after sixty-four years of marriage, she was living alone. Yet she was not afraid. Every night before going to bed she recited the Twenty-third Psalm ("Though I walk through the shadow of death, I will fear no evil for thou art with me"). She fell asleep in perfect assurance that the Lord had her in charge and would let no harm befall her.

It was this faith that was communicated in Sunday School, during the hour before the eleven o'clock service. The teachers of the seventy enrolled students were mostly women, often parents of the children who were being taught. The older children met in the church, the younger grades in the old frame church that had been built in 1880 and then moved behind the brownstone structure in 1907 to serve as a parish house. Cleared of pews, its auditorium was now a multipurpose room for congregational meetings, Vestry meetings, and Sunday School classes. With six classes of lively children seated around six tables in an unpartitioned room, it is difficult to see how any teaching and learning went on in the buzz of conversation and inevitable noise. But we are assured that it did, through illustrated Bible stories; memorization of Bible verses (for which several pupils received prizes), the Ten Commandments, and the catechism; and study of the seasons of the church year and of a list of 101 questions and answers Bost had prepared.[21] Meanwhile, the men of the congregation met in the Men's Bible Class and the women of the Altar Guild prepared the altar for the service. Sunday evenings at 6:30 the young people of the church met in the parish house for candy pulls and games. The Sunday School year concluded with a grand congregational picnic at Lakewood Park, which was then the western terminal of the city's trolley cars and had "a merry-go-round, a roller coaster, a lake for swimming, a rink for roller skating, and a pavilion for dancing."[22] At the picnic, while the women assembled the food—fried chicken, ham, boiled eggs, deviled eggs, and potato salad—and tended the young children, the men and the older boys and girls "gabbled" and played games.

In the haze of golden memory, these days were recalled nostalgically as a time when the congregation of St. Philip's Church was one large family where everyone had known everyone else for years and years. When the Hope Valley contingent seceded in 1958 to form St. Stephen's it was in order to recapture their youth. "Wouldn't it be wonderful," they said, "if we had a church of our own, so that our children might have the wonderful experience of a family church that we had."

Yet in 1916 there were problems. They appeared in the annual congregational meeting, in the monthly meetings of the Vestry, in the semimonthly meetings of the Brotherhood of St. Andrew, and in the day-to-day life of the parish and its parishioners.

Since the fiscal year began on December 1, the annual meeting of the congregation was held on the first or second Monday of December, at 7:30 P.M. in the parish house. Those who attended listened to the Rector's report on the state of the parish, heard the treasurer's report, and approved the budget for the upcoming year. The male members of the congregation then elected four of their number to serve on the Vestry for a three-year term. Some of the problems became visible here. For example, there was a growing sentiment in the Diocese, and perhaps in St. Philip's, that the suffrage in parish elections should not be restricted to males. Moreover, because at St. Philip's the same vestrymen were reelected to succeed themselves, term after term, some members of the congregation had begun to feel that the church was being run by a clique.

Another problem grew out of the distant past. Since medieval times the vestry in Roman Catholic and, in turn, Anglican churches had been instituted to handle the property and finances of the parish, leaving to the priest-in-charge or rector the worship services, including the music, and the Sunday School. On the whole, St. Philip's Vestry worked within that tradition, keeping the buildings in repair, subjecting each bill to minute scrutiny, preparing an annual parish budget, and collecting the annual pledges. Through its elected officers—senior warden (nominated by the Rector), junior warden, treasurer, and secretary, it executed its decisions. Although its budgetary choices affected policy, especially in the money given the organist and choir and in the physical plant allotted to Sunday School classes, the Vestry (it is important to note) rarely intervened directly in the church's program or even expressed an interest. Because St. Philip's Sunday School was nearly self-sustaining, from the weekly offerings of its teachers and pupils, it generally functioned outside the Vestry's deliberations.

Because the Vestry administered the church's property, the congregation tended to elect vestrymen whose acumen had been sharpened by handling substantial property in their daily lives, men such as William A. Erwin, J. Harper Erwin, E. K. Powe, and Kemp Lewis of Erwin Cotton Mills; J. A. Robinson, owner and editor of the *Durham Sun*; E. I. Bugg, proprietor of the Malbourne Hotel; and E. D. Pusey, superintendent of the Durham City Schools. Then too, as Bost never had a secretary, much of the correspondence of St. Philip's was typed by business secretaries on the letterhead of Erwin Cotton Mills, the *Durham Sun*, the Malbourne Hotel, and the Durham City Schools—a symbol, perhaps, of the belief that there is no fundamental separation between the secular and the spiritual: in both spheres we are doing God's will.

However, Bost also needed a band of committed men who would help him with the church's program and do small but indispensable tasks around the church. He thus formed at St. Philip's a chapter of the national Brotherhood of St. Andrew and recruited as members C. H. Burcham, Lester F. Butler, Noble L. Clay, Charles M. Herndon, Jr., W. C. Lindsey, Jr., James Michaels, and E. D. Pusey.[23] They took an oath to follow in their daily lives a Rule of Prayer and a Rule of Service. They met with Bost two evenings a month. After devotions, they identified tasks to be done around the church, then went out and did them. They located areas of the church's program that needed strengthening and worked to build them up. For years the Brotherhood quietly and effectively served as Bost's militia, the extension of his hands and feet and spirit.

A comparison of the early church of the pre-Bost years with the larger congregation of 1916 reveals that many of the latter's problems were a function of its growth and size. Whereas the smaller, closely knit early congregation had immediately identified newcomers and welcomed them, newcomers to the larger church recalled with some bitterness how they had been ignored and "left out" by the busy, happy families who knew their pews and each other. Once aware of the problem, the Vestry began a rotation system for the ushers (three new appointees every three months) and established a welcoming Hospitality Committee. Bost went out of his way to visit Episcopalian families who had recently moved to Durham. The Brotherhood of St. Andrew delegated one of its number, usually Charles M. Herndon, Jr., to leave cards each Saturday night at the Durham hotels inviting guests to attend the Sunday services. To further diminish perceptions of exclusion and cliquishness the congregational meeting in 1917 introduced a system of rotation in Vestry elections,[24] and in 1919 it admitted women to the vote. Also, every three years a representative of St. Andrew's Mission was now one of the four vestrymen elected that year.

In the early days, attendance at St. Philip's Sunday service and Sunday School was one hundred percent. If someone was absent, it was assumed that he or she was sick, and a visit followed that afternoon. In the new, larger church, new communicants were lost. Attendance at the Sunday service, outside the old guard, whose presence could always be counted on, fell off. Parents did not bring their children to Sunday School. The Men's Bible Class, which had averaged nineteen participants (53 percent of the thirty-three enrolled in the autumn of 1915), dropped in 1916 to a meager eight. St. Andrew's and St. Joseph's were both doing better than the mother church, St. Philip's. To the Brotherhood of St. Andrew, C. H. Burcham, teacher of the Sunday School at St. Andrew's, reported a steady attendance of forty. In West Durham Will Erwin's Sunday School class was booming, and he was telling everyone who would listen that the teacher should interest the child.

The situation was complex, and so was the response of Bost and his associates. The Vestry instructed every church agency (the Altar Guild, the Sunday School, the Woman's Auxiliary, the Junior Service League) to report to Bost anyone who was sick so that he or members of the newly formed chapter of the Brotherhood of St. Andrew might visit them. During the influenza epidemic of 1918, which killed more than half a million people in the United States, Bost risked his life to bring comfort and aid to stricken families not only in St. Philip's Parish but outside as well. One of the Brothers, E. D. Pusey, superintendent of the Durham City Schools, had been appointed in 1914 superintendent of the Sunday School of St. Philip's. In 1917 he became teacher of the Men's Bible Class, and Lester F. Butler, another Brother of St. Andrew, succeeded him as superintendent of the Sunday School. The Brothers of St. Andrew undertook each Sunday to bring at least one other communicant to the Men's Bible Class. As the national Episcopal Church as yet had no published teaching series, the Sunday School strengthened its curriculum by adopting the *Christian Nurture Series* of Morehouse Publishing Company, with definite lessons, "Pupil's Illustrated Leaflets, and a Teacher's Manual" on an ordered sequence of subjects: "The Fatherhood of God, Our Father's Gifts, Trust in God, Obedience to God, God with Man, God's Great Family, The Christian Seasons, Church Worship and Membership, The Life of Our Lord, The Long Life of the Church, The Winning of the World, The Bible in Outline, The Creed and Christian Convictions, The Christian and the Community, and The Work of the Holy Spirit in the Church." [25]

Finally, to vitalize the eleven o'clock Sunday service Will Erwin persuaded the Vestry to appropriate one thousand dollars, one-fifth of the budget, to pay not only an organist but also a choir director and a choir. Miss Rosa Warren and Mrs. Yancey were among the singers who helped create a strong and distinguished music program at St. Philip's. The organist continued to be Mrs. John M. Manning. Born in New Bern, she had received her music education at St. Mary's in Raleigh and before her marriage had been organist at Christ Church in her native town. When as a young bride she came to Durham in November 1889, she sat in the congregation at St. Philip's for only one Sunday before she was asked to take over the organ, which she did and continued for thirty-seven years, a record unmatched by any other organist in the history of St. Philip's. "With her," the ECW Scrapbook of 1952 tells us, "it was a labor of love, and she was at the organ whenever the Church was opened. Choir practice was held in her living room at home, to the delight of all the neighbors. She died suddenly on May 11, 1927, soon after giving her Easter music, which had always meant so much to her"—and to the congregation.

Meanwhile, the Vestry was tackling the most ineluctable problem: an increasing slackness in payment of pledges. This had not been characteristic of the early church and, for that matter, remained unproblematic at the two mission churches, St. Andrew's and St. Joseph's. But at St. Philip's the fiscal situation in 1916 was truly desperate. A pledge is a pledge is a pledge, as Gertrude Stein might say, but not for every St. Philippian. Year after year, a number of regular annual pledges went variously delinquent: not paid on time, or in full, or ever. The report of the treasurer, Kemp Lewis, on October 8, 1915, bleakly described the situation:

> I am not at all optimistic as to the finances of the Parish. The Episcopal and Contingent fund assessment has been materially increased again this year, the mission assessments get greater every year, we have to shoulder the burden of rising interest on rectory debts, and in the face of these, the percentage of people who take any interest in paying up and running the Parish seems to me to be less than when I was Treasurer a few years ago. Our people seem to take no interest whatever in missions and special collections for these funds usually amount to nothing. My own opinion is that the unsatisfactory payments is [*sic*] due more to a lack of spiritual interest than to lack of money.

The situation did not improve in 1916: collections ran 12.5 percent short of the amount pledged ($500 out of $4,000, in round numbers), payment of Bost's salary was always a month in arrears, and the deficit on December 31 stood at $529.57, *which the vestrymen paid out of their pockets.*

If the problem of fiscal irresponsibility had been developing over the years, so had its solution. The Vestry, on the recommendation of the Diocese, introduced the Every Member Canvass. Each November every member of the parish was visited by a vestryman and a partner nonvestryman to secure his or her pledge. The Vestry elected two able treasurers—Kemp Lewis and later Hugh White—to introduce business practices of accounting, accountability, and punctuality into the treasury's operations.[26] At the suggestion of the two Erwins the Vestry set up a three-vestrymen Finance Committee to prepare the annual budget and, in general, to oversee the church's financial operations. Two special campaigns extinguished the $6,000 debt on the rectory. (In the second campaign of 1918, West Durham—that is, Will Erwin, J. Harper Erwin, and E. K. Powe—pledged $2,000 if St. Philip's matched it with an Easter offering of $1,200; the Brotherhood of St. Andrew pitched in to make certain the offering was a success.) By 1921 the shortfall on delinquent pledges had been reduced to 7.5 percent of the amount pledged.

But what directly floated St. Philip's into financial equanimity was the wartime prosperity of 1917 to 1920. Thanks to military needs for cloth, textile mill stockbrokers were flush with money, which in Durham they shared with their churches. In January 1920 Will Erwin donated $5,000 to build a parish house for St. Joseph's. During the same year J. Harper Erwin chaired a committee to raise $7,200 for the University of the South (Sewanee), and Kemp Lewis chaired another committee that collected $6,500 for the Nationwide Campaign of the National Episcopal Church. In each campaign the quota for St. Philip's was oversubscribed. To top it all, in January 1921 Will Erwin established a $30,000 trust fund for St. Joseph's. Three-fifths of its income was to be applied to insurance, repairs, and maintenance of its facilities. The general level of giving at St. Philip's rose and did not falter even during the depression of 1921. Bost's salary could now be raised from $1,800 to $3,000 plus a rent-free rectory, and the treasurer of St. Philip's Parish could now report each month: all bills paid on time.

All these measures and the hard work of many people lifted St. Philip's Parish into another era of well-being. The number of baptized persons rose to 1,000 (1920) and of communicants to 675 (1919). At St. Philip's Church, attendance at Sunday School set new records each week: 110, 117, 125 out of an enrollment of 165. Attendance at the Men's Bible Class ran steady at 20 to 25. There was even talk in the Vestry of building a new parish house to replace the increasingly inadequate old one.

Success also lifted Bost into local prominence. As Phyllis Bowman wrote:

When the United States entered [the conflict] in 1917, Bost was active in the sale of liberty bonds. Speaking in a theater in behalf of bond sales, he called for cooperation of all and asked the audience to conserve food, pay taxes gladly, buy bonds, give unstintingly to good causes, and answer their country's call eagerly and bravely. "Whoever loses his life for righteousness' sake shall find it," he said. "We are making war on war." The following year he headed the Chamber of Commerce gardening committee to promote the planting of war gardens.

At the end of the war Bost served on a committee of the Durham Ministers Association which tried to get the city to call off a masquerade dance planned to climax the day of welcoming home Durham's Company M and Battery C in April 1919. The ministers opposed such a dance on the grounds that costumes promote licentious behavior. However, fifty of the most respected ladies volunteered to chaperon, and a block of Duke Street was roped off and brightly lighted, and the dance was held.

Throughout the 1920s Bost was often quoted in the *Durham Morning Herald*, since he had by then become a respected . . . leader of the community. He served as chair of the Red Cross and on the Board of Associated Charities. In 1924–25, he served as president of the local Rotary Club. He was a member of the Public Library Committee. The only church services in Durham upon the death of Woodrow Wilson (February 3, 1924) were held at St. Philip's, although all the churches tolled their bells and a community memorial service was held later at Trinity College with W. T. Laprade as eulogist. Later that year, when the Scopes trial was making headlines, Bost tried to calm violent feelings. "He is a foolish man who would hinder and hamper the scientist in his lawful pursuit of all that he can find. But he is equally foolish who accepts for ultimate truth that which is only the reaction of the human brain." Bost felt that if proper Christian spirit had prevailed, the fight could have been prevented.[27]

STABILIZATION OR HESITATION?

What appears as hesitation to the historian may be simply a hiatus in the evidence. The Vestry minutes are missing from December 7, 1921 to May 7, 1930. The minutes of the Brotherhood of St. Andrew cease after January 30, 1923. Yet we know from other sources that both the Vestry and the Brotherhood continued throughout Bost's tenure.

Nevertheless, statistics concerning church membership do raise questions and provoke a search for answers. The number of baptized persons in St. Philip's *Parish* peaked in 1920 at 1,000, the number of communicants at 675 in 1919. In the next few years there was a decline. The figures are:

	Baptized Persons	Communicants
1919	997	675
1920	1,000	612
1921	900	629
1922	940	656
1923	750	541
1924	762	553

In 1925 St. Joseph's and St. Andrew's, while remaining parochial missions, reported separately, and for the first time we have the enrollment for St. Philip's *Church*. In that year it reported 586 baptized persons and 390 communicants. In the next ten years, the number of communicants, which is the more reliable and interesting figure, hovered around 400. The exact figures are:

	Baptized Persons	Communicants
1925	586	390
1926	592	409
1927	568	423
1928	586	438
1929	628	462
1930	NA	NA
1931	627	383
1932	654	396
1933	672	401
1934	596	415
1935	640	438

This stabilization of enrollment at approximately 400 occurred during a period when the population of Durham was still rising, from 21,719 in 1920 to 52,037 in 1930 and 60,195 in 1940. The question arises: Why was there a cessation of St. Philip's growth? Several factors come to mind.

One: the motor idea that had inspired Cheshire, Murdoch, Bost, and Erwin—namely, to extend God's Kingdom by founding parochial missions among the unchurched—had exhausted its power to animate as missions were in fact established. In the Diocese the number of new industrial missions leveled off during the 1910–20 decade. In Durham St. Philip's itself and its parochial missions in West Durham and East Durham and among the deaf had been firmly set in place. Bost, to be sure, was still moved by the idea. In 1916 he suggested to the Brotherhood of St. Andrew the foundation of a Sunday School mission in Bragtown, north of Durham. The suggestion was strategically sound, and a chapel that could be used was identified. But apparently there were no Erwins or Burchams in Bragtown nor supporting animators in St. Philip's, and nothing was heard of the proposal again. Its quiet demise marked the end of aggressive expansion of St. Philip's in that way.

Two: St. Philip's ceased to be a neighborhood church. In the early church, families who worshiped together lived together. But now as parishioners moved in the 1920s to new developments in Trinity Park and Morehead Heights, and in the 1930s to Hope Valley and Forest Hills, the old neighborhood simply melted away. The nurturing influence of viewing each morning the tower of your church as you picked up the newspaper in the front yard was gone, as was the close intimacy that came with waving to your neighbor, friend, and fellow parishioner as you walked by his place in the evening. New means of reinforcing a sense of Christian community needed to be found.

Three: Bost was distracted from concentration on St. Philip's Parish by his new civic responsibilities (the Red Cross, the Chamber of Commerce, the public library, the Rotary Club, etc.) and by his diocesan offices. Men honor their fellows by giving them work to do. They honored Bost by appointing him member of the Standing Committee of the Diocese, chair of its Finance Committee, member of its Executive Council, and delegate to the General Convention of the Episcopal Church (deputy in 1910, 1919, 1922, 1925; alternate deputy in 1913, 1916, 1928, 1931). Bost's focus on things spiritual stayed intact. He was gratified by a more pleasant financial situation and increased numbers in the parish and by the honors bestowed on him, but he was not taken in by them. As he remarked to the Brotherhood of St. Andrew on September 13, 1920: "While the financial side has been provided for, we will keep up the spiritual work."[28] Also, as we shall see, until the end of his life he was an innovating builder of institutions. Nevertheless, in the closing fifteen years of his pastorate he was a busy, busy man. One of our interviewees even remarked that he seemed too busy to see her.

Four: There came the death of three men with whom Bost had closely worked ever since his arrival at St. Philip's. The deaths of E. K. Powe (September 28, 1929), Will Erwin (February 28, 1932), and Bishop Cheshire (December 27, 1932) were a great blow to Bost and to St.

Philip's Parish. As general manager of Erwin Cotton Mills, Powe had stood in the shadow of its formidable president. However, gentle by nature, he had a sturdy Christian personality and role. When an employee of the Erwin Textile Factory was absent by reason of sickness, it was "E. K." who visited the family that evening to bring what help he could. He taught Sunday School in St. Philip's Church for years; he and his wife, Claudia, repeatedly recruited singers for the choir, and he served as junior warden in 1914, 1915, 1916, and 1917, and as senior warden in 1919, 1920, and 1921. Will Erwin, of course, was the great and intelligent giver of his time, energy, and money to the Episcopal Church, not only in Durham but also throughout the Diocese of North Carolina. He had served as senior warden of St. Philip's Parish in 1918, 1922, 1925, and 1926, and 1930, and he was a member of the Vestry at the time of his death. Bishop of the Diocese of North Carolina for thirty-nine years, Cheshire represented, as Bishop Penick reported to the 1933 Convention, "the best of the patriarchal type of Episcopate which is fast becoming obsolete. So ended an era in the life of the Diocese." [29]

Finally, a fifth factor in the cessation of St. Philip's growth was the Great Depression, which imperiled the finances of the Diocese of North Carolina and of its member parishes, as the level of giving fell off. When in the autumn of 1930 the diocesan Executive Council asked member parishes to contribute $72,000 in 1931, only $62,000 was accepted, and of that only $50,000 was actually paid in. As the depression deepened, the figures became more alarming: in 1932, for example, of the $68,000 requested the Diocese received only $41,650. [30]

In Durham the effect of the depression was at first cushioned by the prosperity of the tobacco factories. Durham then produced one-fourth of the nation's cigarettes, and during the depression's early months more were smoked. As late as September 9, 1930 the treasurer of St. Philip's reported that its treasury was in an "unusually good condition." [31] But in 1931 the old sad litany of pledges not subscribed, pledges not paid on time, pledges not paid in full, and pledges never paid was resumed, as was the year-end deficit—in this case, $1,000. In what may have been his last act for his old church, Will Erwin offered in January 1932 to give it $500 if the Vestry raised a matching sum to erase the deficit. After his death the treasurer raised the matching $500 from delinquents, and Erwin's estate honored his promised gift and in addition paid out his pledge for the entire year—an example of fiscal morality for others.

The Vestry, meanwhile, was severely retrenching. In September 1931 the paid choir was discontinued, the organist, Mr. Howell, was dismissed, and the director of the new volunteer choir, Alice Hundley, assumed her duties at a monthly salary of $50. A once splendid music program, which in 1921 had cost $2,300 and as late as 1931 $1,450, was placed on a shoestring budget of $750.

In January 1932 Bost's assistant who had been in charge of St. Joseph's since 1928, the Reverend Edwin W. Hurst, was let go as he answered another call—thus saving his salary of $1,425.[32] It seems that lay deacons assumed many of his duties at St. Joseph's. At Bost's request the Vestry eliminated his own car allowance of $240 and reduced his annual salary from $3,600 to $3,000. He still enjoyed a rent-free rectory, however. The sexton's weekly pay was cut from eight dollars to five.

In a complex operation the Vestry renegotiated its debt owed to the Fidelity Bank. In 1923 the Vestry, in a protective move to safeguard room for expansion, had purchased the Guthrie property at the corner of Main and Queen Streets and borrowed approximately $17,500. Though this formidable debt killed any possibility of erecting a new and badly needed parish house, nothing was done to pay it off. In September 1931 it still stood at $17,473.30, with an annual interest charge of $1,114.[33] In December of that year the Woman's Auxiliary gave $1,000 to reduce the debt. In September 1932 the Vestry leased the Guthrie property for ten years to the Sinclair Oil Company, which promised to erect a filling station and pay a minimum monthly rental of $62.50. Before signing the lease the Vestry was advised by Kemp Lewis to seek the approval of the Woman's Auxiliary: "I think it would be a mistake for the Vestry to go ahead without consulting with the women of the congregation."[34] Through its corresponding secretary, Esther Cowles Bost, the Auxiliary replied: "The entire Auxiliary looks with favor upon the proposition, and I am instructed to write on behalf of the Auxiliary and say that its entire membership will heartily concur in and co-operate with the Vestry in anything which they may decide to do."[35] The Vestry then negotiated a new loan with the Fidelity Bank that bound St. Philip's to pay interest at 6 percent on the debt of $16,473 and to amortize it at the rate of $62.50 a month. Thus, by the autumn of 1932 progress was being made toward the amortization of the debt. By February 1935 the parish budget was balanced at such a level that Bost's salary of $3,600 could be restored.

Even during these difficult years Bost's pioneering and forward-looking spirit remained alive. In his annual report to the parish on December 1, 1930 he urged the construction of a new parish house "within the next five years" and of a brick church for the parochial mission of St. Andrew's in East Durham.[36] If the congregation failed to rise to the challenge, as it had failed earlier to respond to his proposal to sponsor a Bragtown mission, he did not show his disappointment but led it into other projects that coincided with those of Cheshire's coadjutor and successor, Bishop Penick.

While Penick kept in touch with his clergy, he was more an administrative bishop than Cheshire. He thought in terms of programs whose direction was firmly in the hands of the diocesan central office. Responding to the change of needs and of opportunities arising from them, he shifted the diocesan emphasis from sponsoring parochial missions in rising industrial towns to strengthening pan-diocesan activities for young people, for college students, and for men as well as women.

It is testimony to Bost's zeal for extending God's Kingdom and to his flexible adjustment of means to new conditions that he and his close associates, men and women, *anticipated* the new strategy at St. Philip's. As early as 1930 the men of the church were transporting by automobile up to twenty Duke students to the Sunday morning service. The *Diocesan Journal* of 1932 reported:

> Mention must also be made of the works of the Rev. S. S. Bost and of the women of St. Philip's Parish for what they are doing for the students at Duke. Through teas and socials many contacts have been made with our Church students there, and in spite of the distance between the college and the church, many students have been attending the services. The organization of a College Students' Auxiliary has been found very helpful.[37]

The work was sustained in ensuing years. "For Duke," the *Diocesan Journal* of 1934 reported, "Mr. Bost provides a monthly corporate Communion, social gatherings in the homes of members of St. Philip's, and opportunities of service in the choir and in other ways."[38] The formation of the chapter of the Laymen's League at St. Philip's also accorded with Bishop Penick's policy and Bost's intentions. At Bost's last congregational meeting, on December 10, 1934, "Mr. Bost and E. M. Hunter made a few remarks about the Laymen's League and expressed the desire that every man in the congregation join the

League which would begin to function in January."[39] This was several months *before* Penick, at the Diocesan Convention of 1934, expressed the "earnest hope" that chapters of that organization might be formed in every member parish.[40] Until the end of his life Bost was pioneering new institutions that endured.

However, the closing years of his ministry at St. Philip's were clouded by controversy, triggered by a factional debate over the declining Sunday School attendance and by the failure of the Vestry to do anything effective about it. In a series of letters dating from October 4, 1932 Lester F. Butler, superintendent of the Sunday School, defended the teachers and blamed the parents for failure to bring their children or to bring them on time and prepared by study at home.[41] The Woman's Auxiliary suggested the formation of a Parish Council to consider this issue and others that lay outside the Vestry's financial/property focus. The Young People's Service League, led by Ellerbee Powe, Jr., and E. Lawson Moore, concurred with the Auxiliary's proposal and recommended the annual election of a general superintendent for the Sunday School.[42]

By January 1933 agreement was reached by representatives of all concerned parties: the Vestry (J. Harper Erwin, Jr., and Bailey W. Hobgood), the Woman's Auxiliary (Mrs. Murray Jones and Mrs. L. A. Tomlinson), the Sunday School teachers (Mrs. George Watts Carr and Mrs. J. A. Robinson), and the YPSL (Ellerbee Powe, Jr., and E. Lawson Moore). The outcome, approved by the Vestry, was a Parish Council composed of two elected representatives from the Woman's Auxiliary and from the Sunday School teachers and one representative from each of the other agencies of the parish: Vestry, Brotherhood of St. Andrew, Choir, Altar Guild, YPSL, St. Joseph's Church, and St. Andrew's Church. The belief was expressed that "the organization of the Parish Council . . . will stimulate interest in the Church and its activities and enable them to function to better advantage at present."[43] The Council's first act was to supervise the election of Bailey W. Hobgood as superintendent of the Sunday School. In ratifying the action the Vestry voted unanimously to thank Lester F. Butler "for his long and excellent service to the Sunday School."[44]

One senses in the controversy and in the remarks of several interviewees a growing dissatisfaction with Bost's style of leadership, especially among the younger generation. Gentle, firm, and persevering in personal work, he was not appreciated by those among the parishioners who expected a more forceful and dramatic presentation. One interviewee, young at that time, remembered him as "colorless." Another recalled that Bost was being criticized for not having attended a seminary, as if a year's apprenticeship to Francis Murdoch would not mean more in any man's life than three years in a seminary program. In the closing months of his illness from cancer before he died on June 7, 1935, Bost could still recall that like his mentor he had been a faithful shepherd of his flock and a sound builder of a congregation that would endure.

3
Mission to the Deaf
JUDITH HOBART PEARSON

The Episcopal Church has long been recognized as a pioneer in its mission work to the deaf. The first worship service for the deaf was conducted by an Episcopal priest. Dr. Thomas Hopkins Gallaudet, an Episcopalian, founded at Hartford, Connecticut, the first school for the deaf in the United States in 1817. His elder son Thomas began a Bible class for the deaf in his parish in 1849; after his ordination to the priesthood in 1852, he organized and became rector of St. Ann's Church for deaf persons in New York City. In 1864 his brother Edward founded Gallaudet College, the only college for the deaf in the world. The Episcopal Church was the first to ordain a deaf man, and as late as 1964 it was the only church that was willing to do so. The Diocese of North Carolina was the first to build a church solely for the use of the deaf. The church was named Ephphatha, an Aramaic word meaning "be opened," used by Christ when He healed a deaf person (Mark 7:34–35).

In the South, mission work among the deaf was started by the Reverend Job Turner in 1876. He covered the territory from Maryland to the Gulf and from the Atlantic to Arkansas. After Turner's death in 1903, the Reverend O. J. Whildin from Baltimore took over his charge.

The year 1906 may be regarded as the advent of definite and organized efforts in the Diocese of North Carolina, when Whildin made his first trip to Durham and held services in St. Philip's Church. After repeated visits and with the assistance of the Reverend Sidney S. Bost, Whildin prepared and presented to Bishop Joseph B. Cheshire, on May 20, 1906, seventeen deaf persons for confirmation. Roma C. Fortune was a member of that class.

Touched by the religious needs of these isolated people, Bost continued services for the deaf at St. Philip's once a month. He was assisted by Mr. Fortune, who became a lay reader, and by Robina Tillinghast, of Morganton, the daughter of deaf parents. Fortune interpreted the order of worship and Miss Tillinghast the sermon. In addition, Miss Tillinghast conducted Sunday School and Bible classes each Sunday afternoon. In the next four years the mission grew to forty deaf persons.

In October 1910 Bost cited St. Philip's as the best illustration of what could be done in mission work with the deaf. He proposed to diocesan authorities that the diocesan Woman's Auxiliary become responsible for half of Miss Tillinghast's salary and that St. Philip's pay the rest—each giving $300. It was planned that as "Mission Teacher to the Deaf" she would extend her work to larger towns in the Diocese where the deaf lived and would organize Sunday School and Bible classes for them. She would prepare them for baptism and confirmation and interpret the services and sermons. By this time Fortune was conducting the Sunday School classes in Durham. In addition, weekly society meetings were held at St. Philip's for literary and social purposes.

In the spring of 1911 Robina Tillinghast began work with black deaf people. She taught a class of five at St. Titus in Durham, and under her direction a class of fourteen in Charlotte was taught "by a very intelligent colored deaf woman." The rest of her classes also continued to grow, to twelve members in Greensboro and eight in Raleigh. In Winston-Salem she met with five people, and in High Point she met twice with seven.

By 1912 her work had grown to include 125 deaf persons distributed throughout the Diocese. Her counsel was sought in all matters pertaining to their welfare—problems met in the community, in the education of their children, in caring for the sick, and in earning a living. In explaining her mission she said, "They must of necessity have some interpreter between them and the outside world whom they can love and trust to help in the solution of their problems." That year Fortune signed at a Christmas celebration in Sunday School, saying that the mission "benefits us in every way, not only in our business and social life but it helps and inspires us in our religious life."

In 1915 Miss Tillinghast resigned her position and moved to Spartanburg, South Carolina, because she was needed by her parents. For nine years she had worked unceasingly and laid the work on broad, strong foundations. By then St. Philip's mission in Durham was regarded as the most prosperous mission to the deaf in the South.

Fortune, who had become president of the State Deaf Association, succeeded her. After several years he was approached and asked to consider prayerfully the matter of being ordained to the ministry. After months of reflection, study, and prayer he resolved to do so. He studied theology under Bost and on February 13, 1918 was admitted as a candidate for Holy Orders. On May 8, 1918 the Diocese's work among the deaf was crowned when he was ordained deacon by Bishop Cheshire in St. Philip's Church.

The Bishop assigned Fortune to the Durham mission as the center and base of his operations. There he would continue to work under and with Bost. But the Bishop also commissioned him, as Diocesan Missionary to the Deaf, to take charge of work with the deaf throughout the Diocese. In addition, he was authorized to work in neighboring dioceses if his services were requested.

In a letter to the *Carolina Churchman* in 1919, Bost proudly remarked that he had "found the deaf liberal contributors to Church work, conscientious in the observance of Church duties and desirous of the highest possible development of themselves and their children. . . . Mr. Fortune is an able, conscientious and capable worker, a wise leader, well known to the deaf throughout the state, and trusted wherever he is known."

By 1920 the statewide mission had grown to 290 members, and by 1921 a Sunday School class with a leader was operating in Greensboro at St. Andrew's Church. Fortune was traveling to Burlington, Greensboro, Kannapolis, Winston-Salem, Concord, Charlotte, Salem, Kenly, and Princeton. He also began to visit the Deaf and Mute School at Morganton, and the Deaf and Dumb School for the "colored" people in Raleigh. In 1923 he preached to an audience of nearly a thousand outside the Durham mission, which now had sixty members. Monthly he visited the Bible study class in Burlington, where he held services for eighteen to twenty members.

In 1926 it was reported in the *Carolina Churchman* that Bishop Cheshire had long been known for his special interest in the work being carried on for the deaf in St. Philip's Parish. On his list of one thousand things that needed to be done in the Diocese, the erection of a church for the deaf numbered twenty-third. He was anxious that no time be lost in giving this worthy group a church of its own.

In May 1926, in an address to the to the National Council of the Woman's Auxiliary, in session at St. Philip's Church, Fortune described plans to erect a beautiful and substantial church in Durham, to be the center of church life for the deaf in the Diocese. Indications were that this structure would attract other deaf persons to Durham to partake in the finer spiritual life that would be made possible. He related that the deaf church members were elated and felt it would assist them greatly in their church activities.

The Diocese put forth great efforts to raise the money to build such a church, and the estimated cost of $15,000 was shared by its entire church family. The Woman's Auxiliary gave $3,000, another $3,000 was pledged by a prominent layman in Charlotte, and $1,000 was given by deaf people themselves. The Advent-Epiphany offerings were designated for this purpose. Added incentive was given by making the church a memorial to Bishop Cheshire.

On January 27, 1927 Fortune was ordained priest by Bishop Cheshire at St. Philip's Church. James R. Fortune, his son, interpreted the service and sermon in sign language.

In March 1928 Bost, on behalf of the Advance Work Committee of the Executive Council of the Diocese, sent a letter to all parishes reporting that a balance of $5,656.31 was needed to erect a church for the deaf. He urged each parish to earmark its Easter Offering for this building.

The cornerstone for a brick church was laid at the corner of Geer and North Streets in November 1930, and the building was completed the following year. The consecration of Ephphatha Church on May 17, 1931 marked the happy culmination of twenty-five years of planning and faithful labor in the erection and furnishing of the only church exclusively for the worship of the deaf in the entire South, one of four in the United States. The service was led by Bishop Cheshire. The Reverend J. M. Koehler, of Pennsylvania, the oldest minister for the deaf in the United States, preached the sermon in sign language. Alexander Tillinghast, the brother of Robina Tillinghast, acted as interpreter for the hearing. The service included the singing of hymns in sign language.

Later, the Church of the Holy Comforter in Burlington restored St. Athanasius Church, an old church building that had not been used for public worship since 1911. It was donated to the deaf congregation in Burlington and reconsecrated in November 1934. There were now two churches for the deaf in the Diocese of North Carolina.

Bost died on June 7, 1935, four years after the consecration of Ephphatha Church. At the Annual Convention Bishop Penick made this
observation:

> I suspect that Mr. Bost's most lasting service to his generation
> was his personal concern for the deaf people of his community
> that widened through the years to embrace the great silent parish
> of the Diocese. It was his sympathetic interest in this afflicted
> group that introduced and interpreted the Church to them until
> today the Diocese of North Carolina is nationally conspicuous
> for its ministry to the deaf. Although there is neither speech nor
> language, God's voice is heard among them, saying "Ephphatha,
> be opened."

Through the persistent work and devotion of Roma Fortune the
deaf mission continued to grow. As automobiles became increasingly
available, more and more of the deaf who lived in remote areas were
able to attend services at central points, some traveling as far as fifty
miles. In 1938 Fortune reported that he had ministered through service
and sermon to 1,340 persons outside Durham and Burlington.

In 1942 more than two thousand deaf persons across the state suffered the loss of their beloved clergyman. On October 27, at the age
of sixty-three, the Reverend Roma C. Fortune died while calling on a
parishioner of Ephphatha. Bishop Penick praised him for his unflag-
ging zeal and effectiveness in carrying out his ministry:

> Considering the handicap under which he labored Mr. Fortune's
> ministry was not only dramatic and appealing, but far-reaching
> in its extent and substantial in results. We honor him as one of
> the outstanding pioneers of the Church to our brethren who live
> in perpetual silence. We never heard the sound of his voice, but
> we never failed to catch the muted sweetness of his personality
> and the message of a life that was eloquent above words.

Funeral services were conducted on October 29 by Bishop Penick and
the Reverend David Yates, Rector of St. Philip's, and given in sign language by James Fortune. The service was described as follows:

> It seemed to us as we beheld the "suffering in silence" that that
> wonderful service never meant as much to us at that moment.
> The choir standing in front of the communion rail facing the

congregation "sang" in sign language as Bishop Penick read the hymn. Their graceful movement of arms and figures, with faces rapt in reverent keeping with hearts that had been sorely smitten, produced a silent harmony that caused one's nerves to tingle and made one feel the reality of what their religion meant to them.

After the death of his father, James R. Fortune, already a licensed lay reader, left the dairying industry and set out to receive the necessary training to become the speaking leader for the deaf so that his father's ministry might be continued. Bishop Penick was instrumental in making him feel the call to serve these people who had been left rather helpless. As James explained his decision, "It was in an interview with Bishop Penick that I realized the vacancy created by my father's death was of real concern to the Bishop. He made me see that the work among the deaf was an integral part of the missionary program of the Diocese." In the six months between his father's death and the next Annual Convention, Fortune conducted twenty-eight services, preached outside the Diocese once, and presented a paper to the North Carolina Sunday School for the Deaf Convention.

James Fortune was ordained deacon, by Bishop Penick, on February 22, 1944. Yates preached the ordination sermon, and Roma C. Fortune, Jr., interpreted. Members of the deaf congregation, assisted by the Woman's Auxiliary of St. Philip's, served a luncheon to the participating clergy at St. Philip's Parish House.

Fortune succeeded his father as Diocesan Missionary to the Deaf, while keeping the Durham mission as the center and base of his operations. He extended his field of mission work to include regular services in the parish house of Grace Church in Morganton. These services were attended by the deaf in the community as well as by the adult students of the Deaf and Mute School. Afternoon chapel services in the school auditorium were attended by about three hundred students, ranging from eight to eighteen years, and by about thirty adults. In addition, he gave several talks to hearing congregations in church services and Sunday Schools, making the work among the deaf more widely known in the Diocese.

In 1944 the Diocese provided full scholarships for three deaf persons to attend the Diocesan Leadership and Teachers Conference. These teachers then acted as leaders on the Sundays when Fortune was not present at their parishes in Durham, Greensboro, and Winston-Salem.

James Fortune was advanced to the priesthood at Ephphatha Church on April 12, 1945, thus becoming one of two speaking clergy out of the fifteen in the Episcopal Church who were occupied full-time in the work among the deaf. A significant feature of the ordination was that it took two people to do each part of the service, as the deaf in attendance had to be provided with the same words as those who could hear. Fortune's mother led in the "singing" for the deaf, and his three brothers were ushers. During the service a silver ciborium was dedicated by Bishop Penick in memory of Robina Lenoir Tillinghast, who nearly forty years before had helped Bost start a Bible class for the deaf at St. Philip's. A reception for the visiting clergy was held at St. Philip's following the service. St. Philip's had also hosted a reception the previous Wednesday for the visiting deaf ministers and about one hundred guests from Durham, Burlington, and Raleigh.

In 1946, after attending a Conference of Church Workers among the Deaf of the Protestant Episcopal Church of America, Fortune visited New York City and conducted a service at St. Ann's, the first mission for the deaf in the United States.In 1947 he was elected first vice-president of the Conference of Church Workers among the Deaf; in 1951 he was elevated to the presidency, an office he held for seventeen years. In 1949 Fortune was elected vice-president of the board of directors of the North Carolina State School for the Deaf in Morganton; he served on that board until 1961.

Between 1946 and 1949 money collected from Advent offerings throughout the Diocese was contributed to the Rectory Fund for the Missionary to the Deaf. A lot on Wilson Street in West Durham was bought and a rectory was built. In his report to the Annual Convention in 1949, Fortune gave special thanks to the Reverend C. Alfred Cole for his personal interest in conducting the campaign for the funds. He also thanked the many parishes, missions, and individuals for their contributions to the Rectory Fund and noted that the plans were in the hands of the contractor. On April 22, 1950 Bishop Penick, assisted by the Reverend Clarence Haden, Jr., of St. Philip's, conducted a dedication service for the newly completed rectory. James Fortune was the only minister to live there; the house was sold by the Diocese in 1978 when he retired to Littleton, North Carolina.

In 1952, 5,469 deaf persons attended Fortune's services throughout the Diocese. In addition to providing regular services, he answered many calls for assistance in counseling, interpreting, and visiting the

sick—a very important need among the deaf. He expressed their gratitude to the Diocese for making those services possible. Moreover, he
continued to educate more people about the Episcopal Church's work
among the deaf by speaking to numerous Woman's Auxiliary groups
and civic clubs.

The fiftieth anniversary of missionary work among the deaf in the
Diocese of North Carolina was celebrated in 1956. Six members of
the original confirmation class of 1906 were still living and active
in church work. The Bible classes in Durham, Burlington, Winston-
Salem, Greensboro, and Statesville were thriving. Fortune held services
in each of these towns once a month, traveling approximately 22,000
miles a year on circuit.

In July 1958 he began serving as consultant to the Department
of Audiology at Duke University. Preschool deaf children are often
doubly handicapped, as their parents may lack understanding of their
needs. Fortune administered hearing tests, informed parents of special
educational methods available, and offered instruction on how they
might begin the necessary teaching of their preschool deaf children.
This was a real missionary service of our church, as these children came
to Duke from all over the Eastern Seaboard. As Fortune expressed
it, "The Church is serving as it has always done, from the cradle to
the grave."

The year 1960 saw another first in the field: beginning on February 1,
a full-time chaplain was installed for the Episcopal students at Gallaudet College. That year our Church's missions among the deaf became
a cooperating agency of the Home Department of the National Council. This gave stability to our work through centralization of direction
and provided access to all the resources of the National Council.

In 1960 James Fortune was also appointed an instructor on the faculty at Duke University and continued to conduct specialized audio-
logical testing at Duke Hospital and Murdoch Center at Butner. He
served as chair of the Presiding Bishop's Advisory Committee to the
Home Department of the National Church, which assessed the needs
for strengthening and advancing the work with the deaf throughout
the Church.

In 1962 Episcopal deaf persons of the Diocese hosted the Annual
Convention of the Conference of Church Workers among the Deaf,
held at Kanuga. The participants included 125 members of the clergy
and laity throughout the United States. That year Fortune traveled to

Texas to meet with a committee interested in establishing work with the deaf in that diocese. He also appeared on radio and television in New York to explain the work of the Episcopal Church with the deaf.

Meanwhile, through these years from 1944 to 1967 the Ephphatha congregation in Durham, consisting of approximately forty communicants, continued its regular Sunday program of worship service and church school classes. Attendance at both was 100 percent of the church's membership, so great was the congregation's faith and zeal. In the legal categories of the Diocese, Ephphatha was never more than an "unorganized mission," but its dedication exceeded that of many organized missions and parishes.

But as older members died and younger ones moved away, Ephphatha's enrollment dropped sharply, from 38 communicants in 1967 to 22 in 1974. Job discrimination in employment, generated by prejudice and workman's compensation regulations, was part of the reason. Young deaf persons, Fortune reported, did not want to come to Durham because of the prejudice against them: "This is a sad situation. People don't understand them. The Northern states are hiring deaf people but not around here."

In addition, vandalism to the church structure had become a continuous problem. Fortune reported that "half-bricks" had been thrown through windows, copper gutters and the copper wiring to the air-conditioning system had been stolen, and bottles had been broken against the building. He said, "Every time I go over there to the church and unlock the door—they've tried to break it in, too—I hold my breath. I tell you, it's a bad feeling." Women were afraid to go to the church to plan and participate in programs, and an air of apprehension hovered over the premises. Finally, the desecration and vandalism became more than the congregation could stand, and in 1975 a "heartbroken, disappointed and disgusted" Fortune gave up and recommended to the Bishop that Ephphatha close its doors. The Diocese deconsecrated the church and it was sold.

The congregation met at St. Philip's briefly and then at St. Joseph's, where James Fortune continued to conduct services in Durham, though after a heart attack in April 1976 he was forced to curtail his activities throughout the Diocese. Like his father before him, he served as Diocesan Missionary to the Deaf until his health no longer permitted. When he retired in 1978 the Diocese appointed John Barry Kramer as his replacement. Kramer made Winston-Salem the center and base of his operations, as there was now a larger number of deaf persons concentrated in that area of the state.

James R. Fortune died on January 3, 1992. His funeral services at St. Philip's Church were conducted by Bishop Robert W. Estill, Bishop Hunting Williams, and the Reverend C. Thomas Midyette III. He was buried in Maplewood Cemetery.

4

The Rectorship of David Yates
1935–1945

DAVID YATES, THE PERSON
SIBYL G. POWE AND LOUISE NEWTON

"He was one of the few men I have known in my life in whom I found absolute integrity," the Reverend James Cox, Church of the Incarnation, Dallas, Texas, said.

"He stood like a rock for what he believed to be right," the Reverend Thom Blair, former rector of Christ Church, Charlotte," declared.

"Upon a few choice spirits, he made the impact of a lifetime. Upon others, he had a delayed effect—conversions in retrospect," Arthur Ben Chitty, chair of Funds for Episcopal College, recalled.

"What he was, he plainly was, and his convictions were audible, visible, understandable, known," the Reverend Tom Thrasher, former rector of Chapel of the Cross, Chapel Hill, wrote.

"He was the conscience of the Diocese," Bishop Edwin A. Penick avowed.

"My ministry is based in a large part on his ministry. He was a great influence on my life," the Reverend L. Bartine Sherman, former rector of St. Philip's, Durham, offered.

"Whoever knew David Yates was bound to know Our Lord," Kay Brownell, former Durham resident, stated simply.

David Yates was born on September 4, 1904 in Charlotte, North Carolina, the son of David Schenck, a prominent Charlotte insurance man, and Edith May Will Yates. His mother was an Episcopalian and his father a Presbyterian. His mother's brother, Theodore S. Will, was an Episcopal minister.

David had an older brother, William, and a younger sister, Clair (Mrs. Andrew Owen). According to Clair, David was mischievous when he was a little boy but "he never did a *mean* thing in all his life." In her early snapshots of him, he appeared as a cherubic, blue-eyed blond. Even as an adult, he possessed that innocent, sweet expression of childhood.

When and how did David become interested in the ministry? We know he attended the Presbyterian Church briefly when he was quite young, but he spent the rest of his life as a totally committed Episcopalian. His sister Clair said she believed that their mother always wanted him to be a minister, and that Bishop Edwin A. Penick encouraged David to enter the seminary. (Penick was rector of St. Peter's Church, Charlotte, when David was a very active communicant there.)

David grew to be a tall, almost gangly man, yet he had the grace and style of an athlete. He loved sports from all standpoints—as a player, as a coach, and as a spectator. Most of all, he appreciated the human relationships that he encountered in the sports arena. He preferred structured, team sports, and he operated best when playing by the rules of the game.

In 1921, when he was a senior in high school, his mother died of cancer. He had wanted to go to college, and he dreamed of entering seminary. But with his father a tubercular invalid and his sister Clair and brother Bill interested in college too, he had to postpone his own education for awhile. After graduation from Charlotte High School, he went to work at the Thompson Orphanage in Charlotte. He was associated with the orphanage for six years, serving as secretary and athletic director. During this period he lived at home with his ailing father.

Soon after his father died, David enrolled in 1927 at the University of the South, Sewanee, Tennessee, majoring in English, history, and Greek—all three! He was older, of course, than most of his classmates, but that did not deter him from succeeding in his studies or in extracurricular activities. Valedictorian of his class, Phi Beta Kappa, and letters for four years in basketball and tennis were the honors he earned. He also sang in the Sewanee glee club. During those college years he worked at a number of summer jobs, including one with the Duke Power Company in Charlotte.

In the spring of 1934 he received the Bachelor of Divinity degree from Virginia Theological Seminary and was ordained deacon on June 21 by Bishop Penick. Penick ordained him into the priesthood on January 16, 1935. His first clerical assignment was as assistant to the rector of Calvary Church, Tarboro (1934–35). On November 12, 1935 he became Rector of St. Philip's Church, where he served for ten years.

In Durham, he rented a furnished room from Mrs. Ethel Lipscomb on Duke Street. During World War II he often rode his bicycle from the Lipscomb house to the parish house on East Main Street. (The new parish house had not yet been built, and his office was in a little wooden structure behind the church.) Once, on a particularly cold day, with head ducked low and bicycle flying along, he ran into an automobile and was badly bruised and lacerated. Despite his injuries he managed to get to St. Philip's in time to conduct the regular eleven o'clock service, though a bit shakily.

David developed a parish ministry that was unusual, even in the days of small, close parishes. He was a real shepherd to his flock. He knew every family in his church—and he knew them well, including their children, relatives, friends, and neighbors. He was like a member of the family. The amazing thing was that he had the capability of being a part of *everybody's* family in his church. He kept in touch with what they were all doing, and he shared their day-by-day joys as well as their sorrows. He visited them often in their homes. He called on all new visitors at St. Philip's almost before they had time to get home from church.

Since he never married, his ideas about the responsibilities of mothers with young children were somewhat naive. Several parishioners recall his going to the hospital to see a new mother and infant and, while there, trying to persuade the mother to teach a Church School class or undertake some other church duty the following Sunday. When there were objections to his requests, he chided that each of us has duties in the church as well as at home, at work, and in the community.

The practices of religion were an important part of his parish ministry. They were obligatory, and they were intended to cultivate Christian discipline, which he felt was as essential as Christian service. He set rigorous standards for his parishioners, by example as well as by admonition, and though his straitlaced rules turned off some, most parishioners found them guidelines strict enough easily to define their relationship to the Church.

To David, the Church was the pivot on which all action revolved.

His ministry included visiting all Episcopalians, no matter where they were from, who were confined in local hospitals. He even requested diocesan priests to send him names of their parishioners who were patients in Durham, so that he could contact them.

This kind of personal ministry is recognized today as being extremely time-consuming and emotionally draining. It has become full-time employment for many hospital chaplains. But David never complained about the personal toll. He frequently worked a twelve- to fourteen-hour day, tireless, indefatigable, and cheerful in his work with those in need. He made it abundantly clear, however, that being a friend to many was not a technique he used to enhance his own popularity, but a means of translating his Lord's message of love.

No one will ever know how much of his small income he gave away. When there were needs in the Parish that others could or would not meet, he tried to help with what little he had. He lived simply and frugally on his inadequate salary, and his friends and family noticed that sometimes he was actually ravenous when invited "to stay for dinner." His worldly possessions were meager. In Tarboro and Durham, his bedroom was furnished by the landlady. For his efficiency apartment in Chapel Hill, his dear friends Dewey and Lonnie London loaned him secondhand furniture. He never collected any of the material things most of us surround ourselves with. He did not, for instance, have a large library or record collection, or works of art or attractive clothes or even the gadgets that make life easier. If he collected anything, it was people.

An important aspect of the man David was the unwavering manner in which he carried out his convictions. Some people, including those closest to him, considered him stubborn and uncompromising. But almost all respected his integrity and tenacity even when they disagreed with him.

Once at a Diocesan Convention when David was espousing endlessly a controversial point, Bishop Penick admonished him to "sit down, say no more, and let the convention make its decision." Yet the Bishop later described him as the "conscience of the Diocese" and in private said, "David has more Christianity in his little finger than I have in my whole body."

World War II created a difficult moral issue that David felt he must face head-on. He began quietly to preach pacifism. His sermons were often about the wrongs of warfare and the wrongs of conscription. Even if his parishioners had accepted the first as wrong (which was difficult, at best, during a popular war), it was too much to expect them to endorse the individual's wrong in serving when called to combat. Most St. Philippians had family members who already had been inducted into the armed forces, and some had borne a tragic loss of loved ones in the war.

Despite his firm principles, David encouraged dances in the old parish house, arranged for the servicemen stationed at Camp Butner and at Duke University. He always attended those functions. The dances proved to be successful; often as many as two hundred young people jammed into the parish house on Saturday night.

David's earnest and relentless stand on the war made many St. Philippians uncomfortable with him. Yet amid the criticism, some were saying, "I can't go along with his pacifist ideas, but I know he is taking the Christian point of view."

If this period of his life could be termed a "crusade," it would have to be interpreted as a sacrificial endeavor. For the most part, his words fell on deaf ears. There was practically no support for his condemnation of the war, either in the Parish or in the Diocese. He might have found some audience on a national scale, but he rarely worked beyond diocesan lines.

This must have been a terribly lonely time for him. It also must have tested his faith. But his commitment was strong—even without hope of compensation.

In the telling, it might seem that David's ministry was an enigma. On the one hand, he took a conservative stand on a Christian's duty toward the Church; on the other, he was considered by some to be almost radical on moral and social issues of his day. But wasn't he sincerely and simply following the teachings of the Church in all situations?

David Yates will be remembered for his work with young people. He built a strong Young People's Service League at St. Philip's. He was able to do this only because young people genuinely liked and admired him. One of the projects undertaken by the youth of the church was the publication of a lengthy bulletin (sometimes as many as twelve pages) entitled "St. Philip's Press."

During the summer, in accord with Bishop Penick's policy of reaching out to young people through camps and conferences, David directed athletics or an entire camp at Cheshire, Vade Mecum, and Kanuga. His worn blue blazer with padded elbows was a familiar sight to hundreds of North Carolina Episcopal boys and girls. He always wore the old blazer at softball games and other sporting events.

He found it easy to relate to young people on the playing field, but at other times it was difficult for him to communicate. For example, his annual sermon on "Christians and Sex" sent the teenagers into hysterics. They thought his old-fashioned bachelor ideas were funny. But behind their amusement there was a tinge of love and respect. Perhaps it was because they knew he cared.

DAVID YATES AND THE PARISH OF ST. PHILIP'S
HAROLD T. PARKER

When the Vestry of St. Philip's and David Yates interviewed each other on September 30, 1935 in the old, inadequate parish house, a parish that had not had a new rector for thirty-seven years was viewing a friendly, gangly young man, only recently out of seminary, who had never had a parish. The disparities went even deeper than anyone realized: a seasoned institutional church that had lost its momentum was encountering a young idealistic Christian who took the Ten Commandments and the injunctions of Jesus Christ seriously, even to the last word. Without knowing the ultimate consequences of its action, the Vestry stepped forth in hope and faith; or, in secular language, it bet on inexperienced zeal and youth and offered the position to Yates at an annual salary of $2,400. Yates accepted.

The symptoms of the loss of momentum were several. The cessation of the growth in the number of communicants, discussed in Chapter II, was one. At the monthly Vestry meetings, mustering a quorum of the majority of its members had become a problem. In June 1934, since no quorum was present, no business was transacted. Down to 1920 the date of the annual congregational meeting, the first or second Monday in December, coincided with the beginning of the new fiscal year, December 1. Congregational consideration of the new year's budget could be based on the treasurer's annual report for the preceding twelve months and on the results of the Every Member Canvass. Even when the beginning of the fiscal year was shifted in 1921 to January 1, the congregational meeting, from habit, continued to convene in December. The effect was to relegate final budgetary decisions to the Vestry and its Finance Committee, and to reduce the functions of the congregational meeting to listening to the Rector's report and to electing four members to the Vestry. It is no wonder that at one of Bost's last congregational meetings only 27 of the total 417 communicants bothered to attend.

It had not been characteristic of St. Philip's to have a large overhang debt. Thanks to the generosity of Calvary Church (Tarboro), Joseph Cheshire's former church, and of Cheshire himself, the old frame church was paid for in 1881 as soon as it was built. Only five years were needed to extinguish the debt on the new brownstone structure that was erected in 1907 and dedicated in 1912. In 1914, when the Vestry, to safeguard room for expansion, purchased a house on Queen Street and converted it into the rectory, its cost had been covered within four years. But in 1923, when the Vestry borrowed $17,500 to buy the Guthrie property at the corner of Main and Queen Streets in a similar safeguarding move, amortization of that debt was not begun until nine years later, in 1932, and then only at the modest rate of $750 a year. The formidable debt and its 6 percent interest charge stymied efforts to build a new parish house for St. Philip's Church and a brick chapel for St. Andrew's — recognized needs for over fifteen years. Also left untended, almost unrecognized, were the obligations and opportunities for a downtown church to meet the needs, spiritual and material, of its increasingly rundown surrounding neighborhood. Save for Easter baskets for needy children in the nearby Edgemont mill sector, St. Philippians, as a congregation, lived largely unto themselves.

To be sure, within the church, there were promising elements of strength and renewal: veterans of responsible service who could stand firm "come hell or high water" (Col. J. Harper Erwin, Kemp Lewis, and the new treasurer, Bailey Hobgood); an emerging younger generation of leaders who could fill the void created by the deaths of Will Erwin and E. K. Powe (J. Harper Erwin, Jr., William H. Ruffin, Nat Gregory, B. R. Roberts, Richard Leigh, Ellerbee Powe, Jr., and Lawson Moore); the Woman's Auxiliary of one hundred members, meeting monthly in four chapters, who spontaneously voted $1,000 from their treasury toward reducing the debt and constantly peppered the Vestry with suggestions for innovation and improvement; the women of the Altar Guild, faithful tenders of the sanctuary; and the dedicated teachers, men and women, of the Sunday School. Nevertheless, attendance at the Sunday School continued to decline, and the Parish Council, from which so much had been expected, ceased to meet.

David Yates made a difference from his first eleven o'clock Sunday service, in late November 1935. He did not alter the Anglican liturgy, which he understood, respected, and loved, but he enhanced it. "He had a very plain style when reading the service, but it was at once thoughtful, earnest and *sure*. The way he read the prayers, for example, helped to bring out the meaning. The way he emphasized the 'dew of Thy Blessing' in the prayer for the clergy always made vivid the way God's blessings rain down upon us all. He always said, 'Christ Jesus came into the world to save *sinners*,' reminding us that it was those who were conscious of their sin that Jesus came to help. But most vivid of all was the way he said, 'Thou art the same Lord whose property is *always* to have mercy.' One felt, somehow, that every person in the church, David himself, choir, and congregation was in the presence of God."[1]

Yates wrote out his sermon in advance, and he read it. We do not have this very first sermon, but several later ones were published from time to time in the *Durham Morning Herald*. They were well considered, well written, and conveyed a message that Yates thought the congregation needed. After half a century, they still stand up as effective presentations. Of his own accord he later suggested that on Communion Sundays (usually the first Sunday of each month) his sermons not exceed fifteen minutes. After Bost's interminable talks, what a welcome relief!

In the ensuing months and years Yates continued the enhancement of the Sunday morning service. When on February 5, 1936 an anonymous donor offered to give St. Philip's two eucharistic candles, two Vestry veterans, Col. J. Harper Erwin and E. I Bugg, recommended caution and consultation of the congregation, out of respect for the feelings of many low-church parishioners. But the majority of the Vestry, representing a new generation, overruled them and accepted the gift. Later, in his sermon "Silent Aids to Worship," Yates explained: "All candles symbolize Christ as the Light of the World. The candles on either end [of the altar] are eucharistic candles, lighted only at the Eucharist or Holy Communion. They represent the two natures of our Lord Who was both human and divine." The Vestry's acceptance of the candles was a slight but significant step away from low-church churchmanship.

Also enhancing the excellence of the eleven o'clock service was a new direction and vigor in the choir. The resignation of Alice Hundley as choir director and organist gave Yates the chance to secure, in October 1937, Professor and Mrs. W. P. Twaddell as co-choir directors for $40 a month: Mr. Stratton became the organist for a monthly salary of $30. Twaddell was a major figure in Durham's musical history, and to obtain his services and those of his wife for St. Philip's was a major coup. Born in 1879 in Philadelphia, he had studied music at Yale, New York University, and the University of Pennsylvania, where with Dr. G. Edward Stubbs, an authority on boys' choirs, he had "helped to develop a method for training boys' voices in order to control range and tone quality before, while, and after their voice changed." After a career in Northern churches and a year as director of music at Bessie Tift College in Forsyth, Georgia (whence the title of "Professor"), he came to Durham in 1922 as organist and choir director for the First Presbyterian Church, where he remained for twenty-five years. A dynamo of energy, he founded a Durham Children's Choir School (1924–46), directed the Durham High chorus which in three consecutive years (1934–37) won so many state prizes that it was barred from further competition, and for ten years took on the co-direction of St. Philip's choir. His wife, Vera Carr, a native of Durham, was an accomplished musician and music director of the county schools.[2] The Twaddells started at St. Philip's a series of distinguished choir directors that has continued without interruption ever since. Their appointment also signaled a return to paid singers, as the amount budgeted for the choir rose from $750 (1936) to $1,005 (1937) and $1,605 (1938). An additional $200 was appropriated to repair the forty-year-old organ.

Yates made a difference, too, at his first congregational meeting. At his first Vestry meeting, on December 11, 1935, he quietly "announced that instead of holding the congregational meeting in December it would be held in January." This step was itself a revolution, fifteen years overdue. But more was to come. When the congregation assembled in the old parish house on January 6, 1936, eighty-seven communicants attended, a figure equaling that of the best of the Bost years. After opening the meeting with a song and a prayer, Yates called on representatives from each church agency to report on its activities and accomplishments during the past year. Unfortunately we do not have these reports, but a mere list suggests the complex operations of a mature institutional church:

Report on Primary Church School — Mrs. J. A. Robinson
Report on Young People's Service League — George Watts Carr, Jr.

Report on Work of the Choir—Mrs. Hugo Walker
Report on Altar Guild—Mrs. Frank Webb
Report on Women's Auxiliary—Mrs. H. C. Byrd
Report on Laymen's League—Nat Gregory
Report on Vestry—Col. J. Harper Erwin
Report of Treasurer (in printed form)—B. W. Hobgood, Jr.
Report on Every-Member Canvass (in printed form)
    —E. M. Hunter
Report by the Clergy—St. Andrew's and St. Joseph's
    —Rev. A. S. Lawrence, Jr.—St. Philip's—Rev. David Yates

This simple innovation, of annual reports publicly presented, was repeated the next year, and the next year, and the next . . ., until it became a habit, an institution within the larger institution, St. Philip's Church. And no wonder! It compelled agencies and their leaders to reflect on what they were doing. Since their activity was thus opened to public scrutiny and discussion, it made them responsible for what they did or did not do. As a device for stimulus and control, the innovation was invaluable to both the rector and the congregation.

The list also reveals the intergenerational nature of the leadership at St. Philip's. Col. J. Harper Erwin, the oldest person listed, had joined his brother Will at St. Philip's in 1895. In 1900 he had donated the land on which the first chapel of St. Andrew's had been built. He had served as junior warden in 1920, 1921, and 1927, as senior warden in 1928 and 1929, and now was reporting for the Vestry again. The youngest person on the list was George Watts Carr, Jr. Born in 1919, confirmed in 1931, he was at the beginning of a long career of service and leadership in the church. In between in age was Mrs. J. A. Robinson, primary supervisor in the Durham City Schools and for nearly fifty years teacher and chair in the primary department of the St. Philip's Church School. Her husband, editor and publisher of the *Durham Herald*, had been one of the founders of Chapter 225 of the Brotherhood of St. Andrew during the period from 1916 to 1921. And so had Bailey W. Hobgood, the treasurer, the impregnable rock of fiscal integrity. And, of course, there were many others, who will appear later in our story. Yates did not create this pattern of intergenerational effort and leadership, but he continued it and as advisor to the Young People's Service League he attracted other young people into it.

The minutes of his first congregational meeting continued:

After the reports, in accord with custom, Mr. Yates called for nominations for members of the Vestry to replace G. W. Carr, E. H. Clement, E. M. Hunter, Jr., and W. H. Ruffin; the following nominations being made:

W. B. Bass
H. C. Bird
J. M. M. Gregory
Murray Jones
Frank Minter
Lawson Moore
B. R. Roberts
W. E. Seeman

Ballots were distributed and upon motion duly made and seconded, it was decided that the four persons receiving the highest number of ballots would be declared elected. This resulted in the election of the following persons to serve on the Vestry for three years beginning January 1, 1936:

H. C. Bird
Lawson Moore
B. R. Roberts
W. E. Seeman

Mr. Yates announced that the Women's Auxiliary was very anxious to secure a memorial to Reverend S. S. Bost, and that a committee from the Vestry had been appointed to meet with the committee from the Auxiliary. The project was discussed at length, after which a motion was made and seconded that these committees be given power to act. This motion was unanimously carried.

The committees decided on a large window, representing Christ the Shepherd bringing home the lost sheep in His arms. The window was to be placed at the far end of the nave, overlooking the altar. Its cost, $1,075, was soon oversubscribed. Payne-Spiers Studio of New York City was retained to create and install it, and the Vestry approved its appropriate inscription: "I am the good Shepherd and know my sheep" (St. John 10:14).

The minutes of Yates's first congregational meeting concluded: "There being no further business to come before the meeting, a motion for adjournment was made and Mr. Yates announced that members of the Women's Auxiliary would serve light refreshments." [3]

Always the teacher, by word and by deed, Yates also made a difference in the Church School, which then met twelve months a year. At an early meeting its dedicated teachers elected him its superintendent by acclamation.[4] Thereafter he assembled them in monthly faculty meetings, at which he conversed about what it meant to be a Christian teacher. He emphasized three important points for teachers: "1. Our prayer life. 2. To Live What we Teach. 3. Faithfulness and dependability." He also defined demanding policies: before the school year started, a teacher must come to know the families of his or her pupils; a child who was absent once was to be telephoned by the teacher; after the second absence, the teacher was to visit. He encouraged the teachers to form their own productive committees on curriculum and methods, and they responded. He urged them to use the growing Church School Library and suggested they read at least two books during the year, one before Christmas and one after. He even involved the students. He formed an elective Student Council, comprised of representatives chosen by classes above the sixth grade. At that time there were two Church School budgets: the $300 allotted by the Vestry and the $200 in pledges contributed by the students; there was also the student Lenten offering of about $400. The Student Council set the Church School budget. By the 1940s the result of these measures was a vital Church School, with rising attendance.

Yates's relations with the Woman's Auxiliary, Altar Guild, Church School teachers, and Young People's Service League were warm, supportive, and in action cooperative. Indeed, one is tempted to say that the Woman's Auxiliary was so strong during these years and so forward-looking that it shared a co-leadership role with him. His relations with the Vestry were more complex. Only gradually and incompletely could he bring the Vestry to his way of thinking. What happened cannot be defined in a phrase, but only disclosed by an unrolling narrative.

In part, their initial differences stemmed from the complexity of the situation facing them: the magnitude of their problems in the midst of the Great Depression — the inadequate old parish house at St. Philip's, the dilapidated chapel of St. Andrew's, the deterioration of St. Joseph's since Will Erwin's death, and the daunting parish debt, now standing at $14,500 — as well as the greatness of the need and opportunities for service in the environing community. In a letter to the Vestry, the Reverend A. Stratton Lawrence, the new Assistant Rector in charge of St.

Joseph's and St. Andrew's, addressed both the problems and the opportunities:

> It is my sincere opinion that St. Philip's parish has a future that is hardly equaled by any other Church in the Diocese, and it is a future that must be constantly kept before us. We must ever be cognizant of the fact that Durham is the focal point for the Deaf work of the Diocese, that it has a large Negro population, scarcely recognized by the Parish, which is being ministered to by one lonely Negro priest, that it has the largest number of Episcopal students of any town in the Diocese in Duke University, that it has a large number of Episcopalians among the people in the mill sections of the city, that in East Durham and Edgemont, the latter particularly, the Church has a great opportunity for valuable and important work. To carry on this great work in our Parish and Community as Christ's disciples, we must work out from the mother Church. Therefore, I urge the Vestry to do all in its power to help the congregation realize the need and opportunity of the Parish, by full cooperation with the Rector, by planning ahead and mapping out a program for the whole Parish.
>
> Such a glance into the future looks beyond the payment of the Parish Debt, and beyond the construction of the much needed Parish House for the mother Church, and looks forward to the time when the Parish will need not one assistant, but two or three. I would like to see the Vestry work out a ten year program for the Parish, with the first five years specifically and clearly planned.[5]

In this situation fellow Christian parishioners, united in their dedication to the welfare of St. Philip's Parish, might still legitimately differ on the strategy to follow.

To a point Yates and the Vestry were one. Responsible for the maintenance of church property and for the prudent management of its finances, the Vestry in its monthly meetings understandably dealt with repairs, bills, and budget. The rhythm of the fiscal year, January 1 to December 31, formed its central concern. Each November its Finance Committee formulated for the general Vestry's approval a preliminary next year's budget—a wish list. In December one of its members chaired the Every Member Canvass, which rarely obtained enough pledges to match the estimated expenses. Even the amount pledged had to be discounted by 7 percent as uncollectible. In the succeeding January the Vestry realistically revised its proposed disbursements downward to accord with projected income. Then, during the year, not all pledges were paid on time. It was not unknown during the summer for the treasurer to have to borrow from the bank in order to pay the Rectors' salaries. Nevertheless, every fiscal year ended with all projected budget expenses met, a notable achievement in the depression years.

Yates, however, was not satisfied with merely balancing the budget; nor were several reform-minded Vestry members. He tried to persuade the Vestry to widen the scope of its activity, to raise its sights, to speed the discharge of the debt, to hasten the erection of a new parish house, *and* to reach out in social service to the Durham community.

The Vestry minutes and those of the annual congregational meetings, spare as they are, enable us to trace the fascinating story of the interaction of the prudent Vestry with Yates on these major issues. Two important letters (how we wish we had more!) amplify the account.

The story opens during the summer of 1936. At the end of an inconsequential nuts-and-bolts Vestry meeting on August 5, "The Rev. Mr. Yates proposed that we have a definite program of work for the fall." After a few months when nothing happened, a former senior warden, Professor Harold C. Bird, probably impatient with the Vestry's failure to make long-term plans, suggested at the Vestry meeting of November 11, 1936 that "it would be well for the old Parish Council to function again." The Vestry "approved the suggestion and elected Mr. Ellerbee Powe, Jr. and Mr. Lawson Moore, to represent the Vestry on this Council." Back in 1932 Powe and Moore had collaborated with the Woman's Auxiliary to found an antecedent Parish Council, which had ceased to exist. Although the second version remained in existence throughout Yates's ministry, there is no record that it did any more than the first.

Nevertheless, 1937 opened propitiously with the prospect of a budget surplus. At the Vestry meeting of Wednesday, January 6, an illuminating discussion followed on how to spend it. Yates proposed $200 for social service, $100 for work at Duke University, $50 for the Young People's Service League, and an indefinite amount for the Church School. These are clues to the breadth of his thinking and vision. Several vestrymen favored payment of outstanding bills and reduction of the church mortgage. However, prudence prevailed when the Vestry decided that a surplus was not a surplus until it had been accumulated, and it passed to the order of the day.

Persevering and indefatigable, Yates went to the congregation at its annual meeting on Monday, January 11, 1937, only five days later. At its very end, he "stated that he was very anxious for the church to pay off its debt as soon as possible so that we could build a new parish house which is so badly needed at the present time." Since there was no comment, a motion for adjournment was made and the Woman's Auxiliary served light refreshments.

The Vestry's silence on the parish house issue for the next eleven months set the stage for our first important letter, from Glen A. Coan, secretary of the Parent-Teachers Association of St. Philip's, to Mr. Lloyd Williams, secretary of the Vestry, dated December 16, 1937:

Dear Lloyd:
At a Parent-Teacher meeting of St. Philip's Church School held on December 11, the following resolution was passed and I have been asked to hand you a copy: "It being the sense of this meeting that a great need exists for a new Parish House, it is therefore resolved that the Vestry be requested to work out in the near future a plan whereby a suitable Parish House may be procured, said plan to be submitted to the congregation." [6]

When the Vestry at its December meeting again discussed the need for a new parish house and again took no action, Yates went again to the congregational meeting, on January 10, 1938, this time with Mrs. George L. Lyon, president of the Woman's Auxiliary. Together, they "made a strong and timely plea for a new Parish House." But still no action was taken.

Finally, after *eighteen years* of discussion on the need for a new parish house, the Vestry moved. At a specially called meeting not quite two weeks later, January 21, 1938, Yates nominated and the Vestry confirmed William H. Ruffin as senior warden. An executive officer of the National Association of Manufacturers—the first Durham businessman to achieve that honor—Ruffin may have made a decisive difference in the ensuing events. Yates then appointed five three-man Vestry committees with assigned functions: Finance, Worship and Music, Religious Education, Social Service, and Missions (St. Joseph's and St. Andrew's). The appointments were made "with the suggestion that the committees meet and map out programs and plans for activities during the coming year." The innovation here was not to have committees—standing committees on finance, music, and hospitality were common during the Bost years—but to have a comprehensive set that conformed to Yates's overall vision for the Parish and potentially implemented it. That vision included, it may be noted, social service to the community. In addition, the sensitive selection of just the right members for each committee reveals a rector who knew his parishioners well and was thinking all the time about how and where they might best serve.

Yates next "mentioned the need of the church for a parish house and suggested it as an aim for the Vestry for 1938, as our present facilities are entirely inadequate for the Sunday School." The Vestry recognized the need but thought that the debt of $10,943.30 must first be extinguished. It authorized Yates to appoint a Vestry committee to meet with a committee or representative of the Woman's Auxiliary to consider "the advisability of taking action on this question," that is, the debt. This was the background of our second important letter, handwritten from Mrs. George L. Lyon, president of the Woman's Auxiliary, to William H. Ruffin, chair of the Vestry committee:

February 10, 1938

My dear Mr. Ruffin:
In regard to your wish to hear from the women of the parish, the question was raised and discussed at all four chapter meetings. I take pleasure in reporting to you that each chapter voted *unanimously* that *now* is the propitious time to erase the debt on the church property. This result voiced the opinion of over a hundred women who pledge their enthusiastic cooperation in any step the vestry sees fit to take.

Hoping you will give us the privilege of sharing in this great service to our church. I am

Sincerely and loyally,
Elizabeth F. Lyon
Pres. St. Philip's Branch
of Woman's Auxiliary[7]

Thus encouraged, the Vestry acted swiftly. Upon a motion by Ruffin it decided on February 10 to stage a special campaign to wipe out the debt. The drive was to end not later than Palm Sunday, April 10.

Pledges were to be preferably in cash, but if not in cash then in installments to be paid in full by January 15, 1939. Unfortunately, the campaign occurred during a steep decline in business activity— a mini-depression within the Great Depression. The drive, chaired by Dr. Arthur H. London, raised only $7,155.30 in pledges, and of that amount only $5,319.50 was paid in by the end of the year. By special gifts and annual amortization the debt was finally cleared in 1941.

At the Vestry meeting of January 1939, Yates took one step backward. In renewing the five standing committees (Finance, Worship and Music, Christian Education, Social Service, and Missions), he replaced the committee on Social Service with a familiar standby, a Committee on Hospitality and Fellowship. The purpose of the Committee on Social Service had been to lead the congregation into serving the needs of the deteriorating downtown community that surrounded St. Philip's. Its withdrawal signified that Yates was retreating from full implementation of his overall vision of a church strong enough to serve both itself and others. One can only speculate on the reasons for his retreat. Questions abound. Did Yates encounter a basic indifference among the majority of the congregation to the needs and opportunities for service lying immediately to hand in the neighborhood around the church? Or did he decide that at the present juncture he had to make choices and set priorities and that it was more important for St. Philip's to put its own house in order by extinguishing its debt, building a new parish house, and fostering hospitality and fellowship than it was to serve the world outside?

With the extinction of the debt in sight and with sharpened focus, Yates, at the Vestry meeting of March 7, 1940, reintroduced for discussion "the question of the much needed Parish House." (He nearly always "suggests" or "introduces for discussion.") In response, the Vestry appointed a planning committee for a special fundraising campaign but postponed the drive for a year.

This second campaign for a parish house was a replay of the first, though with obvious improvements, the product of lessons learned from the first experience, but ending with the same stunning, incomprehensible conclusion. At the April 1940 Vestry meeting George Watts Carr, a Durham architect and member of the Vestry committee, presented floor plans for a parish house to be erected on a site west of the church (its location today). The estimated cost was $45,000 to $50,000. In June the Vestry interviewed George Ward Stone, head of a

New York firm that had managed similar campaigns and was bidding for the St. Philip's job. But again the Vestry hesitated. At its October meeting it suspended plans for a special parish house campaign, as "inadvisable at this time." At the November meeting the idea was floated that the Church School's immediate needs could be met by building "a rough stained hut" consisting of twelve classrooms and costing only $3,500 to $4,500. Under the outraged protests of the Church School teachers the Vestry dropped the idea in December and referred the entire question to the upcoming congregational meeting.

At that meeting, on January 13, 1941, Yates again "introduced for discussion the important subject of our need for a Parish House." The meeting unanimously instructed the Vestry to return with plans for a special fundraising campaign. At the Vestry meeting of January 17 Yates again named Ruffin senior warden and chair of a Special Committee for the Improvement of Educational Facilities of the Parish. The Special Committee, the Vestry, the Woman's Auxiliary, and a specially convened congregational meeting of February 5, 1941 then enthusiastically endorsed plans for a special drive: Goal, $20,000; George Ward Stone to be manager of the campaign for a commission of $1,000; pledges to be paid within two years of the close of the drive; the remainder of the parish house cost to be covered by a bank loan.

In a whirlwind campaign from February 10 to March 10, Stone and his associates raised not $20,000 but $25,590. Great was the delight and elation and joy at St. Philip's!

But then occurred the incomprehensible phenomenon, which appears again and again in our history: some St. Philippians do not keep their pledged word. After two years, B. R. Roberts, treasurer of the Parish House Building Fund, reported on July 7, 1943 that $9,113 was still past due. As late as 1946 the Vestry was still trying to collect the $6,000 owing on pledges made five years before.

In any case, the outbreak of war in early December 1941 suspended for years all planning for a new parish house. Truly, this history of St. Philip's should bear a subtitle: "How God's Will Was Achieved by Fallible Human Beings, or Pilgrim's Progress."[8]

Yates was rector not only of St. Philip's *Church* but also of St. Philip's *Parish*, which included the two parochial missions, St. Joseph's and St. Andrew's. The same was true of the Vestry and its five standing committees, appointed by Yates: they too were agencies of St. Philip's Parish. The standing committees, first installed in January 1938, were appointed anew with different personnel every January throughout his ministry. They were one of the ways that he tried to involve members of the Vestry in the work of the Parish and thus get things done.

The reports of the Vestry's Finance Committee, dealing largely with bills and budget, were regular, almost monthly. The reports of the other committees — Worship and Music, Christian Education, Hospitality and Fellowship, and Missions (St. Andrew's and St. Joseph's) — were occasional, as some crisis in their field arose. However, when the reports of the Committee on Missions are dovetailed with those of the Assistant Rectors in charge of St. Andrew's and St. Joseph's, we can perceive what developed in that area.

Just as the first chapter of this history was entitled "In Search of a Rector Who Would Stay, 1878–1898," the subtitle of this chapter might read "In Search of an Assistant Rector Who Would Stay, 1935–1945." Three excellent young men came, contributed vitally to the life of the two mission churches, and did so well that they were subject to call elsewhere. A. Stratton Lawrence was the first. From July 1935 he revitalized St. Joseph's, first as deacon and then, after his ordination in 1936, as Assistant Rector. However, during the summer months he was also business manager of the conference/camp of Vade Mecum. He was so successful there that Bishop Penick decided that he would be more useful to the Diocese as manager of the center and minister to the unchurched nearby. So Lawrence resigned from St. Joseph's on January 27, 1939.

On the strong recommendation of Bishop Penick, St. Philip's Vestry then called on February 17, 1939 the Reverend Henry Nutt Parsley, a graduate of the University of North Carolina and Virginia Seminary and currently engaged in parochial and student work at Amherst. At St. Joseph's his work with the students at Duke University became so fruitful that he resigned on October 9, 1941 to become chaplain at Duke.

St. Philip's Vestry on December 2, 1941 next called the Reverend Josiah T. Carter, a rector from Clarksburg, West Virginia, who for several years gave very strong leadership to both St. Andrew's and St. Joseph's.

Nothing could surpass the Christian dedication and zeal of the several families who worshipped at St. Andrew's. They were regular in at-

tendance, prompt in promising and paying their pledges, and supportive of each other. In this, St. Andrew's greatly resembled St. Philip's
Church during its first two decades.

And nothing could exceed the dilapidation of the chapel in which
the congregation met. Erected in 1901, never of sound construction, it
had fallen into disrepair. When Nat Gregory, chair of the St. Philip's
Vestry Committee on Missions, inspected the structure in August 1939,
he was shocked:

> The church building itself [he reported on September 7, 1939] is
> in terrible condition. The ceiling is not sealed, and very poorly
> braced, so that a high wind could very possibly blow it in. The
> front doors are practically rotted away, as are the front steps. The
> joists under the house were never nailed to the foundation sills,
> so that the walls have swelled, leaving large cracks in the floor,
> and considerable irregularity in the side walls. The irregularity
> has caused the plaster to crack all over the inside and in some
> places large pieces are about to fall. The only heating arrange-
> ment is a stove in the center of the floor, with sheet metal pipe
> going straight through the ceiling. It is practically impossible to
> heat the building with these limited facilities, as the heat all goes
> up into the top through the cracks.[9]

At the moment of Gregory's report St. Philip's Vestry was so
strapped for cash that it could not appropriate more than $30 to brace
the building. The Vestry also discussed a long-term policy of raising
money for a new chapel. The congregation of St. Andrew's started its
own church building fund.

Since the Vestry had done nothing effective, the new Assistant Rector, Josiah T. Carter, brought the issue before the congregational meeting of St. Philip's Parish on January 11, 1943, nearly three and one-half
years after Gregory's report and thirteen years after Bost had called
for a new brick building for St. Andrew's. In his report, which in his
absence was read by Mrs. Carter, he praised the congregation of St.
Andrew's ("it would be hard, if not impossible to find a more faithful
and devoted group"), paid a glowing tribute to its Woman's Auxiliary and Sunday School, and recommended the formation of an advisory governing board composed of four men and three women, even
though "such an arrangement may be contrary to certain traditions"
of male dominance. However, he went on, something had to be done

about the building if a permanent, growing mission was to be established in East Durham:

> At present the building is dreadfully out of repair, making it impossible to keep the interior properly cleaned, and kept in churchly order. It is so cold during the winter months that it has often become necessary for all to huddle around the stove during Services and choir rehearsals, and not infrequently have we had to retire to some nearby home. If you will pardon my frankness, let me say that I do not believe we have the right to expect the congregation and especially the children of the Sunday School to risk their health in such surroundings. If we ever expect to do more than minister to the few unusually faithful of the present membership, and entertain a reasonable hope of retaining the children of these families something must be done. Although it may be wise to eliminate from our minds, for the present [wartime conditions], any thought of a new Church building, it would seem to be false economy not to make the present building more comfortable and attractive, that is, if we really want to reach out and lay the foundation for a permanent work in the future.[10]

In response to his plea an advisory board of four men and three women was elected, and St. Philip's contributed $97.50 and the congregation of St. Andrew's added $217.50 to improve the interior appearance of the chapel. But the building itself was still woefully inadequate, and its replacement, so long discussed, was in 1945 still on the Parish's list of unfinished business.

St. Joseph's was in easier circumstances. Thanks to the generosity of Will Erwin, it had a solid granite church building (1908) and parish house (1928) as well as a $30,000 trust fund (1929), which was annually yielding $800 (sometimes more, sometimes less) to a church budget in the neighborhood of $1,400. It had the program and agencies of a matured church: at the Sunday services a dedicated Altar Guild, an organist, a choir of seventeen members, a Sunday School, and a Young People's Service League; and, of course, at all times and for all endeavors, a strong Woman's Auxiliary.

Since it was closer to Duke University than St. Philip's Church was, St. Joseph's had taken over the work with the Duke students. The first Assistant Rector, Lawrence, had offered them its parish house as a meeting place. His successor, Parsley, who had been doing student work at Amherst, lived in a graduate dormitory at Duke. Even before he left St. Joseph's to become chaplain at the university, he had developed a full-fledged program on the Duke campus: Communion at 9:00 A.M. each Sunday in the University Chapel; a meeting of the Canterbury Club each Sunday evening at 6:45; monthly socials and special conferences hosted by the Woman's Auxiliary of St. Joseph's.

St. Joseph's was also moving toward the status of an independent parish, a move fostered and guided by Yates and St. Philip's Vestry. On December 9, 1936 the Vestry approved for St. Joseph's an Advisory Board of ten men and on January 13, 1939, a separate treasurer. Both were to operate under the supervision of St. Philip's officials. In 1942 the Advisory Board and St. Philip's Vestry negotiated a demarcation line between the two jurisdictions: St. Joseph's was to have first visiting rights to newcomers who lived on Watts Streets and west. Also in 1943 and 1944, thanks to a special drive and a gift of $1,000 from the estate of Claudia Erwin Powe, St. Joseph's had raised $5,500 to build a rectory, which then became another item on the list of unfinished business.

Contacts between St. Philip's and the other Episcopal church in town, St. Titus in the black community, were rare. Reverend A. Stratton Lawrence's description of the Episcopal situation in Durham bears this out: in April 1937 he referred to the "large Negro population, scarcely recognized by the Parish [of St. Philip's], which is being ministered to by one lonely Negro priest." Indeed, during the Bost years St. Titus appears only once in the Vestry minutes of St. Philip's: when in the 1920s the Vestry was contemplating disposal of the pews from the old frame church, it decided to donate ten pews to St. Titus, at the latter's request.

During the rectorship of David Yates the customs of a segregated society were not breached. The lowest employee on St. Philip's staff, the sexton, was a black man who did most of the manual labor around the church. When from time to time St. Philip's hosted the Diocesan Convention, the delegates of the North Carolina black Episcopal churches were housed by black families in Durham; white delegates found shelter in white hotels or with white families. But at the Convention meetings, there was no racial discrimination.

However, there are clues that during Yates's tenure the level of consciousness of the racial situation was rising among St. Philippians. Rev. Lawrence's letter, quoted above, is one clue. The minutes of the monthly meetings of the Church School faculty contain others. The minutes of January 6, 1937, for example, are revealing:

> There was a long and involved discussion about a booklet entitled "The Church and the Negro," which is prescribed [by the National Church] for use of the church school in Lenten Studies. Mr. Yates read two of the stories which were immediately pronounced dull and uninteresting by some teachers. Someone suggested that a study of St. Titus Church would be more helpful. This was dropped. Mrs. Carter moved to accept the booklet, but with the provision that each teacher be allowed to adapt the stories according to his or her idea of the subject present. Motion passed 9–5.[11]

There was a follow-up. At the faculty meeting of February 22, 1937, the "motion was made and passed to ask the entire Church School to go on a 'Pilgrimage' to Raleigh on February 28 to visit and inspect St. Augustine's College, the only Episcopal Negro College in America. Inspection of this college is in line with the Lenten Study now going on in the Church School."[12] On November 26, 1940 the Student Council of the Church School budgeted $4.50 for St. Titus, under the heading of "Missionary Work." Later, in a wartime sermon, Yates cited racial prejudice as a cause of war. These clues suggest a drift of opinion and thoughtfulness, but they do not permit us to say more.

Through all the struggles, disappointments, frustrations, and postponements David Yates remained the same friendly, gangly, youthful bachelor who was continually reminding and teaching his congregation what it meant to be a follower of Jesus Christ. He taught by his example. On his initial salary of $2,400 he was not hard up. But notice what followed. At the then current price level, he could save half of it, or more likely give it to those in need. He relinquished the rectory, which the church rented out; he lived in rented rooms; when after several years the Vestry budgeted him for $3,000, he declined the increase; when later it insisted, he requested a reduction. He never took a vacation. As we have seen he was his own superintendent of Sunday School, and in those days the Church School met throughout the year, including the summer months. The Vestry finally in 1943 recommended that their Rector take two weeks' vacation. It is not recorded that he did. He was tireless and genial in doing the Lord's work. He always found time to visit each family in the congregation more than once a year. The parishioners were always glad to see him, and they noted with amusement that he generally arrived shortly before the evening meal, so he had to be invited to join them. To be sure, he thus supplemented his income, but is there a more Christian way toward fellowship than to share a meal together?

He taught also by his sermons, which his listeners remembered long after he had left St. Philip's. Sibyl Powe and Louise Newton remarked that

> he knew that we all needed help, and he preached simple but useful sermons toward that end. He preached, for example, about the need for concentration, especially during the prayers. One was comforted when he said that at first it was difficult to concentrate more than ten minutes at a time. He often preached about the obligation to go to church at least once a week. He said that everyone should go to the eleven o'clock service on Sunday, and that the other services were extras. He wanted to make sure that the congregation met together as a whole, or as near as might be, at least once a week. And at least one of the reasons for this was that he always kept us up on our obligations.
>
> A hymn he often had us sing was "Once to Every Man and Nation," which includes these words: "New occasions teach new duties." David never left us any doubt as to what our new duties were. It was his practice, though, to start early, and prepare us for the obligations; his sermons pointed out where duty lay, and gave concrete helps for carrying out that duty. They always started where the listener was, and then showed the way he should go. Then when the new obligation came up, we were as ready for it as possible.
>
> Sometimes he seemed to set impossibly high standards. But they were always set in perspective. He knew, proclaiming the truths of the Gospel as he did, what sinners we all were. But he sought us out, got us to Church, made us understand the forgiveness of God, and set us on the right path.[13]

His seven extant sermons, originally published in the *Durham Morning Herald*, enable us to confirm and later to illustrate this remembrance. Their subjects ranged from the "Silent Aids to Worship" —the structure and symbols of the church building—through the observance of Lent to keeping the Sabbath and prayer. But whatever the subject and text, the theme of the sermon was always the same, "Living a Christian Life," and so was its focus, "Putting God First." The tone, of quietly reasoning together, was positive and encouraging in pointing the way to go. To be sure, there were alluring temptations: the obsessive desires for money and material goods, for pleasure, for comfort, and for popularity. But there were also many aids: the Bible, the example and injunctions of Jesus Christ, the Book of Common Prayer and its enactment each Sunday in the Anglican liturgy, and the fellowship of other communicants of the congregation. And one might add, as another aid and source of inspiration, the example and the sermons of David Yates, who lived the life he preached.

The War Years, 1941–1945

The Japanese attack on Pearl Harbor, December 7, 1941, came as a surprise to most St. Philippians. J. Harper Erwin, Jr., told how the news came to him. The son of Col. J. Harper Erwin, Will Erwin's brother, he had already served St. Philip's as junior warden in 1932, 1935, 1936, 1940, and 1941, and as senior warden in 1937. As junior warden and chair of the Vestry's Finance Committee, he had gone over to the parish house on Sunday afternoon, December 7, to help total up the returns from the annual Every Member Canvass. As he was figuring, Nat Gregory arrived with his report and with the stunning news of the Japanese attack.[14]

St. Philippians soon had a second surprise. Their beloved Rector was a pacifist! On the second Sunday after Pearl Harbor David Yates felt bound by his principles, "Put God first," and by his loyalty to Jesus Christ to declare forthrightly in his sermon that being a Christian and serving in the armed forces were irreconcilable! His listeners in the pews were not simply astounded, they were red-in-the-face angered and infuriated. They or their sons, husbands, brothers, or fathers were dutifully, honorably, and patriotically answering their country's call, and now they were told they were living in sin! Yates was probably astonished by the violence of their reaction, although foreknowledge would not have stopped him. Bishop Penick came over from Raleigh to counsel him, but Yates never moderated his position. Pacifists are always asked worst-case scenario questions: "If your wife or sister was being raped, what would you do?" Once David was asked, "If the Japs were invading our country and taking over, what should we do?" His reply was short and consistent with his beliefs: "Let them."

It has been said that being a pacifist only in peacetime is like being a vegetarian between meals. Yates's distinction was that in peacetime his pacifism was latent and invisible, lost in his overall genial, caring friendliness to all. Only in wartime did it become overt and vocal. The point is that, like Jesus, he loved and cared for everyone, in both the enemy camp and ours. His sermon, "Let Us Pray," delivered during wartime, is worth quoting at length, as an expression of his thought and as an example of his approach of reasoning together:

> For what, then, ought we to pray, and for whom? Certainly for the people in many parts of the world who are suffering terribly from war, famine, and pestilence. We have seen pictures in *Life Magazine* and elsewhere that portrayed some of this suffering. We have read descriptions of what is being endured by the conquered peoples of Europe, the population of China, those in the other countries that are at war. We can only dimly imagine what is the lot of the sick, the wounded, the dying, the bereaved, the hungry, the starving. This winter cold and famine will sweep over Europe and in their wake will stalk disease and death to take many of the emaciated millions out of their afflictions. . . .
>
> Shall we not extend our intercessions to friend and foe alike? We know that our so-called enemies are God's children and therefore our brethren. We know that they, too, are human and can feel in full measure the crown of thorns that mankind is pressing upon his own brow. Most of them decide this war very little more than we do. We know that we as well as they are guilty of the sin that is the underlying cause of war.
>
> But more than this, even, we have a command from our Master, "Pray for them which despitefully use you and persecute you." He prayed from the Cross for His persecutors. In the name of our common humanity, in the name of our one Father, in the name of our common Savior, we cannot omit them from our prayers.
>
> We are not to pray for the success of their designs, of which God will be the judge. But we are to pray for their forgiveness where it is needed and for their conversion from any wrong paths that they are following. In the words of the Litany we are to ask, "that it may please Thee to forgive our enemies, persecutors, and slanderers, and to turn their hearts." When engaged in evil as we see it, they need our prayers more now than ever before.

This will not be easy. It makes necessary another thing for which we must pray—that we may be without hate. Christ had directly commanded this. "Love your enemies." He says further, "A new commandment I give unto you, That ye love one another; as I have loved you, that ye also love one another." How is it that Christ loved us? He loved us entirely apart from any worthiness on our part. "While we were yet sinners, Christ died for the ungodly." Love of all men is absolute and unconditional in our religion; hate is completely forbidden. But it will take constant wrestling in prayer and God's grace thereby to accomplish it.

Nothing is a more necessary condition of bringing peace than the elimination of hate. If the peace terms are dictated by hate and the desire for revenge, they will lead to a repetition of what we are now going through. Yet it will be hard to avoid and will require all of the power through prayer that we can possibly get. . . .

Shall we not pray also that God will eliminate the other causes of war, in ourselves and in other people? Nationalism, race prejudice, pride, economic greed, selfishness; these are the sins that lead to war, and are wrong, whether they have that effect or not. They are contrary to God's will, and that is their condemnation. We need to ask God to broaden our sympathies, to widen our vision, to enlarge our hearts and those of all men, and to help us to express them in our national and international life. So can we best prepare for the just and durable peace that we long for when this war is over.

We shall surely pray for our own loved ones. We shall not pray for victory. As Bishop Penick has said, that would be judging, which is God's province. But we shall pray that God will keep us all true to Him, and that His will, to keep our loved ones safe but above all that they may be true Christians and so be prepared for whatever may come, will prevail.

One great, simple fact looms up from this war that overshadows every other meaning it could have. It is that our great need and the dire need of the world is to come back to God. That can be done only through prayer.

As World War II followed its own stern necessity and St. Philippians at home anxiously awaited casualty returns, they continued the essential services and institutions of their church and its parochial missions:

the eleven o'clock Sunday worship service and its immemorial Anglican liturgy and choir; the Altar Guild; the Sunday School; the annual congregational meeting; the monthly Vestry meetings, the annual budget; the Every Member Canvass; the Woman's Auxiliary; the Laymen's League; and the Young People's Service League. All these continued. And so did the spirit of devotion, beautifully expressed by a member of the Altar Guild, Mrs. Elizabeth Lyon, on January 29, 1945: "The duties of the Altar Guild are discharged quietly and unobtrusively, and with a deep sense of responsibility and high privilege for being able to contribute to the most important and sacred function of the church — the loving and consecrated care of the sanctuary." [15]

The war brought deprivations. The church services were depleted of young men; gasoline rationing curtailed the number of committee meetings (which may have been a blessing): the shortage of building materials necessarily postponed the construction of St. Philip's new parish house, St. Joseph's rectory, and St. Andrew's new brick chapel.

Yet the war also opened new opportunities for service, to which the Rector and the congregation together loyally responded. The Vestry ordered the installation of the American flag as part of the regular church service. Each Christmas the Woman's Auxiliary dispatched Remembrance Boxes to every St. Philippian in the armed forces. When a succession of infantry divisions, each numbering 30,000 men, was trained at nearby Camp Butner, the Durham streets were inundated with 4,000 soldiers each day and more on weekends. St. Philip's formed a special Soldiers Service Committee, chaired by Mrs. George Watts Carr. "Every Saturday night the old parish house was set up for a square dance or party for the soldiers at Camp Butner. Mrs. J. A. Robinson always stood at the door to receive them, and she was 'Mom' to thousands of these boys. Mr. Yates, Mr. Parsley, and Bailey Hobgood were there to keep things moving, and a number of girls helped with the entertainment." [16] The Vestry detailed two of its members to greet soldiers attending Sunday morning worship services. "On Sunday night the soldiers came again and there was music and singing. In this, Mrs. N. T. Yancey, distinguished soloist and organist at St. Joseph's, was the leading spirit."

The war also widened horizons and brought the world into view. St. Philippians were serving on every continent and on the high seas. That alone was mind-extending. Proposed curriculum changes in the upper grades of the Church School reflected this enlarged interest. At the meeting of its faculty in January 1943 Ethel Reade reported "on the general outline for the Parish, the general theme being Conversion to Christ for World Service. Four units were suggested for study in relation to this general theme: A Just and Durable Peace, Latin America, Christian Family Relations, and Race Relations." Yates, as superintendent, appointed a committee "to look into the feasibility of carrying out this study in the Church School: Miss Ethel Reade, Mrs. J. A. Robinson, Mrs. Leighton Huske, Mr. Glen A. Coan, and Mrs. Frank A. Webb." The committee was to function until September. The outcome of the report was that in February 1943 the Upper Department of the Church School worked on plans for a Just and Durable Peace: in March, during Lent, it studied Latin America. Of the other two recommended subjects, Christian Family Relations had long been a familiar topic and needed no further amplification, while the topic of Racial Relations was apparently dropped.

Meanwhile, as Yates became better known in Durham and in the Diocese of North Carolina he was honored by offices and given work to do outside St. Philip's. He was elected president of the Durham Ministerial Association in 1937 and 1944, and president of the Durham County Churches in 1940–41. In the Diocese he served as a delegate to the General Convention, 1940, 1943, 1946, 1949; as a member of the Standing Committee, 1941–47; and as secretary to the Executive Committee, 1935–38, 1939–40, and 1944–47.

Everything in St. Philip's seemed to be operating smoothly when David Yates again surprised the congregation: he informed the Vestry on February 9, 1945 that he was considering a call from the Chapel of the Cross at Chapel Hill, North Carolina, and on February 16 he resigned from St. Philip's. An outpouring of expressions of love, dismay, and shock followed his last eleven o'clock worship service at St. Philip's on Easter Sunday.

The reasons for his decision to move are speculative. He himself simply told the senior warden, Dr. Angus McBryde, that he thought ten years was long enough for a parson in a single church, which may have been the exact truth.[17] The fact that members of the congregation were surprised twice, by his pacifism and by his departure, suggests that they had not penetrated the inner citadel of his privacy. For all his unfailing friendliness, he apparently confided his deepest thoughts and feelings to no one, except perhaps to Bishop Penick.

Two concepts dear to David Yates were "pilgrim" and "pilgrim's progress." In his delightful sermon "Silent Aids to Worship," he took the pilgrim down the center aisle of the nave, into the chancel and sanctuary, on his way to God. For nearly ten years, two pilgrimages, of St. Philip's Parish and David Yates, had come together, intertwined, and then parted. What his experience at St. Philip's meant to him we shall never know. What his rectorship meant to St. Philip's is clearer. He had enlisted the cooperation of its leading church workers to re-vitalize a seasoned institutional church that had lost momentum and that was facing apparently intractable problems. Vigor and spiritual meaning were restored to the eleven o'clock Sunday worship service and Sunday School. The stagnation in growth was ended as the num-ber of communicants at St. Philip's *Church* increased from 415 (1934) to 608 (1944). The debt of $14,500 was extinguished and replaced by a Parish House Building Fund of $19,000; funds of $5,500 were as-sembled for a rectory at St. Joseph's and of a lesser amount for a brick chapel at St. Andrew's.

Yates had failed to persuade the congregation to recognize the obli-gation and opportunity to serve the needs of a deteriorating downtown neighborhood. Nevertheless, he passed on to his successor a church of renewed spiritual vitality that was poised for the resolution of its major internal problems. And, of course, he left the parishioners with the imperishable memories of living and working and playing with a saint during ten memorable years.

5
The Rectorship of Clarence R. Haden, Jr.
1945–1951

St. Philip's parish was without a rector from April 2 to September 1, 1945. During these interim months tremendous events occurred:

President Franklin D. Roosevelt died of cerebral hemorrhage on April 12 and was succeeded by Harry S. Truman.

World War II was ending in Europe as Germany surrendered on May 7.

The first atomic bomb, produced at Los Alamos, New Mexico, was exploded at Alamogardo, New Mexico, on July 16; the bomb was dropped on Hiroshima on August 6 and on Nagasaki on August 9. Japan surrendered on August 15.

Earlier the war had begun winding down in Durham, North Carolina, as the last troops to be trained at nearby Camp Butner had left in December 1944.

It is testimony to the inner strength of the parishioners and of the institutions of St. Philip's that church services continued without missing a step or a beat and that the Vestry took charge and resumed enterprises that had been placed on hold since Pearl Harbor.

Throughout the interim months Dr. Angus McBryde, the senior warden, presided over the Vestry meetings. Moving very rapidly, the Vestry, on April 9, confirmed the sale of an East Durham lot and ordered that its net proceeds of $2,841.45 be deposited in the St. Andrew's Building Fund. This was a major step toward realizing the dream of a new chapel for that parochial mission. The Vestry next authorized the senior warden "to appoint a committee to study the feasibility of going ahead with solicitation of pledges in a new drive to raise additional funds for the Parish House Building Fund. (Motion by B. R. Roberts [junior warden], seconded by Mr. W. H. Ruffin.)" The Vestry thus independently, without any prodding from a Rector, resumed the quest for a new parish house. On motion from Ruffin the wardens were further instructed "to look into the feasibility of securing a suitable lot for a Rectory," which had not been needed when David Yates, a bachelor, had lived in rented rooms.

The next two Vestry meetings, on May 1 and 14, were equally vigorous. Releasing their pent-up frustrations with Yates's pacifism, the Vestry on May 1 voted (1) to request Mrs. Twaddell, director of music, "to use at least one verse of the hymn 'America' in the worship service"; (2) to incorporate "prayers for the United States Army, Navy, and Air Forces in the worship services"; and (3) to place in the vestibule of the church "a Roll of Honor listing the names of the men and women from St. Philip's in the armed services." They next authorized the purchase of a house in Trinity Park on the northeast corner of Gregson and Green Streets to serve as a rectory. Its cost of $12,825 was to be defrayed by the $4,696 received from the sale of the old rectory and by a loan of $8,129 from the Parish House Building Fund. The Vestry in conclusion sent a committee of the two wardens, Angus McBryde and Ben R. Roberts, and William H. Ruffin to New Orleans to hear the Reverend Clarence R. Haden of that city. They were so favorably impressed that on the spot they extended him a formal call and invited him to visit St. Philip's as soon as he could. After a visit on May 30 and 31, he accepted the call and set September 1 as the date of his arrival.

Throughout the twentieth century St. Philip's was blessed with a succession of able Rectors. Each was a dedicated Christian and priest, each had his own personality and style of operation, and each made a significant contribution to the ongoing pilgrimage of the parish. Haden was no exception. In 1935 the Vestry of St. Philip's, representing a seasoned church that had lost momentum in the midst of a town mired in the Great Depression, had chosen for Rector a young, inexperienced, homegrown North Carolinian. And it had chosen well. In 1945 the Vestry, representing a mature church that was surging with renewed vigor in an economy that was emerging from wartime constraints into postwar prosperity, went with the experience and tested competence of an outsider.

Haden's experience had been in business as well as the church, and he brought skills developed in both fields. Born on May 30, 1910 in Fort Worth, Texas, educated in the public schools of that city and at Baylor University, and originally a Baptist, he had attended Union Theological Seminary in New York City (1932–34) and the Episcopal Seabury–Western Theological Seminary for his S.T.B. degree (1936). Ordained an Episcopal priest in 1936 in Evanston, Illinois, he began his ministry at St. John's Church, Fort Worth. He then served in Texas: as minister-in-charge at St. Barnabas Church, Enton, and St. Paul's Church, Gainesville, in 1936–37, and as rector of St. John's, Corsicana, where he remained for four years. His next parish was St. Matthew's, Houma, Louisiana, for two years before he became rector of St. Paul's, New Orleans, for another two years until the call of St. Philip's. Before entering the ministry he had worked in the purchasing and accounting departments of Armour and Company and in the sales and advertising departments of the Pagburn Candy Company, both in Fort Worth.[1]

A broad-shouldered, friendly, forthright, take-charge person with a smile that lit up his face and shone on everyone around him, he took over St. Philip's even before his arrival. The Vestry had allowed Yates to worry along without a paid secretary. Haden set as a condition for his acceptance the appointment of a personal secretary who would double as director of Christian Education. He even named the person he wanted, Mary Burgess, and her salary, $125 a month. The Vestry had budgeted his annual salary at $2,400, the starting figure for Yates. Of course, that did not last long. Haden's first budget doubled that to $4,800. Upon his arrival he followed Yates's practice of presiding over the regular monthly meetings of the Church School faculty, but with what a difference! Instead of spiritual meditations on the Christian life by Yates, we had expositions of modern pedagogical methods by Haden; instead of teachers' discussions of their programs and problems, we had Haden announces, Haden pronounces, Haden instructs—and the Student Council disappeared. At the Vestry meetings, Haden kept discussion moving along at a safe but rapid pace. After the first year he ceased to renew five of the six standing committees Yates had founded, retaining only the one on finance. The upshot was that the Vestry business fell increasingly into his capable hands. He became the chief source of initiation of proposals and of supervision of their execution.

Yet Haden and his wife, both socially inclined, were well liked by nearly everyone, men as well as women. His sermons were excellent, all our interviewees agree. He was an intelligent, hands-on administrator of marked ability, they add. And his friendly, direct style got things done.

In November 1946, upon the resignation of Mrs. William P. Twaddell, Haden appointed as organist O'Kelley Whitaker, a former acolyte, and recruited Allan Bone, conductor of the Duke University Symphony Orchestra, to direct the St. Philip's choir. Bone, in turn, recruited a core of paid singers, notably Susan Rose, his lead soprano, as well as volunteers from the congregation, including Richard L. Watson, who was to sing in the choir for more than forty-five years. As director of the newly organized Durham Civic Choral Society, Bone was also able to persuade several of its founding members to sing at St. Philip's, including Jane and Charles Sullivan. By 1948 the choir numbered nineteen "voices," including eight sopranos, five altos, three tenors, and three basses. Bone greatly enlarged its repertoire and by strenuous rehearsals sharpened its performance. Previously, it had led the congregation largely in singing hymns and carols. In "the hope that the music of the Church will continue to make an ever increasing contribution to the devotional spirit of the services of the Church," Bone had the choir "perform works taken from the core of religious music" and "chosen for their liturgical significance and for their musical quality." He drew "on the music of several sixteenth- and seventeenth-century composers—Palestrina, Vittoria, Ruffo, Lotti (Italy), Tallis, Byrd, Gibbons, Purcell (England)—J. S. Bach, Handel, Haydn, and Mozart of the eighteenth century, and the nineteenth-century Russian church liturgy." In the autumn of 1948 the choir presented its first full-length cantata, Bach's "Come, Redeemer of Our Race." When this was broadcast over the radio during the Christmas season, the quality of the choir's rendition was so high that listeners thought it was a performance from New York.[2]

Apparently without much prior discussion, Haden sponsored the installation of stained glass memorial windows in the church, meaningful symbols of exquisite beauty created by Payne-Spiers Studios of Paterson, New Jersey. From 1947 to 1951 ten such windows were put in place and dedicated:

Those in the nave of St. Philip's portray the Seasons of the Church Year:

Advent Window portrays Isaiah in the temple with the angel taking live coals from the altar to purify Isaiah's lips. In the right panel St. John the Baptist is shown baptizing our Lord. The dove symbolizes the Holy Spirit. The Agnus Dei is the symbol of our Lord. The Tau Cross and the Rising Sun are the symbols of Advent. The Acanthus is a symbol of heaven, and the pomegranate of immortality, all advent notes. The window was given by Claudia Powe Watkins and Warren Byers Watkins as a memorial to Claudia Josephine Erwin Powe and Edward Knox Powe.

Nativity Window depicts the Holy Family and the Adoration of Shepherds. Its donor was the Kemp P. Lewis family in memory of Lottie Sharp Lewis (Mrs. Kemp P. Lewis).

Epiphany Window portrays the visit of the Magi and the Christ of All nations, the Hope of the World. It is a memorial to James Allen Murdock by the J. A. Murdock family.

Lenten Window shows Christ in the Garden of Gethsemane and Christ on the Cross. It is a memorial to William Powell Twaddell, given by Mrs. W. P. Twaddell.

Ascension Window depicts Christ giving the Great Commission and shows the angels with the risen Christ. It is a memorial to Linda Claire Biggers by Mr. and Mrs. W. P. Biggers.

Pentecost Window symbolizes the Descent of the Holy Spirit to the disciples. Its donors, the R. H. Cowan family, gave it as a memorial to Mabel C. and Robert H. Cowan and his sisters Martha Cowan Kuker and Ida Cowan.

Trinity Window symbolizes the Holy Trinity. It was given by the Saunders family.

The windows in the chancel and sanctuary treat various themes:

The Conversion of Saul depicts the conversion of Saint Paul on the road to Damascus, a memorial to Roland H. Crain, given by Mrs. R. H. Crain. The open book with the inscription, "Spiritus Gladius" with a sword through it, is St. Paul's symbol.

Visitation Window portrays St. Mary calling on St. Elizabeth, her cousin and mother of St. John the Baptist. The fleur-de-lis is the symbol of the Blessed Virgin as is the BVM in the lower part of the window. The inscription, "Remember thy servants, O Lord" is taken from the prayer in the Burial Office. The window was given by the Woman's Auxiliary as a memorial of members departed this life.

The Window of St. Philip is a thank offering given by the Laymen's League.

The Good Shepherd Window above the altar had already been installed in 1935 in memory of the Reverend Sidney Stuart Bost.

From the sturdy, restful simplicity of the Norman tower, which harmonized with the low-key churchmanship of the early years of St. Philip's, the stained glass windows and the professionalized choir were moving the church *toward* the dramatic splendors of a more complex worship service.

At first Haden and the Vestry worked closely together to bring the long-discussed dream of a new parish house into reality. The problems they faced were site, design, estimated cost, and money. Before Haden's arrival George Watts Carr, the architect, had already submitted two preliminary plans, one using the vacant lot west of the church and the other placing the building in back of the church. Initially the Vestry favored the second option, but it acceded to Haden's recommendation to choose the first (September 10, 1945). When Carr returned with revised plans for the new site (November 12, 1945), Haden proposed that the new building be known as "St. Philip's Memorial Parish House" with a plaque listing and honoring those who had served in the armed forces. The Vestry agreed and appointed William H. Ruffin to chair a special campaign to solicit funds for its construction.

The estimated cost, not clearly formulated at that point, was $50,000, a prewar figure. On paper the Parish House Building Fund still had $19,750, but it had loaned St. Philip's $9,000 to purchase the rectory, thus reducing the fund's realizable assets to $10,750.[3] With his usual efficiency Ruffin chose his own campaign committee and in the first ten days of February 1946 secured pledges for the parish house of $55,716.[4] Again, there was jubilation at St. Philip's. Everyone assumed that sum would be enough, even after a basement was added for the choir. The Vestry authorized Carr to secure bids and appointed a building committee of Ruffin, Ben R. Roberts, and R. G. Hurst.

However, postwar shortages of materials delayed construction. And when the bids came in, the Vestry was stunned to learn that inflation had raised the estimated cost to $127,000, double the money on hand. Again the Vestry faltered. It considered buying "The Virginian" for $25,000 as a stop-gap solution of the Sunday School problems. Haden went to the congregational meeting on January 12, 1949 and in an eloquent plea kept the congregation, the Vestry, and the project firmly on track. The minutes of the meeting read:

> Mr. Roberts, Senior Warden, led the discussion concerning the proposed Parish House. Mr. Haden concluded this discussion by pointing out that a whole generation would be handicapped by our failure to build at once and he stated that his personal belief was that we should launch out on faith. Mr. Haden stated that by November of this year approximately half the amount needed will have been raised and that it is reasonable to suppose that the remainder can easily be raised within the next eight or ten years if not sooner. Before putting the question of whether or not the Parish House should be built at once, Mr. Haden carefully explained that he did not wish to overpersuade anyone and that he wanted it clearly understood that a decision to build would mean another campaign without apologies to anyone. The motion was carried with only one dissenting vote.[5]

This was not the first time, nor was it to be the last, that St. Philip's "launched out on faith."

The parish house was completed in the early months of 1949, in time for St. Philip's to host the annual Diocesan Convention on May 10 and 11. Its contractor had been C. H. Shipp, another member of St. Philip's. A fourth drive, again chaired by Ruffin, raised another $51,105 in pledges, and the building, debt-free, was dedicated in 1953.

At the Diocesan Convention of 1949 Bishop Penick placed the completion of the parish house, truly a memorable event, in a glowing historical perspective. In his address he said:

> We have come together under happy and fortunate circumstances, as the guests of this hospitable parish that has often been the host to diocesan gatherings. It helps us to reflect, as we as-

semble here, that we are the beneficiaries today of the missionary vision and enterprise of a young clergyman named Joseph
Blount Cheshire, who, in 1878, was Deacon in Charge of the
Chapel of the Cross at Chapel Hill. By horse-drawn vehicle, over
unimproved dirt roads, and, I suspect, occasionally on foot, he
traversed the intervening miles between Chapel Hill and Durham, and planted here the seeds of the church that, under God's
blessing, has grown into this magnificent parish. The spirit of
its founder has never departed from St. Philip's congregation. In
fact, it has accelerated through the years, as evidenced by the
establishment of missions in East Durham and West Durham, by
the pioneering work among the Deaf, which was started by the
Reverend Sidney S. Bost during his Rectorship here, by the extensive college student work associated with Duke University, and
by a sympathetic ministry to the many patients who come to the
medical centers of Durham for treatment. These are some of the
achievements of the past and activities of the present, the most
recent accomplishment of which is the completion of a modern
and commodious parish house.[6]

The end of the war also offered the Vestry of St. Philip's and the
congregations of its two parochial missions the opportunity to resume
their building plans, a rectory for St. Joseph's and a new chapel for
St. Andrew's. Over the years both had accumulated substantial building funds, awaiting use, $6,291.55 in St. Joseph's and $5,194.64 in St.
Andrew's. Before any discussion occurred, however, the Vestry on the
suggestion of the Assistant Rector, the Reverend Josiah Carter, invited
the two missions to become diocesan missions as a step toward independent parish status. St. Joseph's accepted and with the approval of
Bishop Penick became a diocesan mission in April 1947. It achieved
independent parish organization in 1956. Mother church and daughter
church parted in peace, as the financial details of the separation were
amicably arranged.

The congregation of St. Andrew's decided that for sentimental reasons it preferred to remain a parochial mission of St. Philip's. Yet it was
still treated as a stepchild. When it petitioned the Vestry of St. Philip's
for permission to mount a special building campaign, its request was
denied on the ground that the times were unsuitable. Haden sided

with St. Andrew's and urged that its congregation should be allowed to formulate definite building plans for Vestry authorization. But the Vestry was adamant in its refusal. St. Andrew's lost its most robust champion when Carter died in May 1947, and the dedicated congregation continued to meet, and in winter to huddle around the single stove, in a building that was a disgrace.

Meanwhile, at St. Philip's the work of the major church organizations flourished. The Altar Guild, the Order of St. Vincent, the Adult Choir, the Woman's Auxiliary, the Laymen's League, the Young People's Service League, the Sunday School, and the Sunday School Choir were all doing very well. Thanks to their annual reports to the congregational meeting in January 1948 and in January 1949 and, not least, to our interviews, we can describe their activity in some detail.

If we imagine ourselves at St. Philip's on a Sunday in 1948, we shall notice that six of its major organizations came into action during the course of the day. The preparation for the services was begun the preceding Saturday morning by two members of the Altar Guild. We have already commented on the spiritual devotion of the thirty women who composed that group. It was their "privilege to prepare the altar for all Communion services, marriages, baptisms, and funerals; to decorate the church for Palm Sunday, Easter Thanksgiving, and Christmas; to keep the linens immaculate, the silver and brass polished; and to arrange the flowers on the altar." In December a yearly schedule was made out whereby two members served "together each week from Monday through the following Sunday. Any service coming within that week was taken care of by the two women on the Altar Guild at that time." Each member worked with a different person during her four weekly tours of duty, "so that the Altar Guild would come to know each other better and become a stronger unit of service."

Mrs. R. B. Boyd was among those who kept the brass "bright and beautiful"; Mrs. W. B. Leftwich had "laundered the linen for the altar for over twenty-five years, a service that brought great satisfaction to her" and was deeply appreciated by the other members. The saints of a congregation, obviously, are not only in the pulpit. Six young girls, who formed a Junior Altar Guild, "received a course of instruction under Mrs. George Lyon." "A corporate communion service for members, with instruction from Mr. Haden, was held the second Wednesday in each month" except July and August.[7]

Sunday opened at eight o'clock with a communion service celebrated by Haden and attended, almost invariably, by twenty-three worshipers who preferred a quiet, meditative experience to the glories of a musical exposition.

By 9:20 A.M. parents and their children were arriving for Sunday School, the Sunday School Choir, and two adult Bible classes. Although Haden still met each month with the Church School faculty, he had relinquished the superintendency of the Sunday School to Nat Gregory. In successive years Gregory reported a steady rise in Sunday School enrollment, from 186 pupils in 1948 to 269 in 1949 and 295 in 1950, with average attendance running, respectively, at 64.5, 69, and 71 percent. In January 1951 Gregory warned that if the growth continued at the current rate, the *new* parish house facilities would be soon inadequate![8]

The Sunday School was divided into three groups: the preschool children, aged three to five years; the primary department, comprising the first three grades; and the senior classes to the twelfth grade. The preschool children, with an enrollment of 56 and an average attendance of 39, had its own group service in the large basement room of the parish house opposite the choir room. There, on Sunday, December 18, 1949, the Woman's Auxiliary gave and dedicated in memory of Mrs. J. A. Robinson, teacher in the primary department for nearly fifty years, an altar, a cross, a candelabra, vases, and a dossal. The opening period each Sunday "was devoted to a group worship. Hymns, prayers, and instruction provided meaningful experience. In turn each child participated actively in the service. Stories which illustrated the teachings of Christ were told. By means of dramatizations and other devices, desirable qualities were emphasized. Following the group service, the children were divided into four sections according to age." Mrs. Clarence Haden instructed the three-year-olds, Mrs. William Ruffin the four-year-olds, and Mrs. Charles Steel the four-and-one-half-year-olds, while Mrs. Watts Carr, Jr. taught those who had reached the age of five. Mr. George Lyon, Jr. served as pianist.[9]

The three primary grades met for group activity and service in the assembly room upstairs, and the senior classes met in the church for Morning Prayer with Mr. Haden, before they all adjourned with their teachers to classrooms in the parish house. For the first time in several years the Sunday School had a full complement of teachers:

First Grade	Mrs. W. P. Biggers
Second Grade	Mrs. J. H. King and Mrs. F. B. Gray
Third Grade (Boys)	Mr. John W. Harris
Third Grade (Girls)	Mrs. W. F. Carr, Jr.
Fourth Grade (Boys)	Mr. R. L. Fortune
Fourth Grade (Girls)	Miss Anna Jean Walker
Fifth Grade (Boys)	Mr. L. A. Carr and Mr. S. J. Preslar
Fifth and Sixth Grade (Girls)	Mrs. S. J. Preslar
Sixth Grade (Boys)	Dr. A. M. McBryde
Seventh Grade (Boys)	Mr. J. R. Beaman
Seventh and Eighth Grade (Girls)	Mrs. C. H. Livengood, Jr.
Eighth Grade (Boys)	Mr. Frank B. Gray
Ninth Grade	Mrs. R. E. Quinn
High School Group	Mrs. R. B. Cooke

The Sunday School Choir, founded by Mrs. Charles Moore in 1944 and now (1949) composed of thirty members, accompanied the Morning Prayer service of the senior classes in the church. Its discipline was strict and its morale high. Any child who missed rehearsal on Wednesday afternoon forfeited the privilege of singing the next Sunday.[10] For the adults, a Men's Bible Class was taught by Charles Livengood and a Women's Bible Class by Mrs. Burke Hobgood. Attendance at these classes varied from five to fifteen, depending on the Sunday.

By 10:45 A.M. the congregation was beginning to file into the church for the eleven o'clock service. On a characteristic Sunday (the second Sunday in Advent, for example), attendance had risen from 175 (1946) to 225 (1950) and the church was comfortably filled. As the vested three acolytes, Adult Choir, and Rector assembled in that order in the narthex, the organist (O'Kelley Whitaker or, later, Carol Mackie) played a prelude. With the opening hymn, the congregation stood up and the processional entered the church, led by the acolyte/crucifer, in accord with immemorial Anglican custom. The twelve acolytes, who took turns at serving, were all members of the Order of St. Vincent. Five to seven times a year they met for instruction about the procedures for lighting and extinguishing candles, the proper way to bear and to position the cross, the correct pace for leading the processional and the recessional, and, not least, the requirements of their Order.[11]

Every Sunday evening at six o'clock there was a meeting of the Young People's Service League, whose members ranged in age from thirteen to seventeen. "A service of Evening Prayer followed by supper, a program, and a business session comprised the regular meeting. The average attendance was 20. The League also had Corporate Communion followed by a fellowship breakfast every third Sunday in the month."

The motto of the YPSL was "Not for ourselves, but for others." In supporting this motto "the entire membership was divided into four committees: Program, Service, Membership-Finance, and Social." Each committee had a chair and an adult counselor. In early September each committee chair, counselor, and members met and made complete plans for the year.

The Program Committee had a twofold responsibility: to plan the program for each meeting and to plan and carry out the Evening Prayer service in which each Leaguer took part. The general theme (in 1947–48) was the Prayer Book. The theme and various related subjects were suggested in *Plan*, a special guide to program planning published by the National Youth Council in New York.

The Service Committee was one of the most important. Each month the YPSL tried to pursue at least one project in each of the five fields of service—Parish, Community, Diocese, Nation, and World. Projects in which everyone could participate were most often chosen. They included contributions to the "Bishop's Scholarship Fund, sending Care packages, and giving donations for world relief. Tray favors were made and distributed to the community."

The Membership-Finance Committee took care of the League's finances and by a telephone committee kept all the young people of the parish informed of the League's activities. The socials planned by the Social Committee were "varied and good fun." An outstanding event one year was a "hayride and picnic on Youth Sunday."[12] Photographs suggest that the Leaguers thoroughly enjoyed being with each other, with their adult counselors, and with their Rector, who attended their sessions.

The concluding paragraph of the YPSL's report of January 1949, written by George L. Lyon, Jr., its president, was profound in its implications and, in the light of future events, in its historical irony:

The League would welcome any who would care to visit on Sunday night. Perhaps you should come and see which way we are going for we represent your future Vestry, Laymen's League, Woman's Auxiliary, and your entire church tomorrow.

The passage conveys the participants' sense of belonging to a stable community of faith moving over time. St. Philip's was still a church of families. Their parents and in some instances their grandparents had founded and amid world-shaking crises had maintained that community. In turn the Leaguers would preserve it and pass on the torch of shared faith and worship to their children and grandchildren. But they would pass it on with a difference: with a greater sense of duty and service to the community outside the parish, in Durham and the world. The historical irony lies in the disparity between their expectations and what happened.

The young Leaguers correctly perceived that among the laity the recognized leadership roles at St. Philip's were to be found in the Vestry, the Woman's Auxiliary, and the Laymen's League. Excluded by diocesan canon from service on the Vestry, women volunteers had developed in the Woman's Auxiliary their own organization that performed nearly all the functions of a church: worship, fellowship, religious education, service, and collection and distribution of revenue. Its spirit was defined by Mrs. Urban T. Holmes, Jr., of Chapel Hill, who had just been elected president of the Woman's Auxiliary of the Diocese of North Carolina at its 69th annual convention, held at St. Philip's on April 11, 1951. "The Woman's Auxiliary," she said, "is the women of the Church bound together by their common love for God, their common concern for the welfare of mankind, and their common zeal for the spread of the Gospel. It is an international and interracial fellowship organized for service to the church in every phase of its life and all fields of its activity." [13]

Over the years the Auxiliary's influence at St. Philip's had kept growing. On major policy questions it was now regularly consulted by the Vestry and listened to. Without its very active, forward-looking support, the new parish house might never have been built during that generation.

The Auxiliary's membership on September 1, 1948 was 196, divided into six chapters. "With the assistance of the chapter recruiters and the rector [Haden], sixty new members were enrolled" for a total of 256 in 1949. Of these, an estimated 50 percent were active. Each month each chapter met in the home of one of its members for fellowship, devotions, a program of religious study—in 1948–49 the theme was world evangelism, "Ye shall be witnesses"—and refreshments. To those who attended, it was usually a warm and satisfying meeting, both a devotional and a gracious social occasion that became a significant part of their lives.

The Auxiliary's officers included president, vice-president, secretary, and treasurer, as well as secretary of Christian Education, secretary of Christian Social Relations, secretary of Supply, custodian, chair of the United Thank Offering, chair of St. Margaret's Guild, and chair of Devotions. The six chapter chairs also had their complement of officials.

In 1948–49 the Auxiliary's ways and means committee, known as St. Margaret's Guild, undertook three projects to raise money. Sale of 44,000 pansy plants in October 1948 yielded a net profit of $307.50. Profit from a rummage sale was $635.42. The bazaar held in the parish house in early December netted a profit of $1,411.38. The pre-Christmas bazaar, first held in 1944, was becoming the outstanding event of the Auxiliary's year. Weeks, months, or in some instances the entire year went into preparation of articles for sale at the various booths: needlework, doll clothes, toys, food (plum pudding, fruitcake, roasted peanuts), and white elephant items. The continuous luncheon serving more than four hundred had the reputation of being the best meal in town and the best bargain. The total revenue created by St. Margaret's Guild was thus $2,354.30. Add in the chapter pledges of $1,017.00, and the total income for the Woman's Auxiliary was $3,371.30.

The distribution of this income, the way it was spent, signaled the Auxiliary's interests. Back in 1932 its gift of $1,000 to the Parish House Building Fund had sparked the campaign to extinguish the overhang church debt and erect a new parish house. In 1948–49 it still donated $500 to the Parish House Building Fund—in fact, it did this every year. But at Haden's request it now allotted another $500 to the organ fund, in the hope of sparking a similar campaign to replace the old, decrepit instrument. Thompson Orphanage received $125, plus six boxes of good clothing, Christmas gifts for three children, and clothes for two children during the entire year. Sixteen children of Judge

Mamie Walker's Juvenile Court were given Christmas gifts, and one family was taken from the Welfare Department. Another $225, plus food and clothes, was sent to missionaries in Japan, China, the Philippine Islands, and Puerto Rico. Lesser gifts went to Kanuga and Vade Mecum, and $692 discharged an obligatory diocesan assessment.[14]

Money gifts, however, do not begin to convey the multiple services of Auxiliary members. One member corresponded regularly with missionaries at home and abroad. Another member, known as the Cheer Partner, wrote to persons in the church who were sick or in sorrow; new babies were remembered, too. The Auxiliary chapters took care of the nursery every Sunday morning, and each week they supervised the sexton as he cleaned the church and parish house. Each month women of the Auxiliary cooked and served the Laymen's League supper. Twice a month the Auxiliary's Secretary of Church Periodicals took current magazines to the wards of Duke, Watts, McPherson, and Lincoln Hospitals. And so on and on. The Auxiliary truly lived its ideal.

The Laymen's League met once a month in the parish house for an evening supper, prepared and served by members of the Woman's Auxiliary. Supper was followed by a talk by a visiting speaker. In the fall of 1948 the speakers were Mrs. E. J. Evans, whose husband later became Durham's mayor, on "Zionism"; Dean D. D. Carroll of the University of North Carolina at Chapel Hill, on "Communism"; and Ted Gannaway, provincial chair of the Laymen's Association, on "What the Laymen in the Episcopal Church Can Accomplish by Concerted Action." Attendance was high, averaging fifty-five each meeting. The league usefully took the functions of the defunct Brotherhood of St. Andrew. Its standing committees provided ushers for the church services, aided a successful Every Member Canvass, decorated the church for Christmas, donated a stained glass window for the sanctuary, sponsored a Boy Scout troop, and visited the sick.[15] Haden's achievement in enlisting the men in parish activities was so outstanding that it attracted the attention of the Presiding Bishop of the Episcopal Church, Henry Knox Sherrill.

The minutes of the Vestry meeting of March 12, 1951 read: "Mr. Haden reported that he had been requested to become Executive Secretary of the Presiding Bishop's Committee for Laymen's Work, that he felt he should accept this call, and that he was therefore tendering his resignation effective May 1. . . . On motion, this resignation was accepted with regrets." Haden's career did not stop with this appointment. While he was executive secretary, Seabury-Western Theological Seminary conferred upon him the honorary degree of Doctor of Divinity. In December 1952 he accepted election as Dean of Grace at Holy Trinity Cathedral in Kansas City, Missouri. In 1957 he was elected bishop coadjutor of the Diocese of Sacramento (California), and in 1958 he became its bishop.

Every one of our interviewees who knew Haden spontaneously volunteered: "We always knew he would be a bishop." This chapter should enable us to understand why they thought so. His record prior to his arrival had been that of a person who was always moving on to greater challenges. It was normal to anticipate that "he was going places." His beneficial actions in Durham and the Diocese of North Carolina and at St. Philip's confirmed that impression. Civic-minded, he was a member of Rotary and Kiwanis and in 1951 president of the Durham Community Chest. In the Diocese he was an examining chaplain, chair of the Department of Christian Education, member of the Standing Committee, member of the Board of Trustees of St. Augustine's College (Raleigh), and a leading nominee for bishop coadjutor.[16] At St. Philip's he did not innovate (the only exception being the initiation of a weekly bulletin), but as a friendly, attentive, intelligent, hands-on administrator he toned up the performance of each and every church organization, and he welded the church family together. By putting the church on the way to extinguishing all its debts and by building the new parish house, he gave the congregation economic stability, a resolution of its major internal problem, and a glow that came with great success. Almost as a by-product he continued the trend, initiated by Yates, of increased enrollment and attendance. During Haden's tenure the number of communicants rose from 590 (1945) to 707 (1951), and the total attendance at all three Sunday services (8:00, 9:30, and 11:00 A.M.) increased from 16,175 (1946) to 21,492 (1950).

St. Philip's, its own house now in order, was in a position to take on greater challenges and rise to new heights of service and achievement. The questions were, would the congregation perceive the opportunity, and how would it respond?

6

The Rectorship of Tom Turney Edwards 1951–1956

In several respects the process by which the Reverend Tom Turney Edwards was called to St. Philip's was unique in the history of that church. In selecting the successor to Bost (1935) and later to Yates (1945), the male Vestry had appointed a Search Committee from among its members. The committee had turned up a promising candidate, who in each case declined St. Philip's invitation; the Search Committee then selected its second choice, David Yates and then Clarence R. Haden, Jr. After the Vestry and the candidate had interviewed each other in Durham and were pleased by what they saw, the position was filled.

To find a successor to Haden (1951), the Vestry formed a Search Committee chaired by one of its members, Ben R. Roberts, and composed of all Vestry members plus four non-Vestry communicants, Mrs. John Gregory, Mrs. Robert G. Hurst, Mrs. Ray Quinn, and Mr. Nat Gregory, appointed by the senior warden, William H. Ruffin.[1] The enlargement of the Search Committee to involve non-Vestry members of the congregation was an innovation; so was the inclusion of three women. Once the committee recommended a candidate, the Vestry alone issued the call.

However, when in 1951 its first choice, James Madison of St. Paul's Parish in Holyoke, Massachusetts, declined St. Philip's invitation, Bishop Penick intervened directly. At his request he met with the Vestry after the eleven o'clock service on Sunday, August 19.[2] According to a memorandum dictated by Ruffin the next day, the Bishop "started out by saying that he was going to do something that he had never done before, i.e., make a strong recommendation to a parish with reference to a new Rector. He said there would be available to St. Philip's the Rev. Tom Turney Edwards," a native of Winston-Salem who had been a communicant of St. Paul's Episcopal Church in that city. Educated in the public schools of Winston-Salem and the undergraduate college of the University of the South (Sewanee), he had secured his B.D. from the Episcopal Theological School in Cambridge, Massachusetts, in 1948. Since then he had embarked on a Ph.D. program at Harvard University and was working on his dissertation in Paris, France, while serving there as assistant minister at the American Cathedral.

"The Bishop said that he felt so strongly about Mr. Edwards and his qualifications that he could recommend him to us without reservation. He stated that Mr. Edwards was approximately 31, that his very attractive, sweet, and charming wife was also from Winston-Salem, and that they had two small children. Mr. Edwards himself, a large handsome man, had a positive and engaging personality. . . . An exceptionally fine scholar, he was an excellent preacher — if we got him, we would have the best preacher in the Diocese." To be sure, he lacked extensive experience in parochial work, but the Bishop felt that would be unimportant in a parish like St. Philip's that was already organized. "Mr. Edwards had done exceptionally fine work during two summer vacations at Statesville and at Enfield." Ben Roberts, the chair of the Search Committee, had received "the highest kind of recommendation from these two points" as well as from the dean of the Paris Cathedral.[3]

Doubtless, as Bishop Penick was praising Edwards to St. Philip's, he was lauding St. Philip's to Edwards. The outcome of the ensuing negotiation was that the two parties accepted each other sight unseen, for the first and only time in the history of St. Philip's. Edwards, it was agreed, would enter upon his duties on November 1, 1951.

DEVELOPMENT OF A PROGRAM, 1951–1953

Bishop Penick was right on one score: St. Philip's was a well-organized parish. During the interim period between the resignation of Haden on May 1, 1951 and the arrival of Edwards on November 1, and indeed well into the early months of Edwards's rectorship, the major organizations seemed to go of themselves. The eight chapters of the Woman's Auxiliary continued to meet on the first Monday of each month, and its St. Margaret's Guild continued to raise money by an annual rummage sale, pansy sale, and bazaar. Once a month, usually on the second Thursday, the Laymen's League assembled to eat a supper cooked by the Woman's Auxiliary, to listen to a distinguished speaker, and to share a moment of Christian fellowship. Each Sunday evening the Young People's Service League met for food, fun, and fellowship, and once a month for an eight o'clock Sunday morning corporate Communion. In June 1952 it was "judged the best league in the entire Diocese of North Carolina and awarded the efficiency shield, which was the highest citation given!"

When Edwards entered this complex ongoing society with its long history of family interrelationships, he already had a mature personal theology that sustained and guided his conduct. In a fairly early sermon on the Great Commandment "Thou shalt love the Lord thy God with all thy heart, and with all thy strength, and with all thy mind," he said that "heart" required worship and prayer, "strength" needed to be applied in action—a Christian "must put his religion to work, if it is to mean anything at all"—and "mind" must be set to study: "The more you know about yourself, your fellow man, and your God, the better Christian you are. You cannot serve God by ignorance."[4] As his rectorship unrolled, these activities—worship, prayer, action, and study—intertwined and supported each other, and constituted the major themes of his life and preaching.

Nevertheless, when Edwards and his wife arrived in Durham, they must have experienced a period of personal and professional adjustment. Durham was not Paris, nor even Cambridge, Massachusetts. They had been away from North Carolina for so many years that they might have had difficulty persuading the congregation that they were not Yankees. Though Edwards had preached excellent sermons at Statesville and Enfield and would continue to do so at St. Philip's, there was much more to being a rector than sermon preparation and delivery. His predecessor Haden had arrived with a well-honed administrative style; Edwards, a neophyte, needed to develop his own, to try this or that approach, to discover what worked and what did not. In fact, it was nearly two years before he had in place all the elements of his program.

However, the congregation was friendly and went out of its way to welcome Edwards and his wife. When they were looking over the rectory (at 1102 Gregson Street, in Trinity Park) preparatory to moving in, Watts Carr, former junior warden and current president of the Laymen's League, invited Edwards to the league's monthly supper. On the

Saturday afternoon before he preached his first sermon at St. Philip's, November 4, 1951, the Woman's Auxiliary hosted at the rectory a get-acquainted reception in honor of the couple.

Edwards eased himself into the situation. After opening with prayer his first Vestry meeting on November 1, "he expressed his wish to accommodate the needs and desires of the parish and requested suggestions." Once the usual fiscal and property maintenance issues had been disposed of, the Vestry discussed "the problems of Christian education in the parish, including revival of the Church School choir," which had declined during the interim months between rectors. Edwards agreed to investigate the situation. At the December Vestry meeting he reported that he had conferred with Mrs. Charles Moore, the founder of the Sunday School Choir. They had agreed that its restoration had to be a gradual development. The Vestry left further action to the Rector's discretion.[5]

With the Vestry's approval, he appointed as his secretary Mrs. Matthew West. Loyal and efficient, she soon became for him "the irreplaceable Matt West." She recalled that he, his curate, and herself always began each weekday at 8:30 A.M. with Morning Prayer, which was what the Prayer Book intended.[6]

On November 12 Edwards started attending the monthly meetings of the Sunday School faculty, a practice he continued throughout his tenure. At first he placed himself in a listening and learning mode. He "scheduled conferences with teachers so as to determine what was being taught and to help out anyway he could."[7] Repeatedly, he "asked the faculty for their comments on the way he was holding the opening exercise at Sunday School."[8]

In January he changed the time of the annual congregational meeting. From time immemorial it had met at 7:30 P.M. on the first or second Monday in December or January. Edwards, probably with the Vestry's consent, moved the time to the second or third Sunday in January, immediately after eleven o'clock Morning Prayer. The result was a doubling of attendance, from slightly more than 100 communicants to more than 200. To quote one of Edwards's favorite comments, why hadn't someone thought of that innovation before? He retained the useful format, introduced by Yates, of annual reports by the major church organizations. But he soon limited the reports to two minutes apiece, thus curbing long-windedness and expediting business.

In February he came a cropper. At the conclusion of the Vestry meeting of February 11, 1952

> "Mr. Edwards expressed concern over the lack of spiritual impact on the community. He suggested that we consider the need for and feasibility of a hostel operated by the church for the benefit of visitors to the city, particularly for visitors and relatives of patients who are undergoing treatment in any of our local hospitals. The consensus of the vestry was at the present time there was no acute need for such service and that this undertaking might best be deferred for later consideration. Mr. Edwards urged the vestry to give serious thought to other ways and means by which we might serve people outside our own congregation."[9]

Nothing came of his suggestion, and, like Yates before him, Edwards did not actively return to the question of the role of the metropolitan parish in an urban community. When I remarked to an interviewee that Edwards always seemed to cope, quietly and without tumult, she replied, "Yes, or he went on to other things." This instance can be interpreted as an example of his tentative, flexible, experimental style.

Nevertheless, the reaction of the Vestry to his suggestion deserves attention. To a historian, asking why an event did *not* occur may be as productive of insights as inquiring why one did. On the face of it the Vestry's failure to respond to the needs and opportunities for service in the community was puzzling. Such prospects were certainly visible to two Rectors, Yates and Edwards, and to two Assistant Rectors, A. S. Lawrence in 1937 and, later, John Denham in 1956. Why didn't St. Philip's lead the way? Was it habit, reinforcing reluctance to engage in new ventures? Or adherence to the traditional concept of the role of the church: St. Philip's served Durham best by simply being itself, a nurturing, caring, loving Christian community, with foreign missions abroad? Or, perhaps, ignorance of what a metropolitan church might do?

Or maybe complacency, a comfortable self-satisfaction with what St. Philip's seemed to be doing so splendidly? Jean Bradley Anderson's observation on the leadership of Durham at this time is interesting and perhaps relevant:

> Veterans returning from the World War II found a Durham County that despite all the change already apparent in the coun-

try still clung to its outmoded cultural and material shell. Many people who had not been away were also beginning to feel that changes were needed, particularly in leadership: *complacent*, reacting instead of leading, and dedicated to the status quo.[10]

The congregation of St. Philip's, in particular, was on its own cloud nine. After two decades of struggle and suffering—the Great Depression, World War II, the strenuous, challenging idealism of David Yates, the rigors of four fiscal campaigns—a modern parish house had been built and the church debt was on the way to extinction. No wonder Kenneth Podger, the chair of the Every Member Canvass, could complacently refer in November 1952 to "the peace and tranquillity of the society in which we live."[11] In light of this mood of comfortable self-congratulation, the reluctance of St. Philippians to take on new altruistic ventures can be understood and perhaps forgiven.

Meanwhile, Edwards started visiting his parishioners. In 1960 Elizabeth (Libby) Roberts recalled one of the positive outcomes of those visits:

St. Philip's was Edwards's first charge and he was a fine, conscientious, young man. It is significant that he began his visiting by going to see the shut-ins. About this time, Mrs. Frank Webb, who is always interested in finding new and better ways that we, and particularly herself, can better serve God and St. Philip's Church, talked with someone about the Order of "The Daughters of the King." She went to Mr. Edwards and asked him to write for information about this Order. The Handbook and information arrived.

The Order had two rules. First: The Rule of Prayer—"To pray daily for the spread of Christ's Kingdom, especially among women; for God's blessing upon members of the Order, and for the spiritual growth of the parish to which the chapter owes allegiance." Second: The Rule of Service—"To take regularly some part in the Church; to make constant effort to bring other women within its influence and to render at all times such aid to the Rector as he may deem necessary for the spiritual upbuilding of the parish." This gave us a wide field.

This seemed just the kind of organization needed by Mr. Edwards and the parish. We had no assistant rector at the time, and to have a group of women on whom he could call for special assignments would be invaluable to him and to the parish.

With the help of Grace Carr, twenty women were invited to meet with Mr. Edwards on Monday, January 14, 1952, and discuss forming a chapter at St. Philip's. We met in the Woman's Auxiliary room of the Parish House, and he told us about the Order and how he thought we could help.

All twenty women were interested in the work, but only ten felt they could become members at this time.

The charter members were as follows:

Mrs. Frank Webb (Gertrude)	Mrs. Charles Livengood, Jr. (Virginia)
Mrs. R. B. Boyd (Lizzie)	Mrs. Ralph Van Trine (Leona)
Mrs. Watts Carr, Sr. (Amy)	Mrs. Frank Minter (Margaret)
Mrs. Louis Carr (Grace)	Mrs. B. W. Roberts (Libby)
Mrs. R. E. Quinn, Jr. (Dorothy)	Mrs. J. M. M. Gregory, Jr. (Katharine)

On Thursday, January 17, 1952, we met to officially form the Chapter. We decided to study, pray, and to take assignments given us by our Rector. Mrs. Frank Webb was elected first President, with Mrs. Louis Carr as Secretary. Mrs. Carr has served as Secretary ever since the Chapter was formed.

Mr. Edwards picked the book *Creative Prayer* by E. Herman for our study. Once a month after mid-week communion we met. He read to us and then discussed what he had read. Then he told us where he needed our help.

At this time one of our church members was dying with cancer. Her family had very little money, three children, and not any help. Also we had a young woman to move here whose husband abandoned her just before her third child was born. We saw her through this time. We went with Mr. Edwards with private communion to shut-ins. We prayed every day for members of the parish who particularly needed our prayers. And we also visited out-of-town Episcopalians at Duke Hospital.

We were on probation all this year until activities started again after the summer. At our first meeting in the fall, Mr. Edwards said that all of us who wanted to continue with this work would be received into the Order and would receive a silver cross, the symbol of the Order. All ten of us desired to become active members.

At mid-week service on September 18, 1952, we were installed as members of Chapter 1640 of the National Council of the Order of the Daughters of the King.[12]

As the group lost a Daughter through transfer, sickness, or death, it invited another member of the congregation to replace her. As the years passed the Daughters concentrated their efforts on the shut-ins in the parish. They served in pairs. Every shut-in was visited once a month by a different pair throughout the year. By the end of December each Daughter had visited every shut-in.

The Daughters accompanied the Rector as he took private Communion to shut-ins at Easter and Christmas, and they brought an appropriate gift. The Daughters remembered their birthdays and assisted them in every way possible. It was the hope of the Daughters that there was no shut-in of St. Philip's Church who did not feel loved.[13]

The Daughters of the King did not report at the annual congregational meeting; its members did not attend any national convention of their order; they shunned publicity and public acclaim. Quietly, unobtrusively, unknown to most members of the congregation, they aided the Rector and went about their mission of serving God by serving others. (For a list of members from 1952 to 1993, see Appendix B.)

It is notable that Edwards involved the Daughters of the King in study (a reading of E. Herman's *Creative Prayer*), in prayer (anyone who had perused that Anglican devotional classic knows how it compels the reader to pray), and in action, to the succor of shut-ins. Prayer and action were rules of the order; study through reading was Edwards's characteristic addition.

As Edwards continued visiting his parishioners, he became aware of the immensity, indeed the impossibility, of getting around single-handedly to everyone of his communicants. Even when, twenty-two months after his arrival, he acquired a very able curate, the Reverend Robert Meredith Watson, Jr. (we shall hear more about him later), the two of them could not match the desire and expectation of every parishioner for a visit. In what must be a classic statement of the trials of an overburdened rector, Edwards explained the situation to his flock in an issue of the *Epistle to the Philippians*:

Dear Friends,

I ask you to think for a minute of what is involved in ministering to our congregation. It is a large congregation with about 800 active members every single one of whom has a claim on the minister's time.

I want to get to know everyone, but if I could devote one afternoon to each member, it would still take more than two years to get around. This is barring emergencies and allowing no time for any other activities.

But think of the emergencies that are bound to arise in a congregation of this size. Think of the incidence of sickness, to take only one kind of emergency. We keep a long sick list at all times — frequently as many as 25 or 30 a week, many of whom will be chronically or critically ill and will need constant attention. With our own sick list and the numerous requests from other parsons to visit members of their flocks who come to Duke for treatment, Mr. Watson and I could spend all day every day doing nothing but visiting the sick; we never feel happy about the time we spend with the sick; we always wish we could spend more.

Unfortunately, however, sickness is only one phase of our work. Think of the incidence of troubles of all kinds in a congregation of this size — financial, domestic, moral, spiritual, social. People naturally want to talk these things over with their minister, because that's what he's for, and he had better be ready to spend all day if necessary. Now, the trouble with trouble is that, just as you don't usually get into it in a day, neither do you get out in a day. There aren't any serious problems that can be solved at one sitting or at the first try. Mostly it's a question of working with people over a long period of time with repeated conferences and much soul-searching and brain-racking. A broken life can't be set quite as easily as a broken bone; the minister has to try to hold the pieces together until they knit, and that takes time.

Well, these are only two phases of my ministry, sick calls and counseling, and yet I repeat that I could spend all my time on them alone. But I can't afford to, for there is still so much more that I am responsible for and that you would not care to have me neglect, like for instance the planning and conduct of services. Or the preparation and delivery of sermons, talks and addresses, which increase fearfully in the special seasons. Have you any idea how long it took to compose that little homily which sounded so easy and spontaneous? A well-known preacher hereabouts estimates 15 hours of preparation! Well, it is obvious that no parish priest has 15 hours to spend on a sermon. But the good ones do take time.

As Cicero would say, I shall pass over the entire program of Christian education which it is the rector's sole responsibility to organize, supervise and carry out. I shall not mention the Youth Work either, which devolves upon the rector, nor the cooperation and assistance expected of him from other parish organizations like the Woman's Auxiliary and Laymen's League, Altar Guild and Acolytes. I decline to speak of the manifold details of office administration, the correspondence, records, files and the like without which no organization can tell what it is doing or where it is going. Then, too, there are certain civic responsibilities which ministers, of all people, must not shirk, not to mention diocesan offices and tasks which cannot be left to the other fellow forever. Is your brain reeling? Mine is, just from enumerating all these things.

What is the point of all this? Not to complain but to explain. The point is that the minister is spread awfully thin, and as the Church gets more and more centralized and the lay people turn over more and more of their responsibilities to the professional ministry, it gets spread still thinner.[14]

To alleviate the problems engendered by this situation, Edwards initiated over the years three measures. First, he inaugurated a weekly newsletter. Haden had already started a weekly bulletin, distributed at each Sunday service, listing the next week's activities. Edward greatly expanded the bulletin to a weekly *Epistle to the Philippians*, written by himself, printed at the church office, and mailed to parishioners in time to reach their homes by Friday. In his best experimental style (why not try this?), he explained in the first issue ("A Trial Balloon") its advantages: it would provide a "much more efficient way of communicating information to our parishioners than we now have. . . . it would act as a kind of link between the Church and its members."[15] Always the teacher (he had undertaken a Ph.D. program with the thought of becoming a professor) and brimming over with information he wished to share, Edwards interspersed routine announcements with brief educational essays on church ceremonies, church doctrine, church and Bible history; the meaning of confirmation; the virtues of the Episcopalian burial service; why the purchase of a new organ had priority over air-conditioning the church—on and on. The essays were friendly, scholarly, practical popularization at its best, and a mine of information for the grateful historian.

An excerpt from his essay on the funeral of Kemp Lewis conveys the urbane grace that pervaded each epistle. To understand the essay we must recall that Lewis had been a personage of some importance. An executive officer of Erwin Cotton Mills, he had succeeded Will Erwin as its president; a sturdy church worker at St. Philip's, he had been its treasurer (1914–17), its senior warden (1924, 1925, 1935, 1936), and one of its chief contributors:

> The burial of Mr. Kemp Plummer Lewis which, with the consent of the family, furnishes us with an occasion for making a few remarks on that office of the Church, was a perfect model of simplicity and restraint. In fact, to those who witnessed it must have seemed amazingly simple, considering the place that he held in the community, the business world and the Church.
>
> According to a principle that seems to operate pretty generally in Protestant Churches, one would have expected the last rites of such a prominent man to be marked by more pomp and circumstance. Yet of pomp and circumstance there was none.
>
> The service was utterly unpretentious; it did not proclaim a man of consequence. There were no floral displays in the church, except two vases on the altar; there was no sermon, no eulogy of the deceased. There wasn't even any music! There was just the plain, unadorned Prayer Book service for the Burial of the Dead that would be used for any loyal son of the Church, no matter whom.
>
> Nowhere does the Episcopal Church show its democratic spirit more than in the Burial Office. Whether it be kings and queens or paupers that go to the last resting place, they are all ushered out of this world according to the same rite—the same majestic prayers offered, the same strengthening words of Holy Scripture are read—and have been, lo! these many years. It is important that it should be so, especially at such a time, for it signifies the equality of all men before God. And what comfort there is in the

thought that one is a part of an age-old tradition and is joined to that "blessed company of all faithful people," past and present and yet to come in heaven and on earth, who have been buried by this rite![16]

Edwards's second measure to handle problems arising from an enlarged congregation was to secure the appointment of an Assistant to the Rector. Although an appropriation for an assistant had been budgeted for 1951 and 1952, no one had been recruited, and the Vestry, despite Edwards's desperate need, had dropped the item from the budget for 1953. At its meeting on April 9, 1953, however, Edwards forced the Vestry's hand by pointing out that a suitable candidate, Robert Meredith Watson, Jr., was about to be ordained deacon and was available. At Edwards's request, Watts Carr, Jr., as junior warden, had determined that there was enough money in the general fund to pay for an assistant during the closing months of 1953 and until he was placed on the budget for 1954. After an interview, Watson was called, and he accepted the position, to start on September 1, 1953.[17]

He and Edwards had much in common. Close in age (Edwards was born in 1921 and Watson in 1925), they had attended the same high school in Winston-Salem. Both had been confirmed at St. Paul's Episcopal Church there, both had been taught in Sunday School by a Mrs. Bland, and both had served in U.S. military forces during World War II. And both had scholarly interests: Edwards had attended Sewanee and the Episcopal Theological School in Massachusetts; Watson had studied at the University of North Carolina at Chapel Hill (B.A., 1950) and the Virginia Theological Seminary (B.D., 1953). Both had entered graduate programs, Edwards for a Ph.D. at Harvard, Watson for a Master's degree in history at Duke University.[18] Together with Matt West, the secretary, they made an excellent team.

Edwards's third measure, taken after Watson's arrival, was to call on the laity to minister to each other and to form neighborhood groups. In the *Epistle to the Philippians* of May 9–15, 1954, he explained that they could ease the problem of an overburdened clergy if only they would:

The Bible says that your ministry, the ministry of the laymen to each other, is just as important and just as vital as the professional ministry. When Jesus said, "I was hungry and you gave me food, I was thirsty and you gave me drink, I was a stranger and you welcomed me, I was naked and you clothed me, I was sick and you visited me, I was in prison and you came to me"—when He said this He was not talking to professionals. He was talking to laymen. And He didn't say that these laymen could hire professionals to do their welcoming of strangers, visiting of the sick, clothing of the naked, feeding of the hungry, for them. Sometimes people say to me, "Have you been to see so-and-so," and I always restrain a mischievous impulse to counter with a question: "Have you?" There are two good reasons why you should start thinking seriously about your lay ministry to each other. The first is that your soul's salvation depends on it. The second is that there is a lot of good you can do. I can't make a fellowship of the church. You and you alone can make this church the fellowship it ought to be, and you can do it by your ministry to one another.

We have thought of a way to help you do it. We have divided Durham up into 17 neighborhoods, on the theory that the neighborhood is the most logical basis of community. On a large map of the city we have pin-pointed every Episcopal home. We have asked two or three couples from each neighborhood to serve as captains for a year. If any crisis or emergency arises in your neighborhood, if a sickness strikes or a death occurs, or if a new family moves in, or if someone in the neighborhood is received by confirmation—if any of these things should happen, the neighborhood captains will get in touch with you and tell you about it. Please realize, when they call you, that they have been asked to do what they are doing. Their job is to keep the Episcopalians in their neighborhood informed of what is going on, and the rest is up to you. Will you cooperate? I know you will.

Many good things could come of this plan. Even if the result were only that we should get to know each other better, it would be worth the trouble. Maybe we can have some neighborhood meetings or study groups in Lent; this would save you the trouble of coming down to the parish House.

The Vestry is 100 per cent behind the plan. The neighborhood captains are 100 per cent behind it. Everybody we have discussed it with is 100 per cent behind it. I hope that you will be too.

Sincerely,
Your friend and rector
Tom T. Edwards.

During the same years, 1952 and 1953, Edwards was bringing ahead the musical and educational programs of St. Philip's. Within a few months of his arrival he and the Vestry faced three competing demands for capital expenditures: the replacement of the broken-down sixty-year-old organ ($16,500), air-conditioning the church ($10,000), and removal of the service station at the corner of Queen and Main Streets ($1,500 cost plus annual loss of revenue of $1,800). After careful exploration of costs and available funds, the Vestry gave priority to the music program. A sixteen-rank Moller organ was installed in the sanctuary of the church during May 1953. It was paid for almost immediately by a contribution of $4,158 from the Woman's Auxiliary Organ Fund, by a $5,000 bequest from the Kemp Lewis estate, by a donation of $1,000 from Lewis's daughter, Mrs. Edward S. Orgain, and by a special, almost private campaign to extinguish the remainder. The Vestry then contracted with Moller to install, for $11,000, ten additional ranks in an antiphonal organ at the rear of the church. Payment of this overhang debt was deferred for several years. The Vestry also left to the future the projected air-conditioning of the church and removal of the service station.[19]

Edwards had a discerning taste in music and an appreciation of its role in enhancing the spirituality of the parish. One of the first problems to greet him at St. Philip's—as the Vestry reported in successive meetings—was an unsatisfactory music situation. The Junior Choir, once the pride of the Church School program, had declined in attendance and discipline. The Adult Choir of sixteen paid singers and two volunteers, expertly directed by choirmaster Allan Bone, performed superbly a sophisticated repertoire of classical religious music, but many members of the congregation longed for the old-time familiar hymns (Who wants Johann Sebastian Bach, anyway?). The entire program, it seemed, was costing too much: choirmaster, $1,050 ($150 more than budgeted); Junior Choir director, $495; the paid choir, $1,732.92 (beyond its budget of $1,500); and the organist, $815, for a total outlay of $4,092.92.

As Edwards aided Mrs. Charles Moore to revive the Junior Choir, he won her consent and that of the Vestry to a radical reform: a single choirmaster/organist who would direct both the Adult and Junior Choirs, and an Adult Choir composed of only four paid singers and a complement of volunteers. Merging the three positions (senior choirmaster, junior choirmaster, and organist) into one would give St.

Philip's sufficient funds to secure a highly qualified person who would ensure central direction and control of the music program.

Since Allan Bone was not an organist, he did not fit into the scheme. He resigned from St. Philip's in July 1952 and took most of his choir of paid singers to the First Presbyterian Church down the street. After a year of experimentation with two or three choir directors, Edwards was able to appoint in June 1953 as choirmaster/organist Henry Cook, a graduate of the Oberlin Conservatory of Music, who had "organized at Rocky Mount a boy's choir that was the talk of the diocese." He and Robert M. Watson, Jr., Assistant to the Rector, came to work on the same day, September 1, 1953. Edwards's professional staff was now complete.

But there was more to come that September, in the field of education. During the first twenty-two months of his rectorship, Edwards retained the structure of Sunday morning services inherited from his predecessor: eight o'clock Holy Communion, the Sunday School hour at half past nine, and the standard eleven o'clock service, with Holy Communion on the first Sunday of the month and Morning Prayer on the succeeding ones. The Sunday School was divided into three groups: the preschool children, ages three to five years; the primary department, of the first three grades; and the senior classes, to the twelfth grade. The first two groups each held their own worship service before dividing into individual classes; the senior classes attended Morning Prayer, conducted by the Rector in the church and accompanied by the Junior Choir, before going to their respective classrooms. Adults could attend a Men's Bible Class or a Women's Bible Class.

Working at first within that structure, Edwards cooperated with the faculty to strengthen the education program. He invited the Reverend Edward Jeffress, diocesan director of Christian Education, to attend the monthly Sunday School faculty meeting on March 31, 1952. Jeffress brought the welcome news that, for the first time in its long history, the National Council of the Episcopal Church was "preparing a teaching series which will be available for use at all levels in about two years." The teachers, "practically as one," protested: they needed material *now*, this coming fall. Jeffress referred them to curriculum materials obtainable through the Northern Presbyterian Church and the Diocese of Pittsburgh.[20] Following up his suggestion, the faculty adopted the "Pittsburgh Plan" and its associated teaching material. Upon the opening of the new church school year that fall, in the *Epistle to the*

Philippians for September 14–10, 1952, Edwards described both the problems of the Sunday School and the new material, and invited the parents to pitch in and cooperate. It was a revealing statement, disclosing for the first time in our history of St. Philip's what was happening *within* the Sunday School. Edwards stated his case with characteristic realism and candor:

> We promised to tell you something about the new Sunday School material, because we are counting heavily on the parents' interest. But first let's talk about Sunday School in general for a minute. This business of Christian Education is a hard nut to crack, as anyone will tell you who ever had anything to do with it! How to teach our children the Bible, the History, Worship and Doctrine of the Church, and the Prayer Book, with poor material, with a volunteer teaching staff, with only about 20 minutes of actual teaching time on Sunday morning, and virtually without any parental interest or cooperation—that is the task that has been handed to us! Hopeless? All but! Yet it is only recently that the Church has waked up to the fact that its Schools are in difficulty and calling for drastic remedies!
>
> The truth is that even with the best of everything, with good material, with plenty of time, and with professional teachers, the job of bending these young twigs in the direction they should grow would be a challenge to us; and under the present set-up it is out of the question. Or it has been.
>
> We are telling you this because you should know what we are up against. Did you know that if you added up all the time a child spends in the Sunday School class room throughout his entire life, you would come out with less than a week? In one week we are supposed to impart the whole sweep of Christian knowledge and mould the character? But this is only one of the handicaps. Teaching materials have been woefully inadequate. Children of a past generation memorized passages from Scripture, a practice disdained by modern experts, who have thrown out the old, stern discipline of learning and concentrated on making the lessons so attractive to the children that no urging will be needed to make them learn. The resulting pap has been palatable, all right, but without a particle of food value! After the child has gone through the whole rigmarole, he still doesn't know the first thing about

the Bible or Christian Ethics or anything else. So what's the use? After years of fumbling and groping after a decent curriculum, the new material, though not by any means a panacea, looks very promising. The content is solid—not froth, no meringue! Besides it offers a means of unifying the work. Instead of having a different topic for each class, which isolates each teacher and throws him or her entirely upon his or her resources, the entire Sunday School, except for the first three grades and the adult groups, will study the same topic throughout the year. Our subject for the coming year is "The Life of Christ." In language appropriate to each age group this one topic will be presented to all children from grades 4 to 12. We shall not go further into the details of this plan, but you can readily see how this plan will benefit us.

See how it helps the teachers! Whereas all was chaos before, with each teacher acting independently, sinking or swimming as the case might be, now we can pool our resources, share our ideas, actually use our meetings to prepare for the Sunday sessions.

See how it helps the family! With all the children studying the same topic, the whole family can enter into the project, take part in the discussion. The parents can now participate with their children, without having to be experts on everything from the Old Testament to Christian Symbolism. There can be a meeting of minds at home.

The success of this plan, which, by the way, comes from the Diocese of Pittsburgh, depends on parent cooperation. These are your children, going out to form the citizenry of the future. Help us train them! Ask them what they study, get them to show you their leaflets, find out what they got out of the lesson!

By all accounts the Pittsburgh Plan was a success in 1952–53 and was continued the next year.

The Men's Bible Class, under the presidency of Edmund Taylor and led by Dr. John Hallowell, a member of the parish and a distinguished Duke University political scientist, was also having an outstanding year (1952–53). Using the third volume of the Episcopal Church's new adult teaching series—*The Faith of the Church*, by James Pike and Norman Pittenger—Hallowell presented in the first semester the great doctrines of the Church and applied them to the political "isms" of the modern age: Fascism, Communism, and Socialism. In the second semester he shared the forum with other distinguished faculty from Duke and the University of North Carolina.[21]

However, there were complaints, not about the educational program but about the structure of the Sunday services. "One of the complaints heard most frequently from young couples with children of school age is that it is too hard to see that the children get to Church School and they themselves get to Church, when one comes at 9:30 and the other at 11:00. They can do one or the other but not both."[22]

Edwards hearkened. In September 1953, along with the arrival of his new assistant and the new musical director, he announced the introduction of the Family Service. Parents and their children would come to church together at 9:30 P.M. After Morning Prayer and the singing of some familiar hymns (an adroit touch!), accompanied by the Junior Choir, the children would go to their classes and the parents would remain for a lecture by the ministers on the lesson their children were studying that Sunday according to the Pittsburgh Plan. And Edwards made sure that the Sunday School teachers were prepared by giving them, at the monthly faculty meeting, solid background information for the month's lessons. So a major segment of the congregation—the ministers, the teachers, the parents, and the children—were engaged in a joint educational effort. The theme for the first semester was "Great Stories from the Bible," and Edwards suggested a list of books for the parents to purchase and study. The Men's Bible Class was, regrettably, a casualty, but men could still study the Bible with the ministers at the Family Service. The Women's Bible Class, for women who did not have children of school age, continued under the wise direction of Mrs. Burke Hobgood.

The innovation was in numbers a fantastic success, beyond Edwards's wildest dreams. "None of us was prepared," he wrote, "for the overwhelming response that the Family Service received last Sunday! About quarter past nine people began to pour in, and they kept on pouring in until every seat was taken! The Church hasn't been so full since Easter."[23] Throughout the year attendance at the Family Service, and hence at the Sunday School, remained high, without appreciably diminishing the numbers of those who worshipped at eleven o'clock. The Family Service was one of the major, and most satisfying, achievements of Edwards's rectorship.

But the month of September 1953 was not yet finished. The same *Epistle to the Philippians* that announced the introduction of the Family

Service also listed the regular monthly Vestry meeting for 8:00 P.M., Monday, September 14. At that meeting Richard Baker, Bishop Coadjutor of the Diocese of North Carolina, presented the devastating report of the Diocesan Survey on "the failure of the Episcopal Churches in Durham to keep pace with population growth." "While the city of Durham grew at the rate of 223.7%, from 1920 to 1950, the Episcopal Churches grew at the rate of 52.3%, and from 1949 to 1951, sustained a loss of 20.9%, in the combined membership." [24] It was a blockbuster report, sufficiently explosive to jolt the most complacent congregation into action. To understand it we must first fill in the background before recounting its far-reaching consequences for St. Philip's.

In the early 1950s the Diocese of North Carolina, guided by Bishop Penick, was appraising itself, with an eye to self-improvement. "At the 1951 [Diocesan] Convention Penick asked for and received authorization to form a Commission" [25] that, in the words of the Bishop's address, would oversee "a Diocesan Survey to be conducted by the Unit of Research and Field Study of the National Council, the purpose of which is to discover new fields of opportunity for the future expansion of our Church." [26] With masterly economy of phrase he had set the goal, the direction, and the means, in brief the strategy, for advance. [27]

Bishop Baker, as chair of the commission, spent a substantial portion of the next two years on the Diocesan Survey. In company with Dr. Joseph G. Moore, director of the Unit of Research and Field Study of the National Council, or Professor William H. Dennis, its field director, Baker "visited nearly every congregation in the Diocese, talking with the clergy and representatives of these groups," persuading them to complete three basic steps: the Episcopal Census, the Residence Membership Map, and the Self-Study Form. [28] In Durham he and Moore worked with Robert G. Hurst, a prominent member of the Vestry of St. Philip's and Durham chair for the survey. [29]

After the Diocesan Survey was completed in March 1953 and presented to the Convention in May, Baker set out to visit each parish in the Diocese "for the purpose of interpreting the survey as far as it affects the parish." [30] During his conference with the St. Philip's Vestry on September 14, 1953, he had nothing but praise for St. Philip's *Church*. The survey itself showed why:

> There is no question that St. Philip's downtown location is excellent for a metropolitan parish. Transportation both by road and

bus is excellent to every section of the city. The parking facilities available to this church on Sunday morning are excellent [thanks to the use of the Sears parking lot]; week-day parking facilities are adequate.

The church building is a stone structure, strategically located. The parish house is quite new and the equipment is excellent.

[The membership has steadily increased in recent years:] [31]

	1925	1930	1935	1940	1945	1950
Baptized persons	592	637	530	669	779	890
Communicants	409	383	440	552	570	709
Church school	197	185	124	160	193	317
Parochial budget	$8,775	$7,805	$5,220	$9,397	$12,837	$19,483

Almost all members of the congregation are native-born, preponderantly of Anglo-Saxon, Irish-Scottish nationality backgrounds, with a few of northern and southern European nationality backgrounds. More than ¾ of the adults in the congregation are college graduates or have been to college. Most of the balance are high-school graduates or have been to high school, placing this congregation in the upper 25% of the educational groupings in the city of Durham.

It is a family parish. There are a large number of children in the congregation [children to 9 years of age form 20.8%], slightly less than the normal amount of later-aged teen-agers and young people in their 20s, and a large middle-aged section of the congregation who make up the major portion of the congregation, from 30 to 55 years of age.

The indication is, therefore, that there is an exceptionally fine number of young children, especially for a downtown congregation, with need to review carefully and work on the program for teen-agers and people in their 20s, who in Durham form the largest age block. [However, while it is a church of families], it is not in any way a neighborhood parish. Only 12.5% of the congregation live within a mile of the church. Nevertheless, the good transportation lanes to this church allow the majority to come to the church in less than 20 minutes.[32]

The survey also praised St. Titus Mission. "Located in the central section of the largest Negro neighborhood in Durham, it has gained communicants from 1920 to 1951 at the rate of 137.8%." With better buildings it would have the potential to grow even more.[33]

But the survey came down hard on St. Andrew's and St. Joseph's and on the situation in Durham as a whole. St. Andrew's Mission, it said, "is located in a non-growing section of the southeastern area, unable to serve the people in a growing area. Its church building is a small wooden structure seating 75 persons; with no parish house or rectory, it is inadequate for the church's need in every way. The membership has not grown in numbers: there were 56 baptized persons in 1925 and 60 in 1951; 44 communicants in 1925 and 46 in 1951; 71 in the church school in 1925 and 48 in 1951."[34] The congregation was largely middle-aged and elderly. The church should be relocated and supplied with new and better equipment. Nor was the situation at St. Joseph's any better. Located disadvantageously "in an area surrounded by industry and away from the normal path of the residential traffic in its section of the city," its membership had actually declined: in 1925 it reported 307 baptized persons; in 1951, 154. During the same period its number of communicants fell from 214 (1925) to 128 (1951).[35]

At the same time, two fast-growing residential sections of the city—the Watts Hospital area to the north and along University Drive to the south—were without the services of a neighborhood Episcopal church or mission. Consequently, during recent decades the rate of growth of the combined membership of Episcopal white churches in Durham had been sluggish.

Throughout the report the Diocesan Survey placed the responsibility, and the burden, of redeeming the situation squarely on St. Philip's. As the mother church, it must lead. Specifically, Bishop Baker recommended the formation of a local committee to study the survey's recommendations and propose appropriate action.

For both the Diocese and St. Philip's Parish, 1953 was a significant year for yet another reason: it raised the desegregation issue. From 1940 to the closing decade of the twentieth century the congregation of St. Philip's would be stirred by five controversies in which old ways of thinking, feeling, and acting were challenged by new: pacifism, desegregation/integration, gender (the role of women), Prayer Book revision, and sexual orientation. Before midcentury societal and Prayer Book discipline and order had been almost automatically defined and enforced by training the young in roles that were accepted by nearly everyone as divinely ordained: white/black, men/women, heterosexual/homosexual, liturgical belief and practice. After midcentury, individuals and groups increasingly stepped forth to challenge accepted modes of behavior. They stirred defenders of the old order and supporters of the new to the deepest levels of being. They provoked anger. They raised the question, what should a Christian do? They separated communicants from each other and often from their clergy; they placed the clergy, bishops as well as rectors, under the multiple pressures of conscience and policy as dedicated followers of Jesus Christ, as ordained priests of the Episcopal Church, and as leaders of divided congregations and emotionally torn communicants struggling in novel situations.

David Yates's radical pacifism during the war years of the 1940s had separated the congregation from its Rector, stirred anger, and raised the question, what would Jesus Christ have us do? But since the congregation was unanimously opposed to his position, it did not cause an intracongregational fight. In any case, the issue vanished for most St. Philippians with Yates's departure and the end of the war.

The situation was vastly different with the racial issue: it went on and on and on. For the Diocese of North Carolina controversy was ignited when in June 1952 "the trustees of the University of the South [Sewanee] adopted a resolution that denied black students admission to its School of Theology. As a result, the dean of the school (the Very Reverend Craighill Brown, resident in the Diocese of North Carolina), most of the seminary faculty, and the college chaplain all resigned; a number of members of the student body [including Albert Nelius, later a curate at St. Philip's] also withdrew, to enroll at other seminaries of the Church."[36] Because the Diocese of North Carolina was "one of twenty-two southern dioceses that own Sewanee," Bishop Penick on May 12, 1953 invited the Diocesan Convention "to record its mind and judgment on this issue." "I have complete confidence," he added, "that whatever statement you may issue, it will represent your Christian convictions, courteously expressed in terms of dignity, moderation and constructiveness."[37] A word to the wise and prudent, he hoped, would be sufficient.

In response, the Diocesan Convention—clerical and lay deputies alike—requested "the Trustees of the University of the South to admit qualified students to the School of Theology, regardless of race."[38]

Edwards, in turn, published in the *Epistle to the Philippians* the entire text of the Convention's resolution and gave it the spin he wished the congregation to take:

> We thought the Philippians would be interested in the following resolution, which was presented to the Convention by the Department of Christian Social Relations early the first day:
>
> "Whereas, before a world ridden with racial tensions and color conflicts, our nation stands avowing the equality of all men before God, and "Whereas the Lambeth Conference of 1948 affirmed 'That discrimination between men on the ground of race alone is inconsistent with the principles of the Christian religion'; and
>
> "Whereas the Synod of the Fourth Province, of which we are members, in October, 1951, adopted a resolution saying, 'We consider it unwise to attempt to establish a segregated School of Theology for Negro candidates for the ministry in the Fourth Province, but feel that existing schools in the South should be open to men of all races'; and
>
> "Whereas the Bishops of the Fourth Province declared in November 1952, 'It is our Christian duty and privilege to work together as brethren in the service of Christ and His Church'; and
>
> "Whereas all other Episcopal theological seminaries receive all the laity for training whom the Church recommends, as far as space will permit; and
>
> "Whereas seven white theological seminaries of other denominations of the South have made specific welcome to Negro students;
>
> "Be it resolved that the Diocese of North Carolina, one of the twenty-two owning dioceses, in Convention assembled, requests the Trustees of the University of the South to admit qualified students to the School of Theology, regardless of race."

Nearly everyone was surprised by the ease and rapidity with which this resolution was adopted by the Convention! Indeed, there was scarcely any serious opposition, aside from a couple of attempts to get the wording altered. Some of the delegates were apprehensive of a debate that might turn out to be very extended and heated; but after a few guarded speeches, the question was called for, and the resolution was passed just as it is printed above. Perhaps we should have more faith in the good sense of our people after all!

The same Convention defeated, 95–74, an amendment to the canons that would permit women to serve on vestries. Edwards reported that, too, in the *Epistle*. "Once again the question of women on vestries was broached and defeated by a majority that grows slimmer and slimmer. One feels safe in predicting that in a couple of years the opposition will be worn down" and the motion will carry.[39]

Thus by September 1953 Edwards had marshaled his strengths. While continuing the traditional Anglican services and enriching them with excellent preaching, he had cooperated in founding a chapter of the Daughters of the King, opened by the weekly *Epistle to the Philippians* a channel of communication and education, assembled an excellent staff, restructured the Sunday morning service, strengthened the music and educational programs, and taken a position on the issues of race and gender. He had also been made aware of St. Philip's responsibility toward redeeming the sad state of the Episcopal churches in the city of Durham. In the coming years he would affirm and elaborate the initiatives thus outlined.

IMPLEMENTATION OF THE PROGRAM, 1953–1956

Edwards, Watson, and Cook—the Rector, his assistant, and the choirmaster/organist—were alike in at least one trait: as educators, they enjoyed teaching. This characteristic appeared early in Cook's work with the Adult Choir, which sang at the eleven o'clock service. He had only a quartet of paid singers (including Susan Rose, the lead soprano, who had loyally remained with St. Philip's after Allan Bone's departure) and a group of amateur volunteers, whose only indispensable qualifications were ability to carry a tune and willingness to work. Yet by Palm Sunday, April 11, 1954, the combined choirs of St. Philip's and St. Joseph's churches were able to give an evening performance of the cantata *Christ Lay in Death's Dark Prism* and a short *Kyrie in D* by Johann Sebastian Bach. Edwards commented: "This is the first time in many years that the choir of St. Philip's Church has been in a position to undertake anything so ambitious. It is hoped that our people will appreciate the preparation and work that has gone into this performance and will show that appreciation by filling the Church."[40] That year the choir followed on the third Sunday in Advent with a fine evening performance of sections of Handel's *Messiah* for a congregation of two hundred.[41]

Cook's talents appeared also in his training of the Junior Choir, which sang in the Family Service at 9:30. He held it to a high standard in rehearsals and would not allow it to perform until it could sing with exactitude. He persuaded many members to attend his summer choir camp at Camp Leach, near Washington, North Carolina. (By a coincidence, one of the camp's young counselors was Tom Midyette, who was known as "Captain Tom.") All this training paid off, not only in church but also in the choir's performance in a public Civic Choral Society concert during the Christmas Season of 1954. Edwards told the story in the following week's *Epistle*: "You parents certainly must have been pleased at the way your children behaved themselves. They marched out on the stage as neat and orderly as a squad of soldiers, and they stood up straight, and when the conductor gave the down beat they came in without the slightest hesitation and sang with all their might. And mighty sweet it was, too. As we looked at them up there on the stage with all those adults, in their red and blue robes, it seemed to us that it was likely to be an experience that they would never forget, and that they were receiving training in the choir that they would never forget, either."[42] Behind the scenes a corps of parents and choir mothers (headed by Mrs. William Wallace until September 1953 and after that by Mrs. Richard L. Watson) took the children to afternoon rehearsals on Wednesday and Friday, cleaned and mended choir vestments, and gave moral support. A detailed and invaluable description of the Junior Choir by Mrs. Watson comprises Appendix C.

Cook also attempted, like choirmasters before and since, to lead the congregation to "a clearer understanding and more thoughtful appreciation of what our Church music is, and can mean." To that end he taught a weekly study class on church music for the Woman's Auxiliary each Tuesday morning during Lent in 1955. Lectures, discussions, recorded music, and even a bit of singing featured in the presentation.[43] At the conclusion of the seven-session course he gave a multiple-choice examination. That you may have the fun of testing your own knowledge, it is given below. The correct answers are found in note 44 (don't peek).[44]

Quiz on Church Music
1. Church Music is desirable in our worship when it is
    a) an aid in maintaining the interest of the people.
    b) presented as an offering of Praise to God.
    c) soft and restful in mood.
2. Music may be used effectively in church because
    a) it can inspire in all of us the fear of God.
    b) it can smooth over awkward spots in the services.
    c) it can aid the communicative effect of certain parts of the services.
3. The music of the Communion Service should be
    a) mournful, in remembrance of Christ's death.
    b) joyful, in remembrance of Christ's bringing of Salvation.
    c) mysterious, in remembrance of the Real Presence.
4. Of the two main divisions of music for the Communion Service, the Common or Ordinary belongs to
    a) the Choir.
    b) the Bishop.
    c) the Congregation.
5. Match the musical portions with their proper functions:
    Kyrie Eleison   a) acclamation of penitence.
    Sanctus   b) pre-Communion devotion.
    Agnus Dei   c) post-Communion Thanksgiving.
    Gloria in Excelsis   d) shout of praise and adoration.
6. The Gradual is sung in honor of
    a) the Holy Communion.
    b) the Collect for the Day.
    c) the Gospel.
7. In Morning Prayer, the Venite may be omitted on
    a) Ash Wednesday and Good Friday.
    b) Any Saint's Day for which a Collect, Epistle and Gospel are provided.
    c) Epiphany and seven days after.
8. The Invitatory Antiphons occur
    a) before the Gospel
    b) before the Venite, and are used to

    c) confuse the congregation

    d) set a seasonal tone to Morning Prayer.

    e) give the service a penitential character.

9. The Salutation ("The Lord Be with You," etc.) serves usually

    a) to remind us to kneel for prayer.

    b) as a transition from one part of the service to another.

    c) to give the congregation a part in the prayers.

10. The Creed comes after the Second Lesson or the Gospel

    a) to sum up and ratify the revelation of God's Word.

    b) to remind us of what we believe.

    c) it is a historical tradition to do so.

11. The Litany is usually read from the Nave or Chancel steps because

    a) the minister here prays on behalf of the congregation.

    b) the minister can be heard more clearly from this place.

    c) it is a historical tradition to do so.

12. Ante-Communion is primarily a service which emphasizes

    a) the Holy Communion.

    b) the Holy Scriptures.

    c) the Holy Catholic Church.

13. When rubrics in the Prayer Book specifically use the word "Say," we should

    a) always speak the section following.

    b) not pay any attention to the small print.

    c) remember that no special manner of vocal utterance is meant.

14. Canon Law puts the ultimate authority for the music of a parish in the hands of

    a) the Minister.

    b) the Bishop.

    c) the Vestry.

15. The Hymnal is authorized by

    a) the House of Bishops.

    b) the minister in each parish.

    c) the General Convention.

16. Music for weddings must

    a) be very solemn and soft.

    b) follow the Canon and rubric, but otherwise be appropriate to the nature of the occasion.

    c) be composed by Mendelssohn and Wagner.

Edwards had a discerning taste not only in music but in art and literature as well. In one *Epistle to the Philippians* he told how the design on the cover of our Sunday bulletin came into being:

For years, Mr. George Pyne has been acting as unofficial artist for St. Philip's Church, and though he has always done excellent work, this Lent he has surpassed himself. He drew the beautiful design for the cover of the bulletin, which we shall be using this year. With the same subject matter as before, yet in an entirely different style, it depicts the story of St. Philip, the patron saint of this church, as related in Acts viii, 26–39.

If our parish follows the example of its patron, it should have a very strong interest in missions. The story in Acts says that, in obedience to a heavenly command, St. Philip journeyed to the south of Jerusalem, and on his way ran into an Ethiopian, the treasurer of Queen Candace. This high official was reading the book of Isaiah in the place where it says, "He was led as a sheep to slaughter; and like a lamb dumb before his shearer, so opened not his mouth." Not knowing who was meant, he asked Philip to explain the text to him, and Philip seized the opportunity to preach Christ. The encounter ended with the Ethiopian's being baptized.

The drawing on the bulletin was redone literally several times before the desired effect of balance and rhythm was obtained. It is a symbolic, rather than a detailed pictorial, rendering of the subject; it attempts to state its message tersely, like a trademark, with rigid economy of line. On the left you see a rudimentary chariot, and on the right gracefully carving lines both denote the pool where the baptism took place and give a sense of eternity to the theme. Notice how different lines are repeated in other places and how the artist has achieved great dignity and strength, without sacrificing a particle of grace or beauty.[45]

St. Philip's, of course, was a dynamic congregation, with many other gifted people, in many lines of endeavor. One communicant, Frances Gray Patton, published a best-selling novel, *Good Morning, Miss Dove*, and then attended the southern premiere of the movie based on it. Preceding the showing her friends gave a dinner in her honor and chose Edwards to present their testimonial gift. He responded with a delightful and self-revealing after-dinner speech on humor.[46] We do not wish to deprive you of the pleasure of reading it. Yet we have quoted him so frequently in this chapter that we risk the danger of having to list him as its co-author! So the speech is reprinted as Appendix D. As he would say, do not miss it. You have a treat in store.

During the next three years (1953–56), Edwards continued the educational structures and programs he had set in place in September 1953: the Family Service on Sunday at 9:30, with preschool children in their classroom, Morning Prayer or monthly Communion for parents and older children to the twelfth grade in church, then Sunday School classes for the children with their teachers in their classrooms while their parents remained behind in the church to listen to lectures by Edwards and Watson. Everyone—ministers, teachers, parents, and children—studied the same subject for that week according to an overall theme for the nine-month academic year. In 1953–54 the theme was Great Stories of the Bible and the Major Prophets; in 1954–55, Church Doctrine; and in 1955–56, the History of the Church. At the monthly Sunday School faculty meetings Edwards and Watson provided background instruction on the topics that were to be taught on the coming four Sundays. It is symptomatic of the different educational emphases of Edwards and his two immediate predecessors that at the meetings of the faculty Yates had meditated on the Christian life; Haden had discoursed on methods of instruction; Edwards and Watson, as young scholars, lectured on information and doctrine.

We are fortunate to have in the archives of St. Philip's a copy of the lectures of Edwards and Watson for the first two years, doubtless because they were mimeographed and placed each Sunday in the vestibule of the church, and a set was then filed by some unknown benefactor, perhaps the church secretary, with the Vestry minutes. After four decades the lectures still read well. Those on the prophets Moses, Amos, Hosea, Jeremiah, Isaiah, Second Isaiah, Ezekiel, Nehemiah, and Micah are sound, substantial, and abreast of contemporary scholarship. Those on Church doctrine constitute an amazing adventure. The young ministers tackled with apparent ease all the "big" questions: Purpose of Theology, Reason and Faith, Revelation; the Doctrines of Man, Sin, God, Christ, Resurrection, Atonement, Eternal Life, and Salvation; and the Christian Interpretation of History—two two-thousand-word lectures to each topic. Doubtless, Edwards thought the congregation needed them. In the *Epistle to the Philippians* for January 16–22, 1955, he explained:

> Those of you who have been attending the 9:30 service know that our topic for this year has been Christian doctrine. So far we have talked about the need for clear statement of belief (Theology), Revelation, Man, Sin, God. These topics are hard to get across with the time and resources at our command, but we think that it is important to know what you believe and worthwhile taking the time to find out. Christians should be serious students of their faith, for how can you serve God if you do not know what He stands for or what he expects of you? Some people will tell you that it doesn't matter what you believe; it is what you are and do that count. To that we reply that what we are and do directly depends on what we believe. As William James said, "There is no difference of truth that does not make a difference of fact somewhere."
>
> Will you, therefore, help us in this very difficult undertaking by doing the following: reading the mimeographed talks each Sunday; reading our text week by week: Wm. A. Spurrier, *A Guide to the Christian Faith*; asking your children each week what they have studied in Church School and trying to help clarify their thoughts about religion. Please consider that this is the *last chance* your children will ever have to get what we are giving them now. If they don't get it now, they probably never will. Test the truth of this by your own experience.

He refined his argument in the *Epistle* of October 9–15, 1955:

> Ministers and teachers are constantly amazed at lay conceptions of God, good and evil, sin, hell, salvation, Jesus Christ, the Christian fellowship, faith, prayer, and all the rest of it. Frequently what the layman assumes to be the Church's position on some doctrinal matter has no resemblance to what is being taught; frequently, too, the Church is criticized for a supposed belief which, as a matter of fact, it does not hold or teach. You wouldn't be satisfied with a hazy, cloudy opinion about your health or business, would you? No, you'd go deeply into the matter until you found out the truth. Then you should not be satisfied with hazy opinions about matters that affect your soul's salvation.

Don't get us wrong: we do not believe in salvation by knowledge. There is a lot more to the Christian life than that. Nevertheless, it is important to know what you believe.

Even so, as the course proceeded, Edwards became aware that the lectures were beyond the intellectual training and stamina of many listeners. While he praised the congregation for its patient attentiveness, he set aside the last meeting of the Family Service in May 1955 for questions, "if we have confused you." And he promised a "more comprehensible" series next year.

Edwards filled out the education program by using the neighborhood organizations to form weekly Lenten study groups in 1955 and 1956. Neighborhoods that were too small to constitute a group were merged with others to form ten in all. In the past, neighborhood team captains had functioned to rally support when newcomers arrived or when crises, such as sickness or death, struck. Now, the captains were also responsible for picking the best night for weekly study and arranging a meeting place in a member's home. A leader guided the discussion during Lent 1955, of James Pike and Norman Pittenger, *The Faith of the Church*, volume III of the Church's new teaching series; and during Lent 1966, of Bernhard W. Anderson, *The Unfolding Drama of the Bible*. Leaders for 1955 included such distinguished Duke University faculty as Drs. Katherine Banham (Psychology), Allan Cartter (Economics), John Tate Lanning (History), and Grover Smith (English). Even a partial list of the hosts and hostesses suggests the immense reservoir of talent and energy that was available in the "old church" during these years. They included Kate Herndon, Florrie Jones, Sarah Markham, Reba Hobgood, Ada Shipp, and (as they appeared in the *Epistle*) the husband and wife teams of Mr. and Mrs. A. L. Jernigan, George McAfee, Frank Gray, B. R. Roberts, R. E. Quinn, Jr., Garland Llewellyn, James E. Davis, E. L. Embree, Kenneth Podger, R. B. Cooke, R. L. Fortune, Bailey Hobgood, John Cahoon, W. L. D. Townsend, George Pyne, George Watts Carr, Jr., Nello Teer, Jr., Kenneth Royall, Jr., E. K. Powe, Richard H. Leigh, B. W. Roberts, Arch Bass, Edwin Hamshar, Richard L. Watson, Charles Livengood, and Paul Wright. The meetings were well attended, especially by women, who "as usual appeared in force." Discussion by all accounts was active, and the seven sessions each Lent may well have accomplished the goals Edwards had in mind: "to establish genuine fellowship, to increase our knowledge of the content of the faith and its meaning for our lives, and to become personally committed to it."[47]

Edwards also strengthened the education program all along the line by founding the parish library. As a graduate student at Harvard University and during his summer vacations, one of his favorite haunts was the stacks of Widener Library. No doubt he noted how for over a century that library had been built by donations of memorial volumes, given by a Cabot, a Lodge, a Lowell, or some other eminent alumnus in memory of a family member. Perhaps that gave Edwards the idea to transfer the practice to St. Philip's. Previously, under Yates and Haden, a few precious volumes had been tucked away in the Rector's office, to be signed out by his secretary, when he had one. Edwards had bookplates printed: "Given by . . . in memory of . . ." He advertised in the *Epistle*: give five dollars and buy a bookplate. Month after month he listed books given, their authors and titles, their donors, and their honorees. On Sundays he placed new books in the church's vestibule, to be viewed and signed out. As the collection grew to more than one hundred volumes, he found in the parish house a room for the library, with easy chairs for browsing readers. And he sought among the laity a librarian, who would devote two hours a week to cataloguing books and to other such chores. The quality of the books was high, including classics by Evelyn Underhill, E. Herman, Herbert Butterfield, Reinhold Niebuhr, and Paul Tillich that still form the core of the library's collection.[48] The library ever since has been a refuge for many a lost soul seeking guidance, support, and consolation. Here Edwards built better than he could ever know.

His creative energy seemed boundless. He served on the Diocesan Executive Council from 1953 to 1956. He conducted a five-day teaching mission at Rocky Mount. When the Supreme Court ruled that racial segregation in public schools was unconstitutional, he became prominent in panels of discussion on the subject of desegregation.[49] In an "Essay on the Theology of Segregation," printed in the *Epistle to the Philippians* for October 24–30, 1954, he argued that segregation violated two principal Christian doctrines: *Imago Dei*, that *all* humankind, white and black, was created in God's image, and *Atonement*, that Christ died for *all* persons. He subtly added, though, that just as it was wrong to segregate blacks as a group, so it was wrong to admit them as a group. We should think of all people as individuals, with each person standing equal before God and each assuming the responsibilities as well as the privileges of citizenship.[50]

The reaction of the congregation to his reasonable and reasoning approach does not appear in our archives. Nevertheless, later controversies in the Diocese during the 1960s suggest that while the clergy and white lay leaders condemned racial segregation, many of the laity who had been comfortably reared in a segregated church within a segregated society understandably did not share their opinion. In the disparity between the church's leadership and many of the laity lay the seed of crisis.

At Bishop Penick's request Edwards took charge of the effort to do something about the sad state of the Episcopal churches in Durham, as revealed by the Diocesan Survey of 1953. A strategy session was held on April 27, 1955 in Raleigh, attended by the Bishop, Edwards, and Joseph O'Brien, chaplain to the Episcopal Students at Duke University and priest-in-charge of St. Joseph's. It was agreed that St. Philip's would sponsor a new mission in the Watts Hospital area made up of volunteers from St. Philip's and St. Joseph's, and that the congregation of St. Andrew's would be offered two options: either disband and reaffiliate with St. Philip's, which legally it had never left, or become a diocesan mission, relocate, and build a new chapel.[51] Edwards persuaded the Vestry to accept these conclusions. St. Andrew's chose the second option and in 1955 became a diocesan mission, thus freeing itself from St. Philip's supervision and neglect. Encouraged and aided by Edwards and Watson, forty interested laity, largely from St. Philip's but living in north Durham, held an organizational meeting in the Hellenic Orthodox Church on October 23, 1955. In successive meetings they elected officers, petitioned the Bishop for status as an organized diocesan mission, chose the name of St. Luke's Mission, purchased property on Club Boulevard, and chose Watson to be its first priest-in-charge.[52] Watson assumed his new duties on September 1, 1956.

At St. Philip's he was succeeded as Assistant to the Rector by the Reverend John Denham, a native of Washington, North Carolina, who in June 1956 had graduated from Virginia Theological Seminary and had been ordained to the diaconate. David Yates had been the decisive influence in his life. When as a freshman he had entered the University of North Carolina in Chapel Hill, ordination was the farthest from Denham's thoughts. Lonely and depressed and feeling that no one loved him, he stopped going to church, when Yates, then rector of the Chapel of the Cross, dropped by "to find out why and offer a friendly hand." The opportune visit led Denham to realize that he had not been forgotten by everyone. He took a new interest in the Church and in his studies, as he minored in philosophy and majored in sociology and made Phi Beta Kappa. Through Yates he met Bishop Penick, who also had a great deal to do with his becoming a minister, as did William Poteat, his philosophy professor whose courses were a liberal education in thought. Attendance in his junior year at a youth conference in Bloomfield, Michigan, sealed Denham's determination to be ordained. At St. Philip's, as an ardent and tireless young minister, preaching, visiting, and conducting youth groups, he was soon working "26 hours a day."[53]

Throughout Edwards's ministry the thorn in the flesh, the pain in the neck, the cross he had to bear was the Every Member Canvass. Every year the same procedures were followed: the Vestry appointed in early autumn a chair of the Every Member Canvass, the Vestry's Finance Committee prepared a tentative budget, and the Vestry in early November went over the budget item by item in order to reach a final estimate for submission to the annual congregational meeting in January. Meanwhile, in early November pledge cards were mailed to every communicant household, with the instruction to return them within a week. Some came in early; most did not. As late as February, in one instance as late as May, the chair of the Every Member Canvass was still pleading for return of the pledges. The result was that the Vestry did not know until late how much money was at its disposal. And when the canvass was declared officially over, with an adequate sum raised, it was discovered that one-third of the communicants (30 to 40 percent) had not pledged, and never did!

The spirit of the church seemed high. Church membership had steadily risen. The number of baptized persons had increased from 882 in 1951 to 1,077 in 1956, the number of communicants for the same period from 707 to 819. Total attendance at the three services was steady at about 450, sometimes more, sometimes less; attendance at Church School averaged 75 to 80 percent of enrollment, an excellent showing. Yet one-third of the congregation did not recognize its obligation to support its church financially.[54] Perhaps the fact that the congregation was so large and so affluent that two-thirds could always sustain the budget had something to do with the easygoing laxity of the delinquent third.

Nevertheless, Edwards's ministry ended with a financial triumph. Year after year he had vainly urged door-to-door solicitation of every communicant by informed canvassers. When he announced his resignation from St. Philip's, to take effect on November 1, 1956, the Vestry moved the Every Member Canvass back to September and set the goal at $47,394. It merged that drive with a Capital Improvements Campaign to raise an additional $50,000 to clear the debt on the antiphonal organ, to air-condition the church, to remove the unsightly service station from the corner of Main and Queen Streets, and to donate a parting gift of $5,000 to St. Andrew's for a new chapel and $10,000 to St. Luke's for the purchase of a multipurpose building. *And* the Vestry adopted door-to-door solicitation by informed canvassers (see Appendix E). By a superbly managed campaign, directed by Clarence Cobb with the assistance of Claude Bittle and Watts Carr, Jr., the entire congregation met at 9:30 P.M., Sunday, September 16, 1956, for a brief church service and then returned to their homes; by eleven o'clock well-prepared canvassers were visiting each household. By mid-October pledges had been received for more than $97,394.[55] Once again there could be jubilation and a sense of accomplishment at St. Philip's.

On the eve of Edwards's departure for Chestnut Hills, a prestigious Philadelphia church, he and St. Philip's exchanged farewells that were appropriately published in the *Epistle*. Since they were truthful, they are a fitting conclusion to a chapter in which we have tried sincerely to discover and tell the truth about his rectorship. Representing St. Philip's, John Denham wrote:

A WORD FOR THE RECORD

More will be said concerning the approaching departure of our rector and his family as the time comes upon us. But now, while he still has several remaining weeks in Durham, it is well to remember all that has happened in St. Philip's during his period of leadership. The Family Service, now a permanent part of our worship life, was started; Mr. Cook was engaged and the music of our parish was made a major part of our program and worship; a parish Library now on the verge of expansion and relocation was initiated; the operating budget of the parish was greatly enlarged, enabling the ministry of St. Philip's to expand into new fields of service embracing a growing congregation; St. Luke's Mission was begun; St. Andrew's Mission was revived. These are but a few of the results of the rector's guidance and labor. It would be well to thank him for these contributions while he is still with us.[56]

The Rector responded:

My Dear People:

This being the last time I will write the *Epistle to the Philippians*, I wish to take this opportunity to say how much it has meant to me to be here at St. Philip's and to worship with you Sunday after Sunday. St. Philip's will always have a very soft place in my heart as being my first charge. I appreciate your enthusiastic response in worship, your patient attention to the preaching, your vigorous cooperation in all our parish activities, and all your many kind expressions of encouragement and friendship. It is truly a pleasure and privilege to serve and lead such a congregation, and the minister who enjoys this privilege will always receive far more than he gives.

With the prayer that down through the years this parish may be to many other people the secure spiritual home it has been to me for the past five years, I am

Affectionately yours,
Tom T. Edwards[57]

Deacon Joseph Blount Cheshire Jr., newly assigned to the Chapel of the Cross, Chapel Hill, made his legendary walk to Durham on May 26, 1878 and, by his own description, "read services and preached morning and afternoon" in an upper room known as Duke's Hall.

Thomas Atkinson, the third Bishop of North Carolina (1853–81).

Theodore Benedict Lyman, the fourth Bishop of North Carolina (Co-adjutor, 1873–81; Diocesan Bishop, 1881–93).

The original 1881 frame building, serving what was authorized on February 25, 1880 as the Durham Mission Station, was constructed on a lot at "the edge of town" at a cost of $2,500.

John C. Huske (1884–86) served the Durham Mission as well as the Chapel of the Cross in Chapel Hill until the Durham Mission achieved independence as St. Philip's Parish with Huske as Rector.

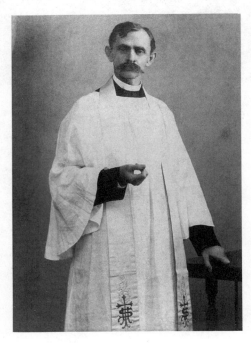

T. M. N. George (1886–90) was an energetic Rector who inspired a growing number of communicants by his own dedication to duty even as he reached out to the black people of Durham in the "Hayti" community.

Charles J. Wingate (1890–91), a mature priest from the Diocese of Kentucky, reported that he found St. Philip's Parish "in a most gratifying condition" but nevertheless left for a Wilson parish after only a year in Durham.

Stewart McQueen (1892–94), a South Carolinian, came to St. Philip's after it had gone a year without a Rector, only to transfer to the Diocese of East Carolina in the space of another year.

Alfred A. Pruden (1895–98) was an enterprising Rector who focused public attention on St. Philip's by advertising special services, both in advance and after the fact. During his tenure the number of communicants increased by 56 percent, even as he did outreach work among the millworkers of Durham.

As bishop, Joseph Blount Cheshire, Jr., was as fervently dedicated to the establishment of missions as he had been when, while still a deacon and assigned to Chapel Hill, he formally organized the mission in Durham that became St. Philip's Parish. Cheshire was elected Bishop Coadjutor in 1893 and became Diocesan Bishop the same year, serving until 1932.

Henry Beard Delany served as Suffragan Bishop under Cheshire from 1918 to 1928.

Bishop Edwin Anderson Penick shifted the diocesan emphasis from sponsoring parochial missions to strengthening pan-diocesan activities for young people, for college students, and for men as well as women. Penick was elected Cheshire's Coadjutor in 1922 and succeeded him in 1932, serving until 1959.

Sidney Stuart Bost was an innovator and a builder who supervised the development of the East Durham and West Durham Sunday Schools into full-fledged parochial missions of St. Philip's even as he sponsored an outreach mission to the deaf and functioned as a respected community leader.

When St. Philip's under Bost outgrew the 1881 frame structure, the services of Ralph Adams Cram were secured to design the present brownstone church building, which was first occupied in 1907.

The interior of the 1907 building as decorated for Easter before the Good Shepherd window above the altar was installed.

Shortly after the turn of the century, Col. J. Harper Erwin bought a lot on Hart Street for St. Philip's mission in East Durham and the parish and members of the Brotherhood of St. Andrew financed a wooden chapel to house what had started as a Sunday School group.

The 1908 church building of Rowan County granite was given to the West Durham mission by textile executive William A. Erwin as a memorial to his parents, Joseph J. and Elvira J. Erwin. The mission itself was designated as St. Joseph's.

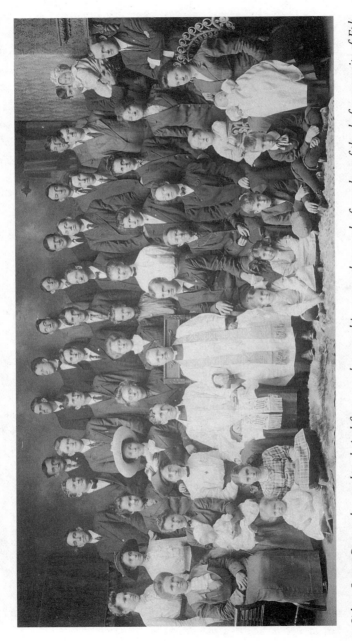

Sidney Stuart Bost and one other clerical figure can be spotted in a 1911 photograph of members of the deaf community of Ephphatha which St. Philip's ministered to with a weekly Bible School.

Roma C. Fortune, who was deaf, was ordained a deacon in 1918 and assigned to the Ephphatha mission. He was ordained to the priesthood by Bishop Cheshire in January 1923 at St. Philip's.

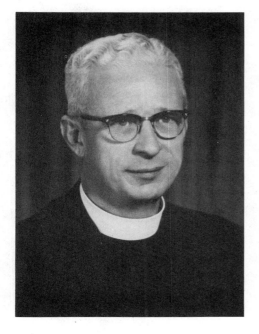

James R. Fortune, son of Roma Fortune, followed in his father's footsteps as a Diocesan Missionary to the Deaf. James centered his ministry in the Durham mission of Ephphatha but worked throughout the state and served the National Church as a representative of the deaf congregation.

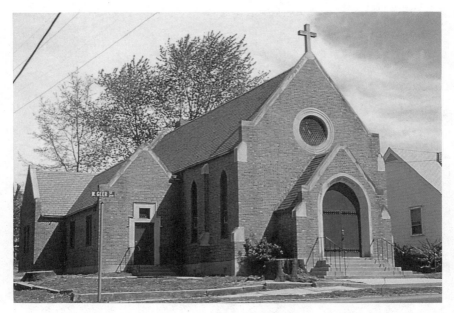

Ephphatha Church, on the corner of Geer and North Streets, was consecrated in 1931, the only church exclusively for the deaf in the South, one of four in the nation. It was occupied continuously until 1975, when a dwindling deaf population and vandalism to the building forced its deconsecration and sale.

The legendary David Yates, "a pacifist saint," touched people by his example. Said to be "tireless and genial in the Lord's work," he declined salary increases and requested a reduction when he was overruled.

Assistant Rectors during the first half of the twentieth century:

Thomas Lee Trott (1905–15)

A. Stratton Lawrence, Jr. (1935–39)

Henry Nutt Parsley (1939–41)

Clarence R. Haden, Jr., a Texan, was described as vigorous, friendly, forthright, a take-charge person with an infectious smile. When the Vestry faltered over the inflation-driven cost of the proposed parish house, he swayed a congregational meeting to vote overwhelmingly in favor of moving ahead to build the structure that was dedicated, debt-free, in 1953.

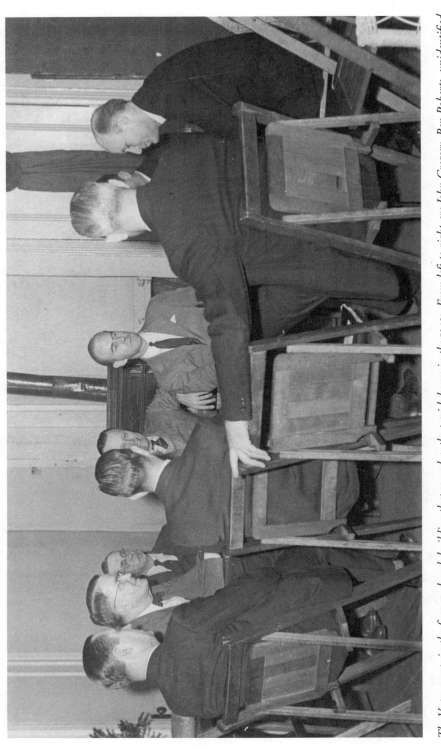

The Vestry meets in the former church building that served as the parish house in the 1940s. From left to right are John Gregory, Ben Roberts, unidentified man, Bill Ruffin, June (Junius) Mallard, Clarence Haden and Bailey Hobgood (back to camera).

Eight different Church School groups meet simultaneously in the old wooden church building that served as the parish house until the present structure was built in 1949.

Kitty Nelson works with pre-schoolers in a kitchen area pressed into service as a Church School room in the old parish house.

In a more cheerful setting, Jo Ruffin teaches a kindergarten Church School class.

The Junior Choir poses for a Christmas season photograph, some members holding gift-wrapped packages. Haden stands in front of the altar; Mary Yancey, longtime organist, is at far left, and "Monk" Moore is at far right.

In the old parish house gatherings were likely to be cramped for space. Here Haden (far left, rear) and Emily Hurst (far right) meet with the Young People's Service League in the Church School primary classroom.

Haden (center at head table) dines with the Young People's Service League in the spacious hall of the new parish house.

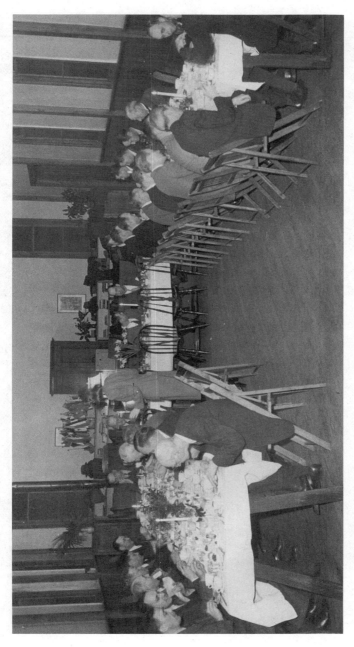

Members of the Laymen's League break bread together in the old parish house on tables improvised from "saw horses" but covered with fine tablecloths and centered with flower arrangements and candles, the handiwork of the members of the Woman's Auxiliary who also prepared and served the dinner.

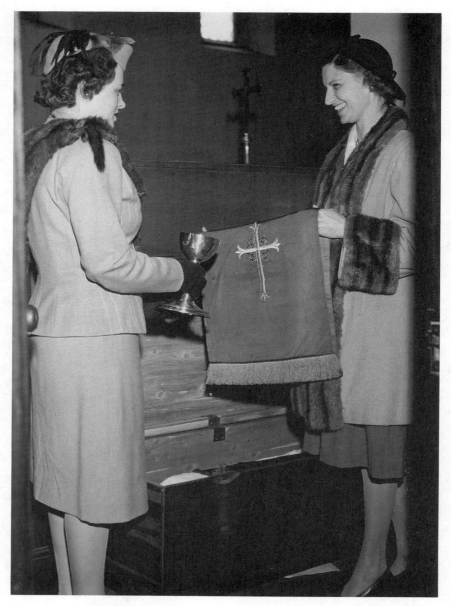

Essie Haden (left) and Libby Roberts take part in the ongoing work of the faithful Altar Guild.

Tom Turney Edwards, scholarly and devout, initiated the Epistle to the Philippians *and used it effectively, introduced a popular 9:30* A.M. *family educational service, and presided over the amicable formation of the mission that became St. Luke's Parish.*

Robert M. Watson, Jr. (1953–56) and John Denham (1956–57) served successively as curate under Edwards, helping him run a parish program serving over eight hundred communicants.

Communicants stream out of the church after dismissal in the "halcyon days"—before the St. Stephen's group left to form their own "neighborhood church" and St. Philip's was on the brink of becoming a parish that would minister to the changed neighborhood that had grown up around it.

Levering Bartine Sherman led St. Philip's through a difficult decade by providing the firm leadership that the problems of the period required and by maintaining a nurturing, liturgical structure in which parishioners could grow in freedom and grace.

Jim Nicholson and Clarence and Mary Lucy Cobb led fellow members of an inspired Cloister Garden Committee to create the Memorial Garden with graceful plantings and benches for quiet contemplation, focused around a beautiful metal sculpture of a dragon-fly emerging from its chrysalis.

Thomas Eugene Bollinger's not inconsiderable problems included the tasks of introducing the Trial Liturgy and handling the reaction to the National Church's support of the Malcolm X University, located two blocks from a parish that had not been consulted. He met the challenges by concentrating on a strong Christian Education program, training a band of lay readers, conducting a self-study that led to a successful campaign to renovate the physical plant and buy available land adjacent to church property, and, finally, cofounding the vital organization that became Durham Congregations in Action.

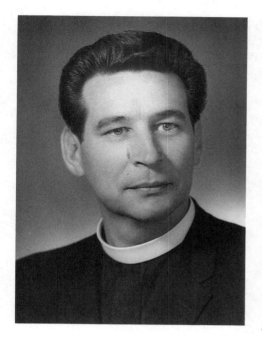

Sherman had for his curate a perfect complement in Albert A. Nelius (1960–67), who relished working with the Episcopal Young Churchmen, visiting the parishioners in their homes, and working with a Fine Arts Commission, chaired by George Pyne, that beautified the church and the parish house.

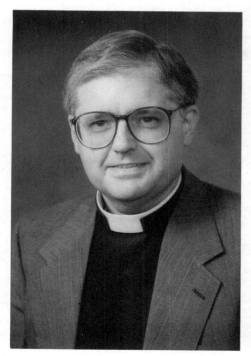

Edward F. Glusman, Jr., was Bollinger's assistant from 1974 to 1975.

Bishop Richard Henry Baker (Co-adjutor, 1950–59; Diocesan Bishop, 1959–65)

Suffragan Bishop W. Moultrie Moore, Jr. (1967–75)

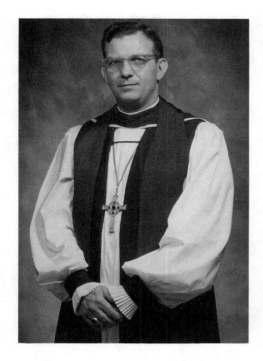

Bishop Thomas Augustus Fraser, Jr.
(Coadjutor, 1960–65; Diocesan
Bishop, 1965–83)

Suffragan Bishop Frank H. Vest, Jr.
(1985–89)

Bishop Robert Whitridge Estill (Coadjutor, 1980–83; Diocesan Bishop, 1983–94)

C. Thomas Midyette III (1978–94) arrived at St. Philip's "a friendly, dynamic, rather brash young man. He departed as a wise guru of deepening spirituality." In the process Midyette taught members of the congregation to move in worship together within the diverse, inclusive community, the Church.

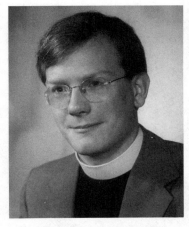

Jonathan Glass was Midyette's part-time assistant from 1982 to 1985.

Victoria Jamieson-Drake (1986–89), part-time assistant to Midyette, cooperated with Amanda Smith to formulate Rite 13, or "Celebration of the Gift of Manhood or Womanhood," and its supporting curriculum, to be followed by the Journey to Adulthood, which proved so successful an undertaking that it attracted attention from across the nation.

Joanne Stearns (1989–92), the first full-time assistant to the Rector at St. Philip's in more than nine years, was universally loved and her departure was generally regretted when she left to take the rectorship of St. Christopher's in Fairborn, Ohio.

7
The Rectorship of Levering Bartine Sherman
1957–1967

Even while Tom Turney Edwards was still present and officiating, the Vestry of St. Philip's appointed a Search Committee to seek out his successor. For the first time several women were full-fledged members of the committee. It included Robert G. Hurst (executive secretary), William H. Ruffin, Kenneth C. Royal, Jr., Watts Carr, Jr., William P. Biggers, Priscilla McBryde, Kitty Leigh, and Libby Roberts.[1]

After a relatively brief search the committee recommended and the Vestry called a priest already known to many of them, the Reverend Levering Bartine Sherman. Familiarly called "Bart," he was the first of three rectors at St. Philip's to be known by the contraction of his middle name.

He came from a family of clergy. His father, a missionary, was dean of St. Paul's Divinity School at Wuchang, China. His brother was an Episcopal priest in Ohio, and his two sisters married clergymen.

Sherman was born in Wuchang on May 23, 1921. He did his preparatory work at Kent School, Kent, Connecticut, before going on to Princeton University. After more than three years in the Navy he returned to receive his A.B. in 1946 (as of 1943) and immediately began his studies for the ministry at the Virginia Theological Seminary in Alexandria. In 1949 he received his B.D. and was ordained deacon on June 3 and priest on December 13. Thereupon he became deacon and then priest-in-charge of St. Andrew's Church, Charlotte, St. Mark's Church, Mecklenburg County, and the mission at Davidson College.[2]

From 1951 to 1954 he served as chaplain to Episcopal students at the University of North Carolina in Chapel Hill. There, for over three years, he was closely associated with David Yates, rector of the Chapel of the Cross. Sherman could not have had a better and more inspiring mentor. He later remarked: "My ministry is based in large part on his ministry. He was a great influence on my life." Once a year, usually in March, Yates and Sherman presented to Bishop Penick candidates for confirmation. On these occasions, in the Bishop's presence, Sherman read Morning Prayer or preached the sermon.[3] At the annual Diocesan Conventions from 1950 to 1954 he was becoming known to the leaders of the diocesan community, including the delegates of St. Philip's. He was elected alternate delegate to the Provincial Synod (1951) and appointed chair of the Committee on Miscellaneous Reports (1954).[4]

After nearly four years of college work, however, he wished to get out and have a church of his own. On September 1, 1954 he became rector of St. Peter's in Charleston, South Carolina. But he felt totally out of place there, and he welcomed the call to St. Philip's as an invitation to "the promised land"—a larger parish, a higher salary, and educated, intelligent leaders whom he knew and could trust. At his meeting with members of the Search Committee, he had asked what they expected of him. Priscilla McBryde replied: "We want someone to come in and love us." Sherman thought he could do that and accepted the call on 13 February 1957.[5]

Bishop Penick immediately assured him that he had not made a mistake. On February 15 he wrote:

> Dear Bart:
> I want you to know how happy I was to hear this afternoon that you had accepted the call to St. Philip's Church, Durham, and that you would begin your work in that parish about the middle of March. That is great good news. Please let me tell you how happy I am to welcome you back to the Old North State, and particularly to this diocese. St. Philip's is one of the major parishes of this diocese. The personnel of the congregation is of a very high quality, and has supplied many top leaders through the years. With affectionate regards, I am
>
> Sincerely yours,
> Edwin A. Penick[6]

Sherman was aware that there were problems at St. Philip's. Before accepting the post he had received from John Denham, Edwards's Assistant Rector who was staying over until Sherman himself could arrive, a balanced, realistic appraisal of the situation of the several Episcopal churches in Durham:

St. Luke's under Robert Watson is still a mission, but will be a parish soon, we hope, and may start to build soon. Presently they are in a converted house.

St. Andrew's is a mission with a new building. Present membership is low. Plans are for a Pilot project in neighborhood evangelism conducted by the Central Clericus of the Diocese to help carry the Gospel from St. Andrew's into the environing area, and hope the people come there to join the People of God. We hope to have clerical and lay help from all over the Central Clericus to "flood" east Durham next May 7th with house-to-house callers. If this plan works there, we may use it elsewhere in the clericus area.

St. Titus is struggling; we could have a house-to-house campaign there; it is much needed, and the Priest-in-Charge, Fred Hunter, is discouraged.

St. Joseph's is thriving under Jack Spong. It is a parish with many Duke University personnel in its membership and great future plans. They may have to build to accommodate the crowds.

St. Philip's is located in a downtown commercial and industrial area, but there is a high concentration of low-income, transient population. The field is ripe here for a pioneering downtown ministry.

St. Philip's membership is scattered all over town but with a concentration in Forest Hills, Rockwood, and Hope Valley. The latter, a posh residential area 5 miles from the parish out in the county, is a controversial issue. At present, it is almost exclusively St. Philip's, although St. Joseph's has several families there. However, there are some top-flight, energetic people who want their own mission out there. [They wish to enjoy once again and to have their children enjoy the close experience of a neighborhood church they had known at St. Philip's when they were growing up.]

The only rub is that the same 50 St. P's families out there contribute substantially to the financial program of St. P's. The group out there has practically guaranteed that all involved families would fulfill their total pledges to our Capital Improvements

Fund (running from 1957–1959), but, of course, they would not necessarily pledge to the operating budget any longer. The sudden lack of their contribution would strain St. P's.

Naturally if the Hope Valley people start their own church, the rector of St. P's will have to depend on the people that are left making up the difference in the operating budget, which I feel they could do. The overall giving at St. P's is mighty low, with very few people even approaching a tithe. With a vigorous overall program at St. P's, I feel that the remaining people could and would support St. P's in love and gratitude.

Most of the old-guard on the Vestry tend to think that when a parish loses 100 people, it is a permanent loss. But the experience of most parishes is just the opposite. When a group of people leave to start another church, the clergy have that much more time to concentrate on the remaining area and its thousands of unchurched people, and they will soon fill in the gap plus some. Besides, when the "wealthy" people of the parish leave, the rest work harder and get a lot more from their parish life than before.

If the Hope Valley mission starts soon, and I personally hope it will, St. P's will be able to concentrate on the Forest Hills and Rockwood area, where many of its supporters already live. And, it may be possible to do some real work in the downtown area, which has been neglected simply because the clergy were spread so thinly over such a large area.

Under your leadership the Hope Valley mission, if you approve of it, could receive an encouraging vigorous, Christian start. But, having the non–Hope Valley part of the parish (80%) give birth to the new mission *gladly* will require a hopeful, intense program at St. P's (which we should have had all along).

I see great things in the future of St. P's. And I hope you will be the man to come here and do the job.

Yours in the Lord,
John[7]

THE FIRST THREE YEARS

Tall, erect, and endowed with an excellent speaking and singing voice, Sherman had a commanding presence. It conveys a sense of his appearance to note that several years after his arrival at St. Philip's he sang the title role in an amateur production of Gilbert and Sullivan's *Mikado*. Very dedicated, very devout, and very firm, he introduced during his first three years at St. Philip's a comprehensive program of study, liturgical tightening, and spiritual renewal. He was working, it must be noted, without an Assistant Rector. His philosophy was that the strength of the Church lies in individuals. The Church provides the structures in which individuals can grow in knowledge and grace. But the individual communicants are free to develop their own talents in their own way.[8]

He expressed his basic theology in his opening *Epistle to the Philippians* (April 7, 1957). If we read it as carefully and thoughtfully as he wrote it, we shall perceive that the key to his sustained spiritual effort throughout his rectorship lay in this kernel of belief:

Dear Friends:

It seems appropriate to me that our new relationship should have its beginning in the season of Lent, for Lent is a time of beginnings, particularly the beginning of new relationships—new relationships with God and with the Body of Christ which is His Church. During the forty days it is possible through our Lenten observance—through Bible reading, prayer, and the worship of the Church—to enter into a closer relationship with God, to feel more keenly His Presence, to acknowledge more clearly His Will for our lives. By the effort to unite our wills with His, we grow into a new relationship of love with Him. As the Holy Days of Maundy Thursday, Good Friday and Easter draw near, it is my hope that this Lent you will have grown into such a relationship with God that these days will have new and significant meaning for you in your lives.

The warmth of your welcome extended to me and to my family has made us feel already at home in your midst. It is difficult for us to express our appreciation for this welcome. I ask your prayers for me and I bid your prayers for this Parish that together we may be a mighty agent for the working out of God's purposes for men.

Faithfully,
Your friend and Rector
L. Bartine Sherman

He continued, of course, the basic, traditional organizations and practices of St. Philip's, even most of Edwards's innovations, but he modified, added, and improved. He continued weekday Morning Prayer at 8:40 A.M. with the staff ("it meant so much to us"), but he invited other members of the congregation to attend, too. He retained the three Sunday morning services: Holy Communion at eight o'clock, Family Service and Sunday School at nine-thirty, and traditional worship at eleven. At nine-thirty and eleven Holy Communion was celebrated and the Decalogue recited on the first Sunday of each month; Morning Prayer was read on the other Sundays.

It was part of Sherman's code to offer on Sunday a good liturgical experience, good music, and a good sermon. He welcomed the strong musical tradition of St. Philip's. When the choirmaster/organist Henry Cook followed Edwards to Chestnut Hills in Philadelphia, Sherman worked closely with Dr. Isaac Manning, chair of the Vestry's Music Committee, to choose a successor. Among those who applied was David Pizarro, who was to become one of the most distinguished musicians in the Episcopal Church. Sherman and Pizarro then worked together to tone up the musical performance, into which they thought laxities had crept. They introduced several changes "dictated primarily by the principles of good liturgical practice." As Sherman explained to the congregation:

> All that we do in church we do primarily to the glory of God, and only secondarily for our own edification. Our service of worship is an offering to God; therefore, our first desire is that it be in the finest form possible. This understanding of the nature of worship governs all parts of the service, including the music. All music for the services is selected with an eye to its appropriateness as an offering to God, rather than the particular musical tastes of any member of the staff or the congregation. . . . This principle that what we do is not to gratify our own desires but is an offering to God, governs our selection of the hymns and the whole conduct of our service.[9]

It suggested also, for example, that the members of the congregation should join with the choir in chanting the Canticles. To guide them, printed cards giving directions for chanting the four Canticles most often used in Morning Prayer were placed in the book racks in the pews. Once the congregation had learned to chant, it was reminded of the "ancient and sensible liturgical role that things said by the minister should have a said response, and things sung should have a sung response. From now on, therefore, at services of Morning and Evening Prayer, the Gloria Patri at the conclusion of the Psalms will be said by the congregation and minister in unison when the Psalms are said, and sung only when the Psalms are chanted." [10]

Sherman's sermons harmonized with his strong sense of form. Carefully crafted, closely reasoned, and intellectually powerful, they could be mentally outlined as they came over. Yet during these years they spoke to the individual needs of his listeners, as he tried to incorporate in each sermon certain phrases that they could hang on to.[11] The author of this chapter still gratefully remembers several such phrases, like "Faith and Constancy," that he worked into his life.

As Sherman conducted his first Sunday service on March 24, 1957, the neighborhood Lenten study and discussion groups, initiated by Edwards, were fading. They did not reappear in succeeding years, but Sherman maintained other opportunities for study and self-education, and opened new ones. He himself was a reader and student and led by example. Even before his arrival he asked the senior warden, Dr. Arthur H. London, to have installed in the Rector's office sixty-five feet of book shelves for his working library: "Not all of my books would necessarily be kept there, but of course the number of books is increasing each year." [12] In various ways he tried to encourage a spirit of study in his flock. In the *Epistle to the Philippians*, he repeatedly referred to the treasures in the parish library and signaled new acquisitions. Like the weekly sermon, the weekly edition of the *Epistle* itself was a teaching vehicle, as he published in it essays on church doctrine and practice. Each year the monthly chapter meetings of the Episcopal Church Women did a concentrated study of a book of the Bible (Jeremiah, Mark, or Romans, for example) or of some work on Christian living. Prior to each monthly session Sherman briefed the chapter Christian Education secretaries on the passage to be discussed. He took this self-imposed duty very seriously and, as he did everything else, prepared carefully. Very early in his rectorship he began a Tuesday evening "Rector's Hour," where he led a group of interested adults in discussion of "Modern Rivals to Christianity."

Out of the Rector's Hour in 1958, the succeeding Adult Study Class in 1959, and the annual confirmation classes grew in 1960 Sherman's superb Course in Christianity, which he regarded as the capstone of his educational effort. The course was nothing if not thorough. Each semester consisted of ten ninety-minute evening lectures, followed by a coffee break and an open-ended bull session. Drawing on his considerable knowledge of theology, history, and church practice, he opened with the disturbing questions asked about the origin, destination, and purpose of man; passed to the Christian answers—Calvary, salvation, Heaven and Hell; and concluded with a detailed description of participation in the Christian answers through life in the Church (see Appendix F for an outline and a list of readings). Though the course was required of all adult candidates for confirmation, it was open to everyone: "Long-time members of the Episcopal Church, new Episcopalians, members of other denominations or other faiths, agnostics and atheists are welcome." [13] Sherman hoped that if every member of the congregation freely responded to a rich opportunity freely offered, St. Philip's would then become a Church community educated in its faith.

Complementing the multipronged educational effort were measures of spiritual renewal. From April 28 to May 2, 1958, for example, a five-night Parish Life Mission was held, attended by seventy-two communicants. In its planning were mobilized all those who held any position of leadership in the parish: vestrymen, Woman's Auxiliary, board members, chapter presidents, Church School officers and teachers, Laymen's League officers, officers of the Junior Choir Mothers' Guild, and Altar Guild officers. On Tuesday, October 28, 1958, Bishop Penick preached in St. Philip's Church at an evening Diocesan Service of Renewal (Revival) for the Episcopalians of Durham, Chapel Hill, Roxboro, and Hillsborough. The primary purpose of the service was evangelical: "to stir up the hearts and minds and souls of our church people to a deeper dedication to God and His Christ." [14] These measures bore fruit—in a revitalized Laymen's League, under the presidencies of Dr. Isaac Manning and Robert Hurst; the creation of a Parish Life Council, under the chairmanship of Josephine Ruffin, to visit inactive St. Philippians and newcomers to Durham; and, most significantly, in the formation of two prayer groups, meeting weekly on Thursday morning after Communion and on Thursday evening. Another sign of vitality was the active Sunday evening sessions of the Young People's Service League, which was honored by diocesan awards in both 1958 and 1959.

All these measures—a firmer liturgy, splendid music, a multipronged educational effort, and means for spiritual renewal—worked together to produce a strengthened attendance at Sunday church services. The total attendance of 575 worshipers at all three services on Palm Sunday 1959 surpassed the record for any previous one since 1936.

Alas! It was to be the last Palm Sunday at which all members of the "old" St. Philip's were together. On April 23, 1959, shortly after Easter, a sizable number of St. Philippians registered as communicants of a new Episcopal church, St. Stephen's, that was being formed in the Hope Valley area.

Initially, Sherman had hoped against hope that the withdrawal would not occur. But once Bishop Penick had decided that the formation of the new parish was a "must," Sherman tried to give the departure a proper "spin." In a memo to the congregation of St. Philip's, he stressed that what was primarily important was not the happening but our attitude toward it:

It would be possible for a long-time member of St. Philip's to be filled with despair, and to feel that this will mean the effectual end of St. Philip's. Or, it would be possible to take a grudging attitude, and to say "This must be, and we must simply make the best of it." Or it is quite possible, and I believe, right, for us to say, "We have been assured by those who should know that this is the right step for us to take in this situation at this time. Let us, therefore, as members of Christ's Church, support this project enthusiastically, for the extension of the Kingdom of God in our community."

Our first concern as Christians is with the cause of Christ; secondly, we are members of the Episcopal Church; only thirdly is our allegiance to St. Philip's Church. What we must be concerned with is the overall effectiveness of the Christian Church in our community, and the strength of our own communion. What we must want is not what is best necessarily for any particular parish, but what is best for the Episcopal Church as a part of Christ's Church. I know that there are many faithful members of St. Philip's who feel that the formation of the congregation could very well hamper St. Philip's permanently. If the remaining members of St. Philip's throw up their hands in despair and say "We have been killed," we may never be able to recover. But if we regard this as an opportunity and a challenge to redouble our own missionary and evangelistic efforts, to strengthen our parish life, and to bring into more active participation in the life of the parish those who have been in the past on the fringe of its membership, then the formation of this new congregation may well be a very great blessing to St. Philip's.[15]

It would be natural for the historian to dwell on what St. Philip's *lost* by the exodus to St. Stephen's. And the loss *was* considerable — in membership, leadership, and money. During the first nine months through January 1, 1960, sixty-eight communicants with their children transferred from St. Philip's to the new mission.[16] They were able, active communicants, and included such outstanding leaders as Paul Wright, Nat Gregory, Nello Teer, and Frank Kenan. As a group the transfers had annually contributed $9,000 to $10,000 to a parish support level of $48,000.

However, it would be more appropriate for the historian to emphasize the *strengths* that St. Philip's *retained* — in membership, leadership, and money. The statistics as reported to the Diocese are illuminating:

	No. of Communicants	No. of Baptized Persons	Parish Support
1957 (after departure of St. Luke's & Tom Turney Edwards)	645	845	$39,450
1958	658	931	39,179
1959	653	929	48,210
1960 (after St. Stephen's)	579	741	53,447[17]

Although the number of communicants dropped from 653 (1959) to 579 (1960), the amount of money contributed by parishioners increased by more than $5,000! Within a year the deficit of $9,000 to $10,000 that might have been occasioned by the withdrawal of the St. Stephen's contingency had been more than made up.

The quality of leadership remained high. Not all Hope Valley people left St. Philip's. J. Harper Erwin, Jr., stayed, as did Dr. Isaac and Dorothy Manning and Dr. Norman and Marjorie Ross. The core of faithful in Forest Hills and Rockwood remained intact: Watts and Ihrie Carr, Robert and Julia Carr, Clarence and Mary Lucy Cobb,

James and Margaret Davis, Angus and Priscilla McBryde, B. W. and Libby Roberts, Kenneth and Julia Royall, and William and Josephine Ruffin. And, of course, there were many others from other sections of Durham: for example, John and Hilda Chatham, Richard and Kitty Leigh, Jim and Betty Nicholson, E. K. and Sibyl Powe, George and Mary Pyne, Ben R. and Louise Roberts, Dr. Julian and Landon Ruffin, and Dr. Richard and Ruth Watson.

The blue-ribbon Vestry of 1959 was largely composed of former or future senior and junior wardens: Clarence Cobb (Senior Warden), Robert Fortune (Junior Warden), Robert Carr, J. Harper Erwin, Jr., Bailey Hobgood, Jack Hughes, Angus McBryde, Isaac Manning, Jr., E. K. Powe, Ben R. Roberts, Kenneth Royall, and William H. Ruffin.[18] It was representative of yet a larger group of available leaders, men who were accustomed to making decisions and standing by them. The presidents of the Woman's Auxiliary, Priscilla McBryde and Louise Roberts in 1959 and Dorothy Manning in 1960, likewise represented the immense pool of ability available in that organization.

Sherman, naturally, was deeply pleased by how well the congregation had stood up to the challenge. Its steadiness under stress was truly a triumph of faith and constancy.

ST. PHILIP'S WAS NEVER MORE BEAUTIFUL

St. Philip's was never more beautiful than during the last seven years of the rectorship of Bart Sherman. His strategy of setting structures in which creative individuals could freely develop their talents and initiatives worked well in the realm of the Fine Arts. There, several parishioners, singly or in unison, created objects of beauty and spiritual meaning.

They worked in several mediums—music, gardening, sculpture, painting, design, the resonant sound of a bell—always suggesting more of spiritual allusiveness and depth than what was directly, concretely perceived. George Pyne, long a member of St. Philip's, its artist-in-residence, was already there, endowing with imaginative grace everything he touched. David Pizarro, the choirmaster/organist, an enigmatic figure, came next in time, arriving in the spring of 1958. The holder of Bachelor's and Master's degrees in music from Yale University, he had been further educated by two years of study of the organ in Germany and France in 1955 and 1956. He already had an international reputation. During the summers of 1958, 1960, and 1963 he went on two-month concert tours of East and West Germany, leaving his duties at St. Philip's to his able assistant, Seth Warner, professor of mathematics at Duke University. While on his travels, in 1963, "he was made Fellow of the Trinity College of Music in London, having successfully passed an examination in organ performance."[19]

Since by church canon the ultimate authority on questions of music in the church lay with the rector, it was important and fortunate that Sherman and Pizarro shared the same philosophy with respect to church music. They both believed that it should express the theology of the service and that musically it should be of the highest quality. In his revealing essay "Wedding Music," Pizarro concluded:

> A noted cleric has stated that people are willing to accept expert advice (and pay for it, too) in all fields except theology and church music. That may well be true, but that does not relieve the church musician of preserving the great charge laid upon him: to preserve what is good, discard the unworthy, and encourage the new. He must ever seek to keep the sanctity of church music. If music cannot meet the most rigid requirements of musicians, then this music is not worthy of performance in God's House. Therein lies the guiding principle for all the church's music.[20]

He was so musical, so talented that he was able to *elicit* superior performances from the church choir.[21] Its members recall the pleasure of working with him as well as the camaraderie of the group. Three or four times a year, usually after Sunday Evensong, they gave a Sacred Concert of the works of Bach, Handel, Mozart, and modern composers. On such occasions vocalists from the black community and instrumentalists often heightened the musical splendor. Characteristic were the two programs offered on the third and fourth Sunday of Advent of 1960: on the third Sunday Johann Sebastian Bach's "Come, Thou, Savior of Mankind" was sung complete; on the following Sunday the program was "made up of music for solo voices. Mrs. Rose sang Tunder's Cantata, 'Sleepers, Wake'; an aria from the Advent portion of the *Messiah*; and an *Advent Chorale* by a North Carolina Moravian composer. Michael Best sang two songs by Vaughan Williams, and Mr. Pizarro played some Advent organ music."[22] Unforgettable, too, was another occasion when the choir, the African American singer Africa Hayes, and instrumentalists performed Handel's *Messiah* Parts II and III. Ms. Hayes, daughter of Roland Hayes of North Carolina Central University, sang frequently with St. Philip's choir.

James Nicholson, junior warden during five years of Sherman's ten-year tenure—"a real leader," Sherman recalled—spearheaded the move to create a Memorial Garden on the church grounds.[23] On April 24, 1961 the Vestry had purchased a vacant lot north of the parish house that was to be used for parking. It would leave between the parking area and the church a small plot of land that might be treated as unadorned lawn. Instead, the idea surfaced that a Memorial Garden might be placed there. Nicholson, a dedicated gardener who was sensitive to the needs and feelings of plants and to their beauty, was appointed chair of the Cloister Garden Committee, which also included Betsy Hansen-Pruss, Mary Lucy and Clarence Cobb, and Dorothy and Nello Teer. A landscape architect, Richard C. Bell, was secured. His plans called for a fifteen-panel brick wall separating and enclosing the garden from the parking lot; a brick walkway leading from the parking area to the church, bordered with plantings of trees, shrubs, and flowers as well as cast stone benches; and in a secluded corner a meditation area with a small circular pool and statuary. "Located as it was just off a busy block of East Main Street and within sound of the loudspeakers and diesel engines of the bus station nearby, the garden was a spot to which one might withdraw for a few minutes of quiet and peace, an opportunity for meditation or prayer."[24]

Donations of money to pay for each panel of the wall as a memorial to the dead, or commemoration of the living, or general thank offering soon flowed in. The Memorial Garden was dedicated, appropriately, on Rogation Sunday, May 19, 1963. The conclusion of the dedication service reminds us of the garden's spiritual significance:

> During the singing of the Choral Respond, the Chairman of the Memorial Garden Committee will plant a shrub in the Garden.
>
> Then will the Rector proceed to bless the Garden, its Furnishing and Plantings, first Saying,
> Our help is in the Name of the Lord;
> *Answer*: Who hath made heaven and earth.
> *Rector*: Blessed be the Name of the Lord;
> *Answer*: Henceforth, world without end.
> *Rector*: Lord, hear our prayer.

Answer: And let our cry come unto thee.

O LORD God, almighty, bless this place that here may abide health, purity, victory, strength, humility, goodness, meekness, fulfillment of the law, and giving of thanks to God the Father, the Son, and the Holy Ghost; and let thy blessing remain on this place and on all who shall pass through it, now and evermore. Amen.

O GLORIOUS God, whose perfect beauty the wonderful design of all thy works proclaim, Bless, we beseech thee, this Garden, its Walls, Gates, Benches, Walks, and Plantings, that it may beautify the place of thy Sanctuary and show forth thy glory; through Jesus Christ or Lord. Amen.[25]

Within a year the meditation area with its small circular pool was completed with metal statuary. Great stalks of metal leaves rose from the water, and in the center a giant dragonfly, its wings outstretched, emerged from its chrysalis. Made by the sculptor Clark Fitz-Gerald of Castine, Maine, the sculpture was conceived as "something more than mere decoration" but as a work of art that, Fitz-Gerald said, "can be interpreted and enjoyed on different levels." He added: "I have used a biological symbol, ecdysis to be exact, to try to give the feeling of the struggle involved in rebirth. Whether an insect emerges from a chrysalis or a Christ revolutionizes man's conscience, the birth pangs are momentous." Although some viewers might view this sculpture as "a pleasant composition of leaves and an insect," he explained, "others may see the deeper symbolism, perhaps even relating the outstretched wings to the cruciform."[26]

When the statuary was dedicated as a memorial to Burton Craige Ruffin, the hope was expressed that as we of St. Philip's "come to live with this sensitively conceived and brilliantly executed sculpture in our Garden, we will become more and more 'impatient with the obvious,' as it begins to speak its variegated meaning to all who really see it."[27]

Enter into our account another actor in the realm of the Fine Arts, the Reverend Albert Arnold Nelius, as Assistant Rector or Curate. After three years of trying to meet singlehandedly the needs of a large congregation, Sherman pointed out to the Vestry that work as hard as he could, many things were left undone, especially in the realm of counseling and visitation. The withdrawal of the St. Stephen's contingent had diminished but did not extinguish the problem; the outpouring of financial support in the recent canvass now made the addition of an assistant feasible. The Vestry, led by Watts Carr, Jr., finally listened and called Nelius in March 1960.

Thirty-four years old, Nelius was a native of Memphis, Tennessee. Educated in the public schools of Memphis and in its Southwestern College, he received his Bachelor of Arts degree in 1951. He attended the School of Theology at Sewanee and then Virginia Theological Seminary, in Alexandria, where he was awarded the Bachelor of Divinity degree in 1954. He served as assistant rector of St. George's Church in Nashville, Tennessee, from 1954 to 1957 and as vicar of St. Barnabas's Church in a suburb of St. Louis, Missouri, from 1957 until accepting the call to St. Philip's. He was married to the former Sigrid von Renner, M.D., a native of Dresden, Germany.[28]

St. Philip's had been fortunate or discerning in its choice of Assistant Rectors — Thomas Lee Trott under Bost; A. Stratton Lawrence, Henry Nutt Parsley, and Josiah T. Carter under Yates and Haden; and Robert Watson and John Denham under Edwards. St. Philip's was fortunate, too, when the Vestry, on Sherman's recommendation, chose Nelius.

Sherman and the new assistant early decided on a division of duties. On Sundays both were present at all three services. Sherman celebrated Communion at the eight o'clock service and once a month at the two other services, and he delivered the sermon at non-Communion services. Nelius gave the sermon (and exquisite sermons they were!) on Communion Sundays and each Sunday evening met with the Young People's Service League. Sherman, as was his canonical right and duty, oversaw the music program.

From Monday through Friday Sherman, Nelius, and the irreplaceable secretary Matt West started each day with Morning Prayer at 8:40. Then Sherman handled the administrative correspondence, relations with the Vestry, the formulation and execution of the budget, relations with the Diocese, the briefing of the Christian Education secretaries of ECW chapters, and the Course in Christianity. Nelius went visiting each and every day, took care of the parish library, and within the structures established by Episcopal tradition and by Sherman did whatever his free and creative spirit suggested.

Nelius later recalled, with a smile, that Sherman did all the work and he had all the fun. He enjoyed meeting with the young people every Sunday night. He unlocked the parish house when they arrived at 5:30 and locked it when they were called for at 7:00. With the four adult advisors, notably Nancy and Walter Mason, he arranged the program, whether it be a speaker, or roasting peanuts to be sold at the bazaar, or going Christmas caroling, or preparing palms for Palm Sunday. The parents prepared and brought food. Attendance was no problem, as twenty-five youngsters enjoyed being with each other and with their counselors and regularly showed up. Nelius also enjoyed calling on parishioners, town-and-gown people whom he found interesting. And he honored those devout women who each Thursday morning at ten o'clock attended the Morning Prayer that Sherman or he conducted: Lillian Cahoon, Ihrie Carr, Mary Lucy Cobb, Aylene Cooke, Betsy Hansen-Pruss, Lillian Hebbert, Mary Pyne, Dorothy Quinn, Julia Royall, Josephine Ruffin, and Gertrude Webb, among them.[29]

He reveled, too, in working with George Pyne and others on the Fine Arts Commission to beautify the church in all possible ways. The commission, appointed in November 1961 by Sherman with the Vestry's approval, had been given a broad charge: "to advise on the selection of memorials, pictures, and other appointments for the Church, the Parish House, and the grounds; to study the relationship between theology and the Arts; and to promote Parish-wide activities in the area of its concern." George Pyne had agreed to serve as chair; its other members included Allan Cartter, dean of the Graduate School of Duke University, Irene Nashold, Marian Scott, Jeanne Smith Whiteside, Frances Woodhall, and Albert Nelius, ex officio.[30]

The marvel is that in the next six years the commission accomplished every single element of its charge. Several passages from the weekly *Epistle to the Philippians* convey a sense of the range of its projects:

(May 6, 1962) I would particularly like to express my own appreciation, and I know the gratitude of the parish, to the Fine Arts Commission and its chairman, Mr. George Pyne, for its work in planning, advising, and designing the new Baptismal Dossal, the Baptismal Candle Standards, the Paschal Candle Standard, and the Processional Torches. LBS

(March 10, 1963) The Fine Arts Commission needs frames that can be used for pictures in the Parish House classrooms. Please let us know if you have frames you can give for this purpose.

(March 17, 1963) There will be a General Meeting of the Women of St. Philip's on Monday evening, March 18, at 8 P.M. Mr. Nelius will speak on the work, plans, and insights of the Fine Arts Commission.

(April 7, 1963) Following the service of Tenebrae on Wednesday evening, the Rev. W. Robert Mill, Episcopal Chaplain at Duke University, will give a *devotional lecture* on the Altar piece, painted by Matthias Grunewald early in the sixteenth century. The discussion will begin at 8 P.M. This work is generally considered the greatest masterpiece of German painting. The portions of it which were shown at Mr. Nelius' presentation of "Portraits of the Christ" evoked great interest; and we are pleased that Mr. Mill will show us more deeply how this work speaks of our Christian faith.

(March 8, 1964) On March 19th at 8 P.M., the *Clergy Hour* [of Lent] will be conducted by Mr. Nelius. In response to so many questions concerning the use of "modern art" in our Parish Fine Arts Program, a remarkable set of slides, borrowed from a minister in Connecticut, will be shown with comments in order to help us better understand the deep spiritual significance of so many contemporary paintings. Others who have been vexed by "modern art" have been prompted, on seeing the pictures, to say, "Now, I begin to understand."

The commission brought reproductions of the paintings and their associated theology to the congregation. George Pyne and Nelius, aided by Marian Scott, lined the walls of the stairwell leading from the first floor to the assembly room upstairs with reproductions of famous paintings of all sorts and conditions of men and women, so arranged that mounting the steps *thoughtfully* was a theological experience in the communion of saints—ordinary men and women, like ourselves, made saints by Christ's outpouring of blood and grace.

On a broad display board placed on the parish hall wall opposite the entry to the library, the same three (George, Albert, and Marian) placed the proper for the week and reproductions of paintings illustrating it. An accompanying theological statement integrated the art and the theology in a process of mutual illumination. The statement for the fifteenth Sunday after Trinity, for instance, is as pertinent today as when it was written:

> The Collect for this Fifteenth Sunday after Trinity reminds us of the plight of man when he is separated from God: "Keep, we beseech thee, O Lord, thy Church with they perpetual mercy; and, because the frailty of man without thee cannot but fall, keep us ever by the help from all things profitable to our salvation."
>
> The stark faces staring out at us from the Display Board interpret this condition of man without God. At the core of each self is a deep inner agony as man faces the fact that all things, and he himself, are temporary. There can be no security, and nothing he can do for himself will contradict this fact. The dread can be tranquillized by foolishly confident self-sufficiency in his prowess at material accumulation; but these efforts of man to save himself by putting his trust in mammon are a self-deception. To achieve relief from his primeval anxiety of the unknown, the terror of helplessness, man must accept his sonship under God.
>
> For it is from this condition of aloneness and the reality of death that God raises man, offering him atonement and resurrection. This is the joy and peace that Jesus, in today's Gospel, offers the man who can commit himself to God." A modern theologian, Roger Shinn, writes: "The lostness of man in the infinite spaces, the wretchedness of the sinner without God are the experiences that lead man to God," to make the leap of faith. The pictures, from left to right:

Edvard Munch (Norwegian, 1863–1944), *The Scream*, 1893. "I want to show men who breathe, feel, love and suffer. I want to bring home to the spectator the sacred element in these things, so that he takes his hat off just as he would in church." Written in 1889, this entry in Munch's journal has the same ring as the letters of Van Gogh, who set forth the aim of his painting in like terms. They reveal a passionate striving towards the essential man—the focal point about which Expressionist painting turned.

Michelangelo (Florentine, 1475–1564), Condemned Sinner, detail from *The Last Judgement*, the enormous fresco on the altar wall of the Sistine Chapel in the Vatican.

Primitive Japanese sculpture from a burial mound 1500 years ago.

Emil Nolde (German Expressionist, 1867–1956), *Strangers*, 1946. Nolde's paintings evoke the mythical element that underlies even the most contemporary reality—a vision of existence that called from his friend Paul Klee the salute: "Nolde, the primeval soul!" . . .

Philip Evergood (American, 1902–), *My Forebears Were Pioneers*. Painted after the New England hurricane of 1938, which had dramatically leveled material possessions into ruins.[31]

George Pyne, meanwhile, was discovering, restoring, and framing photographs of the Bishops, Rectors, and Assistant Rectors involved in the history of St. Philip's. In an adroit arrangement he displayed them across the east wall of the library, while he patiently awaited the time when the parish historian realized his Christian obligation to place these personages in the context of an ongoing narrative.

The Fine Arts Commission drew other parishioners into the orbit of its actions. In a Lenten Creative Art project in the Church School (1966), the drawing of John Steel (first grade) was adjudged the best entry: "His drawing, along with the others entered, was sent to the National Church, for judging in the larger contest."[32] Twelve paintings done by six parishioners—Helen Kendall, Ruth Latty, Ann May, Marjorie Snethen, Elizabeth Willis, and Nancy Woodley—were displayed throughout the Diocesan House (Raleigh) during December 1966.[33]

In addition, Nelius revived the long dormant idea of installing a tolling bell in a tower of the church. He interested Robinson O. Everett, a prominent lawyer and communicant, who contributed substantially to a Bell Fund. Other donations soon followed, and the bell was dedicated, with the name "Sursum Corda," on Sunday morning, May 29, 1966. A van Dusen bronze bell, 38 inches in diameter, 1,000 pounds in weight, it was purchased through the I. T. Verdin Company of Cincinnati.[34] Tentative instructions for its use were immediately issued. It was to be rung for one minute immediately before each Sunday morning service and for ten to fifteen seconds at 8:40 each weekday morning before the reading of Morning Prayer. At weddings, the bell was to be rung immediately following the Benediction and until the organ began playing. At funerals, subject to the wishes of the family, the bell might be tolled as the casket was brought from the hearse into the church and from the church after the service.[35]

The thought occurs: St. Philip's, so adorned, with a church building designed by Ralph Adams Cram, a tolling bell, resplendent stained glass windows and music, memorial garden and meditation area, reproductions of paintings of spiritual significance, and a history of important achievement, all undertaken to the glory of God, would have been in England a legitimate object of serious tourist attention.

ST. PHILIP'S AND THE DIOCESE OF NORTH CAROLINA

Every Rector of St. Philip's during the twentieth century was prominent in diocesan affairs. The signal importance of St. Philip's as a major achieving parish, as well as the ability of its Rectors, ensured that they would serve eminently on diocesan committees and in Diocesan Convention debates.

After his return to North Carolina in 1957, Bart Sherman was no exception. He was one of three diocesan trustees of the Kanuga Lake Conferences from 1957 to 1960 and one of the nine diocesan managers of the Thompson Orphanage near Charlotte from 1957 to 1962. In June 1959 he was elected by the Diocesan Convention to the Diocesan Executive Council to fill out the unexpired term vacated by David Yates, who had transferred to the Otey Parish (Sewanee) in the Diocese of Tennessee. Sherman also succeeded Yates as executive secretary of the Department of College Work of the Executive Council. Bishop Coadjutor Thomas Fraser, who was chair of that department, praised Sherman's work as "outstanding." One of his functions had been to chair the subcommittee in charge of building the Episcopal Student Center at Duke University. From 1960 to 1967 and doubtless beyond, Bishop Baker and then Bishop Fraser appointed Sherman one of six examining chaplains; from 1965 he served as chair of that board, which periodically counseled and then certified candidates for ordination as deacons and priests and thus upheld the high Episcopal standards of an educated and able clergy. In 1965 Fraser again praised Sherman for handling his responsibilities as chair "with his usual capability and care." In 1963 the Diocesan Convention elected Sherman to its powerful Standing Committee, for a term that lasted until 1966. By now he was also serving in a number of other posts: deputy to the Provincial Synod (1961), member of the Committee on the Structure and Organization of the Diocese (1961–62), member and then chair of the Canonical Committee on the (Diocesan) Convention and Dispatch of

Business, which kept the annual two-day meeting on track (1962–65), and dean of the Central Convocation (1965–67). He even resumed his old position as a trustee of Kanuga Lake Conferences (1966–69).

A unique feature of Sherman's rectorship was that he drew an increasing number of lay St. Philippians into the orbit of diocesan activity. To be sure, there had always been one or two St. Philippians who had been prominent in diocesan affairs: Will Erwin during the Bost years, Kemp Lewis under Bost and Yates, and William H. Ruffin under Yates, Haden, Edwards, and still under Sherman. Their contributions to the Diocese and St. Philip's were so outstanding that one is tempted to apply to them the worn term of "statesmen." But other leaders, women as well as men, were coming on, and under Sherman's influence were becoming involved at the diocesan level. A few may be mentioned here, others as they enter the story. As able carryovers from the past, Ruffin and Dr. Arthur H. London were trustees of the North Carolina Episcopal Church Foundation from 1956 to 1968, for a succession of three-year terms. Ruffin was also one of the three trustees of the Diocese during the same period, alternate deputy to the General Convention of the Episcopal Church (elected in 1957), and a member of the Committee on the Structure and Organization of the Diocese (1959). Three St. Philippians were elected to the Diocesan Executive Council: Kenneth C. Royall, Jr. (1956–59) and Dr. James E. Davis and Dorothy Manning (both 1965–68). Mrs. Manning's election coincided with the Diocesan Convention's repeal in 1965 of the canonical ban excluding women from serving on vestries. (The ban on their serving as deputies to the General Convention still remained, a lingering vestige of customs of an earlier patriarchal age.) William P. Biggers was drafted to serve on the newly constituted Board of Directors of the Episcopal Home for the Aging (1958–61), to be succeeded by Dr. Isaac H. Manning, Jr. (1963–65) and Dr. James E. Davis (1965–68). Dr. Isaac and Dorothy Manning were both deputies to the Provincial Synod in 1962. Sibyl Powe was a trustee of St. Mary's Junior College from 1964 until 1968. In the diocesan organization of the Woman's Auxiliary, renamed in 1962 the Episcopal Church Women (ECW), Grace Carr served as second vice-president (1958–60), to be succeeded by another St. Philippian, Libby Roberts (1961–64). Priscilla McBryde was chair of the ECW of the Central Convocation (1966). Not one of these jobs was a sinecure. Each required a considerable outlay of time, energy, and thought.

Other St. Philippians who shared the experience of attending a Diocesan Convention were the delegates annually elected by the Vestry to represent St. Philip's. Those delegates and alternates who attended the Convention more than once during Sherman's rectorship included (in order of appearance) Ben R. Roberts (1957, 1958, 1959, 1963), Kenneth Royall, Jr. (1957, 1958), Robert G. Hurst (1957, 1959, 1960, 1962, 1963), William H. Ruffin (1958, 1960, 1965), E. K. Powe (1959, 1964, 1965), James L. Nicholson (1960, 1961, 1963, 1966), Watts Carr, Jr. (1962, 1964), J. Harper Erwin, Jr. (1962, 1963), and Dr. James E. Davis (1964, 1965, 1966).[36]

To attend a Diocesan Convention more than once and to participate in diocesan activities was to receive an excellent education not only in the Episcopal Church's business but also in the relation of that Church and St. Philip's to five critical issues: desegregation/integration; the double movement of population in North Carolina from rural areas to the cities, and within the cities from the center to the suburbs; liturgical reform, including Prayer Book revision; the theological questioning precipitated by the publication of *Honest to God* (March 1963) by Bishop John Robinson of Woolwich, England, and of essays by the radical "God-Is-Dead" theologians; and the ecumenical movement. Sherman and several St. Philippians paid special attention to the first two issues, while not neglecting the other three. A discussion of all five will enable us to become aware of the broader municipal, state, and national context in which St. Philippians were living during this age of controversies and opportunities that lasted well beyond Sherman's rectorship.

These intense discussions within the Church occurred in the midst of stirring, gut-wrenching events outside. Let us recall a few.

September 24, 1957: President Eisenhower sent federal troops to enforce the Supreme Court's order to admit black students to Central High School in Little Rock, Arkansas.

February 1, 1960: Sit-ins began when four black students in Greensboro, North Carolina, refused to move from a Woolworth lunch counter when denied service. By September 1961 more than 70,000 students, whites and blacks, had participated in sit-ins.

February 20, 1961: Lt. Col. John H. Glenn, Jr., became the first American to orbit in outer space when he circled the earth three times in the Mercury capsule Friendship 7.

February 14, 1962: President Kennedy said U.S. military advisors in Vietnam would fire if fired upon.

October 22–28, 1962: The Soviet offensive missile buildup in Cuba threatened nuclear war until President Kennedy and Soviet Premier Khrushchev reached an agreement ending the crisis.

August 28, 1963: In Washington, D.C., 200,000 persons demonstrated in support of black demands for equal rights. The highlight was Dr. Martin Luther King's speech: "I have a dream . . ."

November 22, 1963: President Kennedy was assassinated in Dallas, Texas.

June 29, 1964: An omnibus civil rights bill was passed banning discrimination in voting, jobs, public accommodations, etc.

August 7, 1964: Congress passed the Tonkin Resolution authorizing presidential action in Vietnam. The U.S. military presence in South Vietnam increased steadily, from 184,000 by the end of 1965 to 475,000 by the end of 1967. Protests against the war mounted.

The intense emotion surrounding several of these events can be conveyed by a single incident. On the Sunday after the assassination of President Kennedy the Great Litany was read in St. Philip's: "From lightning and tempest; from earthquake, fire, and flood; from plague, pestilence, and famine; from battle and murder, and from sudden death, *Good Lord, deliver us.*" After the service, while the author of this chapter was driving homeward Lillian Hebbert, a devout eighty-year-old Episcopalian, she confessed that never before had she been so gripped by the stunning relevance of the litany to a current happening. Events that were commonplace in sixteenth-century England, when the litany entered the Anglican Prayer Book, were becoming commonplace in the twentieth-century United States.

Desegregation/Integration

In response to two watershed events—in 1954 the Supreme Court's unanimous decision declaring that racial segregation in public schools was unconstitutional and in 1955 Rosa Parks's refusal to give her seat to a white man on a bus in Montgomery, Alabama—Bishop Penick stated the theology supporting integration: *Imago Dei*, that *all* humankind, white and black, was created in God's image; and *Atonement*, that Christ died for *all* persons. Ever since then, every clergyman at St. Philip's has adhered to that statement.

However, Penick recommended that the abolition of discrimination should be accomplished through gradual change: "It seems to me that a human problem so vast in its dimensions, involving the welfare of millions of people, living over a wide expanse of territory is far from simple, and cannot, by its very nature, yield to a quick solution. To attempt a speedy answer . . . does not take into account a massive psychological adjustment, affecting basic attitudes and traditions centuries old . . . that make up the pattern of modern society." [37] The Diocesan Convention of 1956 endorsed the principle of gradualism. It formed a Commission on Racial Subjects, which for several years fostered parish-level discussions of the racial problem.

Outside the Church the spirit of gradualism was embodied in the North Carolina Pearsall Plan or Pupil Assignment Law (1955),[38] which placed the burden of integration on black families, who had to petition the local Board of Education for reassignment of their children to a white public school. Under that plan the Durham public schools were integrated.[39]

However, to the oppressed and their supporters "gradualism" was only a nice word for more talk and delay. They were impatient and angry, and the gradualist position was soon eroded and overrun, or gradualists were soon hustled into action, by a storm of demonstrations, sit-ins, and litigation, and by the intervention of the federal government.

The first major blowup in the Diocese occurred over the integration of the camp and conference center at Vade Mecum. For eight years, from 1948 to 1956, there had been two such camps maintained by the Diocese, Vade Mecum for whites and Camp Delany for blacks. For years the facilities at Camp Delany were neglected, until they became disgracefully dilapidated. A succession of diocesan committees investigated and reported and recommended repairs — only to be followed by another investigating committee that reported and recommended repairs and so on, in a human comedy or human tragedy or maybe both.[40] The property was finally sold in 1956 and the camp closed, leaving black children without any diocesan summer camp at all.

In January 1960 the Diocesan Executive Council voted, without dissent, to integrate the Junior Boy's Camp at Vade Mecum.[41] This, of course, would mean social intermingling of races. Shortly after, outside the Church, starting on February 1, young blacks and their white sympathizers in Greensboro, Durham, and other cities in the Diocese were "sitting in" at the lunch counters of Woolworth's, Walgreen's, and Kress's to force integration of their eating facilities. In this storm of protest the Diocesan Convention met in Tarboro on May 10 and 11. A resolution was introduced:

> BE IT RESOLVED by this CONVENTION that it would be unwise and dangerous to racial tranquility to integrate any Episcopal young people's or youth camp at Vade Mecum.

After a heated debate, with amendments, substitute motions, amendments to substitute motions, and a motion to table, the vote on the original resolution was taken. It revealed both a split between the clergy and the majority of the laity *and* a division within the laity. The vote stood: 6 clergy for the resolution and 68 against; 32 lay votes were in the affirmative, 17 ½ were in the negative, and 5 delegations were divided.[42] Upon the admission of seven blacks to the Junior Boy's Camp at Vade Mecum in the summer of 1960, fifteen white boys and girls were withdrawn from the camps by their families. But integration at the Junior Boy's Camp was maintained.[43]

Over the next four to five years a continuing open dialogue among the leaders of differing viewpoints in the Executive Council, the Committee on Racial Subjects, and successive Diocesan Conventions led to the relatively quiet integration of the rest of Vade Mecum and all other agencies associated with the Diocese. The movement toward integration climaxed when the Diocesan Convention of 1964, on a motion introduced by the Reverend L. Bartine Sherman, instructed its Commission on Race "actively to seek" from institutions, wholly or partially owned by the Diocese answers "concerning their admission policy with regard to race." The commission was to recommend to the next Convention such action as it deemed fit.[44] In 1965 the commission duly reported that the Conference Center at the Terraces (Southern Pines), University of the South, Vade Mecum, Kanuga, Thompson Orphanage, Penick Memorial Home, St. Mary's College, and St. Augustine's College had all dropped all references to race in their qualifications for admission. The commission recommended its own dissolution, since the policy of gradualism, which it had been formed in 1956 to promote, had been successfully implemented.[45]

The second blowup exploded close to St. Philip's and stirred Sherman to deliver one of his most forthright sermons. The circumstances were these. On Saturday, May 18, 1963, Wense Grabarek was elected mayor of Durham over Watts Carr, Jr. That night "[black] protesters held a rally followed by a march through the city and sit-ins at six eating places" to force them to integrate their facilities. The sheriff's deputies arrested 130 demonstrators and took them to the county jail, two blocks down Main Street from St. Philip's. Outside the jail hundreds of demonstrators shouted encouragement to the prisoners on the top floor. When the demonstrators dispersed at 10:00 P.M., they promised to return. Return they did, on Monday night, May 20, to the Sears parking lot across the street from St. Philip's, to shout and sing some more. Meanwhile, Mayor Grabarek had persuaded black leaders to tone down the demonstrations for fear of white backlash, had induced seven restaurants to open their service to blacks for fear of black disorder, and had called business and professional civic leaders of both races to a meeting on Wednesday morning, May 22. From that meeting emerged the Durham Interim Committee with Watts Carr, Jr., as chair.[46]

Entitled "The Holy City," Sherman's sermon of the following Sunday, May 26, opened with a quotation from the Revelation of Saint John the Divine:

> I saw the holy city, new Jerusalem, coming down out of heaven from God, prepared as a bride adorned for her husband; and I heard a great voice from the throne saying, "Behold, the dwelling of God is with men. He will dwell with them, and they shall be his people, and God himself will be with them; he will wipe away every tear from their eyes, and death shall be no more, neither shall there be mourning nor crying nor pain any more, for the former things have passed away." (Rev. 21:2–4)

Obviously, Sherman continued, Durham is not the heavenly city described by John. So the Christian must ask, "What can we Christians do to bring our earthly city a little closer in harmony with the Holy City, the new Jerusalem, in which there shall be no mourning or crying or pain? The transfiguring of the city will have to be done by God— but He has already begun this work in Christ, so what is our part in it?"

> First of all, let us remember that the Christian is a realist. We deal not with the world of might-have-been or ought-to-be or wouldn't-it-be-nice-if, but the world as it is. Two experiences this past week brought this very much to my mind. The first was the

General Meeting of the Episcopal Church Women, which was held here in the church last Monday night. If you will remember, Monday night was the night that a large number of the Negro demonstrators came down and sat in the Sears parking lot across the street. In our meeting here, we could hear the singing, the sirens, the shouting. But we kept right on with our meeting. At first it seemed as though the Church was pulling back into its shell, hiding from what was going on. But in a real sense, we were facing facts—the fact that the work of the Church goes on, and that there was nothing one white minister and about twenty white women could do at that particular point—except to pray, which we did: for our city, for justice and order.

The second experience was another meeting I attended—the meeting called by the Mayor Wednesday morning, of a number of business and professional persons of both races. It would seem that this meeting was one which was facing the realities of our present situation head on, in a way that the Church had not. And yet as I listened to some of the remarks made at that meeting I could only wonder what city they were talking about; it did not seem to me to be the Durham I have come to know fairly well in the past six years.

The Christian is a realist, and must face the facts of existence. What are the facts about our city today—what is the reality of our present situation?

Fact Number One: We are not a community. We are two or three or more separate communities living in one city. To say that the Negro ought not to talk about "us" and "them," but just talk about "us" as a whole, is to say something that is greatly to be desired, but which does not meet the facts of the present time. For over a century the white man has been forcing the Negro to regard himself a separate people; to say to him now, "Think about the good of the whole community, not just your own good," is to be not heard. We have conditioned him against this kind of thinking.

Fact Number Two: In any case, the white man is wasting his breath telling the Negro what he ought to do. Since our demonstrations started, I have talked about them only with whites. Nine out of ten people have been concerned with what the Negro has done that he ought not to have done, and what he has left undone that he ought to have done. And so we say to the Negro, "You ought not to try to force us to do something for which we are not ready"; or, "You ought to have tried harder to work things out by conferring with us." Both, perhaps, quite justifiable statements. But the fact of the situation is that the Negro is tired of our telling him what he ought to do, and he is ready to make some decisions for himself. They will not all be right decisions. But he is not going to listen to us, or at least not in the mode of, "Speak, Lord, for thy servant heareth." So this morning, I speak as a white man to white men. I long for the day when I can speak as a minister of Christ without color, to Christians among whom there is neither bond nor free, male or female, Jew nor Greek, black nor white. But that is not the fact of the matter today. Today I can speak only to the white Christian.

Fact Number Three: What the whites want and what the Negroes want are not the same thing. I have heard this said so often — "We both want the same thing, really." But what the average white man wants is peace, with such change as must be to come as slowly as possible; what the Negro wants is much change quickly, with as much peace as may be possible.

Fact Number Four: The problem is a major one, and no solution will be found easily, nor will any solution be found which will satisfy any substantial majority of all of our citizens.

Fact Number Five, and last: This fact is one which I have found to be generally accepted — that the changes which the Negro wants are going to come. Only a small but vocal minority of the whites, and perhaps a handful of Negroes, really believe that it will be either possible or desirable to maintain the status quo.

These, Sherman felt, were the facts of current history which, it seemed to him, were there for anyone to read, whether he be Christian or not. But, he went on, the Christian must recognize another fact: the fact of sin, that we are all sinners, even "men of good will":

So in the specific situation which we face in our city, what does all this mean to us, the white population? It means first of all, that the white Christian must acknowledge his sin — the sin of centuries of repression and paternalism and discrimination. We can only acknowledge our *own* sins. To acknowledge the sins of the Negro is very easy, very satisfying, very dangerous, and completely pointless. We have rather to bear the sins of the Negro, as he bears ours, neither expecting him to act without sin, nor justifying our continued acts of repression and discrimination by reference to his sinful acts.

The final theological fact which we must face is one which I am taking for granted here: that discrimination and prejudice, based simply on a man's color, is sinful. If there are any here who need convincing on this point, I cannot do it in one sermon—or perhaps in any number of sermons. But I, who know myself to be both a sinner and a redeemed child of God, through the immeasurable love of God in Jesus Christ, know that within that love, where I live, there can be no discrimination and no prejudice on any basis whatsoever.

But certainly the Christian can do more, in this troubling of our city, than face facts. Of course we can. The next step is clear— "Take up your cross and follow me." Live the life of the cross—of the denial of self. As we face decisions to be made, we face them on the basis, not of "what I want," or "what will be good for me," but what will be good for the city and the nation and mankind— what is, that is to say, in accordance with God's Will, "not mine." I thank God that it was a member of this parish who said this in the Mayor's meeting, and who had already acted on the basis of it. And I know that there are others who have acted likewise. Not all of us have the opportunity to make this kind of witness; but we do all have the opportunity of giving them our support in Christian love—not just the support of a word of praise, but support in deeds. . . .

Our city is not the Holy City seen by John—and it is a long way from being it. The Holy City will come from God, and not from or through our own actions. But this fact does not excuse us from exerting every effort, under His guidance and with His help, to make this city as close an approximation as may be humanly possible of that city in which there shall be no mourning, no crying, no pain.[47]

Thereafter, Sherman in his sermons hit segregation not once, not twice, but again and again, not in generalized, abstract, theological musings but directly, specifically, and concretely.

The Double Movement of Population

The double movement of population from the rural areas to the cities and from the center of the cities to the suburbs had been recognized by Bishop Penick and by his coadjutor and successor, Bishop Baker (1951–64). The population explosion, focused in a great crescent running from Raleigh along U.S. Highway 70 through Durham and Greensboro and on to Charlotte, had been anticipated. The strains engendered by this drastic demographic change had also been brilliantly discussed in successive Diocesan Conventions from 1959 onward: the plight of the isolated, dwindling rural congregations left high, dry, and bankrupt by the departure of most of their members; the potential distress of prestigious downtown "mother" churches whose leading communicants had transferred to suburban missions. As the official report put it in 1961:

> In some Dioceses the problem has become acute. Some city parishes have been left in a precarious position. There is a ministry to the city as well as to the suburbs. But the shift from being a prestige church to taking on the care of souls who remain in a city is never an easy one.[48]

At the level of diocesan discussion, urban growth was viewed as a challenge and an opportunity, as a beckoning mission field that should not be ignored. As the previous year's report read:

> The last time the Episcopal Church faced a frontier it almost lost its existence. We as a Church refused to blaze the trails into the new West. We were content to be the church of the fashionable set on the Eastern Seaboard. Some have remarked that the Episcopal Church went west only after the trail had been blazed, the railroad tracks laid, and pullman cars [put] in operation. As we prepare to face the new frontier of urban development, we pray that our former frontier experience will not be reduplicated.[49]

If the opportunity was to be exploited, the laity must be engaged:

> The Episcopal Church has the most qualified laymen of any church in the world. . . . Yet somehow, the laity of our Church, this vast reservoir of talent, is not utilized or if it is utilized it is within the mundane things of church administration. We would like to promote the idea of parochial responsibility for new mis-

sion work in the city . . . and that the laity of the churches be encouraged to found and organize and man such parochial mission endeavor.[50]

In its urban mission work the Episcopal Church would have to evangelize all sorts and conditions of men and women. To quote Bishop Coadjutor Thomas Fraser: "We still bear the image in the eyes of many people that we consider ourselves the best church for the best people rather than God's Church for all people. This image which we have earned in the past must be destroyed."[51]

Year after year, in successive Diocesan Conventions from 1959 to 1964, this was the line of argument Sherman and the lay delegates from St. Philip's heard. It was immediately relevant to St. Philip's current situation. Its history had recapitulated the history of the Diocese. Durham had been a village of only 2,041 persons in 1880, but it represented novelty in the North Carolina landscape: the immigration of country people to a manufacturing town that was transforming two native plants—tobacco and cotton—into products salable on national and international markets. As the market and sales expanded, so did Durham and St. Philip's, notably during the rectorship of Sidney Stuart Bost. St. Philip's ceased to be a close neighborhood church, as communicants moved to Trinity Park and Morehead Heights in the 1920s and to the Forest Hills, Rockwood, Hope Valley, and Watts Hospital areas in the 1930s, 1940s, and 1950s. It had responded by sponsoring the formation of two suburban churches, St. Luke's and St. Stephen's, and by revitalizing two older missions, St. Andrew's and St. Joseph's.

Meanwhile, the neighborhood around St. Philip's decayed. Fine residences became rooming houses. Intercity and interstate buses roared in, disgorging into the depot (adjacent to the church) passengers who sometimes needed counsel and money. Street people— bums, boozers, and beggars—lounged about. In the nearby Edgemont district, the closure of the local textile mill, once the community's primary employer and support, had thrust residents into poverty. Personal safety was a thing of the past. Incredibly, from 1880 to 1946 the church edifice had been unlocked, day and night, open to everyone at all times for meditation and prayer. In 1946, on the recommendation of Haden, the Vestry had instructed that it be locked at night. By 1957 both church and parish house were always locked, except during church services, and the church secretary, Mrs. Matt West, was given a buzzer to open the parish house door after she had viewed the visitor. The church was barricading itself against clear and present danger.

The core of loyal communicants still came in from a distance to continue the comfortable round of worship, Vestry meetings, ECW chapter meetings, and bazaars. Alfred Lawrence and David Yates in 1937, Tom Turney Edwards in 1951, and John Denham in 1957 all had pointed to opportunities for mission close at hand, but they had been ignored. "Mission" for St. Philippians meant sending hospital equipment to the wonderful medical missionary, Dr. John Stewart, in far-off Liberia, or corresponding with an equally dedicated Episcopal missionary, Rachel Wolff, in even more distant Nepal. "Meeting needs" meant preparing Christmas baskets for needy families in Edgemont or giving a panhandler a sheet of paper worth a ninety-cent meal at the bus station lunch counter. Strangers to the downtown locality by distance, by class, and by culture, St. Philippians, when they met their immediate neighbors, usually passed to the other side.

The situation was novel. Apparently no one really knew what a downtown church might do, and few cared. But Sherman did care, and he decided to find out what might be done by St. Philip's.

With the Vestry's permission he took an eight-week leave of absence during April and May 1964 to attend the College of Preachers on the campus grounds of the National Cathedral in Washington, D.C. He had been to the college twice before, a week each time, to give one of his sermons and to receive critical comment on its form, context, and delivery. This time he went as a resident Fellow to engage in independent study of a subject of his choice. He was obligated to read voluminously and to prepare a paper. Sherman chose the topic "The City and the Urban Church," and his densely reasoned sixty-page essay became *one of the three most important documents in the history of St. Philip's during its first century.*[52]

In the first four chapters he summarized the technical literature on the subject and stated general principles: the modern city is dynamic and always changing; the Church, while remaining constant to its faith, must flexibly change its approaches; servanthood and evangelism are linked — meeting the needs of people will win them to Christianity and the Church; the homogeneous, middle-class club, which is the modern Church, will give way to a heterogeneous congregation fused into community by a common faith. Chapter 5 described some of the initiatives introduced since World War II in England and the

United States in large cities of over 500,000—industrial chaplaincies, apartment house ministries, and the like. Chapter 6 applied some of the basic procedures running through these initiatives to a hypothetical church in a hypothetical smaller metropolis of fewer than 250,000 people (St. Philip's in Durham, North Carolina). These procedures included the recruitment and empowerment of the laity in numbers and in spirit; the conduct of a formal survey of the characteristics, needs, and resources of the city and the church; the initiation of discussion within the congregation; the invitation to other Episcopal churches in Durham and to churches of other denominations to pool resources in joint efforts to meet urban needs and in the formation of interchurch councils to implement these efforts; and the introduction of liturgical reform to render worship services more relevant and meaningful. It is a tribute to the thoroughness of Sherman's research and the intellectual power of his analysis that all the basic strategies he recommended were in time applied at St. Philip's.

As a starter, on August 13, 1964 he mailed a summary of the first four chapters and a "reprint" of the last two to Bishops Baker and Fraser, "who have the right to see what I did with my time!," to the vestrymen of Saint Philip's, "who are being asked to read them as part of their preparation for a Vestry retreat in September," and to the other Episcopal clergy of Durham, with a request that they pass along copies to their two wardens.[53] He himself was poised to move the congregation of St. Philip's toward the realization of his program and vision.

Liturgical Reform, including Prayer Book Revision

In his paper Sherman observed that "liturgy is a most important means of achieving that community which is important for the church. In order to reach this end, the particular form of liturgy may well be rethought. Even the restoration of such a simple action as that of giving 'The Peace,' as it is used in the liturgy of the Church of South India, can be a significant factor in the building of a sense of community."

Sherman was not alone in "rethinking the liturgy." At the Diocesan Convention of early February 1965, it was reported that the General Convention, meeting in Saint Louis from October 11 to 23, 1964, had "authorized the alternative use of the New English Bible, New Testament, at Morning and Evening Prayer and directed the Standing Liturgical Commission to proceed with developing a plan for revision of the Book of Common Prayer with a special view to making the language and the form of the service more relevant to the circumstances of the Church's present ministry and life." [54]

At the same Diocesan Convention the Committee on the State of the Church endorsed such rethinking of the worship services and strongly urged that the laity be involved with the clergy in the discussion: "The Laity are in the Church not only to be passive recipients of tradition, but also to be active participants in the task of constant rethinking of the Christian message." [55]

Rethinking Christian Theology

Rethinking Christian theology added to the ferment of discussion. The first half of the twentieth century had been a great age in Christian theology, with such giants as Karl Barth, Dietrich Bonhoeffer, and Paul Tillich considering profoundly the drift of Western culture and the relation of Christian dogma to it. The horrors of World War I, the grossness of material civilization, the evils of Nazism, and the threat of a nuclear holocaust had led to a sense of meaninglessness and a feeling of dread. "Life," wrote Reinhold Niebuhr, "is full of contradictions and incongruities. We live our lives in various realms of meaning which do not cohere rationally." Barth urged Christians to stand firm on the foundation of their belief in a transcendent God, "the wholly Other," amid all the wrecks of time and the evils of modern secularism. (At a less stringently intellectual level, American fundamentalists, in their several denominations, took the same course.) Tillich boldly attempted to reconcile old belief and new knowledge in a synthesis that would be spiritually satisfying and intellectually credible.

Tillich's theology came to most Anglicans by way of Bishop John Robinson's small book *Honest to God*. Published in March 1963, it sold 415,000 copies in six months. Within a year Sherman was mentioning it in his sermons. In another year it entered the Report of the Committee on the State of the Church to the North Carolina Diocesan Convention of 1965. [56]

Using Tillich's terminology, Robinson asked his readers to rethink their concepts of God, of Jesus Christ, and of morality. Instead of thinking of God as a Being "up there" or "out there," we should find Him within ourselves in the depth and ground of our being. As ultimate reality we shall find Him there as love. Since Christ Jesus was and is one substance with the Father, we shall find Him there, too. As the ultimate expression of love, he was "a man for others," and we should be so as well. "Life in Christ Jesus, in the new being, in the Spirit, means having no absolutes but his love, being totally uncommitted in every other respect but totally committed in this." "If our eye be single, love will find its own particular way in every situation." It follows that the new morality is neither heteronomous, dictated to us as an absolute code from "out there," nor autonomous, governed by our individual choices, but rather theonomous: discovered within the depth of our being. These changes in theology and ethics need not affect Christian faith or worship: "In prophecy and prayer, in liturgy and worship, the traditional imagery retains its numinous power." But our concept of the Church will change. It will be regarded not as an organization for the religious but as the servant of the world.[57]

The theologians of the "God Is Dead" persuasion were even more radical than Robinson. In their writings they first referred to God's death as a contemporary cultural phenomenon: as a need fulfiller, as a problem solver, as an abiding Presence, God no longer existed in our busy, busy secularized lives. But Thomas Altizer went further theologically: the eternal, unchanging primordial Totality or transcendent Supreme Being had died when God incarnated Himself in Christ Jesus and entered the profane world of time, transiency, and history. For Altizer "God Is Jesus," the sacred Incarnate Word who came to redeem the profane and who calls us to participate in that process of redemption. The centrality of Jesus, rather than the death of God, was in 1966 the key feature of Altizer's radical, embryonic theology.[58]

Sherman tried to understand these new developments in theology and ethics, and in his sermons he attempted by his example and by his words to lead the congregation to reflect upon them too. He explained that we live in a time of revolutionary change both within the Church and without:

> The revolution in the Church is going on in many areas of life: a revolution in the form of the organized church, a revolution in our relationships with other branches of the Christian Church, a revolution in the theological expression of our faith, a revolution in the form of our worship. And at the same time the Church is taking part in so many of the other forms of revolution which are affecting our society and our nation—the racial revolution [the urban revolution, the ethical revolution], the dramatic changes in forms of communication, and so forth.[59]

He commended Bishop Robinson and the radical theologians for raising important questions about the nature of God, of the Trinity, and of Jesus Christ. He agreed that speaking of God "as the ground of all being makes better sense today in our understanding of God than does the figure of God as an old man with a beard sitting [up there] on a cloud." But he feared that Robinson in attempting to free us from the limitations of old forms would simply enslave us dogmatically by new ones.[60]

Stimulated by the discussion and by the popular interest it aroused, Sherman gave a series of sermons on the subject "What about God?" To appreciate their subtlety and depth, they must be read in their entirety. They focused not on the question, Does God exist?—which leads only to a fruitless shouting match—but on how we come to know Him. Through our personal experiences with Him, through the experiences of saints in history and around us, and through our knowledge of Jesus Christ (to *know* is a very strong verb), we learn that God is both transcendent and immanent. From our experiences of Jesus Christ, the ultimate reality, the exemplar of servanthood, we learn to serve others in love and in action.[61]

The Ecumenical Movement

The division of the followers of Jesus Christ into rival competing sects had long been *the* scandal of Christendom. The Church was said to be the Body of Christ, but where in the tangled reality of sectarianism could that Body be found? In the nineteenth century concern for the reintegration of Christendom led in the United States to a variety of movements toward reunion. Cooperation of more than thirty denominations in practical action (Life and Work) had led to the formation of the Federal Council of Churches in 1908, which was enlarged in 1950 to the National Council of Churches of Christ. "In other lands similar organizations were formed: for example, in France in 1905, Switzerland in 1920, Britain in 1942, and Canada in 1944."[62] Meanwhile, in a parallel movement two world conferences were held, in Lausanne (1927) and in Edinburgh (1937), to study the resolution of doctrinal differences among denominations. In a glow of enthusiastic glossing over of differences, the Edinburgh Conference on Faith and Order accepted the generalization "that in the doctrinal realm, the agreements between churches cover over eighty-five per cent of the ground."[63] Led by the Anglican Archbishop William Temple of

Canterbury, the Conferences on Life and Work were merged in 1948 at Amsterdam with those on Faith and Order to become the World Council of Churches, which embraced 147 denominations from forty-four countries.[64]

In the Diocese of North Carolina Bishop Baker, as coadjutor and then as diocesan, made the cause of Church union his own. From August 14 to 31, 1954 he attended the Second Assembly of the World Council of Churches at Evanston, Illinois.[65] He spoke to lay groups in his own Diocese on behalf of Church union.[66] In his address to the Diocesan Convention in January 1957, he quoted the Presiding Bishop of the Episcopal Church: "The Ecumenical Movement is not an alternate extra but a vital part of the ongoing life of the Church."[67] Baker went on to become a member of the Joint Ecumenical Commission of the National Council of Churches (1960) and to serve on the General Board of the National Council (1960–62).[68]

By 1960, however, it was recognized that there were important limitations to the movement toward Church union. Glossing over church differences did not remove them; divergent confessional beliefs on the nature of the Church, the way to worship, and the meaning of sacramental Communion were still tenaciously held.[69] In the United States the Southern Baptists, the Lutheran Church–Missouri Synod, and the Pentecostal churches remained aloof from both the National Council and the World Council. The Roman Catholic Church, commanding the allegiance of the largest body of Christians in the world, refused to participate. It steadfastly held to its uncompromising position that only the return of schismatics and dissenters to its fold could end disunity. Finally, perhaps the greatest weakness of all, "ecumenism was largely the concern of the national leaders in the [participating] denominations, and did not interest the rank and file of their members."[70] Bishop Baker's modest proposal that the Diocesan Convention of 1957 budget a small sum for the North Carolina, National, and World Councils of Churches apparently fell on deaf ears.[71]

It was in this context that Sherman preached two sermons on Church unity, the first in a pulpit exchange at the Trinity Methodist Church (Durham) on January 24, 1965 and the second at St. Philip's on October 2, 1966. He pointed to the strategically practical advantages of Christian Church union—for example, in the missionary field—and to its theological basis: "There is one Body and one Spirit . . . One Lord, one Faith, one Baptism, one God and Father of us all" (Ephesians 4:4–6). He also observed that unity need not bring dead uniformity: within the unity of the Anglican community, for example, there is wide diversity of practice. But he observed, with his usual realism and candor, there are deep hindrances to Church union. One is sinful denominational pride: "Why should we join with anyone else: we have nothing to learn from any other body; nobody can give us anything that we need that we don't already have!" or "While we think Church union is a very wonderful dream and hope, all that is needed is for all those other people to come to their senses and join us." A second hindrance is parochialism. "Most congregations are concerned primarily with their own problems, their own status, the maintenance of their own particular congregational institution. We just are not very concerned about the Church as a whole. Oh, we give to foreign missions, though sometimes rather grudgingly. But our own buildings, our own Sunday School and women's guilds and men's clubs have the first priority." His conclusion was that we must go slowly toward Church unity step by step, yet at each step be ready to take risks in faith. "If we seek to save our lives as denominations, we will lose them. But if we are willing to lose our denominational lives for His sake and the Gospels, then the true life of the one Body will be ours."[72]

THE STORY CONTINUED, 1964–1967

When Bart Sherman came back from the College of Preachers to St. Philip's in June 1964, he returned to a church of declining attendance and stagnant enrollment. The decline in attendance had started before his departure in April and was recorded in the *Epistle to the Philippians*: average attendance in all three services during the first five Sundays of 1964 was 395, then dropped to 356 during the first three Sundays in Lent.[73] The decline accelerated in September and October. "Church attendance this fall," Sherman announced, "has taken a nose dive. In years past, there have been more people in church on the Sundays in the fall than at any other time of the year save Lent. This year, *for unknown reasons*, only the 7:45 service has maintained its usual average attendance."[74] Even fewer people were coming to church the next fall. Again, Sherman was quite open in reporting the decrease and in confessing his puzzlement: "Attendance at all three of our services and at Church School is down this year [1965] as compared to last, and last

year showed a decrease over the year before that. At the 11 o'clock service last Sunday, there were 75 people in church, including the choir!
The average attendance at this service this year is barely over 100; three
years ago the average for the 11 o'clock service was about 135. The 9:30
service has also dropped off. What's happened?"[75] Furthermore, the
number of communicants, which had bottomed out at 510 in 1961,
had ceased to grow, standing at 521 in 1967. There seems to have been
a second migration to St. Stephen's and St. Luke's, barely balanced by
new arrivals to the Durham area.[76]

The cessation of growth did not mean that Sherman, Nelius, and
the Church School teachers were ineffective with parishioners and
their children who were attending Sunday services and classes. Several interviewees remembered with gratitude how Sherman's sermons
"came through to them." David Ross, the research associate of this
history, recalled how he caught from Gert Embree, a primary grade
teacher, the idea that helping the poor was one way of being a Christian, an idea that affected the course of his action the rest of his life.
So, like Sherman, the historian has difficulty explaining the statistics
of slowing enrollment and attendance. Unfortunately, he interviewed
only communicants who stayed at St. Philip's; with one exception (Nat
Gregory), he did not interview any who had left. Nevertheless, from
the interviews there are clues that may lead to understanding.

First, there seems to have developed a distance between most members of the congregation and its Rector. Except for a few intimates with
whom he met in his home for Sunday evening Bible study, most interviewees seem to have found it difficult to relate to him. They respected
him as a man of God but did not seek him out for counsel. The decision to delegate visiting and counseling to Nelius virtually ensured
Sherman's exclusion from close relationships with his parishioners that
would have held them to St. Philip's. Distance was accentuated by his
frequent absences from Durham on diocesan business. "The Rector
will not be in his office—on Tuesday and Wednesday, or on Wednesday and Thursday—as he attends a meeting"—of the Standing Committee, or Diocesan Executive Council, or Deans of Convocations, or
Board of Examining Chaplains, or Kanuga—was a frequent refrain in
the fortnightly *Epistle to the Philippians*.

Second, the congregation did not help to make newcomers feel welcome. Several interviewees recalled with bitterness that no one spoke

to them. The charge that St. Philip's was an exclusive club, friendly within itself, seems to have had some foundation in fact.

Finally, Sherman's handling of three crises left three segments of the congregation disaffected. A Young Adults Group was formed under both Edwards and Sherman, with the same result. Their first meeting was enthusiastic, as they rejoiced in discovering each other. The second, more subdued, was a meal. Then, the participants being unable to find anything they wanted to do together, the meetings faded away under Edwards and were abruptly canceled by Sherman. "As a result of the complete lack of interest in the proposed program for the Young Adults," he announced in the *Epistle*, "meetings of this organization have been discontinued."[77] Likewise with the Laymen's League. Sherman worked very hard to maintain it—changed its title, changed its time of meeting, found excellent officers—but when all measures failed to restore its morale and attendance, he dissolved it,[78] an action that long rankled in the memories of several of the laity.

Then there was the David Pizarro incident.[79] Pizarro was the John McEnroe of organist/choirmasters. He played beautifully but had a streak of the gamin. He just loved to vex and exasperate people, especially those he regarded as stuffed shirts. When the chair of the Vestry Music Committee, Dr. Isaac Manning, would remonstrate, Pizarro would contritely promise to be good, only within a week to resume his mischief. His teasing began to affect the worship service. He, Bart Sherman, and the choir would agree in advance on the anthems and hymns to be sung, only for Pizarro at the organ to soar off into other music. Or he would not bring the choir into the narthex on time, ready for processional precisely at eleven o'clock, a violation of the exact execution of the liturgy that both Sherman and the congregation prized. It was finally decided that Pizarro would have to go. Early in November 1964 he was informed that his services would be terminated, and he was given the choice of an immediate departure or continuing in his position until the end of the year. He chose to have the following Sunday his last. At the conclusion of the eleven o'clock service that Sunday, Sherman announced to the congregation that this was the last service Pizarro would perform at St. Philip's and explained the agreement that had been reached. Many parishioners were not sorry to see Pizarro leave, but several of his closest associates resigned in protest: Claude Bittle, chair of the Special Music Committee; Susan Rose, faithful and cooperative lead soprano for fifteen years;[80] and Seth Warner, assistant organist, who transferred to St. Luke's.

Undaunted by adversity, indeed stimulated by it, Sherman moved ahead with his plans for internal reform of St. Philip's and for involving it in service to the community outside. He conversed about his plans in the *Epistle to the Philippians*, in his sermons, and at the Vestry retreat in September 1964. As long as he only talked, parishioners pleasantly listened, but when he proposed to *do* something, he ran into a storm of opposition in the Vestry and in the congregation.

What he proposed was really very simple, very comprehensive, and to some parishioners very disturbing. It was to establish eleven commissions, each composed of a vestryman as chair and other laity, to study needs and to recommend action in eleven areas of parish life. The eleven commissions were listed as follows:

Finance and Administration: First part of title is self-explanatory; in second aspect, will be concerned primarily with office procedure and management.

Stewardship: The Every Member Canvass, an on-going program of stewardship, education, and the promotion of the St. Philip's Fund.

Outreach and Public Relations: Might once have been called "Evangelism" — ways of reaching out and drawing in our own "fringe" members, newcomers, and the unchurched.

Missions: Primarily concerned with bringing the implications of "Mutual Responsibility and Interdependence" down to the parish level.

Christian Social Action: One of the key groups; what needs are there in the community, and what resources do we have to bring to bear?

Worship and the Liturgical Arts: Will include Music Committee, Fine Arts Committee, ushers, lay readers, Altar Guild.

Christian Education (children): Oversight of the Church School, Nursery, Summer Sunday School.

Christian Education (adult): Has a wide-open field! ECW Sec'y of Christian Education will be a member. Includes oversight of the Library.

Youth Work: Oversight and coordination of the EYC, acolytes, college work, and vocations.

Buildings and Grounds: Self-explanatory: will include three subcommittees, on Church and Parish House, Grounds, and Rectory.

Parish Policies and Long-Range Planning: Will recommend policy statements to the Vestry; and will arrange and plan for one or more long-range planning conferences each year.

In explaining his proposal to the congregation, Sherman sought to allay unnecessary anxieties about change:

> Let's give some thought to what the Church might do to enable it the more effectively to fulfill its four primary functions. The Church exists, first of all, to worship God. This task of the Church really includes the other three; but more specifically, it relates to our function of providing the opportunity for the regular corporate offering of our sacrifice of praise and thanksgiving. Secondly, it exists to nurture in the Christian faith those who have been born into the family of Christ, just as this young man was born in baptism this morning. Thirdly, the Church exists in order to fulfill the great commission given us by our Lord, to go and preach the Gospel: to give witness in this community and throughout the world to the beauty and power and glory of our Lord and King. And fourthly, the Church exists in order to serve. Here we have our Lord's own example, and His commandment, recorded time and time again, the commandment to love, a commandment which is not fulfilled by an emotional reaction, but by an act of the will, expressed in service. . . . The change proposed in the organization of the Parish will enable us, it is hoped, to study and to act a little more quickly and efficiently in worship, in nurture, in witness, and in service.[81]

The crucial and dramatic Vestry meeting came on January 13, 1965. Ten members of the Vestry were present. "The next item of business," so run the Vestry minutes, "was the proposed Parish Reorganization":

> Mr. Sherman opened the discussion by relating comments from letters received from heads of Parish organizations in answer to inquiries pertaining to the proposal. Mr. Sherman stated that even though the answers were less than lukewarm for the changes and they showed a general feeling of reluctance to accept the plan for reorganization, he felt we must take some form of action to revitalize the life of the Parish, or attendance would continue to go down, and membership and budget would follow. Two alter-

nate plans were suggested: the first of these was for an Associate Vestry, the second was to stand pat and make existing organizations serve better. The present poor attendance at services and the lack of support evidence the effects of standing pat and [that it] does not answer the major needs now apparent in the Parish.

After a lengthy and intense discussion "concerning the state of the Parish and covering almost every facet of Parish activity," Dr. Kenneth Podger moved "that the Parish Reorganization plan be adopted and that we proceed with the reorganization as outlined, subject to amendment at any time." Jim Nicholson seconded the motion. Seven vestryman voted for it, two opposed it, and one abstained.[82]

Over the next twenty-two months all the commissions were gradually installed and entered into operation. *With what effects?*

For the first time in the history of St. Philip's, the Vestry considered the entire range of parish activities and programs. This was a great gain, for the reform broke the bands of custom that had hitherto limited the thought and energy of some very able men to the important but constraining questions of property and budget. And, a second gain, they were joined in the discussion by a large number of other laity. After a year's operation the senior warden, William H. Ruffin, reported to the annual congregational meeting on January 9, 1966: "We trust that the administrative reorganization of the Vestry on our so-called commission basis is proving to be worthwhile. Certainly a great many members of the Parish are giving it concentrated attention."[83]

The commissions were, thirdly, an administrative convenience. When the Rector or the Vestry faced a problem requiring study, they could refer it to the appropriate commission for research and report.

And fourthly, in their deliberations the commissions generated a treasury of options for action immediately or later. But how many of these options were actually implemented at that time? That question can be answered only commission by commission.

The commissions divided (with some overlap) into two categories: those working to strengthen the internal program, and those reaching out.

Buildings and Grounds was essentially the junior warden made into a committee. Fortunately, the two junior wardens, Jim Nicholson (1965–66) and Bond Anderson III (1967), were among the most dedicated and efficient in the history of St. Philip's. Thanks to them the innumerable petty but ineluctable details of maintenance were accomplished as expeditiously as before: the installation of new florescent lights in the hallway and of shelves in the mimeograph and sexton rooms; the purchase of new boiler relief valves, of a new water heater, of a reconditioned Electrolux for $92.65, and of four window air-conditioning units in the rectory for $615; and the hiring of a new sexton (Mr. Wilkie Nelson) at a weekly salary of $60.[84]

Worship and the Liturgical Arts was another effective commission, chaired by George Pyne for three successive years (1965–67). It worked through four subcommittees: Ushers, Lay Readers, Music, and Fine Arts. Instead of having vestrymen in charge of ushering, the commission changed to a system involving all men of the parish. The chair for the year, J. Harper Erwin, Jr., and the monthly head ushers were all nonvestrymen. Approximately 135 individuals served as ushers at 140 services. Twenty-three competent lay readers read at all Sunday services. Dr. Lionel Stevenson of the Duke University Department of English was their "dean," having served since 1958. A Special Music Committee, appointed by the Rector and chaired by Mary Pyne, found a new organist/choirmaster, Robert N. Capen, who maintained the high standard of musicianship that was a tradition at St. Philip's.[85]

The commission's annual report to the congregation in 1966 recounted the achievements of the Fine Arts Committee:

> Since its inception in 1961 it has procured and hung 55 pictures in the Parish House, bringing visual beauty to all classrooms and corridors. In addition, as a special project for 1965, this Committee selected, matted, framed, and hung the 58 portraits in the East stairwell, turning a once drab area into the glorious All Saints Stairwell which will ever remind all who enter St. Philip's Parish House that we all have our special place in the Communion of Saints.
>
> Displays were presented on the board in the first floor corridor depicting the seasonal emphases of the Church Year. Christopher Fry's play *A Sleep for Prisoners* was presented in the chancel of St. Philip's on May 31, under the sponsorship of the Commission.[86]

Independently of the Commission on Worship and Liturgical Arts, the first small step toward liturgical reform was introduced during Lent 1965. The *Epistle to the Philippians* quietly announced:

You may have wondered recently why we have, in addition to the Prayer Book and Hymnal 1940, a new small black-bound book in each pew rack in the Chapel.

The Calendar and the Collects, Epistles, and Gospels for The Lesser Feasts and Fasts and for Special Occasions was prepared by the Standing Liturgical Commission of our Church and authorized by the General Convention of 1964 for trial use in the Episcopal Church. Bishop Baker more recently has authorized its use in the Diocese of North Carolina; this experiment will last until the General Convention meets again to study its effects and results.

Here at St. Philip's Church we shall observe these "Lesser Feasts and Fasts" on Mondays through Fridays at our daily Morning Prayer services at 8:40 and also on Thursdays at our regular 10:00 A.M. celebration.

An interesting variety to our services will thus be achieved and a wider acquaintance with the great figures of the Christian Church throughout the centuries. Some of these, like William Laud and William Law, William White and John Henry Hobart, are more especially related to our Anglican heritage. Others, like St. Augustine of Hippo, St. Francis of Assisi, St. Joseph of Arimathea, are part of the common heritage of all Christian people.[87]

The Commission on Finance and Administration essentially did the work of the old-time Vestry Finance Committee: it prepared for Vestry consideration a preliminary budget (a wish list), trimmed it realistically to match the amount pledged during the Every Member Canvass, and presented the revised budget to the January congregational meeting.[88] In this process the Finance Commission worked closely with the Stewardship Commission, which nominated the chair of the Every Member Canvass.

The Finance Commission was twice at the center of two crucial canvasses, 1965 and 1966, that illuminate the attitudes of the Vestry, the lay leadership, and the congregation toward innovation. The canvass of 1965 turned on a proposal of the Long-Range Planning Commission, composed of the Rector (ex officio); two vestrymen, B. B. Olive (chair) and William H. Ruffin; and seven lay leaders: Betsy Hansen-Pruss, Julia Royall, Watts Carr, Jr., Noble Clay, James E. Davis, George Taylor, Jr. (EYC), and Warren Watkins.[89] At its second meeting, on

September 9, 1965, the commission strongly recommended the acquisition of a block of land in the rear of St. Philip's that was being
offered for sale by the Urban Renewal Program. The commission's
speculations regarding possible uses for the land revealed a new trend
in the thinking of the church's leadership: it considered not only the
needs of the church for large classrooms and a larger parking area but
also the needs of the community: "erecting a youth building for the
Church and community, an activity room for the elderly in the community, erecting a parish school facility and providing room for future
social agency offices operating at the city level; a children's community
park was also proposed."[90] The Finance Commission and the Vestry
strongly endorsed purchase of the land and added a "challenge" item of
$7,000 to the preliminary budget. When the congregation failed to rise
to the challenge and pledged only enough to cover the church's operating expenses, the Vestry immediately scheduled for 1967 a special
capital improvements campaign to buy the land. Only when Urban
Renewal announced that the land would not be placed on sale for two
or three years did the Vestry defer the campaign to a later date.

The 1966 canvass turned on the proposal of the Christian Education Commission (Children) to hire a professional director of Christian Education.[91] Without such a reform, it was thought, families with
children would not join St. Philip's, attendance and membership in
the church would continue their decline, and the amount pledged each
year would diminish. The Vestry was persuaded and enthusiastically
added to the preliminary budget $5,100 for the director's salary. How-
ever, again the congregation voted negatively with its pocketbook and
pledged only enough to pay operating expenses. Once more Sherman
and the lay leadership were stymied.[92]

The other major commission was that of Christian Social Action,
chaired in 1965 by Haywood Smith and in 1966 by E. K. Powe and
co-chaired in 1967 by Drs. James E. Davis and Richard L. Watson.
The commission early defined its twofold purpose: "to seek ways in
which St. Philip's may more effectively serve the entire community
and to educate the Parish to its responsibilities and the needs of the
city." During its first two years the commission laid before the congregation and the Vestry a wide range of options for St. Philip's: to aid
the relocation of families rendered homeless by Urban Renewal; to act
as a Traveler's Aid at the bus station; with other Episcopal churches
of the area, to provide a rooming house (limited stay) for indigent

patients of local hospitals; to assist the poor in the immediate neighborhood of St. Philip's; to sponsor an Alcoholics Anonymous chapter; to assist prisoners in finding employment; to introduce a "Friendly Visitor" program for visiting elderly single people; to participate with other churches in a senior citizens' housing project; to establish a day-care center in the parish house for preschool children; to participate in the Co-operative Training Center for unskilled workers not qualified for the Industrial Education Center. In his reports E. K. Powe raised the Vestry's level of consciousness with regard to what the national church and the diocesan headquarters were recommending with regard to community action and cited what several other Durham churches, notably Watts Street Baptist, were doing. The Vestry turned down the proposal to locate a day-care center in the parish house when it learned that St. Philip's could not meet the required standards, but it purchased tables and chairs for a day-care center in Immanuel Church to help it combat juvenile delinquency in its neighborhood.[93]

In 1967 the commission began urging the congregation to work in the Edgemont Community Center, a few blocks down the street. In May, Sherman and eight or ten women visited the center to discover and meet in love the needs of "their brothers" there. This simple act was a historic breakthrough: it symbolized that St. Philip's was moving from discussion about doing something in the community to doing it, as John Denham had urged ten years before. Slowly, the door that St. Philip's had kept shut against community action was being opened, and the pressure was mounting on the leadership to do more.[94]

The concluding months of Bart Sherman's rectorship at St. Philip's were filled with exciting events. In early December 1966 he received from the Steering Committee of the Every Member Canvass a report of its interviews with approximately 150 communicants of St. Philip's.[95] This was the first "profile" in the history of St. Philip's of the attitudes of its parishioners. On the whole, the report was a ratification of his leadership and a confirmation of our narrative. The communicants were generally satisfied with the work of St. Philip's (after all, these were people who had stayed): "Those items receiving many favorable comments were: (1) sermons by the Rector, (2) counselling by the Curate, (3) the music program, (4) the conduct of the services, and (5) the work and dedication of the many women's organizations," such as Daughters of the King, Altar Guild, Junior Choir Mothers' Guild, and Episcopal Church Women. Areas mentioned to be in need of improvement were (1) the Church School program, though there was no agreement as to what should be done; (2) overall fellowship, with the expressed hope that a men's organization might be revived; and (3) communication of the Rector and the Vestry with the congregation. Specifically, parishioners wished that Sherman would spend less time on diocesan business and more on visiting them. They wished to see more of him, which was a compliment of sorts.

During the last two weeks of December 1966 Sherman represented the parish, the Diocese of North Carolina, and the Episcopal Church at the consecration of his brother-in-law as bishop of Hong Kong. He carried with him a check for $5,000 as a gift from the Diocese of North Carolina to the Diocese of Hong Kong.[96]

On February 1, 1967, at the annual Diocesan Convention, Sherman himself was nominated for the post of Suffragan Bishop of the Diocese of North Carolina. On the first four ballots he led in both the clergy and lay orders and seemed on the verge of election; then for reasons unknown the Reverend William Moultrie Moore, rector of St. Martin's Church, Charlotte, moved ahead and was chosen by both orders on the seventh ballot.[97]

During the summer of 1967 Sherman was called to succeed Moore as rector of St. Martin's. Sherman accepted the invitation and resigned from St. Philip's on August 10, to take effect on September 15. In accord with canonical custom, Albert Nelius resigned as Curate. Sherman and Nelius officiated at their last service at St. Philip's on Sunday, September 10.[98]

GOD BLESS YOU!

Months of association with a person, it is said, teach much about his character. Months of association as a historian with L. Bartine Sherman have taught me much about his. If I had to choose one word to characterize him it would be "fidelity"—absolutely erect in his faith in God, unswervingly faithful in the execution of His purposes as he understood them. If I am allowed another phrase it would be "analytical intellectual power," which yielded a strong strategic sense in overall planning. These two qualities, fidelity and intellectual power, were central to his character.

They also explain his central contribution to St. Philip's. He succeeded where other Rectors had failed: he brought it into the twentieth century. He saved it from premature senescence, decay, and death. He forced it, by an act of will, to emerge from its cocoon of pleasant sociability. He initiated the process by which it would live out in its own institutional life the metaphor of the statuary in its Memorial Garden. Metamorphosis, birth or rebirth, rarely comes without struggle or pain and may be prolonged, but Sherman started the process of transformation. Thanks to him the pangs that St. Philip's was feeling were birth pangs, not death throes.

8

The Rectorship of Thomas Eugene Bollinger 1967–1978

        After Bart Sherman submitted his resignation to the Vestry of St. Philip's on August 10, 1967, E. K. Powe, the senior warden, immediately conferred with Bishop Fraser and on his advice appointed a Search Committee to seek and to recommend to the Vestry a promising successor as rector. The committee members included J. Harper Erwin, Jr. (chair), Bond Anderson III, Ihrie Carr, Dr. James E. Davis, Harald Hansen-Pruss, Dorothy Manning, George Pyne, and Richard L. Watson.[1] They had long been known for their years of eminent service to St. Philip's.

THE NEW RECTOR

Moving very rapidly, the Search Committee examined the credentials of forty-three candidates for the position and within ten weeks recommended that the Vestry call the Reverend Thomas Eugene Bollinger, rector of the Church of the Holy Comforter in Burlington, North Carolina. Members of the committee who had interviewed him there reported that "he was a dynamic young man, a go-getter who could pick up a project and run with it." He would inspire St. Philippians "to buckle up, get to work, and raise the Church to heights never reached before."[2] In announcing to the congregation Bollinger's acceptance of its call in November 1967, the Vestry expressed its gratitude to "all those who had helped them in their quest for a new minister. . . . We hope that you will agree with our unanimous opinion that our choice is a splendid one."[3]

        Bollinger's previous career gave the Vestry every reason for optimism. Born in Turrell, Arkansas, on January 12, 1932, he had been educated in the public schools of Memphis, Tennessee, and at Memphis State University, gaining his B.S. degree in 1951 at the age of nineteen. He received a sound theological grounding at the Hamma Divinity School, Lutheran Seminary (B.D. 1954), and served Lutheran pastorates from 1954 to 1958. Converting to the Episcopal Church, he attended the School of Theology at the University of the South (Sewanee) for a year (M.Theol. 1959). Moved ahead rapidly by Bishop Baker and the Standing Committee of the Diocese of North Carolina, he was ordained deacon in December 1959 and priest in June 1960. From 1959 to 1961 he served as minister and then rector of St. Stephen's Church, Erwin, a small congregation of 101 communicants,[4] before transferring to the Church of the Holy Comforter.[5] During his six-year tenure in Burlington, enrollment increased from 386 communicants in 1961 to 585 in 1967.[6]

Meanwhile, Bollinger had become prominent in diocesan activities. Named in 1960 a member of the Diocesan Commission on Evangelism, he authored its report to the Diocesan Convention in May 1961.[7] In January 1961 he participated in a clinic for eighty vestrymen in Charlotte and seventy in Raleigh, under the supervision of Bishops Baker and Fraser.[8] In May 1962, at age thirty, he was chosen a deputy to the Provincial Synod and elected to the Diocesan Executive Council for a three-year term (1961–65).[9] When the Diocesan Commission on Evangelism was merged with that on Racial Subjects into the Executive Council's Department of Christian Social Relations, he was named the department's chair for one year (1963–64).[10] With several other clergy and Bishop Fraser, he participated in a Lay School of Theology, whose three-day sessions were attended by nearly one hundred laity (1965–66). He lectured on the Doctrine of the Church.[11] Bollinger was the only other clergyman to accompany Bishop Fraser and several laity on a visit to the companion Diocese of Panama in July 1966.[12] He was again elected a member of the Diocesan Executive Council in January 1967. His three-year term (1967–70) overlapped by a year that of two St. Philippians, Dr. James E. Davis and Dorothy Manning (1965–68), who were also members of the Search Committee that recommended him.[13] Bollinger seemed to be a rising star in diocesan affairs.

His printed reports and essays as well as his activities in Burlington are valuable clues to his thinking upon taking over at St. Philip's. In his report for the diocesan study commission on evangelism (1961), he paid tribute to the Episcopal Church "as a great historic Church, with grandeur of worship, and a majestic drawing power which many of its own members do not quite realize." The Diocese must "find ways of using to the fullest the drawing power we already have, and the building of a Christ-like image before the world so that no man can mistake who we are, and what we have been sent to do." In witnessing for Christ the laity must become involved: "The idea of the 'Lay Apostolate' should be given serious thought throughout the Diocese, and in all its departments." "Within each parish and mission [lay] leaders must be converted and trained." This could be done in part through retreats. "Real winning evangelism will only result from lives that have encountered God in depth through worship, sacramental living, and prayer." [14] These principles were not novel, but they were important to the history of St. Philip's because Bollinger believed them to the depths of his being. They guided his thought and action during his career at St. Philip's. We cannot understand him or much that happened until we recognize this.

Experience with vestries and vestry clinics led him to publish in *The Churchman* (January 1963) an article entitled "Especially for Vestrymen . . . and Those Who Elect Them" (see Appendix J). Against the all-too-common reality of vestries that focus on questions of property and budgets, leaky faucets and unpaid pledges, he advanced the dream ideal of vestries that unite with the rector in promoting creatively the entire church's program and ministry:

> Unfortunately sometimes the vestry and rector look upon each other with some suspicion. The vestry feels it must keep the rector "in hand," and the rector feels he must goad the vestry into action. There is much quoting of canons, and little serious and effective Christian action. The intent of the canons is that the rector and vestry exist in a cooperative and supportive relationship, each looking at the needs of the other, and prepared to help and defend the other. Only in this way can the rector and vestry lead a parish to discover what "community," in the Christian sense, means. [15]

This ideal had been Bart Sherman's too, and in seeking persistently to realize it at St. Philip's Bollinger was attempting to build on his predecessor's initiatives.

At the Church of the Holy Comforter Bollinger had applied his principles in practice. He persuaded the vestry there to invite other communicants to attend its meetings. Working cooperatively with the vestry, the Episcopal Church Women, and the Reverend James A Woggon, Director of College Work, he led his church to reach out in February 1964 with an Episcopal Campus Center at Elon College. The church rented an apartment in the old president's house, and the churchwomen furnished the rooms to create a home-like atmosphere. The students thus found "a place where they could drop in for a cup of coffee, write a letter, or play a game of chess, or learn about special programs and seminars for Episcopal students." [16]

Later in the year, in a more daring innovation, Bishop Coadjutor Fraser led the Diocese of North Carolina to found a new church in the Cum-Park Plaza Shopping Center in Burlington. "He termed the new church 'an attempt to meet needs of the people where they live' and 'an exploratory ministry on a frontier of modern America.' " "Jesus," he added, "got out and met people where they lived . . . in the market place and elsewhere. Shopping centers are where people live and the purpose of this church center is to provide a pure service ministry to all who pass through this market place."It was open to all, regardless of church affiliation, Monday through Saturday from 10:00 A.M. until 9:00 P.M. A 5:15 P.M. worship service was conducted in the chapel daily, and a 10:00 A.M. service was held on Sunday morning. Counseling by a minister was offered to the public.

The new project was the first of its kind in the Southeast and one of only a half-dozen such centers located throughout the United States. It won national attention when it was cited by *Time* magazine. The program was operated by Bollinger and Woggon of Holy Comforter, the Reverend John Stone of Saint Andrew's Episcopal Church of Haw River, and lay volunteers, working together. [17]

Working cooperatively with others, clergy and laity, in outreach adventures was part of Bollinger's style of operation. He brought it with him to St. Philip's. In this, too, he was prepared to continue and to fulfill the initiatives of his predecessor.

THE SITUATION

In a kindly gesture meant to aid his successor, Bart Sherman counseled his parishioners for the last time in the *Epistle to the Philippians* early in September 1967:

One word about your new Rector, whoever he may be: whoever he may be, he won't be Bart Sherman, so don't try to force him into the slot which has come to fit my contours so comfortably over the last ten years. He will have talents and abilities I have lacked, so encourage him to use them, rather than saying, "Well, Mr. Sherman never did that!" He will change some things without even knowing it; others he will change consciously and deliberately. He will have to, in order to be himself, and to maintain his own integrity as a man and a priest. Welcome this change, for anything living that does not change, dies.[18]

The advice was prescient: Bollinger was different, and some St. Philippians did say: "Well, Bart Sherman [or Albert Nelius] never did that!" That early reaction was normal and natural, and in previous transitions the congregation and the new Rector had soon adjusted to each other. But this transition was not normal. The situation was fraught with difficulties.[19]

Several of these difficulties were purely local in origin. Nelius, Sherman's beloved curate and counselor to the flock, had been one of the forty-three candidates for election. When the Vestry passed over him, a considerable number of St. Philippians felt he had been given a raw deal. They would dislike any other rector simply because he was not Nelius. And during Bollinger's tenure they continued to avail themselves of Nelius's loving counsel. Despite Bollinger's efforts at reconciliation, they remained an intractable minority. Then, the Church School, above the level of the preschool department, was in a state of decline. Unlike Yates, Haden, and Edwards, Sherman had not met with its teachers on a monthly basis. Nor did the teachers themselves meet regularly with each other. Despite the efforts of several able and dedicated instructors, attendance had nosedived from 80 percent of enrollment to 60 percent. In contrast, St. Luke's across town had developed a wonderful Sunday School. Partly for that reason, it was attracting young married couples with children, leaving St. Philip's with an aging congregation. This trend had to be stopped if St. Philip's was to survive. Finally, no one told Bollinger, because no one knew, that basic maintenance had been so neglected over the years that the church edifice and parish house were in a state of dilapidation.

Other difficulties were national in origin, though local in expression. Since the 1950s the United States had been experiencing a profound social revolution in role norms, role expectations, and role behavior in relationships of whites/blacks, men/women, parents/children, teachers/students, clergy/vestry, vestry/congregation—and the interlocking concepts of God/Jesus Christ/Holy Spirit as they appeared in public and private worship. There seemed to be an irresistible erosion of the foundations of customs, values, and beliefs.

The parishioners of St. Philip's, struggling with daily perplexities and responding to immediate opportunities, rarely understood the general scene or the movements of which they were a part. But they were acutely and often angrily involved in specific, local manifestations of these trends, such as the Malcolm X Liberation University affair, when the national Episcopal Church awarded $45,000 to an African-American institution located only two blocks from St. Philip's and sponsored by Howard Fuller, a black activist. Or such as the proposed ordination of women; or the inability of parents to command the attendance of their junior- and senior-high offspring at Sunday School and EYC; or the refusal of EYCers who did attend to elect any officers, for that would be a discriminating infringement upon human equality and dignity; or the prolonged process of Prayer Book revision, which was moving public worship from a theology of humility, embalmed in lovely Elizabethan cadences and enshrined in the hearts of many devout Episcopalians, to a theology of celebration and joy, somewhat dampened by its expression in flat American prose. On this issue of revision the congregation of St. Philip's was evenly divided, often bitterly: in a late poll 49 percent thought the Standing Liturgical Commission of the General Convention was on the right track; 49 percent thought not; 2 percent were undecided. In an era of change, challenge, and confusion what should a poor idealist rector who dreamed of Christian harmony and unity do—especially when he wanted to be liked by everyone?

For Bollinger's personality was part of the situation and the problem. An innovative, creative person, persevering in his goals for St. Philip's, he sometimes wavered in his tactics and equivocated in his statements. Subject to highs of elation and lows of depression, he became under pressure a troubled spirit in a troubled age. His rectorship was never dull, often controversial, and not unproductive. As a historian in search of past historical reality, I shall attempt to follow it as it unrolled.

THE EARLY YEARS, 1967–1970

Bollinger celebrated his first Communion at St. Philip's on Sunday, December 3, 1967.[20] During the three months between Rectors, as in previous interim periods, the basic institutional life of St. Philip's had continued uninterruptedly: the Sunday worship services with their excellent music, the Church School, the monthly Vestry and ECW chapter meetings, the annual bazaar, and, yes, the Every Member Canvass, all animated by the spiritual devotion and institutional loyalty of the congregation.

But compared with previous interims this one proceeded with signal differences, the product of Sherman's term. The several Vestry commissions founded during his tenure continued to operate and report, notably those of Worship and Liturgical Arts, Christian Social Action, Christian Education (Children and Adult), and Long-Range Planning. The latter, chaired by Harding Hughes, reported that it "subscribed to the idea of acquiring additional church property." The chair of the Every Member Canvass, James L. Nicholson, not only echoed the familiar refrain of giving "time, talents, and treasure" but also repeatedly stressed "meeting the real needs of our society" and "raising enough funds so that we can carry on [both] a vigorous program and a dedicated ministry in the community."[21] Even after Sherman's departure, the Vestry elite was expressing his concept of outreach to the community. And again, as in 1965 and 1966, the rest of the laity expressed their indifference by refusing to pledge the necessary extra amount of money. Verily, the leaders might exclaim, a stiff-necked people!

As might be expected, Bollinger continued the basic institutions of the church. But as Sherman had predicted, he introduced differences, some intentional, others inadvertent. Arriving with his personal brand of Midwestern breeziness and directness, he introduced in Sunday services a degree of informality that some worshipers found attractively "less stuffy" and others offensive ("just like a town meeting"). His sermons, also less formal than Sherman's, deemed "thoughtful" by some and "too philosophical" by others, were often eloquent, infinite variations on the theme God Loves You, No Matter What!

Brimful with youthful vitality (he was only thirty-five) and imbued with a self-confidence born of years of success, he introduced other changes and began new initiatives during the winter months of early 1968. Like Sherman he recognized the congregation's need for a post-

Sunday School theological education, but in January he replaced his predecessor's learned, primarily lecture-style Course on Christianity with an open-ended Inquirers' Class conducted by himself. "These evening sessions on Sundays," he announced, "are designed to answer questions regarding the faith and function of the Church both for non-members seeking information, and for members wanting to refresh their understanding of the faith. The evenings are designed to be 'free-wheeling.' The rule is: 'there is no such thing as an irrelevant question!' Everybody come; it can be fun." [22]

During Lent he tackled the problem of the gap that had developed between the Vestry elite and the rest of the congregation. In March he invited forty-five laity—old guard and new arrivals—to form two "Christian Community Clinics." Each clinic, numbering approximately twenty-four communicants, explored in four two-hour evening sessions "the quality of life characterized by the Church and their role in it." The evenings were designed to give participants the experience of forming a Christian community, right then and there. [23]

At the first meeting the twenty-four members of each clinic were subdivided into four groups of six. Within each group every member was asked to share with the others his or her most important spiritual experience, thus establishing a bond. In this way, Harold Parker, a shy scholar who had started attending St. Philip's in 1961 and had been confirmed in 1965, was for the first time brought into interactive contact with two veteran church workers, John and Hilda Chatham, who became friends for life. Open-ended discussion of the nature and role of the church followed, first within each group and then among all four groups together. Clinics 1 and 2 were so enthusiastic that during the post-Easter season another set of laity was brought together in Clinics 3 and 4, and by autumn Clinics 5 and 6 had formed. By this simple measure Bollinger had brought at least 120 communicants, Vestry veterans as well as various newcomers, into a shared discussion and understanding of "the Church as a community which is supportive and free." [24] Furthermore, he had discovered and involved a band of relative newcomers who had been previously outside the orbit of church activity.

In a parallel move to engage more people in its routine activities, the Vestry authorized on March 14 the appointment of six Associate Vestry members. Chosen by the Rector with the advice and consent of the Vestry, they would serve for one year from June 1 to May 31, participate regularly in Vestry meetings with voice but no vote, and work actively as members of at least one parish commission. It was hoped thus to facilitate communication between the Vestry and other parishioners, to educate the parish with respect to the St. Philip's program and witness, to enroll additional talents in its implementation, and to provide an ideal training ground for future members of the Vestry.[25] The first Associate Vestry were Priscilla McBryde, Kathy Leutze, Ralph Billeter, T. C. Cook, John R. Locke, Jr., and B. W. C. Roberts.[26] Other parishioners were invited to attend Vestry meetings.[27]

In March, too, Prayer Book revision, long discussed, desired by some, feared by others, hit the parish with practical force. In obedience to the General Convention (1967) Bollinger decided that the Trial Liturgy, authored by the Standing Liturgical Commission of the General Convention, would be used at all services of Holy Communion from Ash Wednesday through the next four to six months. He made himself available for conferences with individuals and meetings with groups wishing to study the service. He pointedly observed that the current draft was not definitive, that evaluations and suggestions for alteration would be collected at the end of the experimental period, tabulated by the parish Worship Commission chaired by Dr. Richard L. Watson, and forwarded through channels to the Standing Liturgical Commission. Thus every St. Philippian could play a role in the formulation of the final version. "Learn about the Trial Liturgy," he urged. "We are ready to help you."[28]

Meanwhile, the commission mode of operation, installed by Sherman, seemed to be working smoothly. "Under the chairmanship of Dr. Norman Ross, the Commission on Outreach met February 21 and initiated a broad program seeking to reach newcomers and prospective members of the parish. Mrs. Ernest Elsevier was appointed Coordinator and will keep records regarding contacts with prospective members and their involvement in parish life. Contacts will be made by the rector and others as each newcomer comes to the parish or when one is referred to the parish office."[29]

"At its regular meeting on March 14, the Vestry approved a recommendation by the Christian Social Action Commission headed by Dr. James E. Davis that St. Philip's allow its facilities to be used for a program for the aging under the Durham Coordinating Council for the Aging." One day a week — as it turned out, each Wednesday — the parish house was buzzing with older people engaged in crafts, games, counseling, and birthday luncheons. St. Philippians were invited to volunteer their services.[30]

"Acting upon a recommendation by Mrs.Ī. H. Manning, Jr., Chairman of the Commission on Mutual Responsibility and Interdependence, the Vestry approved on March 14, a gift of $200 toward the work in the Diocese of Iran where Mr. and Mrs. Gordon Morrison, parish-sponsored Episcopal missionaries, are presently serving. The gift was a portion of the Christmas offering."[31]

And so, to believe the *Epistle to the Philippians*, all was well. St. Philip's, a major parish in the Diocese of North Carolina, seemed to be in splendid shape. That was doubtless the image Bollinger had of it when he accepted the position. However, his first four months were enough to reveal to him the grimy underside of its operation. Its church edifice and parish house were dilapidated and, even after repair and renovation, would be inadequate. Indeed, the Church School teachers in meeting toward the end of the new Rector's first year recommended that the entire physical plant be scrapped and built anew![32] And with what funds? The Church ran a deficit of several thousand dollars in 1967 and was doing the same in 1968. The current level of giving was low. We do not have the figures for 1967, but they were no doubt little different from those of 1968, when $81,000 was the total amount pledged. There were then 317 pledging units. Of these, 58 did not pledge. Of the 259 that did, 91 (35 percent) pledged less than $101, or less than $2 per week; 213 (80 percent) pledged less than $501, or less than $10 weekly.[33] Families were still contributing sums that were respectable and adequate *before* the inflation of the two world wars. Somehow they needed to be pried loose from older habits of thought and giving. And, of course, not all pledges were paid; several thousand dollars were written off annually as uncollectible. More foreboding in its implications was the trend in average Church School attendance, which once had stood at a stout 80 percent of enrollment. By 1967 this had dropped to 62 percent. It declined still further in 1968, to 58 percent.[34] Young married couples with children were naturally joining other Episcopal churches in Durham that offered more attractive educational programs. As Bollinger noted, St. Philip's was an aging congregation, headed, if these trends continued, toward extinction. Finally—not really finally, because there were other troubles— three years of talk about outreach and serving the downtown community had thus far yielded just talk. Like several of his predecessors, he recognized that "in former years St. Philip's had given no indication that it was aware it has a special mission because it was a downtown church instead of a suburban one." [35]

Bollinger's long-term response to a complex situation was to enter into dialogue with the Vestry and attempt to persuade it to become *energetically* the ideal Vestry he had envisioned in his 1963 article, one that studied and then *acted* comprehensively with respect to the entire program of St. Philip's. His first attempt failed.

At a day-long "working retreat" at Quail Roost on Sunday, April 21, 1968, the Vestry, the Vestry-elect, and the Associate Vestry discussed the parish and its future. In his concluding remarks, Bollinger stated that parish unity came through involvement of people working together. He suggested a reorganization of Sherman's commissions that would better meet present needs.[36] His proposed list reduced the eleven existing commissions to ten, dropped Liturgical Arts—a real loss—but added a Commission on Personnel and Training, and rearranged the rest:

Sherman's Commissions	Bollinger's
Finance and Administration	Administration-Finance
Buildings and Grounds	Property
Stewardship	Worship
Worship and Liturgical Arts	Stewardship
Christian Education (Children)	Christian Education
Christian Education (Adult)	Fellowship
Outreach and Public Relations	Outreach
Christian Social Action	Christian Social Action
Youth Work	Personnel and Training
Parish Policies and Long-Range	
Planning Missions	Parish Future [37]

The Vestry at the retreat authorized him "to work up detailed recommendations regarding the Commission structure for the year ahead." [38]

On May 6 Bollinger mailed to the Vestry for consideration at its May 9 meeting what must have seemed an overwhelming document, an elite-typed, single-spaced, ten-page "tentative description" of the functions of each commission (see Appendix K). In many respects the document was admirable. It displayed a masterly grasp of the situation at St. Philip's, of its needs and problems, and the way to meet them. Its detailed descriptions of the functions of each commission were practical and realistic: their implementation would have involved the Rector, staff, Vestry, and laity in a tremendous united effort to move St. Philip's forward.

However, if the document was admirable, Bollinger's language of presentation did not accord with tradition at St. Philip's. In his May 6 letter to the Vestry presenting its agenda for May 9, he wrote:

> Copies of "tentative" descriptions of these commissions, and their assignments, are attached. Please read them carefully IN ADVANCE OF THE MEETING, so you will be in a position to recommend any changes you feel necessary. PLEASE NOTE: each Commission has been given an "immediate assignment," which must be carried out in the next few months [usually by July]. I feel that we must make certain that we do not enter the fall session without concrete plans in every area. I HOPE WE CAN LIMIT THIS DISCUSSION TO TWENTY MINUTES.

In the history of St. Philip's, no Rector had ever taken that tone to the Vestry. A Rector suggested, or presented, or reasoned but never had he commanded. "Must" was not a word that Rectors had used to the Vestry. And to order commissions to report by July, a month when many St. Philippians fled to the beaches, was simply naive.

The result was predictable. The Vestry adopted on May 9 Bollinger's scheme of commissions as its operating structure, but no reports were submitted in July and August. Nor did the church enter the fall session with "concrete plans in every area." Nevertheless, his initiative may have had educational value: it alerted the Vestry to possible future action and gave Bollinger guidelines for operations in the months to come.

Undismayed by his failure to move the Vestry to participate in overall, comprehensive reform, Bollinger resorted to working closely with individuals within and without the Vestry to achieve innovative changes in particular sectors of St. Philip's life. With the Commission on Stewardship and its chair, Ralph N. Strayhorn, he took on the problem of elevating the level of giving. Over the decades stewardship at St. Philip's had become linked to a single fall event: the Every Member Canvass, which asked communicants to pledge enough money to meet the specific needs of the church as stated by a preliminary budget prepared by the Vestry. If there was any discussion, it was in terms of dollars and cents: whether a specific need should be met and, if so, at what dollar amount, and whether communicants hypothetically should tithe and, if so, before or after taxes. However, even before Bollinger's arrival an element of the Vestry, led by Dr. James E. Davis, wished to restore the concept of stewardship to its original glory: that "stewardship" should be understood as the giving of one's whole life to God, one's time, talent, and treasure, and that the congregation should be reminded of that obligation throughout the year.

Bollinger adopted that concept in his document presented to the Vestry on May 9 (see Appendix K, Tentative Description of the Commission on Stewardship). Strayhorn and his colleagues on the Stewardship Commission (Robert W. Carr, John Chatham, James E. Davis, J. Harper Erwin, Jr., J. Caulie Gunnells, Angus K. McBryde, James L. Nicholson, William H. Ruffin, and E. K. Powe) accepted the idea and persuaded the Vestry to do likewise—and to conduct the November 1968 Every Member Canvass on that basis. Communicants were not asked to pledge enough to meet specific dollar-and-cents needs outlined in a preliminary budget but instead were requested to search their hearts and minds and to pledge what conscience told them.[39] As Bollinger explained in the *Epistle to the Philippians* when launching the campaign on November 10:

STEWARDSHIP IS A WAY OF LIFE

A Christian is a person who knows "whose he is." The Confirmation commitment to follow Christ is an acknowledgment that each Christian offers up the whole of his life in service to God, viewing what he has and is as a trust from God. His life is viewed as an area of service for his God, and he interprets everything he does in this context.

We are viewing our canvass this year in that context. Our members are being reminded of "whose they are," and asked to respond on that basis. The Vestry will operate its 1969 budget on that basis.

Please notice what we are *not* doing. We are not telling you that we have to meet a monetary goal. We believe such a practice only inhibits the Christian truth of Stewardship we are trying to teach. The Vestry will put everything in the people's hands, trusting their love of God to motivate them to see giving of their life resources in a bigger way.

This does not mean we do not have needs, or hopes for the future. We honestly believe God has a great mission for us all in the years ahead, and we will need the time, ability and money our people give to accomplish this. But it is less than Christian to twist people's arms to get them to give toward a dollar figure, when, in reality, they must see their giving as a response to God, not to a Canvass Committee, or a Vestry. Every person must answer to his God about his response; that is the big issue for him. Examine what you have and are, say your prayers, and then fill in your pledge cards. The future calls you to great things!

For the Vestry and the elite leadership represented on its Commission on Stewardship, this action was a bold deviation from custom, a leap in faith. They appealed to the congregation to emulate them in their personal giving of themselves, their time, talent, and treasure, to the service of God.

But what resulted from the appeal? To be sure, the Every Member Canvass, ably organized by its chair, John Chatham, went off according to schedule: a well-attended parish supper (November 10) was addressed by the Reverend Charles Penick of the Church of the Good Shepherd (Rocky Mount), who had already won St. Philip's Vestry to the broader vision of stewardship; a Loyalty Sunday (November 17) was held when each person who came to the altar to receive Communion left "his pledge card in a place near the chancel, as a part of his act of worship"; and a thorough follow-up was carried out—persons not presenting a card were called on by canvassers the next week.[40] But when the returns were totaled, it was revealed that the level of giving had not been appreciably raised. Although "the amount pledged was approximately ten percent greater than last year, this amount was not enough to meet the immediate needs of the Parish."[41] It did not assure the retention of the Assistant to the Rector, Mr. William Wells, "whose salary was currently paid by Bishop Fraser." Nor, as it turned out, was St. Philip's able to keep its choirmaster, Robert Capen, who was absent on leave for a year's graduate work at Syracuse University. When he learned that his salary would not be increased, he declined to return. Other plans for maintenance and expansion had to be scrapped.

At the annual congregational meeting on January 19, 1969, the

Commission on Stewardship gamely announced that it was still "dedicated to the proposition that the principle of stewardship is one which should be emphasized year-round and should not be discarded as soon as the Every Member Canvass is over." It had "under consideration plans to carry on its work throughout the year."[42] But this declaration only highlighted the realities of the situation: a radical attempt to change basic attitudes had failed to break the gridlock that had developed during Sherman's last years, one between an elite leadership ready to move forward with increased giving and a congregation reluctant to part with its money.

During the year Bollinger met on several occasions with the Commission on Worship to discuss the liturgy and services of worship. Chaired by Richard L. Watson and composed of the new choirmaster/organist William K. Miller and the chairs of the Altar Guild, the Junior Choir Mothers' Guild, the Ushers, the Lay Readers, the revived Fine Arts Committee, and the Music Committee, this commission kept the Rector informed on all those areas of parish operation. In response to the "immediate assignment" Bollinger had given the commission, "to prepare an analysis of completed returns from questionnaires on the four-month use of the Trial Liturgy" for Holy Communion, Watson reported that "of approximately 500 questionnaires sent out, slightly more than 200 were returned. In answering the question as to whether the Standing Liturgical Commission [of the General Convention] was 'on the right track' in its revision 110 parishioners answered 'yes,' 50 answered 'no,' and the remainder seemed undecided."[43]

At several points Bollinger intervened directly in several areas of the Worship Commission's concern. Meeting with the acolytes in small groups, he trained them in the way they should go. "These training periods," noted Lawson Moore, their advisor, "will continue indefinitely."[44] Week by week Bollinger met with the new choirmaster. A graduate student in music at the University of North Carolina at Chapel Hill, Miller had "extensive experience in both church and secular music."[45] However, being new to the parish, he needed all the counsel Bollinger could give. Together they added to the Junior Choir (third to eighth graders) and to the now totally volunteer Adult Choir and a Youth Choir of high schoolers. By September 1969 the total number of choristers in the three groups broke all previous records.[46]

As usual, Bollinger's interventions provoked diverse reactions. After nearly four years of close collaboration, Miller would write in his letter of resignation: "Mr. Bollinger has been a real joy and pleasure with whom to work."[47] On the other hand, the ladies of the Altar Guild, the soul of Christian dedication and devotion, and of propriety, were offended when after Sunday services Bollinger hurriedly dropped his vestments on the floor, leaving them to be hung up by someone else.

Bollinger's ideal for the Church School was high: its program should be designed to give children "the inner strength to cope with the basic issues of life."[48] At St. Philip's its foundation was already being laid by the teachers of the preschool department. With love, tact, firmness, and imagination, Margaret Davis and her associates (George Pyne, Lillian Cahoon, Nancy Mason, Victor and Anne Moore, and Bill Townsend) introduced the little three-, four-, and five-year-olds to the Episcopal ritual, led them through the wonderful stories of the Old and New Testament, and each year accomplished the miracle of forming their pupils into a Christian community.[49] Here Bollinger did not need to interfere with their great success. For reinvigoration of grades one to six he rediscovered Ethel Reade, who had led the creative renovation of the Sunday School during David Yates's time as Rector. Since then, as principal of Fuller Elementary School, she had demonstrated skill in firmly involving teachers and children in creative activities. She and Bollinger now recruited new teachers for the first six grades, assembled them in workshops on teaching methods, and supported them with counsel throughout the year.[50]

In September 1968 Bollinger attended the EYC's first meeting for the upcoming year before turning the group over to Mark Featherston, its student president, and William Wells, the young new Assistant to the Rector. In place of the faded and fading formal Sunday evening dinner where coat-and-tied young gentlemen and charming, decorous young ladies ate with their counselors in the upstairs parish house assembly room, Bollinger offered to the group assembled in the open-air Memorial Garden the freedom of "doing their own thing" each Sunday in a programless program. He promised his support in anything they chose to do. His approach extended to the high schoolers his philosophy of a church that was free and supportive. It accorded with the spirit of his Community Clinics and Inquirers' Class.

From the young people assembled in the Memorial Garden this proposal drew mixed reviews. Most had arrived expecting the presentation of a definite plan for the year. Upon leaving, quite a few grumbled that the "new administration" had muffed its opportunity to grab them with decisive action. A few others, however, welcomed the challenge of liberty and returned next Sunday to a guitar-playing folk mass. As Featherston explained: "A folk mass is a new and different form of worship. It combines the 'in' sounds of folk music with the traditional form of worship to form a bridge in communication between the church and its youth. Although the purpose of the folk mass is to 'turn on' the young people of the church, many of the older members of the church could also benefit from it."[51] On the third Sunday evening Featherston "led a discussion of a film many had seen earlier in the week, and of the Simon and Garfunkle song, 'The Sound of Silence,' which the movie popularized. The film, the song, and to some extent the meeting were studies in the difficulties of communication both between and within the generations. There was also some tentative discussion of the direction that the group might take for the year. Several concerns were voiced—the need for spontaneity, the desire to include a wider circle of people than those within the parish."[52] And so each Sunday the members of the group continued, improvising as they went, seeking to find their own thing that they might do it.[53] As the *Epistle to the Philippians* sagely observed: "The whole future of 'Youth Groups' in the traditional sense is very much open to question today and a good deal of thinking is needed to develop meaningful, expressive new forms."[54]

The breakdown of communication between generations and the need for restoration became a subject of discussion and of action by the Vestry. At its February 1969 meeting Priscilla McBryde reported on the thoughtful speech Richard Parker (no relation to Harold), president of the Diocesan EYC, had made to the annual Diocesan Convention about the growing impatience of young people with their parents, "who were not listening." At the invitation of Bollinger and the Vestry, he addressed the congregation at a Sunday morning worship service. The Vestry, in response to his observations, added to the four adult members of the Associate Vestry two members elected by EYC, Nancy Jo Chatham and Susan Olive for 1969–70, and Nancy Jo Chatham and Abbott Mason for 1970–71. At the Vestry meetings they could voice the concerns of youth on any subject, although they could not vote. At the request of Susan Olive, who succeeded Mark Featherston as president of St. Philip's EYC, the Vestry accorded the group the room across the hall from the ECW parlor, to paint, to decorate, and to furnish according to its desires.[55] They took their responsibility seriously and one year painted the entire room, walls and ceiling, a dark overwhelming purple, with gold trim.

What rendered this period (September 1968 to December 31, 1969) memorable, however, was the contribution of William Wells, the Assistant Rector.[56] A native of Chapel Hill and the son of a professor of English, he had graduated from the University of North Carolina in 1963. After two years in the Navy in the Caribbean and three years at the Episcopal Theological School in Cambridge, Massachusetts, he was ordained deacon on June 29, 1968. He aided Bollinger in several ways: in an occasional sermon, in visiting shut-ins and patients in hospitals, and above all by counseling EYC. Firm in his faith but still a thoughtful seeker of its implications for his life, he was sensitive to the needs of the youthful seekers in EYC. Warm and genial, he was their leader and companion at Sunday evening get-togethers and on retreats. He is still remembered with affection.

While Bollinger was energetically and imaginatively devising initiatives within St. Philip's, his relations with its Vestry remained difficult. Only seven vestrymen out of twelve bothered to show up at the regular October meeting in 1968. Only six arrived on time in November. In the absence of the treasurer, Bollinger presented the treasury's monthly report. He went on to criticize the preliminary budget prepared by the Administrative Commission as inadequate for a church of St. Philip's size and unrealistic, as it did not allow for several thousand dollars of uncollectibles. The Vestry discussed and after the arrival of its seventh member approved the revised expenditure of $1,042.56 for cabinets to house choir vestments. After a session of only twenty minutes it adjourned.[57] The disparity was glaring between Bollinger's ideal of a Vestry and a Rector mutually supporting each other in broad-range surveys of parish needs and options and the reality of a rump meeting dedicated to finance and the micromanagement of a minor property question.

What galvanized the Vestry and brought it back to long-range planning for the parish future was an event that never occurred: the proposed consolidation of St. Philip's and St. Luke's. In November 1968 Bollinger suggested that the two churches be merged into one. There ensued within and between the two vestries a thoughtful discussion of the project. To explore the implications of the idea, each vestry appointed a liaison committee, that of St. Philip's being chaired by Harding Hughes and that of St. Luke's by its senior warden, Ernie Greup.[58]

In the flurry of speculation and exploratory study, Bollinger presented his vision of a *great* consolidated church:

> He envisaged this hypothetical church as being "heterogeneous" rather than homogeneous as are most Episcopal churches. . . . secondly, he said that the church should do what God is calling it to do; its members must be willing to become leaders. It must base its actions on the "renewal principle" and recognize the need to evaluate itself; and it must be "evangelistic" in the sense of "winning people to the Lord." Thirdly, he insisted that there must be a simultaneous emphasis upon internal and external activities. These activities should be closely related; one is not possible without the other. He concluded by saying that his observations were based on the premise that many Episcopalians (i.e. a consolidated church) can accomplish more than a few.[59]

Bollinger was so taken by his vision of a consolidated church that at one point he volunteered to resign as St. Philip's Rector if that were necessary to bring the consolidation about. His line of thinking accorded with that of Bishop Fraser, who met with the two vestries on December 16. The Bishop was already on record that an ideal parish had 4,000 communicants served by a diversified staff proportionately numerous.[60]

However attractive the vision in Bollinger's persuasive presentation, its implementation immediately encountered practical problems of site, timing, and cost. Where would the consolidated church be located? At St. Philip's the lead in discussion was taken by Watts Carr, Jr., who remembered and valued the tradition that he and his family embodied—he once recalled sitting at age six on Sidney Stuart Bost's lap in his grandfather's house, which adjoined the church. On November 25 he persuaded the Vestry to approve the motion that while the Vestry was interested in the possibility of a merger, it must take place on the present site of St. Philip's. The motion was seconded by Clarence Cobb and at the next Vestry meeting endorsed by James E. Davis.

At first Bollinger supported that general position. At a meeting of the two vestries on December 4, he said that "St. Philip's either as a parish or as part of a consolidated parish must be in the central city;

a church cannot speak to the city, . . . unless it is physically present there; a suburban parish speaks only to that area; because of the race problem, it is essential that the Episcopal Church have a physical presence near the black community."[61] However, St. Luke's indicated that it had no desire to return to the location it had left thirteen years before. St. Philip's then floated the idea that in the short range the two congregations might meet at St. Philip's pending the move to new, larger buildings elsewhere. It was then observed that the church and parish house of St. Philip's were too small to accommodate two congregations and that in any case the inexorable schedule of St. Luke's own building program could not be interrupted. (Those conversations between the two vestries, it should be noted, were exploratory and amiable and never confrontational—a tribute to the leadership of both congregations.) When, finally, Bollinger suggested to the St. Philip's Vestry that the new consolidated church complex might be located in the Gregson-Duke expressway area in back of the Mutual Insurance Building, a site not much more than half a mile from where St. Philip's stood, members of the Vestry questioned "whether such a short move would make a significant difference in the effectiveness of the program." Besides, how could a church that was running annual deficits of several thousand dollars for two years hope to raise $500,000 to $750,000 for new construction?[62] By February 1969 any zeal for a merger had evaporated in the vestries of both churches.

Nevertheless, though Bollinger's merger proposal fell through, the prolonged discussion was a defining moment in the history of both congregations. St. Luke's reaffirmed its mission to be physically and spiritually present in North Durham. The Vestry of St. Philip's, whose meetings were once again fully attended, decided that the church would remain downtown and develop its mission to the center city. As Watts Carr, Jr., emphasized, it was his "conviction that St. Philip's could have a bright future on its present site if it should choose to throw off its lethargy and move in directions which it had not moved before."[63] Paradoxically, it was the vestrymen identified with tradition who had saved St. Philip's for a radical future of innovative service to its immediate neighborhood. Thereafter, Bollinger and the entire Vestry cooperatively buckled down to work to achieve that destiny.

In September 1969 Bollinger reached across denominational lines to the Reverend William Quick of the neighboring Trinity Methodist Church. They agreed to work together on projects that met the needs of downtown Durham. They were soon joined by the pastors of the First Presbyterian and First Baptist Churches and the rabbi of Judea Reform to constitute the Center City Church Council. From that nucleus eventually grew Durham Congregations in Action, numbering more than fifty churches. It was thus the second instance (Bost's mission to the deaf being the first) of St. Philip's being of service by persuading the larger community to serve. Bollinger's action also illustrated a diocesan and national trend toward "grass-roots ecumenism." While interest in the dream of uniting Protestant denominations into a single large union (COCU) was fading, cooperation among congregations doing things together at the local level was increasing. Union of denominations, it came to be thought, should grow naturally from below rather than being imposed by the fiat of national councils from above.[64]

At the Vestry meeting of March 13, 1969 Bond Anderson, senior warden, announced the appointment of a committee for long-range planning on "bricks, mortar, and land." Watts Carr, Jr., Harald Hansen-Pruss, Harding Hughes, Angus McBryde, James L. Nicholson, Kenneth Royall, and William H. Ruffin—all tested leaders—had agreed to serve under the chairmanship of E. K. Powe, another veteran. At the same meeting Bollinger announced the formation of a complementary committee on program. It was composed of Mary Pyne, Edna Podger, Ruth Watson, John Chatham, Walter Mason, and David Robinson.[65] Interrupted in its labors by the Malcolm X Liberation University imbroglio in the fall of 1969, the committee on bricks, mortar, and land was reactivated in March 1970 and divided for study into three subcommittees: Physical Plant (James Pleasants, junior warden, chair), Program (Walter Mason), and Long-Range Building (Powe).[66] Two months later, on May 24, the Vestry approved the idea of having a capital funds drive for the purchase of adjacent land from Urban Renewal (estimated cost, $46,000) and for renovation of the existing plant (estimated at $30,000).[67] Meanwhile, on May 14 Powe reported that his committee on bricks, mortar, and land needed the professional aid of the Strategic Research Services Group of the Executive Council of the Protestant Episcopal Church.[68] After a visit from David R. Covell, Jr., the council's strategic research officer, Powe moved, George Pyne seconded, Watts Carr supported, and the Vestry unanimously voted on June 11 to conduct with Covell's help a formal, comprehensive parish self-study. A directing committee was appointed consisting of Walter Mason (chair), Harold Parker (secretary), and Betty Hodges, Dorothy Manning, and Ruth Watson.[69] Immediately it went to work.

THE MALCOLM X LIBERATION UNIVERSITY AFFAIR

Durham Morning Herald, Tuesday, October 14, 1969:
RALEIGH — Bishop Fraser of the Episcopal Diocese of North Carolina announced Monday that the national church has approved grants totalling $45,000 for Malcolm X Liberation University in Durham.

Fraser said that the grants of $15,000 and $30,000 will come from the $9 million "Urban Crisis Program" approved by the national church at its 1967 general convention in Seattle.
Durham Morning Herald, Wednesday, October 15, 1969:
The rectors of Durham's Episcopal churches Tuesday expressed opinions ranging from cautious acceptance to a fear of financial losses stemming from a $45,000 grant to Malcolm X Liberation University by the national Episcopal church. . . . The Reverend J. E. C. Harris, rector of St. Luke's Episcopal Church, said that strong feelings [of some communicants against the grant] "could result in the church bankruptcy."

Harris was not far off the mark. Because of a $13,000 drop in pledges occasioned by the grant, St. Philip's failed by that amount to fulfill its annual quota owed the Diocesan General Program. As 50 of the 138 parishes in the Diocese likewise fell short of their quotas, the Diocese perforce curtailed its annual contribution to the National Church by $71,000.

Why did a modest grant to a handful of young African American students detonate among Episcopalians an explosion of wrath and fiscal retaliation? There was and still is considerable confusion and misunderstanding about this question, and we must enter into the subject with more narrative detail than usual simply to set the record straight.

The story opens with the evolving attitudes of black students at Duke University. When Duke admitted six black undergraduates in 1963, it was nearly the last major private university in the country to integrate. As late as the fall semester of 1968 the university listed only 101 black students among 3,500 undergraduates and only one black professor. Integration was really not the term to apply to the situation. The black students were lost in a sea of white students, who did not admit them to their fraternities, sororities, and social functions. Lonely, the black students often sought comfort, support, and sociality across town at the predominantly black North Carolina Central University. Back at Duke they formed, in the fall semester of 1967, an Afro-American Society (AAS). They soon learned to use this society to exert collective pressure on the Duke administration to grant reforms that might ameliorate the situation: a Black Studies Program, additional black professors, enlistment of black students in recruiting black applicants for admission, a living/learning dormitory for black students, the hiring of a specialist in black hairstyles for the campus barbershop, the withdrawal of President Douglas Knight from a segregated golf club — a list of twelve items in all. When the administration, "the white power structure," seemed dilatory in considering these demands, some black students occupied the University Records Office in the Allen Building for a day (February 13, 1969). The administration did not suspend the forty or so AAS students involved but placed them on probation.[70]

Meanwhile, as Kara Miles Turner has observed:

> the black students had been having other experiences that were leading them toward a dramatically different solution to their isolating, frustrating situation at Duke. Having come of age during the integrationist phase of the black freedom struggle, these students, no doubt, arrived at Duke believing that it would be the key to their upward mobility into mainstream America. A university education, they thought, would prepare them for successful careers in the field of their choosing, which would in turn allow them to live in a nice, integrated neighborhood, and allow their children to attend integrated schools. But their sharp encounter with exclusion at Duke made them begin to question whether, if this was what integration was like — being physically near whites but socially excluded and culturally alienated — that was what they really wanted. Their negative experiences at Duke predisposed them to accept the vision of an alternate career and lifestyle.

In the summer of 1968 the Durham Fund for Community Development (FCD) offered them that vision. It sponsored a Summer Intern Program in which black college students, including several from Duke, lived and organized in black neighborhoods. There they met "Nathan Garrett, executive director of FCD, and Howard Fuller, its director in charge of setting up neighborhood councils as sounding boards for the problems and frustrations of its inhabitants. An intelligent organizer and articulate, charismatic speaker, Fuller trained the participants to organize, to develop leaders, and to present their grievances to decision-making bodies in order to effect change."[71] He led them, for example, in appearances before the City Council and in marches on the city hall. By his charismatic example he offered Duke's black students the option of having in the "black world" careers similar to his. Then, in November 1968, several of them attended a conference at Howard University, entitled "Toward a Black University," that "dealt with the need to develop an educational institution that would be relevant to the needs of the black community."[72] Finally, the students were reading the writings of Malcolm X, who before his assassination had preached not integration but black independence, black pride, and black nationalism. The students had carried his books into the Allen Building along with a placard reading "Malcolm X Liberation School."

All those influences came together in their minds and discussions during their period of probation. At some point they began to question the relevance of studying Greek literature to working among their own people after graduation. They began to see that even with ameliorating reforms Duke University could never give the education and training they needed for careers in the black world. At this moment of doubt Nathan Garrett suggested that they form *temporarily* an alternate institution to show Duke University what a school relevant to the needs of the black community might be.[73] In March 1969 the students welcomed and amended his idea. They proposed creating de novo a *permanent* black university in which they would have a major role in the educational decision-making process. A planning committee was formed that included two Duke students, Bertie Howard and Chuck Hopkins. Fuller joined the group as senior advisor and administrator.[74]

To the students' vision of an institution that would prepare them for practical work in organizing black communities, Fuller added the perspective of a black nationalism that included Pan-Africanism. He thought in terms of autonomous, self-supporting black groups that would be formed in the United States and then return to Africa, specifically to Ghana, to work with their brothers and sisters in forming an independent nation-state there.[75] The proposed two-year curriculum reflected this enlarged vision of building a nation based on race. The first year would be devoted to African history and to an analysis of those economic, social, and political systems—slavery, colonialism, capitalism, communism—that negatively influence the thinking of black people. It would be accompanied by courses in French and Swahili and followed by a summer in Africa. The second year was to be taught by experts in several technical trades: the school was to produce the "food scientists, tailors, architects, engineers, organizers/teachers/black expressionists/artists, medics, communications technicians, physical development specialists/linguists" that would be needed in an autonomous, self-supporting black community. The second year would also involve extended periods of fieldwork in black neighborhoods.[76]

Theory and practice, ideology and fieldwork would thus complement, enrich, and sustain each other. By education, technical training, and organization blacks would liberate themselves from white thinking, dominance, and control. They would be free and enabled to do their own thing in their own communal way. Or so they dreamed.

Needing start-up funds, the officials of Malcolm X Liberation University (MXLU) applied to the national Episcopal Church, which since 1967 had sponsored a program to help finance enterprises such as theirs. In that year, a year of race riots, burning, and looting in Newark and Detroit, Presiding Bishop John Hines had called upon the General Convention meeting in Seattle to allocate funds "to community organizations involved in the betterment of depressed urban areas, and under the control of those who are largely both black and poor, that their power for self-determination may be increased and their dignity restored."[77] After a vivid, often angry debate over whether Episcopal money should be used for such purposes, the Convention established the General Convention Special Program (GCSP) and allocated to it several million dollars. The GCSP staff in national headquarters in New York then drafted rigorous guidelines for the evaluation of applications (see Appendix L). Grants of up to $200,000 were soon being made to minority urban organizations across the country, and news of the awards was being regularly published in the monthly *North Carolina Churchman*.

The Seattle Convention had also recommended that every diocese establish programs to foster community renewal in depressed ghetto areas. In response, Bishop Fraser appointed in February 1969 an Urban Advisory Committee composed of twelve Episcopal laymen—eight blacks and four whites, a very distinguished group. He also designated the Reverend E. Nathaniel Porter, vicar of St. Titus (Durham), director of the diocesan-level urban crisis program.

In July 1969 the General Convention Special Program staff approved the application of MXLU for an emergency grant of $15,000 without consulting the Diocese of North Carolina. It referred the second application for $30,000 to Bishop Fraser for evaluation. He in turn passed it on to the diocesan Urban Advisory Committee. "After study, the Committee felt the purposes and objectives of Malcolm X Liberation University fitted with the guidelines established by the national funding under the GCSP. The Committee voted unanimously (with ten of twelve members present) to recommend to the Bishop that he give his approval to the grant."[78] Fraser accepted the diocesan committee's judgment and transmitted it to the GCSP staff. Insulated from reality by bureaucratic procedures that did not reach down to the affected parishes, neither the GCSP staff in New York nor Bishop Fraser and members of the Urban Advisory Committee anticipated the storm of controversy that followed.

The news of the second grant reached St. Philip's on October 14 at the worst possible moment—during the annual Every Member Canvass. Up to then the Canvass had been going very well. The Vestry had reaffirmed the policy to conduct it on the principle of stewardship: communicants would be invited to contribute according to their Christian conscience, although they would be informed of parish needs. Arch Bass, Jr., chair of the canvass, had assembled an able campaign committee, and Dorothy Manning had coordinated a series of neighborhood cottage meetings. By October 9, eighty-nine parishioners had already met with Bollinger in seven cottage meetings.[79] They had enjoyed discussing parish goals and problems with him. There seemed to be every prospect that sufficient money would be pledged to pay for the annual parish quotas of approximately $4,500 to the Diocesan Maintenance Fund and $16,500 to the Diocesan Program Fund, from which the Diocese paid its quota to the National Church.[80]

Outrage over the grant accorded to Malcolm X Liberation University wrecked those prospects. Many St. Philippians had felt a growing resentment of the "New York liberals" who seemed to be "running and ruining" the Episcopal Church. In a letter to the Vestry, William H. Ruffin, an elder statesman, "expressed his support of St. Philip's Church, but indicated that he had been in recent years increasingly concerned by the direction being taken by the program of the National Church."[81] This uneasiness and anger was exacerbated by the way the GCSP and diocesan staffs had handled this specific grant, without consultation of or regard for the parishes most closely affected.[82] Locally, it did not help that Malcolm X Liberation University was occupying an abandoned warehouse across the tracks, just two blocks from and within view of St. Philip's. Finally, vivid antagonism to this specific grant arose, not because of the nature of MXLU, which was not really known or understood, but because of its association with Howard Fuller. To black students at Duke he was an admired role model, and to a few St. Philippians, mostly academics, he was a champion of the oppressed. But to many other St. Philippians he was Durham's Number One Black Militant, who repeatedly packed city council meetings with standing-room crowds of followers to cheer threatening speeches so fiery that violence seemed imminent, who led demonstrators in a march down Main Street that resulted in the breakage of store windows along the way, and who thus provoked the mayor to impose a three-night curfew on the town and the governor to activate the National Guard to keep the peace. Fuller, it was felt, could not be trusted.[83] What deep conspiracies was he hatching in MXLU classrooms, from which newspaper reporters were excluded?

Harold Parker, then a novice canvasser, vividly remembered sitting that October for more than an hour in the parlor of a devout Episcopalian as she agonized over her annual pledge. She had been baptized, confirmed, and married in St. Philip's. She loved her church, and she hated Howard Fuller. She wished to contribute to St. Philip's, but she did not want any of her money to go to the National Church program that was supporting him. Today, social psychologists might categorize her state as "cognitive dissonance," but the label does not do justice to her deep distress. Finally, she offered to make a "restricted pledge" of funds that would go to St. Philip's but not to the National Church program.

Since quite a few St. Philippians as well as communicants of the other white Episcopal churches in Durham wished to do the same, their vestries faced a decision: should restricted pledges be accepted? At a crucial October meeting the Vestry of St. Philip's decided to request formally that Bishop Fraser and the Diocesan Executive Council consult the parish about any future grant application, but it refused to accept "restricted pledges" from any of its fellow parishioners.[84] Even though the vestries of St. Andrew's, St. Joseph's, St. Luke's, and

St. Stephen's accepted such pledges, the St. Philip's Vestry steadfastly
stayed on course through all the stormy and trying months ahead.[85]
The canvass concluded in December 1969 with 240 pledging units
contributing $72,340 and 85 units not pledging at all. This left a pro-
spective shortfall of $13,000.[86] The Vestry painfully trimmed expendi-
tures where it could and paid in full St. Philip's mandatory Diocesan
Maintenance quota of $4,450, but cut its payment on the Diocesan
Program Fund from $16,488 to $3,300.[87] As many parishes in the Diocese were doing the same, the Diocesan Executive Council perforce
reduced its contribution to the National Church from $186,375 (1969)
to $115,582 (1970).[88]

In the aftermath both GCSP staff and the Diocesan Council revised their procedures for screening a grant application so as to bring
local parishes into the process. Normal budgetary pledging and payment processes were smoothly resumed at all levels the following year.
Malcolm X Liberation University moved from Durham to Greensboro in 1971 and closed its doors in 1973. Howard Fuller returned to
his home in Milwaukee, where eventually he became superintendent
of public schools. Perhaps the most instructive conclusion on the trau-
matic episode was that drawn by Bishop Fraser in his address to the
Diocesan Convention on January 30, 1970:[89]

> I have never met or talked with Howard Fuller nor have I
> visited Malcolm X Liberation University. My personal opinion of
> Howard Fuller is that he is an educated, frustrated, visionary and
> angry Black. He is educated by hard work and sacrifice. He is
> frustrated and angry as a result of his experience with the white
> power structure. He is typical of an increasing number of black
> Americans. He has his counterpart in young, white America.
>
> Malcolm X Liberation University is an unrealistic experiment
> in education and has a dubious future, but it offers hope to some
> frustrated, angry Blacks. Isolationism or separatism, whether it be
> a new nation in Africa or white American isolationism, is a tired
> and worn-out concept of frustrated people. My Christian con-
> victions on these matters have been made clear to the Diocese of
> North Carolina for the past ten years. Segregation or separatism
> by class, social standing or race is sinful in the Christian family.
> Violence or war is the incarnation of evil. Either of these practices
> in human problem-solving by a Christian demands kneeling at

the foot of the cross and beating one's chest with the confession of *mea culpa*, my fault, my fault. Law and order are essential to a sane society, but there can be no sane society unless law and order are applied equally to all people. However, in all honesty I must say that in my opinion much of the noise about Malcolm X Liberation University is all out of proportion to the size of the grant, the school, and its possible influence. What this noise does, is to hide the real question facing the Christian, and that is whether he is willing to treat his fellowman as his brother.

But, good can be found in almost everything. The Malcolm X Liberation University grant has done the Diocese a Christian service. It has caused us to look at ourselves and what we have not done to solve race relations and to reconcile differences between people. We have been forced to look at our institutions and our parishes and to ask whom we serve. What does it really take to be a member of the Episcopal Church whether you are black or white? Forgiveness of sins? The desire to follow our Lord Jesus Christ? The services our institutions can render people? Or are we more concerned with background, money, and social position? Is the Gospel of Jesus Christ our constitution and by-laws or are we governed by what is comfortable and compatible to our own little in-group? In what direction is the thrust of our convictions? Or are we dying on the vine as the result of a parasitical existence on a tradition of which we boast but of which we are ill-informed? If the Malcolm X Liberation University grant accomplishes nothing else but force us to face honestly these questions, it will be worth ten times the anguish it has caused us. As a member of another communion has observed, "This may save the Episcopal Church in North Carolina."

A SELF-STUDY THAT IS WORTH CAREFUL STUDY

The five-person committee selected to direct the parish self-study did not include any member of the Establishment, the old families who had been with St. Philip's for more than a generation—the Carrs, the Erwins, the Powes, or the Ruffins, for example. Nor did it include any native North Carolinian. In fact, the majority were in background not even Southerners. Walter Mason, the chair, came from Chicago; Harold Parker, the secretary, from Cincinnati and Chicago; Dorothy

Manning, from Wisconsin; and Ruth Watson, from Kansas, Nebraska, and other midwestern states. Betty Hodges, the one Southerner, was a Virginian. They tackled their assigned task with zeal born of ignorance of the long-standing traditions and problems of St. Philip's and of the belief that thorough self-study and careful planning based on it could make a decisive difference. They brought talents developed in five diverse fields: business (Mason), university teaching and committee work (Parker), medicine (Manning), medical social work (Watson), and journalism (Hodges), but they shared a task-oriented, can-do philosophy. They became prophets of planning.

In constant consultation with the Vestry and with David Covell of the Strategic Research Service Group of the National Church and in communication with the congregation, the committee drew up in September 1970 a timetable for the preparation of the self-study report.[90] Marvel of marvels, the step-by-step schedule was adhered to and the deadlines were met:

October 1. Preparation by census districts of a table and a map of the location of each parishioner.

October 15. Tabulation from data already available of information about parishioners: their sex, age, dates of baptism and confirmation, length of time in St. Philip's, prior religious background, location of residence, time it took to reach church, type of home, education, country of birth.

November 1. Preparation of an Attitude Survey that would reveal through interlocking questions the concerns, ideas, and hopes of St. Philippians for their church.

November 8, 15. Administration of the Attitude Survey. After the 7:45 and 10:00 Sunday services parishioners were asked to retire to the parish hall and take twenty minutes to fill out the questionnaire; on the second Sunday afternoon the Self-Study Committee arranged with Victor Moore, chair of the Every Member Canvass, for the canvassers to take both a pledge card and an attitude questionnaire to those St. Philippians who had not pledged; the result was that 305 parishioners (67.7 percent of the congregation) completed the questionnaire. (See Appendix M for Letters of Walter Mason to the Congregation.)

November 9–10. David Covell spent two days in Durham visiting selected St. Philippians, clergymen of other denominations, and city planners; he also made himself available for three hours in a parish house office to any St. Philippian who wished to drop in.

November 15–December 15. Computer analysis of data on the computers of Walter Mason's firm, Home Security Life Insurance Company, and shipment to Covell.

January 16. Presentation by Covell of the report and of the Research Group's recommendations to the Vestry during a long Saturday afternoon session and to the congregation the next day.

Concealed in this bare chronology are the hundreds of hours spent by the committee and especially by Walter Mason and Dorothy Manning in the assembly, analysis, and presentation of data. As Bollinger observed, the result was that "St. Philip's probably had more trustworthy information available about itself than any other parish of the Episcopal Church." [91]

The opening profile of the characteristics of the congregation reveals little not already known to the readers of that history, but it has the merit of offering statistical confirmation. St. Philip's was not a neighborhood church but a metropolitan one. Of its 727 baptized members, only 19 (2.6 percent) resided within the three census districts that formed an area in which the church was located—an area now occupied by buildings devoted to commercial uses and by rundown rooming houses slated for demolition. Other members were dispersed throughout the predominantly white census tracts of Durham city and county, but with a concentration in three fine residential sections: Trinity Park, Watts Hospital, 106 members (14.6 percent); Morehead Heights, Forest Hills, Rockwood, 166 members (22.7 percent); and Hope Valley, 184 members (25.3 percent), for a total of 456 members (62.6 percent). In fact, only 2 percent of the congregation lived within one mile of the church. The rest were distributed thusly: 1–1.9 miles, 16 percent; 2–2.9 miles, 26 percent; 3–4.9 miles, 29 percent; 5–9.9 miles, 22 percent; and 10 miles or more, 5 percent. This was a far cry from the situation existing from 1880 to 1920, when the flock clustered within a few blocks of the church, an easy walking distance. It presented problems of developing other means of attracting and holding a congregation than neighborhood propinquity.

During Bollinger's first three years the number of baptized persons had increased from 676 in 1967 to 727 in 1969, the number of communicants from 489 to 561, and the average Sunday attendance from 360 to 461. Statistically all the membership figures were positive.

Of the 305 respondents to the questionnaire, 43 percent were male and 57 percent female; 23 percent were under twenty years of age, 21 percent aged 20 to 39, 34 percent aged 40 to 59, and 22 percent aged 60 and over. Thus the distribution was somewhat biased in favor of women and of older members of the congregation. Further:

> The socioeconomic status of St. Philip's congregation was remarkably high. Over ¾ of the adult members were college graduates, and the vast majority of employed persons were in professional and managerial positions. The median family income was over $15,000. Thus the educational, income, and occupational levels of the congregation were considerably higher than national and state averages.
>
> St. Philip's was composed predominantly of long-term members. The most frequent reason adult parishioners gave for attending St. Philip's was that their family had attended. Two-thirds of the adult parishioners said they had been members for 10 years or more. Two-fifths had been members for 20 years or more.
>
> Most of St. Philip's parishioners were residentially stable. Of the congregation, 19 percent had lived in the area for over 3 years. Three-fourths had lived in the area at least 10 years, and over half for 20 years or more.[92]

What was passing through the minds of this relatively stable, affluent congregation with respect to the church's program, present and prospective, and to its leaders? The Attitude Survey provides a few clues. The average attendance at the three worship services, 63.1 percent of baptized persons, suggests a reasonable satisfaction with Sunday worship. But a storm was brewing over experimentation with the liturgy, as the Trial Use ordered by the National Church went into operation. When asked whether St. Philip's should experiment with different forms of liturgical worship, 39 percent of the respondents said yes, 39 percent said no and were very vocal in their opposition, and 22 percent were undecided. In view of the fifty-fifty division and the strength of traditionalist feeling, Covell suggested that "perhaps parishioners should be given the option of participation in new forms of worship." Certainly a period of discussion and education was called for.

The congregation's Church School was another focus of study, comment, and recommendation. In 1969, 166 students were enrolled in classes, ranging from three-year-olds to eleventh- and twelfth-graders. On given Sundays attendance extended from a low of 58 (34.9 percent) to a high of 124 (74.7 percent), for a yearly average of 56.6 percent. But since it was difficult to hold students after they were confirmed at age twelve, it was obvious that attendance was a serious problem only in grades seven through twelve.

The enrollment figures were congruent with the opinions of young people about Church School: 55 percent of the respondents aged eighteen years and younger found Church School interesting, 52 percent thought the classwork was meaningful, and 55 percent believed the teachers knew their subject; 67 percent felt free to express their opinion on any subject under discussion, and 78 percent felt welcome. On the other hand, a sizable minority was dissatisfied: 29 percent did not think the classes were interesting, 20 percent found them meaningless, and 12 percent thought the teachers did not know their subject; 21 percent did not feel free to express their opinion. The size of that minority, it was said, should be a cause of concern to every Church School teacher and administrator. Margaret Davis and her associates in preschool classes, as well as Ethel Reade and her teachers in the first six grades, were commended for designing local curricula. They, at least, were holding their own on attendance. But what measures would be taken for the teenagers, grades seven to twelve? Obviously it was necessary to recruit a stable band of dedicated teachers and train them. Parents must be enlisted in support. More adequate classrooms would have to be built. And the curriculum, too, must be improved. But in what direction? Here a generation gap in opinions became apparent:

One-fourth of the youth would like more discussions about the Bible, Church history, and Church teachings, while almost three-fourths of the adults want children and youth to have more discussions of those topics. Of the youth 58 percent would like more discussions about social and political issues such as civil rights, poverty, the war in Vietnam, and politics, in comparison with only 34 percent of the adults. Among the youth, 55 percent want more instruction about personal and family matters such as Christian morals, my life in school, my relations with my parents, sex, and how to live as a Christian in my community, while 81 percent of the adults wish this discussion for their children.

The conclusion was reached that the youth should not only be drawn into curriculum planning but should also have an influential voice in the formulation of all youth programs—a revolutionary thought in those days but consonant with the spirit and movement of the times.

A similar approach was recommended for strengthening the rather small Sunday adult education class: to ask its members and other parishioners what topics they would like to study and discuss. One hundred of the 205 respondents mentioned three subjects: Bible study, Christianity and family life, and Christianity and social problems. The Self-Study Committee thus revealed a market, so to speak, for the Adult Education Committee to explore.

The self-study confirmed another division of the congregation already registered in this history, between parish officials—those who had served on the Vestry and as heads of major parish organizations and who "ran" the church—and other parishioners. For six years, ever since Bart Sherman had returned from the College of Preachers with his master plan, parish officials had talked and talked of the need for repair and renovation of the physical plant, for expansion of facilities through the purchase of adjoining property and the erection of a multi-purpose building on it, and for a capital funds drive to raise money for these projects. A poll conducted by the Self-Study Committee confirmed that while the parish officials had converted themselves, they had had less influence on the rest of the congregation. Seventy-eight percent of the parish officials thought the facilities should be repaired and/or renovated, but only 47 percent of the nonofficials were of the same opinion. These figures presaged trouble if and when a drive was held. The need for leaders who would maintain contact with the congregation, educate it, and *act* was obvious.

This situation led to the question of leadership at St. Philip's. The local Self-Study Committee identified the major leadership problems as "lack of unity, lack of mission or goals as a downtown church, and inability to reach decisions." The Strategic Research Services Group warned that when decisions were made, "the principle of participatory democracy should be utilized so that all the People of God at St. Philip's have a part in the decision-making process."

The polls indicated that a majority of the parishioners understood the challenges of the situation and would support responsive and responsible programs: 70 percent of the respondents thought programs should be more concerned with spiritual welfare; 65 percent believed programs should focus more on the community. Joint religious programs with other churches of the area were supported by 65 percent, joint community programs by 69 percent: "Community responsibility and involvement were of deep concern to the parish. As one respondent so ably put it: 'St. Philip's should make the most of its unique position as a downtown church to make itself servant to the needs of the transient, elderly, poor (black and white); to attempt wherever it can to bind together the community—not just the Christian community.'" Many parishioners recognized that spiritual renewal, sense of mission, community involvement, and expansion of facilities were intertwined. As one respondent said in reply to the question on "desirable changes in the next five years": "To remain here in the downtown area and renovate 'ourselves' as well as our facilities."

In their appraisal of the current leadership, the majority of the respondents gave high marks to the Vestry and even higher to Bollinger. On the question whether the Vestry and Bollinger were responsive to the needs and feelings of the parishioners, the respondents polled as follows:

	Vestry	Bollinger
Yes, very aware	18	39
Yes, somewhat aware	56	46
Not very aware	23	13
Not at all aware	3	2

It is interesting that when asked to rank in importance nine specific activities of a rector from 1 to 9, the respondent's priorities coincided with Bollinger's. All were agreed that conduct of worship services, counseling, and teaching were the most important functions of a rector. Parish administration, attendance at parish meetings, and office hours were less important. Participation in diocesan affairs ranked dead last.

However, the respondents felt that communications between the Vestry and the congregation should be improved. Also, a strong lay ministry should be developed. A majority expressed a willingness to participate in that development and to take on the challenges facing St. Philip's.

In order that this effort not spin its wheels futilely, the Strategic Research Services Group "underscored the need for effective strategic planning to cope, imaginatively and in a disciplined way, with the shifts in St. Philip's mission and ministry." It recommended that "the leadership of the congregation establish a strategic planning commission as an adjunct to the Vestry. . . . The *strategic planning process* implies immediate planning *and action*." The commission would first "develop a statement of purpose for the existence of the congregation. Second, it would establish a set of realistic long-term goals and short-term objectives designed to accomplish this purpose. And third, it would design the structure and/or pattern of organization which would be conducive to the most effective realization of the goals and objectives."

In transmitting the self-study report to the Vestry on January 20, 1971, Watts Carr, Jr., senior warden, issued a call for immediate action. "We must not waste time and allow the steam to go out of the momentum we have gained. . . . This is an opportunity we will not have again and we cannot afford to muff it."[93] Bollinger reinforced this call in his annual report to the congregational meeting on January 24: "As the Rev. David Covell pointed out, St. Philip's clearly has a great future. All the resources and potential are here—it is only for *us* to decide. . . . We all want action and I believe we are going to get it."[94]

ACTION

Several major consequences, seven to be precise, flowed from the information, analysis, and stimulus provided by the self-study process. One result, and not the least important, was the change of mood from the miasma of pessimism engendered by the Malcolm X controversy to an élan of can-do optimism.[95] The Vestry that had taken office on June 1, 1970 and continued at its post until June 1, 1971 began immediately in February 1971 to implement the recommendations of the self-study report. Their names should be noted because their actions constituted a turning point in the history of St. Philip's: Watts Carr, Jr. (senior warden), James K. Pleasants, Jr., Ralph Strayhorn, Richard L. Watson (secretary), Arch Bass, Jr., John Chatham, J. Harper Erwin, Jr., Priscilla McBryde, James L. Nicholson (junior warden), E. K. Powe, George C.

Pyne, and Warren Watkins. When the first four retired at the expiration of their three-year term on June 1, 1971, they were succeeded by Dorothy Manning (who became senior warden), Walter Mason (chair of the Self-Study Committee and of a newly formed Strategic Planning Committee), Harold Parker (secretary to the Self-Study Committee and now to the Vestry), and Victor Moore (chair of a successful Every Member Canvass that had enabled St. Philip's to resume payment of the General Program quota collected by the Diocese for the National Church).[96] The election in January 1971 of the first three of these who had been members of the Self-Study Committee can be construed as a congregational endorsement of the proposed program of action. The election of all four assured the continuance of reform.

At a special meeting on February 4, 1971 the Vestry followed the recommendation of the self-study report and established a Strategic Planning Committee. It was to be composed of the five members of the Self-Study Committee, who presumably now knew more about the subject of strategy than anyone else in the church; the Rector and senior warden ex officio; and three additional representatives of the parish to be chosen by the Strategic Planning Committee itself. At the next Vestry meeting, on February 11, the committee reported that it had added to its membership C. E. McCauley, Carolyn London, and Mary Lewis Pyne,[97] the daughter of George and Mary Pyne.

Losing no time, Walter Mason presented to the Vestry on March 11 a draft statement of "purpose" of the parish, prepared by the committee in accord with the recommendations of the self-study report:

> The purpose of St. Philip's is to bring together all sorts of persons in the worship of God and in Christian fellowship with each other through a ministry of teaching, reconciliation, and service.
>
> Worship, teaching, reconciliation, and Christian fellowship are on-going elements of our purpose which we have always had or we would not have survived for ninety years. Their inclusion in a statement of purpose should reassure the 179 people who agreed that the "programs of St. Philip's should be more concerned with the spiritual welfare of parishioners" of the Church's continuing intent.
>
> "All sorts of persons" means not just present St. Philippians, whom Covell characterized as a remarkably high socio-economic group, but literally what it says. This phrase, plus "service," would

bring within the purpose the means of satisfying those parishioners who believe we should be more concerned with the community.

This statement of purpose is deliberately couched in general terms. Like a corporate charter, it attempts to establish parameters within which we would operate. What we would do within those parameters would constitute our program.

In commenting on the draft, several members of the Vestry complimented the Strategic Planning Committee on its "industry and on the comprehensiveness, sensitivity, yet withal brevity of the statement."[98] It was accepted by the Vestry without amendment or dissent.

Meanwhile, the Vestry approved (February 4, 11, March 11) the staging of a capital funds drive to raise money for the purchase of the quarter of the city block adjoining the parish house and church (estimated cost, $55,000), for the renovation of church and parish house ($45,000–$55,000), and for the erection of a multipurpose, prefabricated Butler-type building ($50,000–$75,000) that might incorporate food services, suppers, meetings, games, movies, meetings for local groups, bazaars, and Boy Scout activities. The goal of the campaign was set at $175,000. William H. Ruffin, a veteran campaigner, agreed to serve as chair of the Capital Funds Committee.[99] In July, when he left Durham for the summer, John Chatham as vice-chair took over his duties.[100] The amount actually raised, $110,000, confirmed the accuracy of the statistics gathered by the Self-Study Committee: the majority of the congregation would support a capital funds drive to raise money for the acquisition of land and renovation of the physical plant; they were lukewarm to the proposed erection of a multipurpose building. The rather drab, mechanical appearance of the proposed Butler-type building may have been a factor as well.

Nevertheless, with the pledged $110,000 to be paid within three years the Vestry proceeded with the purchase of the land, negotiated by Watts Carr, Jr., and E. K. Powe, and with renovation of the church and parish house directed by a Building Committee chaired by Dorothy Manning with R. W. Carr as supervising architect. The process of repair and renovation went on and on and on. The physical plant was far more dilapidated than anyone had anticipated. The red-carpeted wooden floor of the chancel, for example, was so eaten into by termites that worshipers kneeling at the altar rail were at risk of crashing through to the basement! The Building Committee, with the Vestry's continuing approval, eventually spent more than the $110,000 raised by the Capital Funds Campaign. This meant that the church had to incur a debt of $60,000 to finance the acquisition of the land, a debt that was cleared in 1975 by a second drive, the Campaign for Progress.

Concurrently, following the recommendation of the self-study report, Bollinger, the Vestry, and Walter Mason as chair of the Strategic Planning Committee were together restructuring the administration of St. Philip's. This came in several steps. The first, which passed almost unnoticed at the time, was to appoint the choirmaster, William Miller, administrative assistant to the Rector. He was to supervise the sexton in the daily performance of his duties and to deal with daily problems and emergencies of maintenance.[101] He thus freed the Rector for his essential functions of worship, counseling, and teaching. The auxiliary appointment also enabled the Vestry to increase the pay of the choirmaster and thus retain a person of high quality.

The second step was to form an Administrative Committee composed of the Rector, the senior warden, the junior warden, and the secretary of the Vestry. The secretary to the Rector, the Assistant Rector, and the choirmaster usually attended its monthly meetings. The function of this committee was to keep the Vestry up to the mark and to keep things moving. Historically, the Vestries at St. Philip's had sometimes been dilatory—had talked too much, postponed decision, and tried to micromanage every last detail of execution, only in the end to fail to follow up and make certain that the decision had in fact been implemented.[102] The Administrative Committee met at least once a month, a few days before the regular monthly Vestry meeting, to check on the execution of the Vestry's prior decisions and to recommend further legislation and action by the Vestry. The Administrative Committee never acted without prior Vestry authorization, although it was often sorely tempted to do so.

The third step was an ad hoc, temporary arrangement of committees to handle the repair/renovation of the physical plant and the acquisition of the land. A Phase I Committee eventually was formed to supervise repair/renovation. It was soon merged with the Administrative Committee to form a Building Committee, chaired by Dorothy Manning, which met twice a month. A Phase II Committee, composed of Watts Carr and E. K. Powe, negotiated the purchase of the land. Both committees were committees of the Vestry, to which they

reported monthly. One key to the smooth operation of this arrangement was that for three years, from June 1, 1971 to June 1, 1974, the
secretary to the Vestry, the secretary to the Administrative Committee, and the secretary to the Building Committee was the same person,
who happened to be Harold Parker, a professional historian. During
the preceding three years his predecessor as secretary to the Vestry had
been Richard L. Watson, another professional historian. Watson had
set the tradition, which Parker followed, of consciously writing the
type of minutes that would be useful to the unknown future historian
of St. Philip's, that is, a record not simply of decisions but also of the
discussions that led to them. After several interruptions that tradition
was resumed and nobly maintained by Gert Embree, permanent secretary to the Vestry during the rectorship of Bollinger's successor, the
Reverend C. Thomas Midyette III. Meanwhile, during Parker's tenure
his detailed minutes had the practical advantage of giving the Vestry,
the Administrative Committee, and the Building Committee up-to-
the-moment summaries of each other's actions and of the rationale
behind them. The interlocking membership of the three bodies and
the ability of the people involved were also factors in the smooth functioning of a complicated operation.

The fourth administrative step, initiated largely by Bollinger and
Walter Mason, was a permanent restructuring of the administration of
St. Philip's. In accord with the recommendations of the self-study report, the Strategic Planning Committee formed a Subcommittee on
Lay Ministry (chaired by Angus McBryde) and another on Community Action (chaired by James E. Davis) to prepare a list of goals, objectives, and implementing committees in their respective areas of concern.[103] A Subcommittee on Christian Education was not appointed,
since that department was already conducting its own in-house review,
evaluation, and planning.

The Lay Ministry report, submitted in December 1971, gave a
broad, informative picture of the situation in St. Philip's in that area
at that time. It commended the following lay activities "as being well
handled. They needed only to be continued in the present manner:
Lay Readers, Altar Guild, Daughters of the King, Choirs, Visitation
of shut-ins, Driving of older people (more especially Senior Citizens
at Oldham Towers), Cooking." (It might have well included the ster-
ling achievements of the Episcopal Church Women.) The report also
certified that ecumenical relations had best be left to the Center City

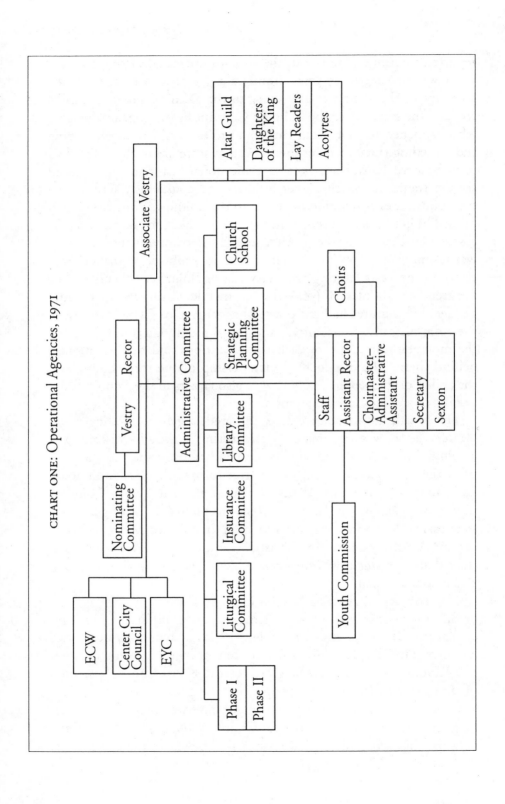

CHART ONE: Operational Agencies, 1971

Church Council, on which St. Philip's was represented, and that counseling, including counseling of alcoholics and drug addicts, was the function of the Rector. In fact, Bollinger was spending twenty to forty hours each week doing just that. However, the report continued, there were certain delinquent areas that badly needed the attention of a lay committee: an Outreach Committee to revive the organization of parishioners into ten or eleven neighborhood groups, who would welcome newcomers, visit the sick, and help each other in emergencies; a Youth Action Committee to discover why junior and senior high schoolers were not attending Sunday School and EYC, and to propose remedies; a Lay*men*'s organization, including a Junior Warden's Committee of men to work with their hands on church property; and, finally, an overall Lay Ministry Committee to identify, classify, and recruit lay talent and to catalyze and coordinate lay activities.

The report of the Community Action Subcommittee, submitted to the Vestry in March 1971, is missing from the parish archives. But judging from what happened next (always a hazardous procedure), the report endorsed the membership of St. Philip's in the Center City Church Council, founded by Bollinger and Bill Quick (Trinity Methodist) in 1969. Probably the report also approved the decisions of the Vestry in May 1971 to appropriate $350 as an annual contribution to the council and to authorize Bollinger to appoint three lay St. Philippians to it. (He named Arch Bass, Jr., John Chatham, and Julia Royall.) Finally, the report may have suggested that these three delegates might concurrently serve on a permanent parish Community Action Committee, thus significantly linking parish action with broader interdenominational involvement in meeting the needs of downtown Durham.

On the basis of these two subcommittee reports and of their own cooperative analysis, Bollinger and Mason submitted to a special meeting of the Vestry on May 7, 1971 two charts: one showing the somewhat diffuse collection of operational agencies that constituted the existing executive arrangements (see Chart I) and the other presenting the proposed clear-cut organization of planning and executive departments (see Chart II and Appendix N). Two minor amendments were suggested by James L. Nicholson, that "(1) the proposed Fine Arts and Memorials Committee be divided into two, the Memorials function to be re-entitled the Property and Memorials Committee in the Administrative Department, and the Fine Arts Function being given to a Fine Arts Committee in the Worship Department, and (2) that the Evaluation Committee be a Planning and Evaluation Committee." Upon a motion by John Chatham, seconded by Mason, the Vestry unanimously approved the reorganization thus amended.[104]

Bart Sherman's pioneer commissions, a major breakthrough, had been *study and planning* commissions to prepare recommendations for Vestry action. Bollinger's and Mason's departments were *planning and action* program departments. Every August each department was to prepare a plan and budget needs for the year, to be reviewed by the Vestry. During the year each department and its committees would implement its plan and, the following summer, prepare an evaluation report on its performance as well as a plan for the succeeding year, both to be reviewed by the Vestry. The departments were thus held accountable. The Vestry would supervise the total program of the church, while being freed from micromanaging the details of its implementation. And Bollinger had, for the first time, the ideal, totally engaged Vestry that he had dreamed of in 1963 and had tried forcibly to install in 1968. Throughout his rectorship he was persevering in seeking to achieve his major goals, though sometimes wavering in day-to-day operations.

At the crucial May 7 Vestry meeting Mason also presented a list of existing Vestry policies, which he had compiled from the Vestry minutes since 1962, along with an ideal list of twenty-seven items on which the Vestry *should* have policies in writing. These would serve as "ground rules within which the Vestry and its Executive Committee can operate."[105] Upon the authorization of the Vestry he then singlehandedly prepared a lucid statement of each policy and secured its enactment by the Vestry, month by month until the task was completed in May 1973. For the first time in its history, St. Philip's had a clear code of the major policies under which its Vestry was conducting its business. Without that reference list the Vestry was "doomed to deciding many issues time after time with possible inconsistencies."

Development of a statement of purpose and a definition of goals and objectives, the launching of a capital funds drive, purchase of land, completion of wholesale repair and renovation, restructuring of administration, and codification of Vestry policies were in themselves actions. They also provided the guidelines, the organizational framework, the agencies, the material means, and the impetus for further actions. Let us consider a few.

Following the new script, all the members of the major program departments—Administrative, Lay Ministry, Parish Education, Community Action, and Worship—met from three to five o'clock, Sunday afternoon, September 10, 1972, in the upstairs assembly room. Seating was arranged according to the organization chart by departments (Chart II) so that everyone could visualize the structure and how they fitted into it. Each department gave a statement of its plans, goals, and needs for 1972–73. All persons involved in programs, including the Rector, Vestry, and Vestry Associates, thus obtained a total view of the situation (Chart III). Departments shared ideas on how they could help each other, and the Rector and Vestry added information and ideas on how they too might function and act within each program area.[106] The reports then became a basis for the preparation of the preliminary budget in November.

During the next summer this annual planning process was reaffirmed and strengthened. On June 1, 1973 all departments submitted substantial evaluations of their performance in the light of their goals and objectives, and they projected their plans and needs for the coming year. On Sunday afternoon, June 10, from half-past noon until three o'clock the Vestry met with each department separately and went over its report. Later, on the basis of the information thus gathered, the Vestry prepared a coordinated plan and a preliminary budget.[107] This planning process, repeated in 1974, was for a time a very useful feature of Bollinger's rectorship. The midyear departmental reports plus those made each January to the congregation enable us to follow the developing action in each area.

The Worship Department (Acolytes, Altar Guild, Fine Arts Committee, Liturgical Committee, Lay Readers, Music Organization, Ushers), chaired by Richard L. Watson, led the congregation through the shoals of the Trial Liturgy. Back in December 1970 Bollinger had appointed a Worship Committee, also chaired by Watson.[108] In an empowering orientation statement he explained to the committee why Prayer Book revision was needed: first, to bring the eucharistic service closer to the liturgy of the early Church, which emphasized the corporate "we" of a worshiping community rather than the individualizing "I" of a single believer; second, to align the liturgy with the discoveries of modern biblical and patristic research stressing that Christ is the real priest at the Eucharist and that "sacrifice" is the key word in the

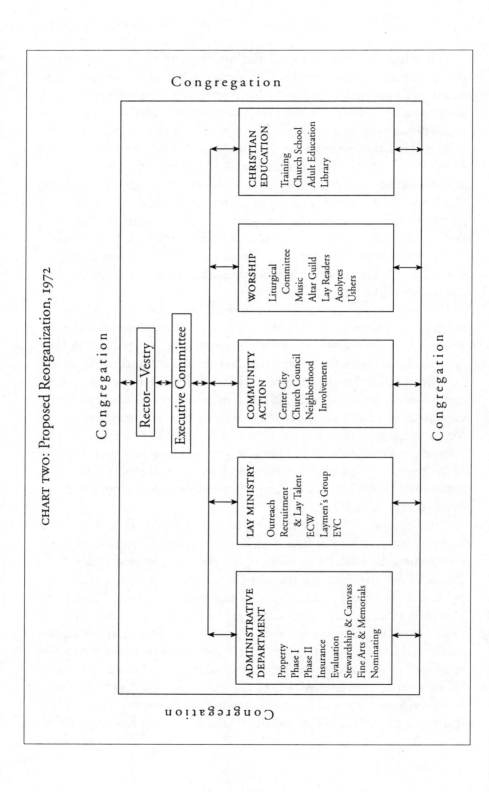

CHART TWO: Proposed Reorganization, 1972

Congregation

Congregation

Congregation

Congregation

Rector—Vestry

Executive Committee

ADMINISTRATIVE DEPARTMENT

Property
Phase I
Phase II
Insurance
Evaluation
Stewardship & Canvass
Fine Arts & Memorials
Nominating

LAY MINISTRY

Outreach
Recruitment & Lay Talent
ECW
Laymen's Group
EYC

COMMUNITY ACTION

Center City
Church Council
Neighborhood
Involvement

WORSHIP

Liturgical Committee
Music
Altar Guild
Lay Readers
Acolytes
Ushers

CHRISTIAN EDUCATION

Training
Church School
Adult Education
Library

CHART THREE: A Congregation in Action:
Representative Personnel, 1972

Executive Committee
Eugene Bollinger, Rector
Victor Moore, Senior
  Warden
Abbott Lloyd, Junior
  Warden
Harold Parker, Secretary
A. L. Featherston, Treasurer

Vestry
Arch Bass, Jr.
Mrs. I. H. Manning
Walter Mason
James L. Nicholson
E. K. Powe

George C. Pyne
Dr. James E. Davis
C. E. McCauley
Mrs. Edwin Hamshar

ADMINISTRATIVE
DEPARTMENT

C. E. McCauley, Gen.
  Chm.

Property and Memorials
Abbott Lloyd, Chm.
Mrs. Watts Carr, Jr.
Insurance
Mr. John Chatham

Building Committee
Mrs. I. H. Manning, Chm.
C. E. McCauley
James Nicholson
George Pyne
Mrs. Angus McBryde
Warren Watkins
Watts Carr, Jr.
James Pleasants
R. W. Carr (architect)
Dr. Harold Parker

Phase II
E. K. Powe
Watts Carr, Jr.

Planning and Evaluation
Walter Mason

Stewardship and Canvass
Frank Gray, Chm.
William B. Jennings, Jr.,
  Co-Chm.
Victor Moore
Arch Bass, Jr.
John Chatham

LAY MINISTRY
DEPARTMENT

Dr. Angus McBryde, Gen.
  Chm.
Mrs. George Pyne
Dr. Norman Ross
Mr. John Chatham
Mr. and Mrs. James Warren

COMMUNITY
ACTION
DEPARTMENT

Mr. Arch Bass, Jr.
Mr. John Chatham
Mrs. Kenneth Royall

WORSHIP
DEPARTMENT

Dr. Richard Watson, Gen.
  Chm.

Liturgical Commission
Wayne Williams
Ethel Reade
Polly Graham
Ruth Bollinger
Mary Lewis Pyne
Priscilla McBryde
Cathy Bollinger
Kent Otto
Francis Newton
Dr. W. H. Willis
W. L. D. Townsend

Altar Guild
Mrs. A. L. Jernigan, Chm.
Mrs. Blaine Nashold,
  Co-Chm.
Mrs. Edwin Bryson
Mrs. R. B. Boyd
Mrs. Goode Broughton
Mrs. John Cahoon, Jr.
Mrs. Watts Carr, Jr.
Mrs. Clarence Cobb
Mrs. R. B. Cooke
Mrs. H. C. Cunningham
Mrs. Charles Dilts
Mrs. A. H. Graham, Jr.
Mrs. Frank Hall
Mrs. Edward Hedgpeth
Miss Florrie Jones

Mrs. John R. Locke
Mrs. C. L. May, Jr.
Mrs. Francis Newton
Miss Ethel Reade
Mrs. Kenneth Royall, Jr.
Mrs. William H. Ruffin
Mrs. Charles L. Steel
Mrs. W. B. Watkins
Mrs. Wayne Williams

Fine Arts
George C. Pyne

Ushers
Mike Troy

Lay Readers
Arch Bass, Jr.
Dr. James E. Davis
A. L. Featherston
Thomas H. Hampton
Abbott Lloyd
Victor Moore
James L. Nicholson
Dr. Harold Parker
E. K. Powe
Charles Steel
Mike Troy
Dr. W. H. Willis

Acolytes
W. L. D. Townsend, Chm.
Lewis Bass
Perry Black
Ricky Black
Bill Boineau
David Bollinger
Ross Carr
Richard Featherston
Tommy Hampton, Jr.
Louis Hodges
Charles Mason

Eric Nicholson
Nicky Nicholson
Bruce Olive
Crawford Parrish
Bill Scott
Tommy Scott
John Steel
Doug Townsend
Bill Warren
Bobby Westrook

ASSOCIATE VESTRY

Mrs. Thomas H. Hampton
Mrs. Blaine S. Nashold
William B. Jennings, Jr.
Dr. David Robinson

EDUCATION DEPARTMENT

CHURCH SCHOOL
C. L. May, Gen. Chm.

Pre-school Division
Mrs. James E. Davis, Chm.
Mrs. John Cahoon
Mrs. Abbott Lloyd
Mrs. Victor Moore
George Pyne
Victor Moore
W. L. D. Townsend
Mrs. Walter Mason

Children's Division
Miss Ethel Reade, Chm.
Mrs. Gertrude Embree
Mrs. Eloise Weiker
Mrs. Barbara Boineau
Mrs. Barrie Wallace
Miss Sara Draper

Mrs. Mina Hampton
Mrs. Sheila Kendrick

Youth Division
Dr. Harold Parker, Chm.
Thomas H. Hampton
Mrs. A. L. Featherston
The Rector

Adult Division
Mrs. Edwin Hamshar,
    Chm.
Dr. David Robinson
Mrs. Angus McBryde
Mrs. Richard Giannini
Dr. Grover Hunter
Dr. Harold Parker

Library Committee
Miss Sara Draper
Miss Louise Kaufman
Mr. Kent Otto
Dr. Harold Parker

YOUTH ACTION COMMITTEE

Mrs. Thomas Hampton,
    Chm.
Thomas H. Hampton
Charlotte Hampton
Tommy Hampton, Jr.
Dr. Harold Parker
Eugene Bollinger
David Bollinger
Amy Anderson
Denise Chatham
Sara Nashold
Kathy Moore
Bill Boineau
John Steel

ceremony; and third, to express the liturgy in modern, understandable English that would enable the Church to carry its mission to unbelievers.[109]

The Worship Committee took Bollinger's message to the congregation in open educational sessions. On the advice of its successor, the Liturgical Committee, Bollinger in the spring of 1972 conducted the worship service according to Trial Use I during nine Sundays in pre-Lent, Lent, and Easter, and according to Trial Use II during eight post-Easter Sundays. Each Sunday he led the congregation "through the service, with short explanations of each portion."[110]

Despite the sensible, educational approach of Bollinger and the Liturgical Committee, the congregation still remained evenly divided, 49 percent in favor of Prayer Book revision, 49 percent opposed, and only 2 percent undecided. Other Episcopal congregations were being torn asunder by the slow process of revision. St. Philippians remained together in their joint endeavors, but many individual worshipers who clung to the old ways were inwardly torn up. They were among the most devout worshipers and active church workers in the parish. They loved God, the Episcopal Church, St. Philip's, and the Prayer Book of 1928 to the deepest level of their being. Any proposed change was gut-wrenching and provoked anger, rage, and fury. The process of "consulting the congregations," they thought, was a charade, a deceptive pretense of concern, a sly maneuver of New York liberal intellectuals to slip a radical change in theology past the men and women in the pews who formed the substance and strength of the Episcopal Church.[111] As it appeared that the General Convention in 1976 and 1979 was indeed approving the revised Prayer Book, their rage and outcries became vehement.

Although Bollinger officially and pastorally and diplomatically took the stance of education and mediation, he personally preferred the revised version. On retreats where he was freer to select the service, he almost always chose the more innovative Rite II and emotionally and visibly savored its eucharistic prayer. His personal preference afforded another reason for his intractable opponents within the congregation to dislike and even to hate him.

Because musical organization was within the purview of the Worship Department, it was natural that when William Miller resigned in June 1972 as choirmaster and administrative assistant to the Rector, Watson should serve as chair of the Search Committee to find his successor.[112] It recommended Kent Otto, who in July accepted the post at a salary of $7,000. Born in St. Louis, he had graduated from Indiana University with a B.A. in organ performance. He had gone on to graduate work at the University of Oklahoma, where he served as a teaching graduate assistant and obtained a Master's degree in music, again with a specialty in organ. Putting his training and knowledge to practical use, he had concurrently played the organ in the church of St. John's Parish. Participation in ROTC qualified him for a captaincy in the Signal Corps and three years' service in Germany, where he was able to continue to study and play the organ. Upon his return to postgraduate work at Indiana University, he became director of music of the First Presbyterian Church in Bloomington. By his training, knowledge of theory, and practical experience as well as by his personal qualities he was amply qualified for the position at St. Philip's.[113] There, rectors have come and gone, senior wardens, junior wardens, and sextons have come and gone, and so have vestrymen, but, Thank the Lord, Kent Otto has continued on and on and on. At present writing (1995) he has served longer than any other official. During Bollinger's tenure he and his wife, Pam, kept the three choirs, Children, Youth, and Adult, to their usual high standard of excellence. In addition, they introduced in December 1973 the fabulously successful Madrigal Dinners, which became a glorious Christmas tradition at St. Philip's.[114]

At the same time Bollinger increased the number of lay readers and intensified their training. Ever since Bart Sherman's time, three parishioners, Arch Bass, Jr., Watts Carr, Jr., and James L, Nicholson, had passed the chalice, and six or seven lay readers had been available to read the lessons during Sunday services. In 1973 Bollinger tripled the number of lay readers, including along the way several women. Then, during the summer of 1973, following a model brought in by Harold Parker from the Church of the Redeemer in Cincinnati, he conducted a mini-college for lay readers. In several hour-long sessions, he taught them basic Church doctrine, Church history, articulate, communicative reading (homiletics), and the practical performance of all the details of the liturgy except the consecration of the Host, which by Episcopal canon was reserved to the clergy.[115] This training increased the efficiency of lay participation in the service. In addition, it paid off later. During the interim seven months between Bollinger's resignation and the arrival of his successor, St. Philip's was able to decline Bishop Fraser's offer of an interim priest and to conduct its own Sunday worship, aided by Barney Hawkins, a lay pastoral assistant, and when necessary paying a priest to consecrate the Host. And, of course, it goes almost without saying, the congregation could also count on the quiet, dedicated devotion and efficient service of the women of the Altar Guild.

The chair of the newly organized Education Department was Harold Parker. His deliberate policy was not to interfere with the success of the Preschool (ages 3, 4, and 5) and Children's (grades 1 to 6) Divisions, and to attend the meetings of those educational committees working in areas that had problems—Youth (grades 7 to 12), Adult Education, and Library.[116]

The Education Department early formulated and each September reaffirmed its statement of purpose:

> Through its several programs the Department attempts to foster the spiritual growth and Christian maturity of the members of the congregation from pre-school age into the adult years. Jesus Christ offered a life and a theology of infinite simplicity and infinite depth. In a sense, once a person has made a decision for Jesus Christ, he or she is a Christian for life; however, to work out what that commitment means in the face of the recalcitrant realities of existence is the adventure of a lifetime. The goal of spiritual growth in a Christian community is in St. Paul: "Till we all come in the unity of the faith, and of the knowledge of the Son of God, unto a perfect man, unto the measure of the stature of the fullness of Christ." (Ephesians 4:13) The Christian Education Department is a band of faithful teachers and workers who are dedicated to this goal of fostering spiritual growth.

In the Preschool Division Margaret Davis, George Pyne, and their associates continued to work their magic of creating a loving, caring Christian community of the very young. "The children became familiar with the Episcopal Service by opening each Sunday with a simplified worship service from the Book of Common Prayer. Through various media which include stories, dramatics, art, and visual aids the children were introduced to the wonderful stories of the Old Testament (in the fall) and the New Testament (from Advent on)."

In the Children's Division Ethel Reade recruited an able band of teachers, including, over the years, Gert Embree and Mina Hampton. Taking as a guide Ronald Goldman's *Readiness for Religion: A Basis for Developmental Christian Education* (Seabury Press, 1968), Bollinger elaborated a bulky (87 pages, elite type, single-spaced) set of objectives for the elementary grades. Ethel Reade and her teachers, using modern media devices, then designed a curriculum to meet those objectives.[117] Bollinger himself taught the children of confirmation age in the sixth grade.

Attendance statistics were kept and tabulated each Sunday by C. L. May, who was also indispensably in charge of audiovisual equipment. Attendance in the Preschool and Children's Divisions was a respectable 60 percent of enrollment.

In the Youth Division Parker and Pat Robinson, a vibrant convert from the Roman Catholic Church, for two years led eight to ten junior high schoolers in individual and group meditation and prayer on the life of Jesus Christ. The group formed only 30 percent of enrollment, but they became so spiritually involved that they even requested the continuance of Sunday School during the summer! Among senior high schoolers, despite the strenuous efforts of several of the finest and most dedicated teachers and parents, attendance remained a lamentable 10 percent.

When Bollinger announced in September 1972 that there would be next Sunday an Adult Education Class, four people showed up: Bollinger and Parker ex officio, and Dr. Norman and Marjorie Ross. But then Bollinger made another of his discoveries—Emmy Lou Hamshar. Monday night after Monday night, in her family room, she held a small committee (Grover Hunter, Priscilla McBryde, David Robinson, and the ubiquitous Parker) with a single question: what do we do next Sunday? The committee soon learned to choose a single theme for four weeks or a semester (let us say, the relation of Christian commitment to life in the family, or in one's occupation, or in meditation and prayer). Discussions on Sunday became active, and attendance soared to a constant thirty-five.

For decades David Yates, Clarence Haden, Tom Turney Edwards, Bart Sherman, Albert Nelius, and now Gene Bollinger had fostered the development of an excellent parish library. Numbering about four hundred books on religious subjects by the 1970s, it had outgrown its rather simple, home-grown cataloguing system. So, singlehandedly, Sara Draper, a graduate student in psychology at Duke University, classified and labeled each book by a modified Dewey Decimal System and typed a new card catalogue. At the same time Louise Kaufmann was recording in her apartment nearly two hundred cassette tapes of sermons and conferences on spiritual subjects, which were placed in the parish library. The unresolved problem was how to persuade members of the congregation to use the books and tapes.

On the organization chart the Youth Action Committee (chiefly EYC) was placed in the Lay Ministry Department, but in personnel, functions, and activities it was tied in with the Education Department and can best be discussed here. A fallout from the Malcolm X affair and the consequent decline in revenue had been the elimination of the position of a full-time Assistant Rector, and hence, to the regret of every parishioner, the forced retirement of Bill Wells after December 31, 1969. Succeeding assistants, usually part-time, were too transient to be effective counselors of EYC, which was allowed to drift in programless sessions without adult guidance. Attendance at the Sunday evening meetings declined, until by the spring of 1972 only five or six young St. Philippians and three or four of their high school friends from other denominations were present. In the spreading drug culture among adolescents, there was the ever-present danger that St. Philippian youth might be persuaded by their peers to experiment with marijuana and LSD unless the positive alternative of Christian living and service were attractively offered.

In response to the situation and to Bollinger's initiative, the Youth Action Committee was formed in April 1972 with Mina Hampton as chair. Composed of representative staff (Bollinger or his assistant), interested adults (Parker and representative parents such as the Hamptons, the Frank Bordens, the McCauleys, and Irene Nashold), and young people, it continued throughout Bollinger's rectorship. Sometimes in the foreground, sometimes in the background, it recruited teachers for the junior and senior high classes, found adult counselors for EYC, and secured Vestry sponsorship of an active "Saints and Sinners Table Tennis Club" (president, David Hall; sergeant-at-arms, Denise Chatham; coach, M. M. Meredith). Under the friendly and concerned supervision of the committee and with the indispensable cooperation of the parents, EYC recovered and had several banner years, notably during the presidencies of Charlotte Hampton (1972–73) and Kathy Moore (1975–76). By the latter years attendance had reached a point that there could be two EYC's, a junior high and a senior high. Attendance at the senior high meetings was a consistent twenty-five; on special occasions the numbers reached as high as forty.

The program of fun and fellowship, projects and retreats came to be organized along four-week units: one Sunday night might be a party, as at a roller skating rink; another Sunday, a weekend retreat to Presbyterian Point at Kerr Lake; a third Sunday, a service visit entertaining the children at the Cerebral Palsy Hospital or the elderly at Hillcrest Haven; and a fourth Sunday, participation in the Sunday worship, even to the point of Ruthie Bollinger writing and delivering the sermon. To these activities were added several fundraising projects. A pancake supper, car wash, bake sale, and waiting on tables at the Madrigal Dinners provided funds that defrayed the cost of their activities. Participation in the CROP WALK-for-the Hungry and a twenty-four-hour Thanksgiving Fast raised $125 for Share Your Christmas. With counselors such as the Mark Featherstons and the John Markhams, Jr., "the activities were conducted and completed with a great feeling of satisfaction."[118]

Although attendance of youth at the Church School continued low, a more optimistic set of statistics was now maintained by the Education Department. It kept track of the number of young people who were participating in the four activities that in addition to worship were open to youth: Acolytes, Youth Choir, EYC, and Church School. More than 75 percent of the church's youth were taking part in at least one activity and quite a few in two. Participation in more than two was regarded as potentially counterproductive.

Following recommendations of the self-study, the Lay Ministry Department, chaired by Angus McBryde, set up the structure of a neighborhood organization and tried to match lay talent with opportunities in volunteer lay work. John Chatham spent endless hours placing parishioners (on paper) into eight neighborhood groups and finding a host family to chair each one. The theory was that these groups could "contact newcomers, visit the sick, and provide needed transportation to various Parish events. The neighborhood groups [it was thought] could be a splendid vehicle for personal lay contact in a variety of situations."[119] Chatham was bitterly disappointed when all his work came to nothing. Except for a few meetings in the first year here and there, nothing happened. He might have taken consolation in knowing that during the first century of St. Philip's history, neighborhood organizations, except for an express ad hoc purpose like the Every Member Canvass or Lenten study, had never taken root. They had quickly faded under Tom Turney Edwards and Bart Sherman and never were established under Bollinger. For some reason co-membership in St. Philip's and propinquity in location were not sufficient to bind parishioners into a local community effort.

Another division of the Lay Ministry, the Committee on Recruiting and Classification of Lay Talent, chaired by Mary Ann Warren, compiled from standing committee chairs a list of all positions needing volunteers. The list was sent to every parishioner with the request that interested people apply. Eighteen volunteered for specific jobs. Their names were passed on to appropriate committee chairs. A follow-up determined whether the chairs had indeed acted.[120] Newcomers were thus provided an easier entry into the work of the church, while the church became more attractive to them and benefited from the infusion of new energies and fresh ideas. A host of new people—for example, Richard and Anne Berkley, Sara Draper, Dwight and Pam Emory, John Isaacs, and David and Pat Robinson—contributed immediately to the church's strength. The congregation was more open than before.

The members of the Community Action Department, Arch Bass, Jr. (chair), John Chatham, and Julia Royall, also served as delegates with Bollinger to the Center City Church Council (CCCC). This council, it may be recalled, had been founded when on September 18, 1969 William K. Quick, Pastor of Trinity Methodist, and Bollinger, as Rector of St. Philip's, wrote letters to each other inquiring about the possibility of the four downtown churches "joining to do some things in Durham that we could not do alone." First Presbyterian and First Baptist soon joined. By January 1974 five other churches had been added to an interdenominational, interfaith, and interracial organization: Judea Reform Congregation, St. Mark's AME Zion Church, Bethany United Methodist Church, Calvary United Methodist Church, and the Catholic Church of the Immaculate Conception (listed here in the order of their entry). For four years Quick and Bollinger had served, respectively, as president and vice-president, to be succeeded in those posts by Nancy Lazlo (Judea Reform) and Victor Moore (St. Philip's), who gave vigorous leadership. Each church annually contributed at first $350 and then $1,000. With that money Duke University Divinity School seminarians were paid to serve the needs of the elderly in Oldham Towers, a high-rise for senior citizens, and to provide supervised recreation for young people in the Liberty Street Housing Project. Both buildings were only a block away from St. Philip's. In another program, Mediport, each member church in rotation took its day in the week to transport the disadvantaged to hospital clinics.[121] CCCC was providing a structure within which St. Philippian volunteers, acting in a spirit of Christian servanthood, could meet the needs of a fellow human being in a face-to-face, one-to-one relationship, and not simply impersonally by donating a sum of money to charity.

In the parish house itself St. Philip's provided the Durham Nursery School with facilities (four basement classrooms, a rest room, and use of the kitchen) for its weekday mission of taking care of young children of working mothers. St. Philip's thus met a desperate, immediate need. As Anne Moore, president of the Durham Nursery School Association and an active member of St. Philip's, explained in her letter of September 12, 1972 to the Vestry, the association operated two day-care centers, the Durham Nursery School on Hyde Park Avenue (East Durham) and the Mary O. Cowper Center on Pratt Avenue (near Duke). When the building inspector condemned the Hyde Park Avenue building, great had been the consternation over what should be done. After a few repairs and modifications the quarters at St. Philip's parish house were made ready and passed inspection, and the young people of EYC soon cleaned up and constructed a playground on the newly acquired land. The Nursery School paid the sexton a fee for extra janitorial services and contributed a modest monthly deposit to compensate St. Philip's for renovations after the school left. But for nearly four years from 6:00 A.M. to 6:30 P.M., Monday to Friday, the basement resounded to thirty to forty young children playing and studying in the security and guidance of professional care.[122]

Concurrently, in December 1972 Victor Moore as senior warden initiated "Share Your Christmas," whereby St. Philippians donated, wrapped, and transported Christmas presents to needy families, whose names were supplied by the Department of Social Services of Durham County. This operation, under Moore in 1972 and John Isaacs in 1973 and 1974, became a model for other churches to emulate.[123]

Meanwhile, outside the new organization of program departments, the Episcopal Church Women continued. Ever since the rectorship of Sidney Stuart Bost, it had been rock solid (a legitimate metaphor, since Jesus Christ used it) in purpose, faith, organization, planning, and action. It performed the functions of a church within a church: fellowship, at the monthly meetings of the five chapters; worship, led by each chapter's Devotional chair; education, in the study of a single book throughout the year (Acts in 1971, Job in 1972), led by each chapter's Education chair; outreach in action, from aid to Rachel Wolff, a missionary in far-off Nepal, to provision of rides to senior citizens in nearby Oldham Towers; collection of revenue, by a splendid Christmas bazaar ($3,689.71 in 1972), pansy sale ($765.12), and United Thank Offering ($903.54)—all efficiently administered by a hierarchy of ECW parish officers matched by their counterparts in each chapter. The variety, immensity, and dedication of the sustained effort of the Episcopal Church Women can be conveyed only by a reproduction of one of its annual reports (see Appendix O).

In April 1973 there occurred in St. Philip's happenings that can best be understood as an invasion of the Holy Spirit. Seventy percent of the respondents to the self-study questionnaire had thought that St. Philip's should do more about the congregation's spiritual welfare. Since his 1963 article on the ideal Vestry, Bollinger had believed that *sustained* organization, planning, and outreach in action must be entwined with spiritual renewal. Now that organization, planning, and creative action were in place, he tossed and turned in his bed at night trying to decide how to awaken St. Philippians spiritually.[124]

He finally opted for a Faith Alive Weekend. To the Vestry on December 14, 1972 he "expressed the hope that 1973 would be a Spiritual Renewal Year for St. Philip's." He added that he was thinking of bringing "to the Church a Faith Alive Weekend, perhaps during Lent." After the Vestry, led by Victor Moore, endorsed the idea, Pat Robinson was named chair of the committee to organize and advertise the event.

At the first Friday evening in April 1973 more than 250 St. Philippians, better than a majority of the active communicants, gathered in the upstairs assembly room in the parish house. They listened as lay witnesses of all age groups from other Episcopal churches movingly testified to their experiences in Christianity. For them Christianity was not the routine recital of creed but a vital living with Jesus Christ in the power of the Holy Spirit. As Robinson wrote, "we heard them praying for one another as they stood to bear witness to Jesus Christ." The next day the witnessing continued with St. Philippians joining in, in several separate groups, meeting at homes. The young people meanwhile went off on their own with their contemporaries from other churches. By Saturday night the assembly room was crowded with St. Philippians transformed, "hugging each other, sharing with one another their thoughts, fears, doubts, joys, sorrows, and faith." On Sunday everyone again came together in a joyous, celebratory Holy Communion. The following Tuesday, Wednesday, and Thursday prayer groups sprang up, meeting in homes, crossing neighborhood lines, continuing on a weekly basis for more than a year. The Faith Alive Weekend and the prayer groups were transforming, vitalizing, blessed experiences for many St. Philippians, individuals and families, and hence for the congregation.[125]

The central theme of these four years of Bollinger's rectorship (1970–73), the central motif, so to speak, was creative study, planning, organization, and action, resulting in the formation of institutions that might endure. In brief, for Bollinger and St. Philip's they were years of creative accomplishment. But there was a secondary theme, almost in contrapuntal inversion: as the line of achievement rose, dislike of Bollinger by an intractable minority of influential and vocal critics descended to extremes of rancor. There were scenes. Let us mention two or three.

By April 1971, when Bollinger was basking in the glow of the successful self-study, Watts Carr, Jr., senior warden, who was always fair, was receiving so many complaints about the Rector that he felt obliged to call the Vestry into executive session to consider them. The majority of the Vestry entered the meeting expecting to ask Bollinger to resign, but Priscilla McBryde pleaded movingly for his retention and others spoke in his support. After considerable discussion the Vestry reached a creative compromise. It authorized the senior warden to appoint a committee of three to five members who would review with Bollinger the questions that had been raised and work with him for constructive action. It also went "on record as supporting the Rector in his ministry at St. Philip's" and directed the Vestry's secretary to spread on the minutes "a resolution of thanks to the Senior Warden for his leadership." Later, in June, when the vestryman who had accepted the post of senior warden changed his mind and at the last moment withdrew, Bollinger nominated Dorothy Manning, a choice the Vestry enthusiastically endorsed. She accepted, she later said, because all factions in the church would speak to her even when they were not speaking to each other. She thought she could serve effectively as mediator, while at the same time bolstering Bollinger's spirits during his moments of depression.[126]

Or again. After a year or two in office as chair of the Christian Education Department, Parker decided that the chiefs of the Church School divisions (Margaret Davis, Ethel Reade, and himself) should meet with Bollinger once a year to gain a sense of working together in a common cause and to consider whether the curriculum was sequentially constructed: the Preschool laying the foundation for the Children's Division, and the latter for the Youth, which would cap and fulfill all grades. He was warned by advisors not to bring Bollinger, Margaret Davis, and Ethel Reade together in the same room. But he persisted. He respected all three, and he felt that he had a good working relationship on a one-to-one basis with each one. (This may have been a delusion; in an Episcopal church one never knows how one is regarded, except in a moment of truth — the Vestry election.) So the meeting was held. And violently blew up in acrimony. Parker obviously needed some training in conflict resolution. Lacking that, he never ventured to arrange another meeting.

Yet, strangely, this secondary theme of the dislike and settled rancor of an intractable minority did not affect the primary theme of creative accomplishment. Whatever their personal feelings toward the Rector, the minority were loyal to their church and their faith, and worked hard at their posts. And, of course, the majority of the congregation approved of what Bollinger was trying to do.

CONSOLIDATION?

Perhaps a bit of modern sociological thought will help us understand what was happening at St. Philip's and why. Sociologists now observe that a crucial factor in the history of a growing church is the increasing number of *active* communicants. As the numbers increase, the church and its institutions pass through four stages.[127] As long as it has up to fifty active communicants it is a *family* church. Governance and admission of newcomers depend on a few family clans, and the pastor is apt to be only a chaplain who performs the services. During its first eighteen years, 1878 to 1896, St. Philip's was in this stage (St. Andrew's always remained there). Then, in 1897, by his aggressive, dynamic evangelism Alfred A. Pruden attracted so many new active communicants and so fixed attention upon himself that he thrust St. Philip's into the second stage, that of a *pastoral* church, centering on the Rector. The blowup that resulted in his departure can be understood in personal terms: Pruden's aggressive style was both attractive and abrasive. But it can also be interpreted as arising from a tension between parishioners who clung to the old ways and old lines of dominance of a family church and a Rector who was trying to introduce the practices of a larger, pastoral church.

By his sympathetic, mediating counseling Sidney Stuart Bost in his turn won the families, old and new, to acceptance of his pastoral leadership and authority, while yet encouraging, indeed evoking, the free play of their initiatives. David Yates and Clarence Haden worked within the forms of the pastoral church that Bost had created. Haden's rectorship can be understood as the personal triumph of an excellent administrator. But it can also be interpreted as the perfect matching of an able Rector with the situation—with the number of active communicants and of the few essential agencies of a pastoral church. Singlehandedly he could still remain in touch with every family and by personal participation with every agency—Vestry, Worship Service, Choir, Church School, Laymen's League, ECW, and EYC. Except for initiating a weekly bulletin, he did not innovate—with perfect matching of form and function, he did not have to. He had only to tone up by his personal presence the operation of each agency. So he was remembered with admiration.

However, burgeoning growth in the number of active communicants, their dispersion over the landscape of Durham County, and the decay of the immediate neighborhood around the church presented problems that no single Rector, be he Tom Edwards, Bart Sherman, or Gene Bollinger, could handle within the forms of an old-time pastoral church. Temporarily, the problems were mitigated by siphoning off members to St. Luke's and St. Stephen's, and by the appointment of Assistants to the Rector (Robert Watson and John Denham under Edwards and Albert Nelius under Sherman, and of an administrative assistant to the Rector (William Miller, Kent Otto). But these were palliatives. Neighborhood organizations—a route that might have been taken—were tried under Edwards, Sherman, and Bollinger but failed. Both Sherman and Bollinger perceived that what was needed was creative institutional change: the establishment of program organizations that would match the institutional forms of St. Philip's to the needs and opportunities of an enlarged downtown church. Sherman proposed study and planning commissions; Bollinger and the self-study team recommended study, planning, and action program departments.

From 1896 to 1900 St. Philip's had passed from a *family* church to a *pastoral* church. From 1970 to 1973 it was attempting to move into the next stage, becoming a *program* church, where the Rector and Vestry supervise but do not micromanage the lay organizations that do the work of the several program departments. The tensions between Bollinger and some members of the congregation can be interpreted as difficulties arising from discomfort with his breezy approach and style. But the tensions can also be interpreted as the response of parishioners who were clinging to the forms, practices, personal relationships, and expectations of a pastoral church, to a Rector who was creatively trying to bring them into the new world of a program church. The two interpretations, of course, are not mutually exclusive, and both could be valid.

The question now before Bollinger and the St. Philippians was: would the changes be consolidated and endure? Bollinger himself realized that his rectorship was entering a change of phase. At the annual congregational meeting on January 23, 1974, he said: "I see 1974 as a year of consolidation and development of program. We need to improve our weak points, and add areas of program where there is need. I ask your prayers for me; be certain that you have mine."

He passed through the first year of this new phase in a mood of increasing elation. In his report to the congregation on January 26, 1975, he said: "1974 was by far the best, most-fulfilling year of my priesthood to date. Your esprit de corps, faith, response, sense of mission, love, support, creativity, hope, good humor, etc., has put me into a stance out of which I have had to struggle against becoming a braggart."[128] Yet less than three years later, on December 8, 1977, he announced to the Vestry his resignation as Rector, and in his last sermon in January 1978 he took leave of the congregation in a bitter, angry speech that showed a frustrated man. What had happened to provoke this change, and why had Bollinger's rectorship ended in this way? To a degree the answer remains shrouded in mystery, but we may offer a few clues.

First, let us say, 1974 was for St. Philip's indeed a wonderful year, one of the best in its history. Along with the sustained effort of the several program departments and their committees, several events rendered the twelve months between the two congregational meetings outstanding. One event was the arrival of Reverend Edward F. Glusman, Jr., first as part-time and then as full-time Assistant to the Rector. A candidate for the Ph.D. in the Duke University Department of Religion (his dissertation topic being the Gospel of Mark as a narrative form), he had Christian dedication, brains, scholarship, and an engaging personality. As he was "a man Bishop Fraser would like to get in the Diocese," Glusman was financed in part from diocesan funds.[129] He immediately made his influence felt in the life of St. Philip's.

A second event was the Teaching Series that Bollinger and Glusman conducted during Lent 1974: five sermons, each one accompanied by a syllabus, detailed biblical references, and suggestions for further reading from books in the parish library. Bollinger's sermons were eloquent theological-philosophical discourses on the Meaning of Life, Redemption, and the Church, emphasizing living in and with Jesus Christ and quoting liberally from Dietrich Bonhoeffer, Teilhard de Chardin, and Jacques Ellul. Glusman's, on the Meaning and Experience of God's Self-Disclosure and of Discipleship, sharply brought the message home through personal anecdote. The totality was a powerful sequence.[130]

A third event, in June 1974, was the smooth transition of office from what might be called the "Self-Study Generation"—Dorothy Manning, Walter Mason, Angus McBryde, Victor Moore, and Harold Parker—to two experienced officials, Richard L. Watson and James R. Pleasants, who were to be, respectively, senior warden and junior warden for the next two years.[131] As part of that transition the four program departments (Worship, Christian Education, Lay Ministry, Community Action), under the supervision of Bollinger and the Vestry, again evaluated in June their past year's performance and presented plans for the upcoming twelve months.[132]

The fourth event was the resurgence of the Youth program, visible in the continued recovery and strength of EYC, previously described.[133] At the same time, the Youth Division of the Church School (grades 7 to 12) adopted the curriculum of the Educational Center of St. Louis. In early September 1974, twenty-one participating teachers took nineteen hours of intensive training administered by a representative of the St. Louis outfit. The lead teachers of the senior high schoolers were Daniel and Judy Pearson; of the junior high schoolers, Lynn Hughes, Harold Parker, and Sam Simmons. A special course for adults, modeled after the Educational Center's approach, was offered in the fall by Glusman and Parker.[134] Glusman also joined Dorothy Manning and Dana Ripley to maintain the high level of programming in the Adult Education Class that had been set by Emmy Lou Hamshar.[135]

The fifth event, occurring on January 14, 1975, was the initiation by Glusman and Anne Moore of a twelve-week course entitled "The Experiment in Practical Christianity." In it twelve people together worked through the experience of studying the Gospel according to Mark and in the process became a sharing Christian group. Two graduates of the course then led a second group; two graduates of the second then led a third group, and so on, until within two years six groups, seventy-two members of the congregation, had engaged in a profound spiritual encounter with Jesus Christ and with fellow parishioners.[136]

The sixth event, also occurring in early January 1975, was the Vestry's decision to stage a capital funds drive to raise $75,000 to extinguish the debt incurred by the purchase of adjoining property and the renovation of the existing physical plant. The ensuing Campaign for Progress, chaired by the veteran fundraiser John Chatham, quickly secured pledges of $60,000, which was sufficient to clear the overhang debt within five years.[137]

To the *active* communicants of St. Philip's—and there were quite a few now—1975, 1976, and 1977 were fulfilling years as they built on foundations already laid down. Glusman in his first report to the congregation commented on how "St. Philip's continued to impress him with the high percentage of parishioners who are active not only in worship, but also in program and in pastoral awareness and care."[138] Within every program department except Lay Ministry and within ECW there was solid, satisfying accomplishment and fruitful innovations. Only a few examples need be cited.

The Worship and Christian Education Departments perfected the jointure of the Sunday worship services with the sessions of the Church School. In September 1970 Bollinger, in order to acquire a full hour for Christian Education, had abolished the Family Service introduced by Edwards and continued by Sherman. Thereafter the Sunday morning schedule was as follows: 8:00 A.M., Holy Communion; 9:45–10:45, Christian Education Hour; 11:00–12:00, Holy Communion on the first and third Sundays of each month, Morning Prayer on the other Sundays, with a full music program integrated into the service. At 9:45 the children and young people attended the excellent instruction of the Preschool (Margaret Davis, chair) and Children's (Ethel Reade, chair) Divisions and the much-improved classes of the Youth Division (Harold Parker, chair),[139] while their parents and other adults took part in the discussions of the Adult Education class planned by Dorothy Manning and her committee.[140] At eleven o'clock the adults and teen-agers went off to church. But what became of the children during that hour? The innovative solution was to create a Second-Hour Division

(Joan Troy, chair) for children from age three through the sixth grade. "Its program was planned to complement that of the first hour. The students worked at their own pace in learning centers on activities which are designed to increase capability in the use and understanding of the Prayer Book and Bible. The students were actively involved in reading, doing research, writing, playing games, singing, completing 'fun sheets,' and other activities which might serve to facilitate the achievement of the goals of the program."[141] Thus an attractive schedule was arranged that provided the children and young people "with a spiritual and educational experience while enabling parents to attend both an educational hour and a service of worship."[142]

The members of the Christian Social Action Department (formerly the Community Action Department) continued to serve with Bollinger as St. Philip's delegation to the Center City Church Council. The department's chair, Victor Moore, became president of CCCC, which added yet other Durham churches and changed its name to Durham Congregations in Action (DCIA). As DCIA it inaugurated Meals on Wheels, by which individual volunteers transported "to shut-ins a hot nutritious noontime meal on weekdays." Meals on Wheels became a popular outlet for individual St. Philippians who wished to serve their fellows in need. Back in the parish, the Christian Social Action Department sponsored an increasingly tremendous and joyous Share Your Christmas endeavor.[143]

Into the midst of these activities Bollinger introduced the parish to a new program that had great potential for nurturing sustained spiritual renewal. The initiative came from Bishop Fraser. Disturbed by the antics of the extremist religious "crazies" of the 1960s and 1970s, he had been seeking for several years a means of spiritually awakening the congregations of the Diocese along the strong, well-balanced lines of his own faith. In late August 1975, hearing of the Roman Catholic weekend retreat called "Cursillo," Fraser sent Bollinger and Fred Wedler, a president-to-be of the Episcopal Laymen's Association, and their wives to a Cursillo in San Antonio, Texas.[144] Bollinger returned to St. Philip's on a personal cloud nine.[145] This was the normal reaction to any retreat. What distinguished Cursillo from other retreats was that it offered a complete Christian religious experience: there was prayer and worship, there was study, there was rejoicing in spirit and song, and there was follow-up action. After a retreat, *cursillistas* from the same hometown formed small prayer groups of two to eight people. At their weekly meetings they prayed *and* reported what they had done the preceding days to win others to Jesus Christ. This revived an element previously neglected by St. Philippians and the Center City Church Council. As we have seen in previous chapters, back in the diocesan discussions of the 1950s and 1960s it had been argued that meeting people's needs was only the first step toward bringing them to the Gospel, the Good News of Christ's redeeming action and power. St. Philippians had served but had not proselytized or converted. *Cursillistas* were obligated to do so.

Bollinger was now in his element, doing what he loved to do and did best: creatively building and promoting a new religious institution. The first four Cursillo weekends, held at the Betsy Jeff Penn Center north of Greensboro, were administered by Roman Catholic clergy and laity, but soon enough Episcopal priests and laity had been educated to conduct the weekends on their own. Several laypersons from St. Philip's were drawn in, although not as many as Bollinger hoped, and even more from Episcopal congregations in Charlotte, Greensboro, and Raleigh. Cursillo soon became an established institution of the Diocese and one of Bollinger's major contributions to diocesan spiritual life.[146]

However, back at St. Philip's there was slippage after January 1975. For example, in 1975, 1976, and 1977 there was no formal annual performance/planning review by the program departments under Bollinger's and the Vestry's supervision. To be sure, the departments continued to exist; they submitted annual statements of budget needs, they reported to the congregational meeting, and they may or may not have conducted their own planning review, but the Vestry was cut out of the loop of discussion. This had serious consequences: the ideal Vestry of which Bollinger had dreamed in 1963 and which had been achieved by the self-study reforms, one that discussed in an integrated way programs *and* bills and budget, no longer existed in fact. Also, communication of Vestry to congregation and congregation to Vestry was impaired. Watson, as senior warden, was aware of the problems. He formed a Parish Council, composed of members of the Vestry and the heads of the several departments and agencies, but after his retirement as senior warden in June 1976 the council ceased to function. The Vestry also published a summary of its decisions in the monthly

Epistle to the Philippians, but this did not ensure communication of the congregation *to* the Vestry. On its retreat in February 1977 the Vestry talked of becoming "more informed and involved" in the life and programs of the parish, but along that line nothing effective was done.[147]

Also, the level of giving remained low. The Every Member Canvass was still an annual agony of "making the budget." The yearly talk of stewardship and dedicating time, talent, and treasure to the Lord fell on deaf ears. In the afterglow of his Cursillo experience, Bollinger volunteered to chair the Every Member Canvass that was conducted in the fall of 1975 for the fiscal year 1976. He organized "a model campaign," centered on the theological significance of stewardship. But the congregation responded by pledging only $88,327, nearly $7,000 less than the year before ($95,000) and only slightly greater than the year before that ($88,164). Consequently, the Vestry had to let Glusman go, as it could no longer guarantee the salary of an Assistant to the Rector.[148] The following year, when the Every Member Canvass in the fall of 1976 at first yielded a shortfall of $17,000, the Vestry next eliminated the position of parish secretary.[149] Under the concept of an expanded lay ministry Anne Moore then organized an Office Ministry, a group of dedicated women who volunteered "with love and commitment" to serve in the parish office on weekday mornings, taking telephone calls, making appointments, answering questions. But not one of the volunteers could type. The Vestry discussed hiring a typist for eight hours a week—but where was the money to pay her? Throughout 1977 we have the spectacle of an affluent congregation unable or unwilling to provide its Rector with an Assistant, a secretary, or even a typist![150] Statistically, there was another disturbing signal: the decline after 1975 in the number of communicants and in the average attendance at Sunday worship services.[151]

There were yet other strains. In September 1976 the General Convention of the Episcopal Church had approved the new Prayer Book. There was every prospect that in 1979 the Convention would give the necessary second endorsement for it to become the Church's official Prayer Book. Bollinger had the difficult task of pastorally visiting parishioners distressed by that prospect, seeking to alleviate their pain. He spent much of the summer of 1977 doing so.[152] Then there was the drumbeat of personal criticism from the intractable minority of parishioners. There were scenes. Rancor reached the point that a few vocal opponents refused to support Bollinger even on policies they had long approved, because now they were his too. Church gossip, not always kind, circulated about his wife, Rita, who did not fit the traditional mold of a rector's spouse, and about his three oldest children, Catherine, Ruth, and David, who were brilliant mavericks—gossip that Bollinger resented. Under multiple pressures, beset and depressed, on one occasion in November 1977 he accused his most loyal supporters of actions that he himself had taken and that had never entered their minds. In this darkness of his personality, which moved so easily from elation to depression to realistic analysis, he decided, as he told the Vestry on December 8, 1977, that it was best for himself, his family, and St. Philip's for him to resign as Rector, effective on January 31, 1978. The Vestry accepted the resignation with "great regret." [153]

It was fitting that controversy attended the details of arranging Bollinger's departure. Vestry members agreed that he should have severance pay, but they differed on the amount. At the next Vestry meeting, on December 18, 1977, several non-Vestry members of the congregation, "E. K. Powe, Richard Watson, Lester Butler, J. Harper Erwin, Clarence Cobb, and Hugh White, . . . each spoke to a favorable and generous amount to be given to Mr. Bollinger. . . . The Senior Warden read letters from William H. Ruffin, Priscilla McBryde, and Angus McBryde supporting generous continuation of pay for Mr. Bollinger. He also advised that he had received two telephone calls from members of the Parish opposing such continuation of compensation."

One member of the Vestry then moved that Bollinger be given $2,000; the motion died for want of a second. A second motion, for $10,000, provoked considerable discussion. The Vestry finally approved a $10,000 bonus underwritten by St. Philip's for up to $6,000 with the balance ($4,000) to be voluntarily contributed by the congregation. This motion passed with one dissenting vote, the dissenter resigning from the Vestry in protest at the magnitude of the church's obligation.[154] As it turned out, in a few weeks $7,050 was raised from the congregation, leaving only $2,950 to be paid by the church.[155] The incident had revealed, once again, both the support Bollinger enjoyed as well as the opposition he excited.

If the Truth is the Story and the Story is the Truth, perhaps the narrative should stop here, without any further comment from the narrator. Obviously, for Bollinger the story of his rectorship was one of triumph and tragedy. For St. Philip's his rectorship meant controversy, spiritual renewal, and a breakthrough into new areas of creative Christian servanthood.

REFLECTIONS ON MEANING

The professional historian is equipped by training to discover what actually happened, and he is honor-bound by his code to present it as honestly as he can. But when he comes to questions of meaning he is no better off than anyone else. He is restricted, furthermore, not only by the limitations of his personal resources but by his localization in time and space. The meaning of an event depends not only on what came before but also on what came after, and what came after is constantly changing. And in space, where is the historian: an insider? an outsider? or empathetically both, within and without?

In the course of telling the story we have suggested several meanings. St. Philip's is a congregation that has passed through three stages (family, pastoral, and program) and is entering the fourth, as a corporate institution. As its garden statuary suggests, it was passing through successive metamorphoses, in agonizing struggles of birth and rebirth (Chapter VII, Sherman). Or, the congregation is engaged in a pilgrimage in faith (Chapter IV, Yates). Or, it is the story of a people who over the years, through joys and tribulations, have found sustenance, support, and consolation in the liturgy of a Book of Common Prayer (Prologue).

But there is a gritty underside to the story, too. It reveals how uncharitable St. Philippians, avowed Christians all of them, could be to each other (the Bollinger years) or to outsiders (the Malcolm X imbroglio). There is nothing more bitter and unrelenting than a church quarrel, because each faction believes it is righteously doing God's will. Then, St. Philippians *as a group* too often fell short of their professed standards of stewardship and of evangelism. Almost never did they make a positive effort to win others to Jesus Christ or even to the Episcopal Church. Perhaps it was not considered good form to do so.

So, what is the meaning of the history of St. Philip's? Let us continue to think about it, in a further adventure of inquiry, reflection, and prayer for illumination. The question *is* important. Meaning is related to a sense of identity—identity (who we are) is related to action—action reinforces a sense of identity and of meaning. Meaning, identity, and action are thus mutually reinforcible. Memory, too, should play a role. We are a congregation that in the past has taken risks and not taken risks, stepped forth in faith and not stepped forth in faith, listened to its prophets and let them down, struggled, fought, repented, survived, and ultimately moved forward in faith, a true pilgrim's progress toward a growing sense of mission.

In all this did we not parallel the history of the Israelites of the Old Testament?

9

Some Thoughts on the Rectorship of C. Thomas Midyette III 1978–1994

"Epilogue" is not the correct word to characterize what happened during the rectorship of Tom Midyette. Webster defines "epilogue" as "a concluding section that rounds out the design of a literary work." But Midyette, who is now a historical personage in our narrative and can be referred to by his last name, did far more than round out; he went on to new creation. A better subtitle than "Epilogue" might be "A Changing Yet Constant Rector Lives with A Changing Yet Constant Congregation."

THE RECTOR

The Rector changed. He arrived as a friendly, dynamic, rather brash young man. He departed as a wise guru of deepening spirituality. The change was reflected in his sermons. Those of the last two years were simply at another, deeper level of thought, emotion, and expression.

Yet in his sermons, which were short, to the point, and distinguished by a personal touch, he was constant in stressing the active side of Jesus' ministry: Feed the hungry, visit the sick, and reach out to those in prison. Midyette's favorite scriptural passage was from the Gospel according to Matthew, where Jesus is speaking to those at His right hand at the final judgment: "Come, O blessed of my Father, inherit the kingdom prepared for you from the foundation of the world: for I was hungry and you gave me food, I was thirsty and you gave me drink, I was a stranger and you welcomed me, I was naked and you clothed me, I was sick and you visited me, I was in prison and you came to me."

As the years passed Midyette developed the implications of that passage. A classic route of spiritual growth has been to walk alone in meditation and prayer. Midyette taught members of the congregation to move in worship together within the diverse, inclusive community, the Church, which incarnates the Body of Christ. Sustained by worship together, the congregation moves outward in love to service of others. Service to others, in turn, confirms and deepens inner spirituality. "It is through our praise and thanksgiving [in worship together] that we finally realize our call to ministry in the City of Durham." "A church which exercises its outreach and ministry to all people is a church which realizes a spiritual rejuvenation within its own body."

This teaching enabled the congregation to handle divisive issues of race, gender, and sexual orientation, which might have torn it asunder, and instead to celebrate its diversity and its inclusiveness and its service in love, as Jesus wished. The celebration appeared in a new statement of mission, formulated in 1992 by the Vestry under the influence of Midyette: "St. Philip's is a holy place where we worship God. Our worship forms us into a community of Christians. By prayer, sacrament, and fellowship we nourish and sustain one another in our individual lives and ministries. We obey the Gospel call to bring the light of hope in Jesus Christ to all people. We offer welcome, support, food, and shelter to all in need without pride, prejudice, or judgment: we have responsibility to the entire Durham Community, especially our downtown neighborhood." In this statement meaning, identity, and action are fused, and the problem presented in the conclusion of the preceding chapter is resolved.

THE CONGREGATION

The congregation changed. Chronologically the narrative divides into two periods. (1) The first seven years (1978–85), when with existing membership the metamorphosis into a program church was confirmed, fulfilled, and completed with the opening of the Urban Ministries Center and the inauguration of the Prison Ministry (September 1985)—in the metaphor of its parish garden statuary, The Dragonfly Flies. (2) The next nine years (1986–94), when with zooming membership, staff, budgets, and diversity, the congregation was moving toward a corporate church. This new metamorphosis placed strains on the congregation, which did not realize what was happening and did not always rise to the new challenges and opportunities, and on the Rector, who had to manage the transformation and might not wish to be relegated to the post of an inspiring preacher/supervising general manager who was distant from the personal counseling that he enjoyed and did so well.

A BRIEF NARRATIVE OF DECISIVE ACTION AND ACHIEVEMENT

The interim seven months between the departure of Bollinger in January 1978 and the arrival of a new Rector in September were unlike any other interim in the history of St. Philip's. The Vestry, with Ralph Strayhorn as senior warden, immediately took charge.[1] It constituted itself the Search Committee. When Bishop Fraser recommended that the Vestry call an interim priest, it thanked him but said that an interim was not needed: the Vestry and other laity would run the church. With Bollinger, the chief source of division, gone, parishioners pitched in and cooperatively worked together. Barney Hawkins, a friendly, popular candidate for ordination who had a B.D. degree from Duke University Divinity School and was studying for a Ph.D., was continued as lay pastoral assistant. A priest, usually Peter Keese, the Duke Hospital Episcopal chaplain, was obtained to consecrate the Host for Holy Communion at the eight o'clock and periodically at the eleven o'clock services, but Hawkins (who often preached the sermons), the Altar Guild, the lay readers and passers of the chalice, acolytes, choirmaster, and choirs conducted the Sunday worship. The other major agencies of the church—the Vestry itself and its wardens, the treasurer and his collection of pledges and payment of bills, the Daughters of the King, the volunteer Office Ministry, Christian Education teachers and classes, parish librarians, Episcopal Church Women, EYC, delegates to Durham Congregations in Action, and volunteer deliverers of Meals on Wheels—continued as before. The laity did not innovate any new agencies or programs, but they strongly maintained existing institutions on which the incoming Rector could build, and they had a wonderful time doing so. Bishop Fraser graciously complimented them: "I did not think you could do it."

After an extensive search, the Vestry called the Reverend C. Thomas Midyette III. A native of New Bern, North Carolina, "he completed his undergraduate education at the University of the South with a major in philosophy and his seminary training at Virginia Theological Seminary. After his ordination, his priestly ministry began in 1966 at

St. Stephen's in Goldsboro where he was Assistant Rector for two years. He was then called to St. Paul's, Clinton, where he remained Rector until 1971. A call from another St. Paul's took him to Beaufort where he served as Rector for seven years" and "packed them in."[2]

An engagement between a new Rector and a congregation resembles a marriage: the two partners like what they see without really knowing each other. The Vestry of St. Philip's saw a dynamic "go-getter" who would be very useful to the parish for perhaps five years before moving on to a larger enterprise. It never anticipated that he would stay for over fifteen years and lead in creating at St. Philip's that larger enterprise. Midyette, on the other hand, had read the parish Profile that the Vestry had prepared for priestly applicants. The parish purpose stated in the Profile was "To bring together all sorts of people in the worship of God and in Christian fellowship with each other through a ministry of teaching, reconciliation, and service." The Profile stated three parish goals:

1. Attraction of new members, especially families with young children.
2. Pastoral care to the entire congregation, especially to members who were formerly involved in St. Philip's but are no longer participating.
3. Social service, with a particular emphasis to improving methods of relating to many transients who come to our doors.

As Midyette read this purpose statement, along with the three goals of the parish, he thought that this was a parish whose rector he would like to become.[3] He probably did not foresee the struggles that lay ahead to achieve those goals. He probably did not recognize how difficult a parish St. Philip's was. At times it would require all his faith, education, and vision to persuade parishioners to live up to their Profile of innovation, outreach, and inclusiveness.

To continue the metaphor: the first year of a rectorship may be a honeymoon period. Some new rectors "play it safe" and try not to "rock the boat." "Playing it safe" was never one of Midyette's attributes. As E. K. Powe, senior warden in 1993, recalled:

I remember so well the first Sunday Tom held services at St. Philip's. Prior to that time, one of the big issues confronting St. Philippians was whether or not the altar should be moved out from the north wall of the Church to be freestanding. The congregation was divided down the middle on this issue and was literally torn asunder by it. Well—perhaps Tom had not heard the furor over the altar or perhaps he had a touch of divine guidance, but as his first unofficial act as Rector at St. Philip's he engaged the services of a couple of carpenters, moved the altar out from the wall and conducted his first service from behind it facing his congregation. . . . To this day we have enjoyed having the clergy perform our communion services by looking us straight in the eye. I think this says much for the man, his decisiveness and his ability to carry them out.[4]

Midyette, in an interview, recalled that in the first week he also switched the crosses, transferring the large cross in the side-aisle chapel to the high altar in the sanctuary and replacing it in the chapel with the smaller cross that had been in the sanctuary. When an eminent parishioner protested that the parish Memorials Committee should be consulted, Midyette replied that by the Episcopal canons he, the Rector, had the authority to make the change, and he strode on ahead. This sequence of events became a pattern that was repeated again and again: a decisive initiative or action by the Rector; a murmur, sometimes a strong murmur, of protest from a portion of the congregation; the Rector persists and the change enters the ongoing life of the church. Let us mention several of the major innovations.

Before we do, however, let us recall another quality of his ministry that was manifested very early: his capacity for friendly, discerning, and helpful counseling of persons in trouble and distress. Both within St. Philip's and throughout Durham his reputation as a caring counselor spread. Even in these recent decades of regionally automated telephone service, Durham's "information" operators soon learned with whom to connect a troubled caller who asked for the number of "that pastor on Main Street."

The first major innovation was the parish house Soup Kitchen. For several years the need for it had become obvious. Since the days of Bart Sherman and Albert Nelius, a few beggars had drifted through the parish house seeking a handout, and stranded families had sought food, temporary shelter, counsel, and directions where to go and where to apply. When Urban Renewal leveled the ramshackle buildings along Pettigrew Street, across the railroad tracks, the trickle became a swarm, as panhandlers, often on booze, hung about the bus station next door or even slept on the benches in the parish garden. Individual chits of paper worth a meal at the bus station restaurant, a pantry of canned food stored in the parish secretary's office, an occasional purchase of a motel room for several nights for a stranded family, even taking a drying-out alcoholic into one's home—these individual measures simply failed to meet the elemental needs of hunger, warmth, counsel, and recognition of a crowd of homeless men whom the district attorney's office labeled "derelicts." The clergy, staff, and individual unorganized parishioners, despite the echoing injunction of Jesus Christ to feed the hungry, simply could not cope individually with an overwhelming problem.

In mid-1979 Midyette sent a delegation of St. Philippians, including William and Mary Harrison, to study a celebrated soup kitchen in Atlanta. They worked in the kitchen itself and returned enthusiastic about introducing one in the upstairs kitchen and assembly room of the parish house of St. Philip's. During July or August 1979 Midyette brought the proposal before a parish meeting, attended by nearly two hundred parishioners. Immediately there were questions, mostly negative in implication. Who would clean up "our" kitchen? Would dirty men use "our" toilets? Would there be fights? Would property be stolen? What would it cost? The momentum seemed to be turning against the project. But then

> Jacqueline Harris stood up and told about her experiences in her native Holland during the post–World War II confusion. She stated that after the Nazi withdrawal, there was widespread food shortage in the cities. Food was then donated by the Allies and was made available at a number of soup kitchens. One of these was in the chemistry building at the University of Leyden. The professor of chemistry and his assistant dished food out of a barrel to the 350 medical students who not only had classes in that building but also lived and studied there. Jacqueline said that she was one of those students. She therefore learned at first hand what it means to be hungry and to be grateful to all who were responsible for a soup kitchen. Her talk was most moving. There was not a word in reply and the motion to install a soup kitchen at St. Philip's for a trial period of six months passed unanimously.[5]

Over the years the Soup Kitchen Committee, chaired successively by Harold Parker, James David Barber, William Harrison, and Richard

Watson, supervised its installation and operation, but the Soup Kitchen's effectiveness was owing to its two directors, first Clifford Wesley Sanderson and then Betsy Rollins. Sanderson, as a member of the Vestry, member of the choir, verger (the only one in St. Philip's history), former manager of Dalton Bookstore in Northgate Mall, and publicist extraordinary, was well suited by his varied experiences to be director and alcohol counselor (such was his title) of a center serving homeless "street people." The center started simply enough, in September 1979: five St. Philippian volunteers in the upstairs parish assembly hall and kitchen from 10:00 A.M. to noon, Monday through Friday, serving 20 to 30 men a light lunch of soup, a large sandwich, and a hot drink. Within a month the center was averaging 40 to 50 clients a day, with 106 on Thanksgiving and 75 on Christmas for a banquet of turkey and all the "fixings." Sanderson contributed valuably to its operation. He initiated the practice of persuading Durham groceries, fast-food outlets, and restaurants to donate surplus food. Modest in amount at first, donated food reached by 1984 an annual value of $104,137.47. The operation could not have survived without it. He also talked to church groups throughout Durham, attracting an increasing number of volunteers from outside the parish and compelling the change of name from Soup Kitchen to Community Kitchen. In addition, he understood the difficulties of alcoholics. He and other counselors helped them sort out their life-problems and even drove them to meetings of Alcoholics Anonymous.[6]

In February 1980 Sanderson was succeeded as director of the Community Kitchen by Betsy Rollins. Sensitive to the needs of others and indomitable in organizing resources to meet them, she became nationally known for her work as director and for her advocacy of feeding the hungry. In 1983, when the Community Kitchen was still located in St. Philip's parish house, she was named to President Ronald Reagan's Committee on World Hunger and to his Task Force on Food Distribution. By 1987, after the kitchen had moved into larger quarters and better facilities in the Urban Ministries Building, it was serving three meals daily from Monday through Friday: breakfast, a very substantial lunch, and a light supper, the latter designed chiefly for people in the adjacent night shelter. In June 1990 a noontime meal on Saturday and Sunday was added. Aside from the service the Community Kitchen performed locally, it became a model studied by other churches and civic bodies in the United States and abroad.[7]

Although the Community Kitchen had been started by St. Philip's, the entire Durham community became involved. By January 1983 approximately 90 percent of the volunteers came from outside the parish, and the Durham Congregations in Action (DCIA) was appointing two members of the twelve-person Kitchen's Board of Directors. By 1989 that number had increased to five, and the number of outside volunteers to nearly three hundred, with only a handful of St. Philippians. Looked at in one way, it might be said that St. Philip's was better at initiating an innovation of outreach than in sustaining it. That observation, however, misses an essential point: in meeting a particular need—the hunger of street people who drifted into its garden and offices—by a particular measure, the Soup Kitchen—St. Philip's not only had reached out in service to the downtown neighborhood, it had persuaded the larger Durham community to become involved and thus had assured a broad-based and enduring support. This pattern had already appeared in the mission to the deaf (Bost) and in the foundation and expansion of Durham Congregations in Action (Bollinger) and was to appear again and again in later innovations.

The second major innovation under Midyette was the Urban Ministries Building. Again, the need was obvious. The Community Kitchen clientele was crowding the St. Philip's parish assembly hall almost beyond its capacity. The other downtown churches had charitable enterprises—such as the Clothing Closet and Food Pantry of Trinity Methodist Church and Financial Aid at First Presbyterian Church—that would benefit from being housed together. Durham Congregations in Action, now numbering nearly forty churches, needed a headquarters office, and Meals on Wheels, an operating base. A large, high-ceilinged room could serve not only as a dining and meeting area but also as a basketball court for the Church Basketball League and for downtown neighborhood youth. *And* the land for a multipurpose building was available in the quarter of a city block purchased by St. Philip's in 1970 from Urban Renewal.

Again Midyette prepared in advance. The building's estimated cost of nearly half a million dollars exceeded that raised in Durham by any previous drive. It loomed across the path like a cliff that had to be scaled. Foundations and business corporations that might be sympathetic were reluctant to give to churches. So, Midyette invited Charles Steel IV, a member of St. Philip's and a lawyer, to attend the Vestry retreat, to be held from Friday, February 19 to Sunday, February 21, 1982 at The Islander on Emerald Isle.[8] On Friday evening Steel lucidly presented the concept of a possible solution: that a campaign be held to raise money for building a United Ministries Center; that a nonprofit corporation, Urban Ministries, Inc., be chartered; that Urban Ministries, Inc., would receive money from the campaign, lease the land from St. Philip's for a nominal sum, erect the multipurpose building, and be in charge of its use. A stormy meeting followed, lasting until three o'clock the next morning. For the Vestry the sticking point was that St. Philip's, which owned the land, had to relinquish control of the building that was to be erected on it.

In the discussion the Vestry hammered out a set of resolutions (see Appendix Q) that accepted Steel's basic strategy but introduced certain safeguards designed to protect the influence of St. Philip's while bringing in the rest of the Durham community: (1) there was to be a campaign to build the Urban Ministries Center, but only if the Community Kitchen and Meals on Wheels were tenants and the campaign was chaired by William M. Harrison, Jr., a member of the Vestry; (2) the committee formed to explore the center's organizational structure would include three members of the Vestry and the Rector of St. Philip's in addition to members of Durham Congregation in Action and other interested parties; (3) Charles L. Steel, the Vestry's attorney, would draft the necessary articles of incorporation for United Ministries, Inc., and the lease between it and St. Philip's and their terms were subject to the Vestry's approval; (4) the possible occupiers of the building were to include the Community Kitchen, Meals on Wheels, the Church League Basketball Program, DCIA office space, *and* other uses to be approved by the Rector of St. Philip's.[9]

In the ensuing fundraising campaign, whose chair was Harrison and whose executive officer in charge of administrative details was Harding Hughes, former senior warden of St. Philip's, every effort was made to involve the entire community: newspapers, radio, television, and the Durham Congregations in Action. December 5, 1982 was designated Urban Ministries Sunday throughout Durham, and special pleas were made in the thirty-seven churches of DCIA. Contributions were sought from businesses as well as individuals. By December 1983, $400,000 had been raised, the goal of $600,000 seemed attainable, and planning for construction by the architect, R. W. Carr, also of St. Philip's, could begin.[10]

Meanwhile, Steel had drafted three essential documents for Vestry approval on December 19, 1982: the Articles of Incorporation of United Ministries, Inc., its Bylaws, and the lease between it and St. Philip's. The Articles of Incorporation named the first Board of Directors. Their names should be preserved in this history as the incorporators of a significant institution that has endured:

Name	Sponsoring Agency	Term of Office
Mrs. Margaret Keller	First Presbyterian Church, Durham	1 year
Mrs. Louise McCutcheon	Trinity Methodist Church, Durham	2 years
Mr. Maceo Sloan	DCIA	2 years
Mr. Tyrone Baines	DCIA	1 year
Rev. Haywood D. Holderness, Jr.	DCIA	3 years
Mrs. Elna Spaulding	Women in Action for the Prevention of Violence and Its Causes	3 years
William M. Harrison, Jr.	St. Philip's Episcopal Church, Durham	2 years
Charles L. Steel IV	St. Philip's Episcopal Church, Durham	1 year
George Watts Carr, Jr.	St. Philip's Episcopal Church, Durham	3 years
Rev. C. Thomas Midyette III	Rector, St. Philip's Episcopal Church, Durham	Term concurrent with rectorship of St. Philip's

The Articles of Incorporation provided that "upon the expiration of the term of each initial Director, the remaining members of the Board shall elect a successor from a slate of nominees proposed by the sponsoring agency for each initial Director." St. Philip's was thus guaranteed four representatives on a ten-person board, while the larger Durham community had six. As with the Soup Kitchen, so with the Urban Ministries Building: in responding to a particular need with a particular measure, St. Philip's had reached out and served the Durham community by persuading the larger community to be of service. At the same time St. Philip's had preserved the means to exercise its own influence.

During the three and a half years of hard campaigning, from February 1982 to the opening of the Urban Ministries Building in September 1985, there had been within the Vestry occasional voices of caution and dissent: "Aren't we moving too fast?" "Do we really need such a fine and expensive building?" But boldness had paid off, or, theologically speaking, another venture in faith had been justified.

In December 1983 Midyette reported to the parish that "St. Philip's Vestry had applied for status as a Jubilee Ministries Center in the name of the Urban Ministries of Durham, Inc. We received this designation from the Presiding Bishop and the National Executive Council of the Episcopal Church. There are only nine such centers in the country which serve as an outstanding example of outreach ministry within the Episcopal Church." [11] Personal recognition came to Midyette in several ways. When in 1986 the Dioceses of North Carolina and Belize became companion dioceses, he was the first North Carolina clergyman to serve for a month as interim rector of the Church of St. Mary's the Virgin in Belize's capital city, in order that its priest might have his first vacation in seven years. Midyette also officiated at four mission churches in the countryside and was struck ("stricken" would perhaps be a better term) by the incredible poverty in which people lived. Upon his return to the United States, St. Paul's Episcopal College in Lawrenceville, Virginia, granted him the honorary degree of Doctor of Laws for his life, work, and service in the field of urban ministries.

The third major innovation of the Midyette rectorship was the Prison Ministry. In obedience to Jesus' instruction to visit those in prison (Matthew 25:36), Midyette in the autumn of 1984 observed to Richard Watson, chair of St. Philip's Service Commission, that here was a mission to explore. Jesus' instruction was explicit but open-ended. To Jesus and his disciples in their first-century Palestinian setting it meant one thing. What it specifically meant in the twentieth-century Durham environment Watson and his associates would discover only through long conversations with Sheriff Roland Leary and his deputies, who were cordial and cooperative, and through action.

At first they explored the idea of having a Prison Ministry Program that consisted of two elements—a "Prison Families Anonymous," which would provide support for the families of prisoners, and a "Prison Visitation" undertaking. Although the expenses of the first element were subsidized by a $1,500 grant from the Diocese, so few families availed themselves of the proffered counseling sessions that the first element had to be dropped. "Prison Visitation," however, took off from its start in September 1985. From then on, each Saturday morning from nine until eleven o'clock, three to eight members of St. Philip's and of other churches visited the seventh floor of the county jail, where each person talked individually with prisoners who had signed up for the privilege. The conversation took place through a mouthpiece set in bulletproof glass. The prisoners, numbering thirty to seventy on a given Saturday, were mostly young men and women, poor and hence unable to afford bail, and charged with nearly every conceivable crime. Except by their example the visitors neither preached nor taught, but they listened sympathetically as the prisoners voiced their concerns and personal problems. In addition, when requested by an inmate, the visitors made telephone calls to "moms," fathers, sisters, brothers, friends, and employers. Usually the call was received with thanks. Also on request the visitors gave out Bibles, generally donated by the Gideons, and distributed paperbacks given by the North Carolina News Service, the Public Library, or parishioners, or purchased from Acclaimed Books, a prison ministry organization in Dallas, Texas. Not infrequently the prisoners asked for dictionaries and even Bible concordances. Though the Prison Ministry could not give money, it was permitted to parcel out one stamp per prisoner per week. For whatever reason, the weekly interlude was welcomed by the prisoners. By 1989, of the sixteen persons who visited with some regularity, eight were St. Philippians, one came from the First Presbyterian Church, two from Epworth Methodist Church, two from Fuller Memorial Presbyterian Church, and three from Duke University Chapel.[12] Once again St. Philip's had involved members of the larger Durham community in an enterprise that can only be regarded as blessed.

Tom Midyette's report to the Parish on January 15, 1989 closed with a letter from a man imprisoned in the county jail:

To St. Philip's Church:

I wish to thank all of you for your prayers and blessing that you have shared with me.

For I am a stranger in this town but yet you all open your arms and welcomed me with love and support when I really needed some one the most and I thank God for you with all my heart and I pray that he will open up the windows of heaven and pour out an abundance of blessing upon all of you. I pray for you all after finding out your church name and address I could not hold my peace, I had to tell somebody that one day if it be the will of God you will see my face in the midst of you. I feel as happy in the spirit of God till I just wanted to testify to somebody. Thanks for all that you have done for me.

A fourth set of innovations came in the field of Christian Education broadly conceived. At first the initiative still lay with Midyette. In November 1982 he informed the Vestry that he intended to ask that $1,000 be introduced into the budget for a part-time Christian Education director.[13] In September 1983 he appointed Mina Hampton,[14] who with Ethel Reade had rebuilt (under Bollinger) the program of the first six grades of the Church School. At the beginning the usual murmurs of dissent were heard within the congregation, in this case at paying one of its own volunteers to do what she would do gratis anyway. But Midyette's judgment was correct: St. Philip's did need a paid Christian Education director who would think steadily and responsibly about the problems of that division, and he was justified in the event by the conscientiousness, resourcefulness, and achievements of his appointee. The Hamptons, Mina and Tom, were what the congregation termed "church workers." Tom was always wherever someone was needed, as usher, chair of ushers, gardener, organizer of a Men's Group that met monthly on a Saturday morning to work in the garden and on the buildings, junior warden, and senior warden; the same was true of Mina in her field of activity. Once when Harold Parker was walking out of the parish house after an afternoon of working in the parish library, he met the Hamptons coming in. To Parker's remark, "Well, St. Philip's is becoming your second home," Tom replied, "No, it is our first," which was correct.

Initially, in 1983, Mina Hampton supervised only grades one through six, but with the retirement of Margaret Davis and George

Pyne she extended her jurisdiction to the preschool years, then to junior and senior high schoolers and informally to adult education and the library. For the Church School she recruited an able band of nearly twenty-five teachers, met them in workshops, and led them to adopt the printed curriculum of the Colorado series that was based on the weekly Scripture lessons for the Lectionary.

Attracted in part by a restored Church School, new families flooded in, twenty in 1985 and fifty in 1986, to raise the number of communicants from 706 in 1984 to 801 in 1987 and the number of children in Church School from an average attendance of 100 per Sunday to 130. On occasional Sundays the number exceeded 160, and classes had to be held in the Urban Ministries Building! To meet the needs and desires of the new families, Midyette, Mina Hampton, and the choirmaster, Kent Otto, revived in September 1986 the morning Family Service at nine o'clock, with a Children's Choir trained by Patricia Bartlett and an emphasis on Christian Education and instruction. Although attendance at this service was never greater than 90, it offered to worshipers another Sunday morning option: together a family could attend the Family Service at nine and then divide for Christian Education at ten o'clock, children to the Church School, parents to the Adult Education Forum (successively chaired by Harold Parker, Donna Hicks, and David Shumate); or parents and older children could attend their respective Church School and Adult Education classes at ten and together enjoy the regular eleven o'clock service with its volunteer Adult Choir and musical splendor. The quiet, meditative early communion service at eight was still attended by 25 communicants, who, in numbers neither more nor less, had been there since the days of David Yates.[15]

The congregation as a whole was changing. It was becoming not only larger but younger. And young people not only had children, who filled the Church School classes, they had new ideas and the willingness and energy to carry them out. A revolution was occurring at St. Philip's: the initiative for major innovations was shifting from the Rector to the laity—a shift that placed Tom Midyette in a new role, of welcoming, co-promoting, and coordinating the initiatives of others, a role he willingly accepted.

The first member of the laity to propose a *major* innovation was Amanda Smith, who had joined St. Philip's with her husband, James David Barber, in 1974. Her proposal can best be understood in terms of the historical context in which she was moving and of what she brought to it. In the rural, small-farm, small-town culture of the patriarchal family that lasted in the United States into the 1920s, everyone — father, mother, son, and daughter — knew the traditional family roles *and accepted them*: the son entered his father's trade as farmer or craftsman, the daughter followed her mother as dutiful spouse and mother, and marriage came early; except for the mavericks, there were no institutional problems of prolonged adolescence and single living, of prolonged career choice, and of identity. The religious rite of confirmation then had real meaning as a certification of entrance upon adult membership in the church and society. But in modern urban civilization, with the dissolution of roles and of their acceptance, people, parents as well as offspring, did not always know who they were, what they might be, or what they should be. They needed guidance and definition. However, the Church (and specifically St. Philip's) was not helping. The well-intentioned, well-organized programs of EYC did not grapple with the central, tormenting problems of gender and sexuality. Confirmation had become "an exit rite, the last thing young people did to please their parents before they left the church" and the Church School, where attendance always drooped in the junior and senior high classes. The old forms had lost meaning and power.

Amanda Smith came to this situation as a professional specialist in gender problems.[16] Upon her arrival in Durham she was employed by the North Carolina Department of Public Instruction to direct a program to open vocational education programs to both sexes. From that post she moved in 1978 to become an independent consultant on building partnerships between the sexes, in which she worked with education, industry, community organizations, and churches in forty-odd counties and five countries. From these experiences, she decided that reformers working with gender issues should stress not equality between the sexes but partnership and friendship, and that one should begin to form the attitudes of men and women when they were young, aged thirteen to eighteen, by having two rites of passage and supporting curricula. The first rite would celebrate the gift of creative manhood and womanhood at age thirteen; the second would recognize the attainment of responsible adulthood at sixteen. She also decided that the two rites should be placed within a Christian faith community. As she later explained:

The church is one of the few remaining multi-generational institutions in the United States, which means it can provide "elders" to function as friends and leaders for young people when they must move out beyond their parents. It can provide peers to share the journey. The church can deal comfortably with moral and spiritual issues because its membership is self-selected and has an agreed-upon set of values. Furthermore, the church already has rituals that mark other life changes, most notably birth, marriage, and death.

So, in 1986 she went to Tom Midyette, "a man of courage and imagination who likes new ventures. He understood the potential of these new ideas immediately." As he explained to the congregation, the program "would prepare young people to meet the challenges of adolescence by supporting them as a Christian family and through the nurture of the church, and then would give them skills for adulthood that would enable them to carry forth the love of Jesus throughout their adult lives." [17]

With his support a committee of parishioners was formed. It was decided that the new program would have four basic areas of study — Society, Self, Sexuality, and Spirituality — and three two-year units: Introduction to Manhood and Womanhood, for young people aged eleven to thirteen; Journey to Adulthood, for ages fourteen to sixteen; and Young Adults in the Church, to age eighteen. It would be accompanied by two rites of passage: the first, "A Celebration of the Gift of Manhood or Womanhood," informally known as Rite 13, was to be celebrated soon after each person's thirteenth birthday; the second was to be performed at the end of the Journey to Adulthood, for the whole graduating class. In addition, confirmation was then offered to graduates who wished it. Starting in the fall of 1987 the new Assistant Rector, the Reverend Victoria Jamieson-Drake, and her husband David, a graduate student at the Duke Divinity School, began on Sunday mornings and alternate Sunday evenings to lead a group of sixth- and seventh-graders through the curriculum of the first unit. The two leaders and Amanda Smith also drafted the liturgy to celebrate the Gift of Manhood and Womanhood, "spending hours on the telephone hammering out phrases." Amanda later recalled its first performance:

Our first Celebration of Manhood and Womanhood, affectionately known as Rite 13, was celebrated for Heather Corry. The ceremony in the church started with a prayer to give thanks for the gift of womanhood. (The service is exactly the same for young men, with the words "woman" changed to "man.") Heather was charged with the knowledge that as a woman she had been given the power of creation, and that because she was made in the image of God, she had a choice as to how to use that power. She was asked if she was aware of the challenge that this gift implied, and she answered "I am." She then led the congregation in portions of Psalm 139, which declares that she has been marvelously made.

Rites of passage for children are also rites of passage for parents, but parents are often given little help in making these transitions, so the ceremony included a prayer for Heather's parents as they began to let go of their child, praying that they would all be carried safely through the journey and one day stand together as adults and friends.

To reinforce strong group formation among the young people, the other members of the group were challenged to be loyal to her. They swore, "We will."

To underscore that Heather was now a young woman and recognized as such by the community, the Congregation was charged to share the wisdom of their years with her as she became a woman, and they affirmed, "We will."

Finally, the priest laid hands upon her head, praying that Almighty God would fill her with courage, wisdom, and joy and that Jesus Christ would be with her as her "strong companion and never-failing friend."

We held our collective breath to see what the congregation's reaction would be. A few people huffed ("I don't see what's so great about starting your period," said one older woman), but most found the experience unexpectedly moving. The most common comment was, "I wish we'd had something like this when I (or my child) was that age." Over the following months we polished and shortened the service and the congregation began to take ownership of these strange new ideas.

We also began to hammer out a curriculum based on the categories of Society, Self, Sexuality, and Spirituality. The ideas about male/female partnership and friendship and proving gender were discussed directly and also reinforced by supportive remarks and activities.

By September 1991 there was a sufficient number of graduates from three Manhood/Womanhood programs to start a Journey to Adulthood group. "Its lay leaders were Amanda Hughes, an exceptionally gifted youth leader, and David Vryhof, a member of the Order of St. John. Having defined Manhood/Womanhood in terms of the *gift* of creative energy, the curriculum for the second two years could stress Adulthood as meaning responsibility which must be *earned.*" "To prepare the candidates for adulthood the program now sought to teach them six basic skills: active listening, negotiation, assertion, research/information management, partnership, and leadership." In June 1993 the seventeen graduates of this stage of the program were presented to the congregation as self-assured young adults. As the first graduates from a rigorous and revolutionizing program, their names deserve to be recorded in this history: Luke Barber, Rachel Brown, Anne Fisher, Jason Hatfield, Chris Heaney, Jennifer McCann, Nick Register, Sarai Rightmyer, Margo Rundles, Katherine Steel, and Michael Steel; and Selby Conrad, Jonathan Feifs, Timothy Feifs, Kathy Sanders, Korto Scott, and Daphne Triplett. Most of them chose to be confirmed. In response to their achievement, the congregation showed its support by presenting the entire group with round-trip plane tickets to Jerusalem. The first eleven graduates listed above accepted the invitation and took part in a youth program run by St. George's College, which retraced the steps of the historical Jesus. That St. Philip's should help place eleven of its young people on the distant Palestinian pathways that Jesus had once trod was as stunning an achievement in its way as the United States Government's placing a man on the moon.

The seventeen graduates resumed their attendance at St. Philip's to complete the final two years in the program as Young Adults in the Church. "They were now encouraged to take on adult responsibilities in all aspects of parish life and the local community. They were challenged to become good stewards of their time, talent, and treasure. Guided by adult advisers, they used the Anglican model of Scripture, reason, and the tradition of the Church to begin a lifelong pilgrimage in their faith."

The effects of the program rippled outward from St. Philip's into the Diocese and the nation. The young St. Philippians themselves had been steadied and strengthened in a Christian life, their friendship with each other and their parents had been bonded, and an older EYC that had been excellent in its time had been replaced by a program with a vastly greater potential for individual assurance and growth. Other parishes in the Diocese of North Carolina and in the nation, facing similar problems, wished to know more about the program, and in response to the demand a 600-page copy of the detailed curriculum with lesson plans was prepared for publication by David Crean and Amanda Hughes.[18] Once again, as with the Community Kitchen, in responding to a local need, St. Philip's had originated a program that had national resonance. Once again it was serving the community by persuading the larger community to be of service. Tom Midyette and the families of the parish had once again ventured on faith and had been justified.

The Journey of Adulthood was just the beginning of other programs at St. Philip's that were lay-inspired and lay-sustained. They became so numerous that neither the Rector nor the Vestry could be expected to manage them, though they did try to be aware of their existence. Only a few can be mentioned here. Dating from 1989, St. Hilda's chapter of the Episcopal Church Women coordinated the work of volunteers who picked up day-old bread from Kroger stores for redistribution to the poor in Durham's housing projects.[19] Another group of women prepared food for AIDS victims and delivered it regularly.[20] At the Vestry retreat in February 1992 it was decided that St. Philip's should look into the possibility of a transitional housing program for homeless families who were drifting into hopelessness. With the approval of the congregation, the Vestry authorized in October that "this program be separately incorporated as the Durham Episcopal Housing Ministries. Elected to its initial board of directors were Ed Embree, Neil Boothby, Katherine Johnson, and Bill Scott." David and Bets Crean, "two Episcopalians who had a long history of involvement with housing and other services for homeless people," accepted DEHM's invitation to move to Durham and serve as volunteer (unpaid) directors. The program's focus initially was to provide housing and training to two or three homeless families for twelve to eighteen months until they were qualified to return to productive lives.[21] (The program was just getting under way when Midyette resigned.)

In 1993 the Diocese of North Carolina gave back to St. Philip's the responsibility of operating St. Andrew's as a parochial mission. Martha Clark-Boothby, first as deacon and after February 14, 1994 as priest, undertook to develop there a ministry to and for Latino (Hispanic) members of the Durham community. Bilingual in English and Spanish, she was a perfect choice for the mission.[22] Reaching across the Atlantic Ocean to West Africa, yet another group of St. Philippians took part in the rescue of Liberian children who had fled the violence of civil war in their native country to take refuge in Abidjan, a major port of the neighboring state of Ivory Coast. To provide instruction for these involuntary dropouts, a privately supported Liberian Refugee Tutorial Program had established a school to heal the children psychologically of the traumas they had suffered during the war and flight; to teach them reading, writing, mathematics, and science; and to provide them with such marketable skills as carpentry, bookkeeping, secretarial practices, and computer science. Led first by James David Barber, who has often appeared in this history, and then in close association by Chester Woyee, a native Liberian employed as a psychiatric social worker for Durham County and a member of St. Philip's, St. Philippians donated basic school supplies (pencils, pens, crayons, paper), typewriters, computers, dictionaries, encyclopedias, *and* money. Their slogan was: "Children cannot wait. Children have needs."[23] Meanwhile, meeting the needs of children and their parents back in Durham, Share Your Christmas continued to be a vital expression of a united parish effort.

Changes in society in the United States brought not only new programs but also transformation of the role of women in the church. To be sure, throughout the changes several essential church institutions at St. Philip's that had always been staffed by women survived intact. The Daughters of the King, which operated as a special religious order under the direction of the Rector, devotedly followed its schedule of visiting shut-ins. Nancy Mason also quietly and effectively continued as its president. The Altar Guild, with equal devotion and care, prepared the altar for all religious services. And, of course, in the volunteer Adult Choir, women continued to outnumber men nearly two to one. But during the Midyette years the organization known as the Episcopal Church Women was profoundly affected. An ECW that had been a church within a church, with its hierarchy of officers and budget, its monthly chapter meetings and programs of Christian devotion, education, and fellowship, and its annual bazaar, had harmonized with a family pattern in which women were confined to household duties and excluded from positions of authority and from certain activities in the church. ECW had been a power within the church, but it had exercised its power from outside the male organization. However, with the opening of the vestries and Diocesan and National Conventions of the Episcopal Church to women, they could now find influential and exciting careers of service in the church's main organization. Moreover, within the Sunday worship they could now serve as ushers, acolytes, lay readers, and passers of the chalice, in addition to their traditional roles in the choir. Opportunities for service were also opening in the innovative new programs outside of ECW. At the same time, wives who were engaged in rewarding employment outside the home lacked time, energy, and interest in chapter meetings and preparations for the annual bazaar. There was also the special difficulty of assuring the safety of the chapter women who met once a month at night in the parish house. For one reason or another during Midyette's rectorship the number of ECW chapters declined to two, attendance at meetings slipped to five or six, and the bazaar with its wonderful luncheon was reluctantly, regretfully abandoned for lack of support. ECW still existed as an organization with a hierarchy of officers, but at the close of Midyette's rectorship it was groping toward new forms of expression that would attract new or revived interest and have justifiable meaning.

The same problem confronted the men of the church. The Laymen's League had flourished during the rectorships of Yates, Haden, and Edwards, only to decay and disappear under Sherman. Attempts to revive it under Sherman, Bollinger, and Midyette repeatedly failed, until Tom Hampton in the mid-1980s organized a Men's Group that assembled one Saturday morning a month to clean up the parish buildings and grounds. The monthly Saturday meetings over the years gave the group shared fellowship and a sense of significant meaning.

The increase in the number of communicants (from 502 in 1978 to 925 in 1992) and of new programs necessitated increases in staff. Here, too, Midyette innovated. He welcomed and continued Kent Otto not only as organist and choirmaster but also as administrative assistant to the Rector, with daily oversight of the sexton and problems of maintenance and finance. Midyette also continued the Office Ministry of dedicated lay volunteers. From Monday to Friday they answered the telephone, greeted visitors, collated papers, sent out notices and mailings, and in general indispensably supplemented the work of the parish secretary. In addition, Midyette persuaded the Vestry and the congregation to fund a parish secretary—first Bea Hall, a member of St. Philip's, and then Anne Henrich, who were both in many ways responsible for the smooth running of the parish administration. He also added a volunteer permanent secretary to the Vestry, Gert Embree, who not only stabilized the Vestry minutes at a high level of accuracy and thoroughness but also preserved them and associated reports in the parish archives. Parish historians will be everlastingly grateful to her fidelity and skill. In 1981 Midyette negotiated an arrangement with Duke University Divinity School whereby each year one of their most qualified aspirants to the ministry would serve his (or her) year's internship at St. Philip's.[24] At first the Divinity School (traditionally a Methodist institution) named its most qualified candidates for the Methodist ministry: William Hanway, Timothy Kimbrough, and David Tucker. But when at the close of the year at St. Philip's they each converted to the Episcopal Church and became Episcopal priests, the Divinity School began to have second thoughts about sending its best. But it continued annually to supply a seminarian and to pay the stipend. According to their various capacities, these too performed valuable services—in Sunday worship, Church School, and Adult Education, and in working with young people.

Midyette also persuaded a distinguished group of Episcopal priests to serve as volunteer Priest Associates. They included Earl Brill, Episcopal chaplain at Duke University and author of *The Church's Moral Vision* in the second Episcopal Church Teaching Series; Thomas Rightmyer, who had retired after serving for nearly a quarter of a century in other Episcopal churches; Harmon Smith, professor of Christian Ethics at the Duke University Divinity School; and John Sharpe, curator of the Rare Book Collection at Duke University.[25] They were glad to step in from time to time and share in the work of a vibrant, ongoing church, preach a sermon, celebrate Holy Communion, or conduct a four-Sunday unit in Adult Education. They lent to the church tone and substantial knowledge.

To the Priest Associates should be added the four or five monks of the Episcopal Order of St. John. For ten years (1982–92) the spiritual influence of their example radiated from St. John's House on Morehead Heights. A small band of parishioners from St. Philip's and other Episcopal churches in the area daily attended their morning Eucharist and sought them out for confession and counsel. The monks themselves were engaged in active service at St. Philip's—attending Sunday worship, preaching an occasional sermon, leading a Lenten meditation at Adult Education, working on the curriculum of the Journey to Adulthood, or dishing out food at the Community Kitchen. They were sorely missed when they left Durham and retired to their "mother" house in Cambridge, Massachusetts.

Intermittently, Midyette was able to persuade the congregation and/or the Diocese to fund an Assistant to the Rector. The first, as a lay pastoral assistant, was Barney Hawkins, a B.D. who was writing his Ph.D. dissertation for the Duke Department of Religion.[26] However, when Bishop Fraser overruled Midyette, the Vestry, and the congregation and refused to admit him to candidacy for ordination, Hawkins left to be ordained in the Diocese of Western Carolina. After service in several of its parishes he moved on to Baltimore, where he became rector of the Church of the Redeemer and its three thousand to four thousand communicants. At St. Philip's he was succeeded as Assistant to the Rector by the Reverend Jess Gaither, who stayed a year.[27] Later in 1982 the incredibly learned Jonathan Glass, who contributed mightily to Adult Education,[28] and in 1986 the Reverend Victoria Jamieson-Drake, who cooperated with Amanda Smith to formulate Rite 13 and its supporting curriculum, served as part-time assistants.[29] Jamieson-Drake's refreshing bright youthfulness (everyone soon simply called her Vicky) was perfectly complemented by the mature wisdom of the Reverend Peter Robinson, who joined the staff the same year (1986) as Associate Rector.[30] He had already served churches in Sanford and Greensboro and had founded St. Francis Church in Greensboro. Since Jamieson-Drake did not wish to be a full-time assistant, she gave way in 1989 to the Reverend Joanne Stearns, who became the first full-time assistant at St. Philip's in more than nine years.[31] Universally loved by young and old, newcomers and the old guard, men as well as women, she was universally regretted when she departed in 1992 to take on the rectorship of St. Christopher's in Fairborn, Ohio.

With so much staff and so many ministries and programs, St. Philip's needed a coordinator of ministries. In 1990 Katherine Bradley Johnson, who had long been associated with St. Philip's and was studying to be ordained as permanent deacon, assumed that post. She served without pay even after her ordination.[32] When we add Betsy Rollins as director of the Community Kitchen and Martha Clark-Boothby as director of Hispanic Ministries to the group that included Joanne Stearns, Peter Robinson, Katherine Bradley Johnson, Kent Otto, Mina Hampton, and Anne Henrich as well as the Priest Associates and the seminarians, we can understand why Midyette bragged that St. Philip's staff was one of the best in the United States: energetic, committed, intelligent, and creative.[33]

The increase in the number and diversity of communicants and the increase in staff brought tremendous achievement and an aura of success but also caused strains, both financial and social. Upon his arrival in 1978 Midyette inherited a church that was running an annual deficit of several thousand dollars.[34] Within a year or two that deficit was eliminated, and the bank loan of $66,770 incurred by the renovations of 1972 was finally paid off: the bank note was publicly burned by the senior warden, Tom Hampton, to the congregation's applause.[35] By the close of 1982 the treasurer, Robert Bailey, was reporting an excess of income over disbursements of $11,136.76, quite the best fiscal year in his remembrance.[36] For the next three or four years the annual Every Member Canvass had no difficulty "making the budget," easily obtaining sufficient pledges to match estimated expenses. The financial situation was also eased by the unanticipated bequests, gratefully received, of Dea Townsend for $50,000 and of Mildred and Paul Glenn for more than $250,000. Not only did these gifts pay for a new organ ($187,000) and the paving of the parking lot ($60,000), but also they enlarged the St. Philip's trust fund to $75,000.[37]

Yet, starting in 1987 the Every Member Canvass became, to quote Midyette, "an ever more grueling experience."[38] At the beginning of 1992 the proposed budget was balanced only by eliminating raises for staff and the traditional grants of $1,000 dollars apiece to the Community Kitchen and Meals on Wheels and of $1,200 to DCIA, deletions that were a stunning insult to historical memory. (Midyette and Tom Rightmyer stepped forward and fulfilled these three obligations out of their discretionary fund.)[39] Even with these budgetary cuts, the treasurer, David Shumate, had to borrow $22,000 from the bank at the close of the year because important pledges had not yet been paid.[40] Perhaps worst of all, over the years the budget was balanced only by neglecting needed maintenance and repairs. The physical plant became so dilapidated that the junior warden, Dorothy Smith, realistically estimated in 1993 that it would take more than $200,000 to put it in shape.[41]

The Vestry's Stewardship Committee, chaired by Tom Metzloff, undertook in November 1989 to analyze why the fiscal strain had occurred. Its intellectually powerful report suggested several factors;[42]

aided by the statistics shown in Appendix R, we can surmise several more. From 1978 to 1992 expenses more than tripled, from $95,350 to $308,835. Whereas the number of communicants had nearly doubled, from 502 to 925, the number of pledging units had risen only slightly, from 212 to 228. This meant that the average pledging unit had to triple its contribution. When the pledging units were examined more closely, however, it was noticed that each year the church was losing significant givers by death or migration. Newcomers, who were not yet caught up in a momentum of giving, did not replace the losses thus incurred. Moreover, the "lifestyle" of young couples with children did not permit them to give significantly—they had a family to maintain, a loan on the purchase of two cars to pay, the mortgage on their home to discharge, not to mention saving for daunting college tuitions and paying off their own college loans. Meanwhile, patterns of philanthropy among the very affluent were changing: in the nineteenth century they gave chiefly to their churches and later to educational institutions as well, but more recently they were giving to a greater variety of competing charities and enterprises. So, the burden of increased expenses and of giving at St. Philip's was falling on the middle class of donors. And they were becoming fatigued by the annual exhortation to increase their contribution yet another 10 percent and by annual appeals by the Rector for money to support yet another new program. As one loyal parishioner remarked to a canvasser: "I have learned that no matter how much money you give, *they* will always find ways to spend it," an observation that reflected a dangerous cynicism toward the Vestry and its leader.[43]

The Vestry responded by attempting to raise the level of discourse. On May 10, 1990 it adopted as its personal standard a goal of a proportional giving that was moving toward tithing. It repeatedly invited the congregation to follow its example.[44] Whether these invitations had any appreciable effect except on those already converted is unknown. The annual agony of "making the budget" continued.

Diversity of communicants also yielded what might be termed social strains. Ethnic diversity occasioned the least difficulty. The few black families who attended were welcomed at worship services and in church work. William Scott was appointed to the Board of Durham Episcopal Housing, and in 1993 Cora Scott was elected a member of the Vestry.[45] Latinos and Asian-Americans (also few) were likewise easily accepted. Gender differences produced more tension. The selection of a woman priest, Vicky Jamieson-Drake, to be Assistant Rector caused some stir. When in her inaugural sermon she chose to make a strong feminist statement, one male parishioner was heard to mutter as he walked out of church, "This will show up at pledge time." But whatever tension her appointment may have occasioned was dissolved by the arrival of Joanne Stearns, who won all hearts. The national debate over the use of "inclusive language" in the Scripture and the liturgy was taken very seriously by a few idealists at St. Philip's but was regarded as "academic," that is, as relatively unimportant, at worst as a minor irritant, by most St. Philippians. Midyette did not believe the canons authorized him to alter the language of the Bible and Prayer Book, although on their own a few parishioners might murmur "she" when referring to the Holy Spirit.

The source of greatest social strain within the congregation was the sexual orientation of several of its members. For years it had been St. Philip's policy to make its parish house available for meetings of such support groups as Alcoholics Anonymous, Overeaters Anonymous, and the Coalition of Battered Women. Should it open its facilities to Integrity, a support group for gays? At its retreat in Beaufort (1984), several members of the Vestry strongly recommended that Midyette not do so. But exercising his canonical right of control over church facilities, he honored Integrity's request to meet in the parish house and had Bishop Robert W. Estill address the group. This was an opening wedge. By one means or another Midyette then persuaded the members of the congregation to tolerate the presence of gay couples in their midst at worship services and on retreats, and even gradually to change their minds about them, their sexual orientation, and their Christianity. In time the congregation would even celebrate its diversity and inclusiveness.

What it meant to the congregation to live through fifteen years of interaction with Tom Midyette can be conveyed in part by the homily he delivered at the burial service for Tom Hampton, who was Mr. Everyman or at least Mr. Everyman's Parishioner:

> Tom Hampton and I shared in both being from Eastern North Carolina. We shared those roots together. A wonderful person! An irascible man! A great friend! A conservative, but a person who understood the Gospel for today. He understood what faith

was about. He knew that the Lord was the way, the truth and the light, and Tom began his journey in life with that overall commitment. Once you understand that the Lord is the way, the truth and the light, it does not matter if you come from Plymouth or New Bern or Hyde County, it matters that your life has been altered forever and you can accept the changes of the world. He came to those changes in his wonderful way, kicking and screaming. He became an integrationalist from a conservative background. He did not particularly like the ordination of women and ended up supporting it wholeheartedly. He was not raised to be inclusive but saw in his faith the need for the Church to accept everyone. Because, you see, when you are raised with Jesus as the way, the truth and the light, then your life is altered. It is changed, and you know that no matter what you do in your life, that what is most important is that you walk in the teachings of Jesus.

One last remembrance of Tom, he truly loved his family—his wife and his two children—but one thing that was true about him, he loved the Church more. He loved Jesus more and it was because of that faith and because of that love, he gave to all of us a kindness, and gentleness and soft irascibleness that he brought us all. We are better for knowing Tom because we know then what he knows that Jesus is the way for all of us. That Jesus is the truth and the light of us and that Jesus is our light. We rejoice in Tom's coming into the kingdom of God. AMEN.[46]

Living with Tom Midyette for a decade and a half and reflecting on that experience enabled the Vestry to compose that dense, sophisticated reaffirmation of purpose which gave to the life and work of the congregation meaning and support for action. This history cannot be better concluded than by quoting it again:

St. Philip's is a holy place where we worship God. Our worship forms us into a community of Christians. By prayer, sacrament, and fellowship we nourish and sustain one another in our individual lives and ministries. We obey the Gospel call to bring the light and hope in Jesus Christ to all people. We offer welcome, support, food, and shelter to all in need without pride, prejudice, or judgment. We have responsibility to the entire Durham community, especially our downtown neighborhood.

ENVOI

Every moment is immediate to God and derives from that relationship its own meaning and significance. But its meaning also is related
to what came before and what came after. In its relationship to the
past of St. Philip's the rectorship of Tom Midyette was fulfillment and
novelty, and it gave significant meaning to what had come before.
Whether it will have lasting significance will depend on what comes
after. And that fact places upon posterity the solemn obligation not
to allow the accomplishment of Midyette's rectorship to stagnate or
dissolve. His generation responded faithfully and triumphantly to the
needs, necessities, and opportunities of the hour in the spirit of Jesus
Christ. Can we do less?

Appendixes

APPENDIX A. TABLE OF OFFICERS

	Senior Warden	Junior Warden	Secretary	Treasurer
Dec. 1914– Dec. 1915	E. G. Muse	E. K. Powe	J. A. Robinson	K. P. Lewis
Dec. 1915– Dec. 1916	E. G. Muse	E. K. Powe	J. A. Robinson	K. P. Lewis
Dec. 1916– Dec. 1917	E. G. Muse	E. K. Powe	L. F. Butler	K. P. Lewis
Dec. 1917– Dec. 1918	W. A. Erwin	J. M. Manning Resigned Mar. 1918	N. L. Clay	H. M. Jensen
Dec. 1918– Jan. 1920	E. K. Powe	E. D. Pusey	L. F. Butler	H. E. White
1920	E. K. Powe	J. Harper Erwin	L. F. Butler	H. E. White
1921	E. K. Powe	J. Harper Erwin	L. F. Butler	H. E. White
1922	W. A. Erwin	J. M. Manning		
1923	K. P. Lewis	J. M. Manning		
1924	K. P. Lewis	J. M. Manning		
1925	W. A. Erwin	H. E. White		
1926	W. A. Erwin	H. E. White		
1927	H. E. White	J. Harper Erwin		
1928	J. Harper Erwin	Clarence E. Boesch		
1929	J. Harper Erwin	Clarence E. Boesch		
1930	W. A. Erwin	E. I. Bugg	C. A. Moore to May; then W. H. Ruffin	C. A. Moore to May; then J. Harper Erwin
1931	E. I. Bugg	H. E. White	W. H. Ruffin	H. C. Bird
1932	E. I. Bugg	J. H. Erwin, Jr.	Murray Jones	H. C. Bird to June; then W. B. LaFar
1933	W. B. LaFar	H. C. Bird	Murray Jones	B. W. Hobgood, Jr.
1934	H. C. Bird	K. P. Lewis	E. M. Hunter, Jr.	B. W. Hobgood, Jr.
1935	K. P. Lewis	J. H. Erwin, Jr.	E. M. Hunter, Jr.	B. W. Hobgood, Jr.
1936	K. P. Lewis	J. H. Erwin, Jr.	Lloyd Williams	B. W. Hobgood, Jr.
1937	J. H. Erwin, Jr.	W. H. Ruffin	Lloyd Williams	B. W. Hobgood, Jr.
1938	W. H. Ruffin	B. R. Roberts	N. A. Gregory	B. W. Hobgood, Jr.
1939	W. H. Ruffin	A. H. London	N. A. Gregory	B. W. Hobgood, Jr.
1940	A. H. London	J. H. Erwin, Jr.	Ellerbee Powe, Jr.	B. W. Hobgood, Jr.
1941	W. H. Ruffin	J. H. Erwin, Jr.	Ellerbee Powe, Jr.	B. W. Hobgood, Jr.
1942	W. H. Ruffin	J. H. Erwin, Jr. B. R. Roberts	R. G. Hurst Noble L. Clay	B. W. Hobgood, Jr.
1943	W. H. Ruffin	B. R. Roberts	Noble L. Clay	B. W. Hobgood, Jr.

	Senior Warden	Junior Warden	Secretary	Treasurer
1944	A. H. London, Jr.	Robert G. Hurst	Richard H. Leigh	B. W. Hobgood, Jr.
1945	Angus McBryde	B. R. Roberts	Richard H. Leigh	B. W. Hobgood, Jr.
1946	B. R. Roberts	Robert G. Hurst	Clarence H. Cobb	B. W. Hobgood, Jr.
1947	B. R. Roberts	Robert G. Hurst	Clarence H. Cobb	B. W. Hobgood, Jr.
1948	A. H. London	Robert G. Hurst	J. A. Murdock Watts Carr, Jr.	B. W. Hobgood, Jr.
1949	W. H. Ruffin	N. A. Gregory	Watts Carr, Jr.	B. W. Hobgood, Jr.
1950	W. H. Ruffin	N. A. Gregory	Watts Carr, Jr.	B. W. Hobgood, Jr.
1951	W. H. Ruffin	Wm. P. Biggers, Jr.	Charles H. Livengood, Jr.	B. W. Hobgood, Jr.
1952	Wm. P. Biggers	Clarence Cobb	Charles H. Livengood, Jr.	B. W. Hobgood, Jr.
1953	Wm. P. Biggers	Watts Carr, Jr.	Charles H. Livengood, Jr.	B. W. Hobgood, Jr.
1954	W. H. Ruffin	Watts Carr, Jr.	Robert L. Fortune	B. W. Hobgood, Jr.
1955	W. H. Ruffin	Cleveland C. Kern	Mattie West	B. W. Hobgood, Jr.
1956	A. H. London, Jr.	Kenneth C. Royall, Jr.	Mattie West	B. W. Hobgood, Jr.
1957	B. R. Roberts	Robert W. Carr	C. E. Bittle	B. W. Hobgood, Jr.
1958	Robert G. Hurst	Robert L. Fortune	Robert W. Carr	B. W. Hobgood, Jr.
1959	Clarence Cobb	Robert L. Fortune	Robert W. Carr	Richard H. Leigh
1960	W. H. Ruffin	James Nicholson, Jr.	Richard Watson, Jr.	Richard H. Leigh
1961	Kenneth Royall, Jr.	James Nicholson, Jr.	Richard Watson, Jr.	Richard H. Leigh
1962	Watts Carr, Jr.	James Nicholson, Jr.	Richard Watson, Jr.	Richard H. Leigh
1963	James E. Davis	Haywood C. Smith	John N. Chatham	Richard H. Leigh
1964	James E. Davis	Haywood C. Smith	John N. Chatham	Harald Hansen-Pruss
1965	W. H. Ruffin	James Nicholson, Jr.	Billy B. Olive	Harald Hansen-Pruss
1966	Angus McBryde	James Nicholson, Jr.	Billy B. Olive	Harald Hansen-Pruss
1967	E. K. Powe III	Bond Anderson III	James Pleasants, Jr.	Harald Hansen-Pruss
1968	Bond Anderson III	James Pleasants, Jr.	Richard Watson, Jr.	Harald Hansen-Pruss
1969	Harding Hughes	James Pleasants, Jr.	Richard Watson, Jr.	Harald Hansen-Pruss
1970	Watts Carr, Jr.	James Nicholson, Jr.	Richard Watson, Jr.	A. L. Featherston
1971	Dorothy Manning	Warren Watkins	Harold T. Parker	A. L. Featherston
1972	Victor Moore	Abbott Lloyd	Harold T. Parker	A. L. Featherston
1973	Angus McBryde	James Pleasants, Jr.	Harold T. Parker	A. L. Featherston
1974	Richard Watson, Jr.	James Pleasants, Jr.	Merrell Patrick	A. L. Featherston
1975	Richard Watson, Jr.	James Pleasants, Jr.	Irene Nashold	A. L. Featherston
1976	Ralph Strayhorn	John Chatham	Irene Nashold	A. L. Featherston
1977	Ralph Strayhorn	John Chatham	Irene Nashold	A. L. Featherston
1978	Ralph Strayhorn to Sept.; then Richard Watson, Jr.	Richard Watson, Jr., to Sept.; then Thomas Hampton	Harold T. Parker	Margo Rundles

	Senior Warden	Junior Warden	Secretary	Treasurer
1979	Richard Watson, Jr., to June; then Thomas Hampton	Thomas Hampton	Gert Embree	Robert F. Bailey
1980	Thomas Hampton		Gert Embree	Robert F. Bailey
1981	Watts Carr, Jr.	Walter Mason	Gert Embree	Robert F. Bailey
1982	Angus McBryde	Walter Mason	Gert Embree	Robert F. Bailey
1983	John E. Markham, Jr.	Thomas Hampton	Gert Embree	Robert F. Bailey
1984	Richard Watson, Jr.	Thomas Hampton	Gert Embree	Robert F. Bailey
1985	Charles L. Steel IV	Thomas Hampton	Gert Embree	Camilla J. Peete
1986	E. K. Powe III	Harry Stallings	Gert Embree	Camilla J. Peete
1987	Daniel Pearson	David Mangum	Gert Embree	Camilla J. Peete Warren Pope, Ass't
1988	Edward Embree	David Mangum	Gert Embree	Camilla J. Peete Warren Pope, Ass't
1989	Edward Embree	David Mangum	Gert Embree	Jean Barber
1990	Charles L. Steel IV	Thomas Hampton	Gert Embree	Rhodes Craver
1991	John Chatham	Thomas Hampton	Gert Embree	Rhodes Craver
1992	John Chatham	Dorothy Smith	Gert Embree	Rhodes Craver to June; then David Shumate
1993	E. K. Powe III	Daniel Pearson	Gert Embree	David Shumate

	Chair of Every Member Canvass (chosen preceding October)	President of Woman's Auxiliary or ECW	President of Laymen's League	Choir Director–Organist
Dec. 1914–Dec. 1915	NA			
Dec. 1915–Dec. 1916	No Chair			
Dec. 1916–Dec. 1917	No Chair			
Dec. 1917–Dec. 1918	No Chair			
Dec. 1918–Jan. 1920	No Chair			
1920	NA			
1921	NA			
1930	K. P. Lewis	Mrs. L. A. Tomlinson retired, had been head of Auxiliary for 21 years		

	Chair of Every Member Canvass (chosen preceding October)	President of Woman's Auxiliary or ECW	President of Laymen's League	Choir Director–Organist
1931	J. H. Erwin, Jr.	Mrs. Murray Jones		
1932	H. M. Kramer	Mrs. Murray Jones		
1933	H. M. Kramer H. C. Bird, Vice-Chair	Mrs. Murray Jones		
1934	E. M. Hunter, Jr.	Mrs. Harold C. Bird		
1935	E. M. Hunter, Jr.	Mrs. Harold C. Bird		
1936	E. M. Hunter, Jr.	Mrs. Harold C. Bird	Nat Gregory	Mrs. Hugo Walker
1937	Lloyd Williams	Mrs. George Lyon	Nat Gregory	C. E. Moore
1938	Lloyd Williams	Mrs. George Lyon Mrs. Hugo Walker	Lawson Moore Angus McBryde	W. P. Twaddell
1939	N. A. Gregory	Mrs. Hugo Walker	Angus McBryde	W. P. Twaddell
1940	N. A. Gregory	Mrs. Hugo Walker	George L. Lyon	Mrs. W. P. Twaddell
1941	Noble L. Clay	Mrs. Hugo Walker	William H. Ruffin	W. P. Twaddell
1942	J. H. Erwin, Jr.	Mrs. B. W. Roberts	Glenn A. Coan	Mrs. W. P. Twaddell
1943	B. R. Roberts	Mrs. B. W. Roberts	Glenn A. Coan	Mrs. W. P. Twaddell
1944	R. G. Hurst	Mrs. R. E. Quinn	Angus McBryde	Mrs. W. P. Twaddell
1945	R. H. Leigh	Mrs. R. E. Quinn	Clarence H. Cobb	Ethel Reade
1946	A. H. London, Jr.	Mrs. George Watts Carr	Robert G. Hurst	Mrs. W. P. Twaddell
1947	W. H. Ruffin	Mrs. George Watts Carr	T. A. Ricks	Allan H. Bone
1948	Watts Carr, Jr.	Mrs. R. G. Hurst	R. H. Leigh	Allan H. Bone
1949	H. V. Stoever	Mrs. R. G. Hurst	Frank H. Kenan	Allan H. Bone
1950	Wm. P. Biggers	Mrs. J. M. M. Gregory, Jr.	I. E. Harris, Jr.	Allan H. Bone
1951	Angus McBryde	Mrs. J. M. M. Gregory, Jr.	B. R. Roberts	Allan H. Bone
1952	Frank H. Kenan	Mrs. W. H. Ruffin	George Watts Carr, Jr.	Allan H. Bone James Wood
1953	Kenneth Podger	Mrs. W. H. Ruffin	E. M. Holt	John West Henry Cook
1954	E. K. Powe III	Mrs. W. P. Biggers	Jack Hughes	Henry Cook
1955	Arthur H. London	Mrs. E. K. Powe, Sr.	C. L. May	Henry Cook
1956	NA	Mrs. E. K. Powe, Sr.		Henry Cook
1957	NA	Mrs. Louis A. Carr	C. L. May	Henry Cook
1958	NA	Mrs. Louis A. Carr Mrs. Angus McBryde	George A. McAfee I. H. Manning, Jr.	David Pizarro
1959	Paul Wright	Mrs. Angus McBryde	I. H. Manning, Jr. Robert G. Hurst	David Pizarro

	Chair of Every Member Canvass (chosen preceding October)	President of Woman's Auxiliary or ECW	President of Laymen's League	Choir Director– Organist
		Mrs. Ben R. Roberts Mrs. I. H. Manning, Jr.	(Men of St. Philip's November 1959)	
1960	James E. Davis	Mrs. I. H. Manning, Jr.	Robert G. Hurst Gordon Woody	David Pizarro
1961	John Chatham	Mrs. I. H. Manning, Jr. Mrs. Julian Ruffin	Gordon Woody B. B. Olive	David Pizarro
1962	Haywood C. Smith	Mrs. Julian Ruffin	William R. Crabtree	David Pizarro
1963		Mrs. Julian Ruffin Mrs. Gordon Woody	William R. Crabtree	David Pizarro
1964	James Nicholson	Mrs. Gordon Woody	John N. Chatham (Laymen's Activities)	David Pizarro (to Nov.)
1965	NA	Mrs. Gordon Woody Mrs. C. C. Ainsworth		Robert Capen
1966	NA	Mrs. C. C. Ainsworth		Robert Capen
1967	Bond Anderson III	Mrs. C. C. Ainsworth Mrs. Watts Carr, Jr.		Robert Capen
1968	James Nicholson	Mrs. Watts Carr, Jr.		Robert Capen William Miller
1969	John Chatham	Mrs. Watts Carr, Jr. Mrs. George Pyne		William Miller
1970	Arch Bass	Mrs. George Pyne		William Miller
1971	Victor Moore	Mrs. George Pyne Mrs. Kenneth Royall		William Miller
1972	Victor Moore	Mrs. Kenneth Royall		William Miller Kent Otto
1973	Frank Gray William Jennings	Mrs. Kenneth Royall Mrs. John E. Markham		Kent Otto
1974	William Jennings	Mrs. John E. Markham		Kent Otto
1975	John E. Markham, Jr.	Mrs. John E. Markham		Kent Otto

	Chair of Every Member Canvass (chosen preceding October)	President of Woman's Auxiliary or ECW	President of Laymen's League	Choir Director– Organist
		Mrs. James E. Davis		
1976	Thomas E. Bollinger	Mrs. James E. Davis		Kent Otto
1977	Daniel Pearson	Mrs. James E. Davis		Kent Otto
1978	Daniel Pearson	Mrs. Edwin B. Hamshar		Kent Otto
1979	Watts Carr, Jr.	Mrs. Edwin B. Hamshar		Kent Otto
1980	Watts Carr, Jr.	Mrs. Robert F. Bailey		Kent Otto
1981	Victor Moore	Mrs. Alton L. Jernigan		Kent Otto
1982	Watts Carr, Jr.	Mrs. Francis E. Bowman		Kent Otto
1983	Victor Moore	Mrs. B. W. C. Roberts		Kent Otto
1984	Richard Watson	Mrs. William M. Harrison		Kent Otto
1985	John Chatham	Mrs. William M. Harrison		Kent Otto
1986	John Chatham	Mrs. James R. Pleasants		Kent Otto
1987	Robert W. Carr	Mrs. James R. Pleasants		Kent Otto
1988	E. K. Powe	Mrs. Thomas Hampton		Kent Otto
1989	Thomas Metzloff	Mrs. Thomas Hampton		Kent Otto
1990	Thomas Metzloff	Mrs. James Davis		Kent Otto
1991	John Chatham	Mrs. Dwight Emory		Kent Otto
1992	E. K. Powe	Mrs. Dwight Emory		Kent Otto
1993	William M. Harrison E. K. Powe	Mrs. Dwight Emory		Kent Otto
1994	Mike Woodard	Mrs. Charles Wood		Kent Otto

APPENDIX B. DAUGHTERS OF THE KING, ST. PHILIP'S EPISCOPAL CHURCH, 1952–1993

*Mrs. Frank Webb
Mrs. R. B. Boyd
*Mrs. William H. Ruffin
Mrs. John Gregory, Jr.
*Mrs. R. E. Quinn, Jr.
Mrs. Louis Carr
Mrs. B. W. Roberts
*Mrs. Frank Minter
*Mrs. Ralph Vantrine
*Mrs. Gordon Woody
Mrs. John B. Cahoon
Mrs. Reginald Potts
Mrs. Kenneth Podger
Mrs. Angus McBryde
*Mrs. H. C. Cunningham
Mrs. I. H. Manning
*Mrs. Rita Odiorne
*Miss Ethel Reade
*Mrs. Kenneth Royall, Jr.

*Mrs. P. C. Spencer
*Mrs. Haywood C. Smith
Mrs. Virginia Stephens
Mrs. Will London
Mrs. Blaine Nashold
Mrs. James Warren
Mrs. Grover Hunter
Mrs. James E. Davis
Mrs. W. B. Watkins, Sr.
Mrs. Walter Mason
Mrs. Jack Markham
*Mrs. George C. Pyne, Jr.
Mrs. Clarence Cobb
*Mrs. Frank Bowman
Mrs. Ed Embree
*Miss Helen Kendall
*Mrs. Robert G. Hurst
*Miss Lillian Lee

*Deceased.

Leaders, 1953–1993

1953—Mrs. Frank Webb, with Grace Carr as secretary and treasurer
Mrs. R. B. Boyd, with Grace Carr as secretary and treasurer
Mrs. W. H. Ruffin, with Grace Carr as secretary and treasurer
Mrs. John Gregory, with Grace Carr as secretary and treasurer
Mrs. B. W. Roberts, with Margaret Minter as secretary and treasurer
Mrs. R. E. Quinn, Jr., with Grace Carr as secretary and treasurer
Mrs. H. C. Cuningham, with Libby Roberts as secretary and treasurer
Mrs. John Cahoon, Jr., with Julia Royall as secretary and treasurer
Rita Odiorne, with Libby Roberts as secretary and treasurer
1981–93 Mrs. Walter Mason, with Phyllis Bowman, Mary Ann Warren, and Lillian Lee in succession as secretary and treasurer

APPENDIX C. DESCRIPTION OF THE JUNIOR CHOIR, SEPTEMBER 1955

Memo to Parents of Junior Choir Members Regarding the Choir
From: Mrs. Richard L. Watson, President of Junior Choir Mother's Guild

The Junior Choir under the leadership of Mr. Henry Cook is one of St. Philip's major projects in Christian Education. In the Fall of 1954, there were 22 boys and 24 girls enrolled in the choir. Twenty-four boys and 24 girls are the maximum number that can be accommodated. In January 1955, 3 boys graduated, and later 1 boy was added. In the Spring 1 girl who moved out of town was immediately replaced. Other than these changes there has been no turnover in membership. Attendance at the rehearsals, which occur twice a week, and at the Family Service on Sunday, which is a major responsibility of the choir, has been remarkable. The record indicates that the children have worked diligently to develop an outstanding choir. In their efforts to sing to the glory of God they have enriched our Church Program immeasurably.

The choir year begins in January when the oldest group graduates, and when the new members, who have been in training since September, officially become regular members of the choir. Through their study and participation in the music of the Church they learn the meaning and traditions of the seasons and ceremonies of the Church Year, become familiar with the order of different services, and acquire a feeling of responsibility for them. A unique example of this occurred last year when, at the beginning of the Family Service, it was discovered that no acolyte was present; one of the choir boys was asked to fill in; and he took over with poise without any formal preparation other than his observation and understanding of the service.

One of the most concentrated opportunities for study is at the Choir Camp held during the summer at Camp Leach. Although the usual camp activities attract the children here, considerable time is spent in training them as choir members. This camping experience in which they work and play with the children from other choirs is something to which they look forward all year. In 1954, 23 boys and girls went to camp from St. Philip's, and in 1955, 24. The concentrated preparation which this group, as a nucleus, receives in the summer helps the choir as a whole to carry on during the busy year.

It would be most unfortunate if any child did not join the choir or did not go to the camp because of the expense involved. The strain on the family budget is particularly great where there are several members of one family in the choir. Yet because of the value of the choir camp it is important to emphasize it as a part of the year's program and help make it possible for each child to attend. With this in mind, a Junior Choir Fund was established in 1954 to help pay camp fees. The Junior Choir Mother's Guild has had several church dinners and has helped the children with a booth at the Woman's Auxiliary Bazaar in order to make money for the Fund. Parents of choir members who have gone to camp, interested church members, and the Woman's Auxiliary have contributed to this Fund. In 1955, the Fund was large enough to pay about one half of the camp fee for each child and a part of the transportation of the choir to the Music Festival held in 1954 at Tarboro and in 1955 at Rocky Mount.

The choir program offers an opportunity for Christian Education at an age when it will have its effect in establishing the child as a regular participant in church activities. The children as a group get pleasure and enjoyment out of this work. They can take pride in doing a good job and in being an important part of the Church. They do much to earn the contributions the Church makes to their activities, but more important, they themselves gain from serving the Church in this way. Finally, anyone close to these children knows the affection they have for their choir director and the influence that he has upon them. His knowledge of music and how to teach it, his ability to work with people, both young and old, his Christian ideals and principles combine to make him a rare individual for whom St. Philip's can be thankful.

APPENDIX D. EDWARDS SPEECH HONORING FRANCES GRAY PATTON

After dinner speech of the Rev. Tom Turney Edwards at the testimonial dinner given in honor of Frances Gray Patton, a member of St. Philip's Church and author of *Good Morning, Miss Dove*.

Mrs. Patton, Ladies and Gentlemen,

When I was invited to accept the high honor and privilege of making this presentation, a quotation flashed across my mind. Well, at any rate, after frantically ransacking my mind for something to say, I at length came up with this quotation, which I would like to share with you. It's a definition of humor, and it comes from an article which was written for the *New York Times* Book Review section in August 1952 by Walt Kelly, the famous humorist who draws the cartoon *Pogo*. Kelly is quoting from Robert Paynes' book *The Great God Pan*. It goes like this:

"What is humor? Humor is a kind of gentle and benevolent custodian of the mind which prevents us from being overwhelmed by the apparent seriousness of life."

I have cherished this quotation ever since. I take it to mean that humor is much more than the laughs and fun you get out of it. It is therapy for tired minds; it is sanity and reality in a cockeyed world. Humor, by enabling us to see the comical side of things, particularly our own antics, saves us from the sin of deadly seriousness, which ends in self-righteousness and censoriousness. What is tragedy but a human situation that does not have its ridiculous side? Pity the poor Russians—the most ponderously, grimly, deadly serious nation of people in the world.

Humor is indispensable for all, but it is especially crucial for those who occupy dignified stations in life. The more dignified you are, the harder you fall, the funnier it is to other people, and the harder it is for you to recover—unless you can laugh at yourself. I belong to a profession which, because of its weighty calling, is always in danger of being overwhelmed by the apparent seriousness of life. My sympathy goes out to clergy who have no sense of humor; they are about as well qualified for their jobs as a one-legged man at a cotillion.

I always rejoice to hear of men like the bishop who was entering a store one winter day when the streets were sheathed in ice. As he was going in, a woman was coming out, and they both slipped and fell simultaneously and in such a way that she was sitting astride the bishop's chest. They went slipping off down the slick street, tandem, as it were, and finally brought up against a telephone pole. The woman was too stunned and horrified to move, so the bishop, still lying on his back, doffed his hat politely and said, "I am sorry, Madame, but this is as far as I go."

I cannot think of any thing more overwhelming in its apparent seriousness than bringing up children and all that goes along with that—PTA School, lunches, crayons cunningly planted where you are bound to skate on them when you go down in the middle of the night to see why the furnace is making that odd noise. Speaking personally, my greatest need of therapy is in this area. Sometimes it is very hard to see anything funny in children.

A little boy came in from school, and his mother said, "I've some bad news for you—

Laddy was run over this afternoon." She expected her son to be crushed, but he took it without turning a hair, and went on out into the yard to play. Soon he was back, asking for his dog. "I told you Laddy was run over this afternoon." The little boy burst into a loud wail: "I thought you said Daddy."

Well, into this virgin territory moves Mrs. Patton with her characters so like us in *The Finer Things of Life* and *Good Morning, Miss Dove*. Men, if your wife is threatening to buy a new dress, have her read "Music of the Spheres" in *Finer Things of Life*.

Many's the harassed, heavy-laden parent you've bridged over a trying period with your gentle satire. It is the therapy we need, and on behalf of your friends gathered here—your patients, I should say—it gives me great pleasure, Mrs. Patton, to present you to them, and from them to you this token of their appreciation for the pure pleasure you have given them and the honor you have brought to our town. Ladies and Gentlemen, Mrs. Frances Gray Patton.

APPENDIX E. THE CAMPAIGN AND CANVASS OF 1956

ST. PHILIP'S EPISCOPAL CHURCH
Corner East Main and Queen Streets
DURHAM, NORTH CAROLINA
September 10, 1956

Dear Fellow Member of St. Philip's.

By this time, you should have received your copy of the brochure setting forth our ambitious, but realistic, plans for (1) a "dowry" for St. Luke's and St. Andrew's, our two offspring and (2) improvement of our Church property.

Ten years ago we met a challenge calling for the remaining $50,000 needed to build our Parish House. Wouldn't it have been a serious failure if we had not done so? At that time economic conditions, in general, were substantially below the present level. Today there are many in our Church family who are enjoying more favorable financial circumstances. So, if we "Give As We Are Blessed," we most certainly will realize our present goal of $50,000.

Recently, I reviewed with interest the study of the Episcopal Church in Durham which we made just three years ago by the Rev. Joseph G. Moore, Director, Unit of Research of the National Council of the Protestant Episcopal Church. The present plans for St. Luke's and St. Andrew's are in keeping with the top recommendations made. Among other favorable observations concerning St. Philip's were—"This is the parent Church of all Episcopal work in the City of Durham—strategically located—There is no question that St. Philip's down-town location is excellent for a metropolitan parish—Transportation both by road and by bus is excellent to every section of the city. The parking facilities available to this Church on Sunday are excellent; week-day parking facilities are adequate." In my opinion these statements are very reassuring.

Consider the respected opinion of our Senior Warden, Dr. London, who stated—"The Vestry spent many hours of thoughtful deliberation before authorizing this drive, and it is my belief that the advancement of the Episcopal faith in Durham and the stability of St. Philip's Church are bound up in the success of this undertaking."

Many people are being called upon to help with this campaign. The response is most encouraging, and there is ample evidence of a high level of interest throughout the congregation. I am convinced that the progressive steps we are taking will afford all of us a large measure of personal satisfaction.

It's *your* church. It should come first. These plans are worthy of your thoughtful consideration and your strong financial support. A fellow parishioner will call upon you Sunday, September 16. Please be prepared for him.

Sincerely yours,

Clarence H. Cobb, Chairman
Every Member Canvass

September 10, 1956

MEMO TO ALL CANVASSERS:

As a Canvasser, you have pledged yourself to perform a service of utmost importance to your Church. The future of St. Philip's depends in a large measure on how well you carry out your canvass.

You cannot conscientiously ask others to be generous unless you, also, are expending the best of your special gifts. One thing that will give you added assurance is to make your own pledge before your first call. Otherwise you feel a secret sense of apology even though you fully intend to make a generous pledge later.

When you knock on a door, introduce yourself and your purpose with the assurance that your story will be heard. It goes without saying that people respond to a friendly approach. A smile opens hearts as well as doors. Approach people as a friend who is going to talk about something of special interest to both of you and them. Demonstrate enthusiasm and confidence. With copy of brochure in hand, ask if it has been seen and invite discussion of its contents. Listen patiently to any suggestions or criticisms. Decide, as you listen, what your most dramatic appeals might be.

Most of your canvass will be routine in that those on whom you call will be ready and willing to make their pledges. It is likely that any problem prospects will fall into one of these three categories: (1) *I've got too many obligations now to take on any new debts.* Your answer is that this Church should not come last but should be one of his very first obligations. (2) *Maybe I'll be able to see my way clear to give something a little later.* Explain that the Church cannot plan a program on the basis of possible future income. It must know how much it has to work with. (3) *How big a pledge do other people make?* It is well to recognize that people ask this question for two different reasons; some want to get by as cheaply as possible; others are sincere in wanting to be sure they don't give too little. Call attention to pledge table in back of brochure. Explain that for our 1957 operating budget we will need as much as was pledged this year and a little more than an equal amount for our Capital Improvements Fund which, however, is payable over a 3 year period. Note that there are two separate pledge cards. Read carefully and be familiar with each of them. Also, fill in the parish census card.

Make your calls Sunday (September 16) preferably in the morning immediately after the 9:30 service. There will be no 11:00 service. If pledge cannot be obtained on first call, be sure to make a definite date for your return visit to pick up the cards. Follow through, please, and make your report to your section captain.

Thank you and good luck.

Sincerely yours,

Clarence H. Cobb, Chairman
Every Member Canvass

APPENDIX F. SHERMAN'S COURSE IN CHRISTIANITY:
OUTLINE AND LIST OF READINGS

(*Epistle to the Philippians*, September 18, 1960)

ANNOUNCING A COURSE IN CHRISTIANITY

WHAT IS IT? . . . A presentation, in terms relevant to the present-day situation of the individual and society, of some of the basic elements of the Christian Faith, with their application to the problems of living and dying. It begins with a lecture presentation, and ends with coffee and a give-and-take bull-session in which no holds are barred, and there are no demands that you take any propositional statements of faith.

WHEN IS IT? . . . Come Tuesday or Wednesday night of any one week at 7:30. Identical presentations on the two nights each week, and you can change as suits your schedule. This also eliminates babysitting problems. Coffee-break at about 9:00; you can leave then, or stay for the bull-session.

WHO MAY COME? . . . Anyone. No obligation. Long-time members of the Episcopal Church, new Episcopalians, members of other denominations or other faiths, atheists and agnostics will all be welcome. Only requirement: a willingness to try to listen and respond.

TUES. AND WED. Sept. 27 and 28. THE QUESTIONS ALL MEN ASK. Dealing with the problems of origin and destination, purpose, and alienation/separation, with some of the factors which complicate the latter.

WED. AND THURS. Oct. 5 and 6. THE CHRISTIAN ANSWERS: THE PROBLEM ANALYZED. The shocking truth about mankind. Painful; you won't like this one.

TUES. AND WED. Oct. 11 and 12. THE CHRISTIAN ANSWERS: THE SOLUTION. Calvary. What is meant by salvation? What are some of its consequences?

Oct. 18 and 19. THE CHRISTIAN ANSWERS: THE PROBLEM AND SOLUTION RE-STATED. We turn to the Bible. Christian Living: what and why?

Oct. 25 and 26. THE CHRISTIAN ANSWERS: HEAVEN AND HELL. A guided tour.

Nov. 1 and 2. PARTICIPATION IN THE ANSWERS; THE CHURCH. Is Baptism symbolic? What is Confirmation? The Holy Communion: some different views.

SUN. AND MON. Nov. 6 and 7. (Sunday, 8 P.M.). PARTICIPATION IN THE ANSWERS: HISTORY. From Jerusalem to Durham. Is the Episcopal Church "Catholic" or "Protestant"? What is our relationship to other denominations?

TUES. AND WED. Nov. 15 and 16. PARTICIPATION IN THE ANSWERS: CUSTOMS. Colors, vestments, vessels; Church polity and organization; Mr./Dr./Rev./Rector Sherman?

Nov. 22 and 23. PARTICIPATION IN THE ANSWERS: MORNING PRAYER. How to follow Morning Prayer in the Prayer Book. Chants. The Church building.

Nov. 29 and 30. PARTICIPATION IN THE ANSWERS: HOLY COMMUNION. How to follow the service. Etiquette in the service. "Tithes and offerings."

COURSE IN CHRISTIANITY

BIBLIOGRAPHY

I. For Confirmation Candidates:
  The Episcopal Church—George Atwater—A1
  Other books in "A" section in the Parish Library.

II. For first four lectures:
  Man's Need and God's Action—Reuel Howe—F4
  The Creative Years—Reuel Howe—F5

III. By lectures:
  Lecture #1:
  The Late Liz—Elizabeth Burns—B11
  The Nature and Destiny of Man (Part I, 1–4)—Reinhold Niebuhr—TP30
  Christianity of Main Street—Theodore Wedel—G28

  Lecture #2:
  Down Peacock's Feathers—D. R. Davies—G52
  Screwtape Letters—C. S. Lewis G10
  Plain Christianity (Chapter 5)—J. B. Phillips—G2
  The Scandal of Christianity (Chapter 3)—Emil Brunner—G48
  The Faith of the Church (Chapter 4)—Pike and Pittenger—TP1

  Lecture #3:
  The Man Born to be King—Dorothy Sayers—L5
  Christus Victor—Gustav Aulen—TP16
  God was in Christ—D. M. Baillie—TP17
  The Faith of the Church (Chapter 6)—Pike & Pittenger—TP1

  Lecture #4:
  Christian Living—Stephen Bayne—F1
  Living the Creed—Carroll Simcox—G4
  The Cost of Discipleship—Dietrich Bonhoeffer—G24
  Life Together—Dietrich Bonhoeffer—G37

  Lecture #5:
  The Great Divorce—C. S. Lewis—G63
  Is Death the End?—Carroll Simcox—G3
  The Faith of the Church—Pike & Pittenger—(Chapter 11)—TP1

Lecture #6:

The Prayer Book: Holy Baptism, pages 273–282 Offices of Instruction, pages 283–295 Confirmation, pages 296–299

Lecture #7:

Chapters in Church History—P. M. Dawley—H6

The Descent of the Dove—Charles Williams—H5

Anglicanism—Stephen Neill—A10

Lecture #8:

The Worship of the Church and Its Work—P. M. Dawley—A2

Lectures #9 and #10:

The Worship of the Church—Massey Shepherd—W20

The Words of Our Worship—Carroll Simcox—W8

"At All Times and in All Places"—Massey Shepherd—W26

NOTE: "The Church's Teaching Series," in six volumes, is the nearest thing we have to an authoritative statement of the teaching of the Episcopal Church. These six volumes, some referred to above, include:

1. *The Holy Scriptures*—Robert Dentan
2. *Chapters in Church History*—P. M. Dawley
3. *The Faith of the Church*—Pike & Pittenger
4. *The Worship of the Church*—Massey Shepherd
5. *Christian Living*—Stephen Bayne
6. *The Episcopal Church and Its Work*—P. M. Dawley

Copies of all of these are available for sale in the parish library.

APPENDIX G. SHERMAN'S ACCOUNT OF THE FORMATION OF ST. STEPHEN'S

MEMO   (October 14, 1958)

FROM: The Rector of St. Philip's Church

TO: All Members of the Parish

SUBJECT: The Proposal for a New Episcopal Congregation to the Southwest of the City of Durham

At a special meeting of the Vestry of St. Philip's Church on Monday night, October 6th, 1958, certain action was taken to be described below, looking towards the possibility of the formation of a new Episcopal congregation in the county area to the southwest of the City of Durham. At this meeting, the Vestry requested me to write this summary of the history of this movement for a new congregation, and to explain exactly where we are now and what we plan to do.

On January 31st., 1957, certain communicants of St. Philip's Church who reside in this area met with the Vestry of St. Philip's. They stated that a meeting had been held to discuss the establishment of a mission in their neighborhood, and that the majority of those at the meeting had been in favor of the project; that a group of these men had discussed the project with Bishop Penick; and that Bishop Penick had requested the group to prepare information on the effect of this mission in general and the timing of its establishment. No action was taken by the Vestry at this meeting.

In February, a delegation from the Vestry met with Bishop Penick to discuss this matter. It was reported to the Vestry that it was understood that the Bishop would require those desiring the formation of this new congregation to complete their pledges to the Capital Improvement Fund of St. Philip's, to secure the approval of the Vestry of St. Philip's, to secure the approval of the new Rector of St. Philip's and to wait at least one year.

In the same month, a communication was received by the Vestry, signed by seven residents of the southwestern area. This petition presented the desire of certain residents of the area to establish a new congregation, and requested that the Vestry give consideration to certain proposed action. The Vestry took no action on the petition at this time, believing that it should be postponed until St. Philip's had a Rector.

After I had arrived in Durham as your new Rector, I thought that I would require some time to familiarize myself with the City, as well as with the congregation, before I could give approval to any action, either positive or negative. In October of 1957, I made an abortive attempt to meet with the seven signers of this petition, to discuss their hopes and plans with them, and to suggest certain alternative action to that which was requested in their petition. For various reasons, this meeting was never held. As a result, the proposal was shelved for nearly a year.

At the regular meeting of St. Philip's Vestry in September of this year, the subject was re-introduced, and after some discussion, a motion was passed requesting the Rector and the Senior Warden to confer with Bishop Penick to ascertain his present views concerning this proposed new congregation, and then to report at a special meeting of the Vestry, to which would be invited the seven men who were the signers of the original petition. Mr. Hurst and I, therefore, met with Bishop Penick in the middle of September. In a letter which he wrote subsequently, summarizing what he had said at this conference, he stated: "The immediate and pressing question is the answer that should be given by the Vestry to communicants (of St. Philip's) who, for two years or longer, have felt that they would like to organize a separate congregation of our Church, to be located in (their) general section of the City. To me, this impulse is vital, and denotes a fine degree of Church interest." At the same time, however, Bishop Penick stated that he did not feel competent to advise us on the need for this new congregation, nor did he feel that a completely unbiased and objective evaluation could be made by the Rector, the Vestry, or any other individual or group of individuals in the Parish. He recommended, therefore, that the Vestry secure the professional advice of the Rev. Joseph G. Moore, Ph.D., Executive Secretary of the Unit of Research and Field Study of the National Council.

At the special meeting of the Vestry, referred to earlier in this letter, Bishop Penick's letter was read, Mr. Hurst and I reported on our conference with him, and the history of the movement for this new Church was summarized in much the same fashion as I have done it here.

(1) The main objections to the formation of this congregation are:
(a) How seriously would this division of the congregation of St. Philip's damage the financial structure of the Church? Roughly $15,000 of our present budget of $48,000 is contributed by members of the congregation living in the area which would be served by the proposed church. Of course, there is no way of knowing at the present time how many of the families in this area would affiliate with the new congregation.

(b) The possible loss of a considerable portion of our present leadership.

(c) St. Luke's and St. Joseph's both have members living in this area also. As smaller churches, the former still in its infancy, the latter only recently a parish, they can ill afford to lose any more of their members than they already do through transfer or death.

(2) Advantages which are seen to be possible results of the formation of this new congregation are:

(a) The new church would be much closer physically to Episcopalians in this area, and therefore would tend to draw them closer spiritually to the Church. It is probable that it would become a much more integral part of the community life.

(b) There are a number of unchurched people living in the area who might be attracted to a neighborhood church, and who are not now being attracted by any of the city churches.

(c) It is possible that the division of the congregation of St. Philip's might tend to increase the feeling of responsibility to the Church of those remaining in St. Philip's, and that new leadership and a new attitude towards stewardship might be developed.

It was generally agreed that what we must be concerned with is not what is best for St. Philip's, or what is best for the residents of this area, but what is best for the Episcopal Church in Durham and in Durham County.

At the conclusion of this discussion, a motion was offered and unanimously passed to the effect that the Rector of St. Philip's be authorized to call into being a Durham Episcopal Council, to be composed of the Rectors or ministers-in-charge of the four white Episcopal churches in Durham, along with two laymen from each Church. This Council is to be asked to invite Dr. Moore to return to Durham and initiate a survey, comparable to the survey which he made of the Diocese five years ago. The main questions for which answers would be hoped for from the survey are as follows:

(a) Is there a real need for another Episcopal Church in the greater Durham area?

(b) What would be the effect, both immediate and long-range, of the formation of such a new church on the overall work of the Episcopal Church in the city?

(c) If the formation of this new church is desirable, what should be its relationship to the other Episcopal Churches of the city?

(d) Should such a new church be desirable, what should be its approximate location?

The members of the Vestry and the seven representatives of the southwestern area seem to be in agreement that, should the recommendations of the survey be adequately supported by good reasons, both groups will be ready to accept these recommendations. This, of course, does not commit either group to the automatic acceptance of Dr. Moore's final recommendations.

I have been in touch with the ministers of the other Episcopal congregations, and have called the first meeting of the Durham Episcopal Council for Thursday night, October 23rd. This will be an organizational meeting, and at this meeting it is expected that an official invitation will be extended to Dr. Moore. The Council will be charged with the local oversight of the survey, and has no authority to take any action on the basis of the results of the survey. Presumably, it will make recommendations to the Vestries or Mission Committees of the various churches, and to the Bishop.

I have already been in touch with Dr. Moore, and he informs me that he can probably visit Durham on Sunday, November 9th. I have asked him to hold this date for us, subject to the action of the Durham Episcopal Council at its meeting on the 23rd.

Dr. Moore will only be in Durham for a brief visit. He will outline for the Council the information that he needs to arrive at his recommendations. After the Council has gathered this information, through the survey which it will then make, all the facts and figures will be forwarded to Dr. Moore. He and his staff will study the survey, and then send us their analysis and recommendations.

This is where we stand as of this minute. We are not in the process of forming this new congregation. What we are doing is initiating an unbiased study of the situation, so that we may have expert advice as to whether such a new congregation should be formed or not. I bid your prayers on this matter, that we may be guided by the Holy Spirit to know and to do what is best for the spread of God's Kingdom in our community.

MEMO   (December 16, 1958)
FROM: The Rector of St. Philip's Church
TO: All Members of the Parish
SUBJECT: The Proposal for a New Episcopal Congregation to the Southwest of the City of Durham

Quite a bit has happened concerning the establishment of the new mission since my last memo on this subject. I am writing you now to bring you up to date on these events, and to try to explain some of the reasons for the action which has been taken.

Our first step, as foreseen in my last memo, was to convene the Durham Episcopal Council, under the chairmanship of Mr. William P. Biggers, which issued an official invitation to Dr. Moore to visit the City. Dr. Moore had requested that we obtain certain information for him, and the Council went to work on this. Prepared and on hand for Dr. Moore's visit were membership maps of all the Episcopal Churches in Durham, a breakdown of the pledges of each Church as to the areas of the city from which they came, and certain statistics from the City Planning Board concerning the proportionate increase in population of Durham County and of Patterson Township, which is roughly the area which will be effected by the proposed new mission. These latter figures were in terms of growth over the past twenty or twenty-five years, with estimated growth over the next ten or twenty years.

Dr. Moore arrived in town shortly after noon on November 13th. After going over the information which had been gathered, he then was taken on a very thorough tour of the area, including present building, areas for future expansion, present churches in the area, major routes of traffic flow, etc. He was also shown three possible locations for the new mission. At the conclusion of this tour, he then spent time in further study of the maps, of the report of his earlier exhaustive survey of the city of Durham made in 1952, and other information. [In] the evening he met with the members of the Durham Episcopal Council (composed of all the ministers, and two laymen from each Church) for dinner. Mr. N. A. Gregory, one of the laymen from St. Philip's Church, representing the residents of the area desiring a new church, told of their reasons for proposing it. The laymen from St. Joseph's told of their parish's desire to aid in any missionary activity in the city. The Rector of St. Philip's expressed some of the reasons for hesitation on the part of some members of our parish, because of a possible threat to the continued life of St. Philip's.

After much conversation, Dr. Moore said that normally he would want to give further study to such a situation, and to gather further information. In this particular case, however, he did not feel that any further study was necessary. He believed that the establishment of the new congregation was a "must." The desire, the enthusiasm, the potentialities, the prospect for growth, all spoke in favor of the formation of this new church. He appreciated the real concern of some members of St. Philip's, but he believed very strongly that, with certain safeguards, there would be no real permanent threat to the continued existence of St. Philip's as a strong and effective parish. The major safeguard which he proposed concerned the location of the new church. One site which had been proposed was too close in to town, and he advised most strongly against any further consideration of that spot. In effect, he stated that the site for the new church should not be closer in town than the general area of Hope Valley itself. As long as St. Philip's is left a fairly large residential area which it could serve more advantageously than any other church, it will be able to continue as a strong and effective parish.

The informal committee of seven residents of the area desiring to promote the formation of this new church thereupon wrote to Bishop Penick, asking his advice on how to proceed, and his approval for their proceeding toward the establishment of the church. At the same time a letter was addressed by them to the Vestry of St. Philip's, asking for their approval. At an informal luncheon meeting on December 2nd, the Vestry and these seven men discussed the whole matter. Some real communication and interchange of opinions took place at this meeting, and there appeared to be a very general agreement on the desirability of the formation of the new mission.

On the afternoon of December 5th, Bishop Penick met with three members of the committee and with the Rector, Senior Warden and Junior Warden of St. Philip's. He expressed his approval of the proposal for the formation of the new church, and his enthusiasm for the project. He suggested a detailed procedure which is to be followed. The first action called for by his suggested procedure will be a meeting of all interested persons in March of 1959. Formal organization of the new diocesan mission will be anticipated for late April or early May, and services will start presumably in early June.

At the regular meeting of the Vestry of St. Philip's on December 8th, the request of the committee for the approval of the Vestry was discussed at some length. There was a strong expression of hope that the new mission would choose a site to the south or southwest of Hope Valley, which would place it in a strategic location to minister to the expansion of the residential area in that direction, and to minister also to the fringes of the Research Triangle when it is developed. It was suggested that this location would also be less likely to drain parts of the "living area" of St. Philip's. At the conclusion of this discussion, the Vestry voted its unanimous approval of the formation of the new mission, along the lines suggested by Bishop Penick.

This is what has actually happened so far, and what will probably happen. But my concern as a Priest of the Church and Rector of St. Philip's, is not primarily with your knowledge of these facts. What is far more important is our attitude towards these facts. It would be possible, perhaps, for a long-time member of St. Philip's to be filled with despair, and to feel that this will mean the effectual end of St. Philip's. Or, it would be possible to take a grudging attitude, and to say "This must be, and we must simply make the best of it." Or it is quite possible, and I believe, right, for us to say, "We have been assured by those who should know that this is the right step for us to take in this situation at this time. Let us, therefore, as members of Christ's Church, support this project enthusiastically, for the extension of the kingdom of God in our community."

Our first concern as Christians is with the cause of Christ; secondly, we are members of the Episcopal Church; only thirdly is our allegiance to St. Philip's Church. What we must be concerned with is the overall effectiveness of the Christian church in our community, and the strength of our own communion. What we must want is not what is best necessarily for any particular parish, but what is best for the Episcopal Church as a part of Christ's Church.

I know that there are many faithful members of St. Philip's who feel that the formation of the congregation could very well hamper St. Philip's permanently. If the remaining members of St. Philip's throw up their hands in despair and say "We have been killed," we may never be able to recover. But if we regard this as an opportunity and a challenge to redouble our own missionary and evangelistic efforts, to strengthen our parish life, and to bring into more active participation in the life of the parish those who have been in the past on the fringe of its membership, then the formation of this new congregation may well be a very great blessing to St. Philip's.

What the exact effect will be on St. Philip's Church, of course, we have no way of knowing. There is no compulsion placed upon any resident of the area to join the new church; there is no compulsion placed upon residents of this or other areas to remain in St. Philip's. Whether to stay as a member of St. Philip's or to transfer to the new mission will be in every case, and must be, an individual decision. I admonish you all to refrain from placing any pressure on any individual or family in the making of this decision. The temptation may at times be great for the two congregations to compete against each other for members. This will in no way benefit the cause of Christ or of the Episcopal Church.

St. Philip's will continue its ministry to its remaining members, and can find a new evangelistic challenge among the people living, permanently or temporarily, in its immediate area. The new mission will be able to seek to extend the ministry of the church to residents of its area who are not now active members of any church. Both congregations will be seeking growth, not primarily from the transfer of those who are already Episcopalians, but through evangelism among the unchurched.

Above all, we must remember that our attitude towards the formation of this new mission as evidenced by the successful experience of parishes in several major cities in this diocese, would not be either what it can do for us, or what it can do to us, but what we are, as members of the Episcopal Church, and as congregations of the family of Christ, will be able to do together in carrying the ministry of the Church more deeply into our community.

I bid your constant prayers both for St. Philip's and for the new mission, that they may both be powerful witnesses to the strength of the Christian fellowship, and our mutual love in Jesus Christ.

APPENDIX H. WEDDING MUSIC, BY DAVID PIZARRO

The Order for the Solemnization of Matrimony as contained in the Book of Common Prayer is complete without the embellishment of music. Indeed, a quiet wedding, unless great expense is to be incurred for the accompanying festivities, is not completely undesirable.

Any music which embellishes the Service must express the theology of the service. Trite, sentimental music is always out of place in the church. Great damage is done to the worship of the church by the use of inferior music. Too often the Marriage Service seems to be a time when all principles of taste in music are cast aside. The music of the church is, even for the wedding service, still the concern of those to whom the moral responsibility for upholding the integrity of the music is given.

It is a common error today to assume that the norm for church music was established for all time by our ancestors of the Victorian Era—an epoch when the music of the church actually sank to its lowest ebb. Though church music has improved in quality in the last few years, the majority of our churches present a musical program which is more indicative of that type of music than it is of music of this day. Aside from textual considerations (which are regulated by Rubric) the music must also be good. Much music performed at church weddings does not come under the heading of good music. In addition to the vocal trivialities which often precede the rite (and sometimes interrupt it—though this is illegal in the Episcopal Church), the so-called "traditional" wedding marches leave much to be desired. The Mendelssohn is at least good music, coming from that composer's best work. The Wagner "Wedding March" has little ground to stand on as a musical composition. Both become inappropriate when one considers the situations out of which they arise.

The music which accompanies the entrance and departure of the bridal party need not be martial music; the more quietly it is done, the more appropriate it will be. There is no reason why the entrance of the bride should not be accompanied by congregational singing; there is much to commend it. This would give the congregation opportunity to sing a song of praise. An illustrious example of the effective use of a hymn at this point was at the wedding of Queen Elizabeth II. It is also fitting to accompany the departure of the bridal party with a brilliant instrumental "sortie."

As for music prior to the ceremony, that had best be instrumental. There is little good solo vocal literature for weddings. There is some choral music, though the hiring of choristers will entail an expense.

This organist, in his brief ministry of music, had heard a number of well-intentioned people say "I just wouldn't feel married unless" . . . this or that musical composition were played. The Marriage Service does not concern itself with sentimental or romantic attachments, but rather with the stark realities of publicly taking solemn vows, and the establishment of a Christian Family. Therefore, the music, if there be any, must express the church's view of marriage, and disassociate this view from popular sentiment.

A noted cleric has stated that people are willing to accept expert advice (and pay for it, too) in all fields except theology and church music. That may well be true, but that does not relieve the church musician of preserving the great charge laid upon him: to preserve what is good, discard the unworthy, and encourage the new. He must ever seek to keep the sanctity of church music. If music cannot meet the most rigid requirements of musicians, then this music is not worthy of performance in God's House. Therein lies the guiding principle for all the church's music.

APPENDIX I. EXCERPTS FROM THE NOTEBOOK OF THE DEVOTIONAL
LIFE CHAIRMAN OF THE EPISCOPAL CHURCH WOMEN
(MRS. WATTS CARR, JR.), 1961–1963

The ingredient of WORSHIP or DEVOTION must remain in its proper perspective if the Episcopal Churchwomen are to be different from every other civic or secular organization in which we become involved. We do not exist for the purpose of doing good works, but to bring people to Christ. To this end everything else is subordinate. In the Episcopal Churchwomen we find a *discipline for worship and study*, and an organization of *giving effectively*.

"Even So Send I You." It is our Lord's own command and we dare not ignore it or pretend that it was not meant for each one of us individually. Let us think NOW especially of where we are sent and how and specific ways we can carry out our responsibilities better, individually or together as members of the Body of Christ in all our work. Perhaps most of all for personal evangelism which we have not always acknowledged as our task.

Let us begin by asking ourselves some questions and by facing up to some hard and not-so-comfortable facts about the world we live in and more specifically, our personal condition in relation to society. Please remember, we explore the situation in an effort to meet ourselves face to face and secondly, to be confronted with the recognition of our *deepest need*.

Are we being forced, through what we hear, what we read, and through the actual situations we are daily involved in—into a disturbing awareness that the values of the western civilization have seriously declined, that the moral standards of adults and youth are in a state of erosion, that we are living in a society that has for the most part expelled God, a society that is doing its utmost "to purge and sterilize out of its Christian heritage the concept of Original Sin"? (Arnold Toynbee, *A Study of History*). Of Christ's victory for us? Or do we have eyes and see not and ears that hear not? Or are our hearts so hardened that we feel not? Or is it too uncomfortable to be honest with ourselves about ourselves?

Are we yet to be shocked into recognition of our condition? Are we still so insulated that we further delay the real confrontation of ourselves as we are by saying, "Well—maybe all this is true about the condition of the world, but that really doesn't involve me—I certainly try to be a good person—I practice the golden rule—I'm not alcoholic—I don't steal or commit adultery—I'm actually not what you would call a sinner—why so much emphasis on sin and evil instead of the goodness in the world?"

Again we must stop and establish a clearer understanding of what we mean (and what the church means) by sin. First, by sin we do not mean immorality. Sin is our rebellion against and self-centered separation from God—sin is being self-centered, grounded in concern for self and our own will and NOT grounded in God and in concern for His Will in our lives. Now we can say immorality is to sin as the pock or scab is to chicken-pox—it is the indication or symptom of the deeper disease. True, we may not be murderers or adulterers, but can we continue to say we are not sinners? As an exercise, let's take one single day and be honest— how many times in this one day have I rebelled against God by refusing to let Him into my life—by practicing the absence of God in the countless on-the-spot decisions I made concerning my husband, the children, my in-laws, my friends and business associates—in the way I accepted, neglected or ignored my responsibilities at home, at work, at the church and in the community—how many times during this one day did I call out to God for His help in doing those things I ought to have done and leaving undone those things I ought not to have done?

(Were we too busy and preoccupied to *really listen* to those around us—our children, husband or a troubled friend? Were we in such a hurry at the market we failed to see the clerk as a person—with needs for courtesy and love just as deep as ours? Were we so overcome by a friend's beautiful new house, we made snide, unkind remarks about her color scheme to her other friends? Did we say we couldn't come to a Worship Committee meeting and accept an invitation to a coffee-hour, bridge party or movie?)

If this examination of a day does not convince us that we sin boldly, let's be more personal and examine our prayer lives. And I hastily confess this exercise brought me to my knees in tears of contrition asking "God, be merciful unto me, a sinner!" How much time do you spend each day in communion with God—in prayer, reading the Bible—in meditation using devotional books as helps? Do you think that it is essential to turn to God in prayer each day? As essential as eating three meals a day? Do you think that it is as important to read the Bible each day as it is to read the newspaper—the society page—the comics? Do you think that it is as helpful to meditate over devotional writings such as *Christian Perfect* as to meditate over *Vogue, The Ladies' Home Journal* or *Readers' Digest*? Now let's be very personal and ask ourselves—How much of my prayers is monopolized by ME, the small circle of *my* needs, *my* family's needs, *my* friends' needs? How much time is given to GOD—loving, praising, thanking Him—being quiet and listening to Him—seeking His Will and purpose in every area and relationship of my life—asking for forgiveness—praying that I be filled with His Grace and outgoing love and that I become more aware of my need for Him—that I become less self-centered and more concerned with the real needs of others—that I be given the strength to be responsive to these needs.

Do I constantly pray for blessings to be used only for my happiness and welfare and not the Christ's service? Can I say in my prayers "I am third—God is first—neighbor is second—I am third." When I pray do I give my prayers my undivided attention? The president of Harvard University several years ago told the graduating class "Wherever you are—be 'all there.'" In may prayers am I "all there"?

Perhaps you will be surprised by what you are discovering as you honestly answer these questions. Like me, you may rebelliously insist: "Yes—my prayer life is thin, self-centered and irregular, but it is not altogether my fault. Life is so complicated in an advanced technological age—an age of speed and wheels—I just live in the car—when I do everything I have to do every day, there's little time left for quietness and reading the Bible and that sort of thing."

Yes, TIME does seem to be a real problem. Indeed, we do seem to be capsulated in terms of time—spending our every breath trying to break through and conquer time—either by driving ourselves to distraction being involved in more commitments and projects than there are hours in the day—or by struggling to fill the long, empty hours of the day with activities that plunge us into even deeper loneliness and anxiety.

When we say we don't have time for prayer, Bible reading and meditation, aren't we in truth saying we care more about these other concerns and activities than we do about knowing God? "Martha, Martha, you are troubled and uneasy about many things. Only one thing is needed." Jesus Christ knew that He needed to go apart to be quiet and pray. He knew He could not do without the Bible. Jesus Christ was concerned with the problem of time, for He had much to accomplish, and in terms of the world "so little time." Jesus Christ was more concerned with seeking God's Will and in doing God's Will: He redeemed time for us. Therefore can we not accept what Christ has done for us and let Him free us from our constant struggle with time? We must here and now acknowledge that "the one thing that is necessary for us" is turning to God in prayer each day. We must open our whole being—mind—heart— soul to receive God each day—we must give ourselves to Him anew each day to be used in His service, in the sure knowledge that His unlimited Grace will be available to us each day to give us the strength and time to do that for which we were created.

"The steadfast love of the Lord never ceases, his mercies never come to an end; they are new every morning." (Lamentations 3:22). Let us step out in faith. Let us discipline and commit ourselves to prayer, Bible reading, meditation each day and know first hand the freedom and peace that comes in giving ourselves to God. Peter Day in *Saints on Main Street* reminds us that "the real work of the church is *to know Jesus Christ* and make Him known by those paradigmatic actions which show forth His Love and His promise of abundant life."

For if we now are aware that our deepest need is God—His Love, Forgiveness, Acceptance—we can agree that "there will never by any peace for those who resist God" (*Christian Perfect* by Fenelon). We can recognize that Grace is the fact that God never leaves us alone. (Read Job or Francis Thompson's *The Hound of* Heaven.)

If we now can understand that (J. B. Phillips, *God Our Contemporary*) the deep fundamental problems in life are neither intellectual nor technical but are always in the last resort problems of human relationship (what bit of knowledge or electronic mechanism can give you the power to love a mother-in-law you can't stand?—what amount of money can ease the broken heart of a parent as she learns her child will never be normal?—what college degree can help you comfort a friend whose husband unexpectedly died with a heart attack?). We can know that apart from Jesus Christ no man can have a real relationship with another, and only as we find our center in Jesus Christ can we find the power to be related to those beyond us and to heal the broken relationships that make us lonely and anxious. (Have you ever had a serious disagreement with your husband or a neighbor that couldn't be healed until you went to Jesus Christ for the power to die to yourself?)

In these critical days we can ill afford to be immobilized by any sense of purposelessness and meaninglessness. Nor can we fail to respond to the urgency of our mission as Christians, as churchwomen and as Worship Chairmen. "What the world expects of Christians is that Christians should speak out, loud and clear, and that they should voice their condemnation in such a way that never the slightest doubt could rise in the heart of the simplest man; that they should get away from abstraction and confront the bloodstained face history has taken on today. The grouping we need is a grouping of men resolved to speak out clearly and to pay up personally" (Albert Camus, *Resistance, Rebellion and Death*).

As Dr. Russell Bowie puts it, in his book *Jesus and the Trinity,* "The roots of what would grow into the Doctrine of the Trinity were present from the beginning, in what Christian disciples—not only seers and saints, but also the *simple people*—felt and inwardly knew. They were inheritors of the Profound faith of Israel in one God, the Almighty. They had learned in a new way the Grace of God that had come to them when they thought of Jesus Christ and tried to follow Him. They were *sure* that there was something stirring in their souls, to bless them and to strengthen them, which was not of their own making and could be nothing less than the Spirit of God. On the ground of daily reality, all that was plain.

"But on another level, all was not so plain. How could that which had been experienced be intellectually interpreted? To believe that what man experienced spiritually must be true was one thing; to get it into an intellectual framework which could seem consistent with the whole truth was something further."

So you and I as Christians, can no longer merely give vague lip-service to our profession that our purpose is the extension of God's Kingdom. We must be willing "to rush to the jagged edges of human need, stand beside one caught in strife, walk where darkness descends, and when all else fails to speak God's name in a world where He may have been forgotten; utter with your own stumbling tongue what you know of Him" (Samuel Miller, *The Great Realities*).

As we go our separate ways to fulfill our life's purpose, knowing Jesus Christ and making Him known, let us pray together.

> May Christ give to us
> At this time, and for always,
> His peace in our souls,
> His presence in our hearts
> His power in our lives.
> Amen.

APPENDIX J. ESPECIALLY FOR VESTRYMEN . . . AND THOSE WHO ELECT THEM, BY THOMAS E. BOLLINGER
(*The Churchman*, January 1963)

The Episcopal Church has as a basic part of its life and structure a force which has yet to be used to its fullest potential toward the fulfillment of the Church's mission—the parish vestry. Though the history of the American Church is filled with the work and concerns of vestries, there is still lacking a general sense of mission in being a vestryman, and the place of that responsibility in the overall mission of the Church.

Part of the problem seems to be the human tendency to look at the letter of the law, and thus limit ourselves. The Canons of the Episcopal Church and of the Diocese of North Carolina are very sparse in defining the purpose of a Vestry. National Canon 13, section 2, simply states that "the Vestry shall be agents and legal representatives of the Parish in all matters concerning its corporate property and the relations of the Parish to its clergy." Other canons, both National and Diocesan, give directions for the number of vestrymen (Diocesan Canon 21, Section 1), appointment and election of officers (Diocesan Canon 21, Section 2), and procedures for vestries to follow when a cure becomes vacant (National Canon 47, Diocesan Canon 22). With the only official definitions regarding vestries couched in legal terms for legal purposes, it is not surprising that these important groups in our parishes have often remained confused as to their proper role, and limited in their outlook.

Canons do not intend to define the entire scope of the Church's life and work, and by no means intend to give a complete statement about the function and potential of a parish vestry. Normally the canons merely state the limits of authority, and point out certain basic standards. They do not intend at any time to say all there is to say. For example: no one is supposed to be content with persons who commune only three times a year. They may qualify as communicants, to be sure, but the Church remains concerned that they grow into more than occasional communicants. Actually, the broad area "beyond the canons" is the area of the relationship of the parish vestry to the total mission of the Church. "Ministry" is the key word giving a broad description of the thought world underlying the work and planning of a vestry. Though operating within the Canons, the Vestry must be committed enough to work in the vast area of the Church's mission which no canon attempts to define.

The work of the Church, therefore, is *ministry*, and the vestry as the leaders of the laity in a parish church, must point the way to their fellow laymen so all may take a creative part in that ministry. In our time the stress on the work of the laity in the ministry of the Church is receiving great emphasis, and promises an impact of revolutionary proportions. No longer can the parish vestry afford to be that group which discusses the proper type of grass seed, a leaky faucet or unpaid pledges, and refuses to face up to the true needs of their people and community in the light of the Gospel.

What can a vestryman do to help lead his parish into a deeper commitment to the great mission of the Church? FIRST, he must be a layman and make full use of the fact! The layman is the churchman who daily continues his struggle in the world outside the walls of the parish church, and comes into contact with certain brutal realities which often never reach ears within those walls. Due to his experiences in this situation, the layman knows how people feel, what they don't understand, and what they long for. Whenever he brings these realities into his parish meetings and insists something be done about them, he is helping to make the Church relevant and, therefore, meaningful. Politicians and public relations men often know more about how people really feel and think than do those who plan and direct the program of the church. The vestryman who takes his "laymanship" seriously will make certain this does not remain the case. In that way a vestry exercises real spiritual leadership among its fellow parishioners, along with the parish priest.

SECOND, the vestry as a conscious unit must exist more than one meeting a month. Unfortunately vestries sometimes allow themselves to become a once-a-month board of directors, watchdogs of the treasury or Star Chamber, who do not carry a consciousness of leadership and responsibility through the other days of the month. Occasionally parishes elect vestrymen who seldom attend worship, never attend parish organizations, but come to the vestry meeting once a month to complain about what is going on. It is dangerous to elect a man to the vestry to "get him active in the church." This not only downgrades the standards which a parish places on its lay leadership, but tends to discourage seriously creative Christians from wanting to serve on the Vestry. The proper image of a vestryman is that of a man who is a regular communicant, and who takes an intelligent leadership in the life and work of the parish church.

THIRD, the vestry, along with the parish priest, must see that the parish's program is lived on a highly creative level. Compared to the standards of art, business, public education and industry, many of the things which take place under the heading of "church work" often are mediocrity personified. The man who would be extremely upset over a poor high school curriculum and facilities in his town, which make it difficult for his son to get into college, may not even raise an eyebrow at a mediocre and poorly-equipped church school in his parish, which will probably fail to give his son the inner strength to cope with the basic issues of life. The businessman who would refuse to hire an untrained worker in his firm, is totally undisturbed by the fact that those who teach, and plan the parish work are often harried people pressed into service without training or support.

Look at some of the areas where the vestry can see that it gives creative leadership to a parish:

Administration: It is surprising how many well-trained businessmen fail to bring their creative business "know-how" into play when they serve as vestrymen. They may be all for efficiency in their businesses, but fail to take the time or the interest on a vestry to analyze the soundness of the administration of their property and finances. Often they equate efficiency with cutting down expenditures, and merely starve the program to death. Efficiency means getting rid of the superfluous things so the REAL job can be done. The REAL job of the church is the ministry of reconciliation to the world in Christ's name. Anything that hinders this mission, no matter how important, must be placed in its proper perspective or eliminated. Sometimes parishes have drained the creative energy of their priest by not providing him with at least part-time secretarial assistance and good equipment to take care of such things as bulletins and other necessary materials. Poor records on communicants, and other persons for whom the parish is responsible, means that a parish cares only about those persons whom it can remember offhand. The parish church seldom takes advantage of up-to-date filing and card systems which business long ago found time-saving and efficient. Good administration to the businessman means getting details out of the way so he can get down to the business of selling his product. The same is true of the parish church—only the business is relating the Gospel to people.

Pastoral care: The vestry bears much more responsibility here than simply letting the priest know when someone is sick or mad. Whether one may have experienced it yet or not, the Church is called to be the "community of concern," meaning it is that body of people who, because of the love of God shown to them through Christ, react in love and responsibility toward each other. Everyone is responsible for the whole and the whole is responsible for the individual. The vestry which does not see part of its function as the nurture and the comforting of its people is doomed to plan forever in unreality.

Worship: Adoration is the dynamic center of the Church's life—in sacrament, prayer, and praise. A vestry which lives apart from this fact cannot possibly lead its parish toward its mission. One good trend in the church today is the "vestryman's retreat." At the beginning of the new year the vestry goes off together with the parish priest for a day or two of prayer, Sacrament, and serious consideration of their call as lay leaders in Christ's mission. This, along with greater use of prayer at the time of vestry meetings, would transform most vestries. Imagine a vestry facing a troublesome decision taking time to stop and pray about it! A few vestries even hold Evening Prayer and sometimes Corporate Communions regularly just before their business meetings. A priest who fails to pray soon finds his ministry withering; the vestry which does not seriously worship cannot possibly be relevant.

Education: Christianity too often has been mediocre in its education when the times called for greatness. The tragedy of poor education is well known to the whole Church, and calls for some humble examination on the part of all vestrymen. A concerned vestryman is acquainted with what is going on in this area of his parish's life, the philosophy and techniques behind it, and its weaknesses. He is prepared to insist that his parish provide what is needed for a truly creative job of Christian training for all its people. Few vestrymen are known to have taken the trouble to look over the curriculum, teaching aids, and classroom space in their church schools, not to mention discussing the deeper issues with the Rector or church school superintendent. The possibilities here are infinite.

Unfortunately sometimes the vestry and rector look upon each other with some suspicion. The vestry feels it must keep the rector "in hand," and the rector feels he must goad the vestry into action. There is much quoting of canons, and a little serious and effective Christian action. The intent of the canons is that the rector and vestry exist in a cooperative and supportive relationship, each looking at the needs of the other, and prepared to help and defend the other. Only in this way can the rector and vestry lead a parish to discover what "community," in the Christian sense, means.

We believe in Incarnation. This not only means that God became flesh in Jesus Christ, but implies that God does not reject any of His creation. We learn from the Incarnation that God uses the human process for the working out of His Will in time and space—through the relations of human beings with Him, and then with each other. The Incarnation is the key to the understanding of the Sacraments, since there we learn God uses earthly things to convey His presence and Will. In the parish vestry we have another example of the implication of the Incarnation—God using men and their relationships, abilities, and concern, for the purpose of fulfilling His Church's mission, and thus the vestry's mission.

APPENDIX K. BOLLINGER'S TEN COMMISSIONS

TENTATIVE DESCRIPTION OF THE COMMISSION ON ADMINISTRATION

This Commission will be responsible for:

1. Development of administrative philosophy and policy for recommendation to the Vestry;
2. Supervise the expenditures in keeping with the annual budget and vestry authorized items;
3. Study both immediate and long-range needs in equipment and other facilities needed to implement ideal administrative operation;
4. Develop job descriptions for non-professional personnel; and develop salary ranges and schedules, vacation periods, etc., for all personnel for approval by vestry and rector;
5. Study administrative procedures for efficiency in line with philosophy and policy;
6. This committee will be the core group to draw up budgets to be approved by the vestry.

NOTES:
Definitions:
  a. "Philosophy"—This is to be a statement of precisely what we are administering, and what we intend to "say" to the parish and community by the way we do it. For example: The accessibility of rector and staff could be a way Administration can indicate genuine concern for people; also, the development of a system so many minor decisions can be made (in line with overall policy) by others than the rector, can free him for more important duties.
  b. "Policy"—is a set of concrete statements about the implementation of the philosophy. It can range from "the office will be open from 9 A.M. to 5 P.M. Monday through Friday, and 9 A.M. to noon on Saturdays" to "information on parishioners will be given to no outsider."

  Job Descriptions of Non-Professional Personnel—These people should have clearly stated job descriptions which are discussed with each one in conference, so there will be no misunderstanding about what is expected of them. Along with this, we need a clear policy regarding salary raises, vacations, sickness, health insurance, pensions, and other items generally considered under the category of personnel.

Professional Personnel—These people are paid for "results," and not for hours worked. They are expected to produce the results, which sometimes means they will have to work long hours, and other times they will have more leisure than the non-professional staff. In most cases they should work under contract, which defines duties and expectations, and even evaluation guidelines, clearly.

Equipment and Facilities—Every aspect of the administration operation should be studied from this point of view, and the needed items listed and priced, along with a description of their purpose.

TENTATIVE DESCRIPTION OF THE COMMISSION ON PROPERTY

1. This Commission shall be shared by the Junior Warden and will be made up of persons with specialized interests in the maintenance of the property presently owned by the Parish. This property includes both the church and parish house grounds, as well as the rectory and grounds.
2. This Commission is to determine the policies of the use and maintenance of this property, and establish a philosophy, or point of view, on the manner in which these facilities should be maintained. The only right witness which a church can make through its buildings is that they shall be kept in such a condition that they become a shining example of the very best we can give as Christians in the service of our Lord. Anything less than the best, particularly in a congregation which is basically affluent, is a statement of poor evangelism and stewardship. In the determining of these policies and regarding the use and maintenance of the buildings, the Commission should be specific about their use and care, and be able to publish this information, once it is approved by the vestry, for all the parish to know.
3. In the course of its duties, this Commission is to study all present facilities and determine precisely how they may be put in the most modern condition. This would include the fixing of what needs fixing, the development of any new facilities necessary, such as storage, the better lighting of some areas, making sure that heating and air-conditioning is working properly, providing for janitorial equipment that is necessary to do a good job, etc. In the process of this, the Commission is to determine specifically the costs and details of such items and report the same to the vestry. The cost information should reflect professional estimates regarding each item.
4. The Commission should provide for suitable personnel to work in each area of its responsibility. It is recommended that the areas of responsibility be made specific, such as nave of the church, electrical and heating systems, parish house, grounds, and rectory, with perhaps different persons responsible for each and reporting regularly to the Commission.
5. There should be at least annually an inspection and evaluation of all properties according to previously established guidelines and these should reflect definite recommendations which the Commission makes to the vestry regarding future budget items.

IMMEDIATE ASSIGNMENT:

This Commission is to organize along the lines suggested, and to set as their first priority the putting of all present facilities in modern condition, and reporting to the vestry regarding the details of same by its July meeting.

TENTATIVE DESCRIPTION OF THE COMMISSION ON WORSHIP

1. This Commission is to become knowledgeable regarding the ethos and spectrum of Worship in the Episcopal Church, and its appropriate uses. In this way this Commission can meaningfully assist the rector and vestry in determining worship's creative application to the needs of the parish.
2. This Commission will see that appropriate training is given to ushers, choristers, lay readers, altar guild members, acolytes and any other persons ancillary to the worship of the parish. This is to be done in conjunction with the Commission on training.
3. This Commission is to determine personnel needed to fill the various positions in the groups ancillary to worship and to see that such positions are filled.
4. In the course of its duties, this Commission is to make a serious study of equipment, facilities, and other resources necessary for an excellent program of worship, and will specifically determine details regarding these items and their costs. This information will be reported to the vestry.
5. This Commission will determine responsibilities of the various ancillary groups and set down same in writing, as policy.
6. This Commission is to at least annually conduct an evaluation of the areas of its concern, report same to rector and vestry, and revise or institute programs accordingly.

IMMEDIATE ASSIGNMENT:
1. To secure Chairmen for ushers and lay readers, and to have them functioning by June.
2. To establish, in conjunction with the personnel and training commission, training program for lay readers this fall.
3. To report to the vestry, in writing, at its August meeting, regarding the specifics of #2, and other recommendations.

TENTATIVE DESCRIPTION OF THE COMMISSION ON CHRISTIAN EDUCATION

1. This Commission is to become knowledgeable in the field of Christian Education, in the sense of Christian Education's being a philosophy embracing a total parish spectrum.
2. This Commission shall make a study of the membership makeup of this parish and determine specific types and structures of Christian Education needed. Some obvious areas are:
   a. Teaching of children,
   b. Adult Education,
   c. Program for aging and shut-ins,
   d. Program for the community,
   e. Uses of seasons and other events

This would include selection of curriculum and appropriate resources.

3. This Commission shall determine the type of parish personnel needed to carry out necessary programs, and work with the Personnel and Training Commission to select and train them.

4. This Commission shall determine both immediate and long-range needs and facilities, financing, equipment and other resources, and report the same to the vestry and appropriate Commissions. In doing so, this Commission shall be specific regarding items needed and exact costs involved.

5. This Commission shall determine if professional staff personnel is needed, and if so, prepare a job description of such a person or persons.

IMMEDIATE ASSIGNMENT:

This Commission shall work with the Commission on Personnel and Training in initial phases of determining its philosophy and Christian Education personnel needs—with specific responsibility of staffing and training the Church School and Adult Education program for 1968–69.

A preliminary progress report is due, in writing, at the July vestry meeting.

TENTATIVE DESCRIPTION OF THE COMMISSION ON STEWARDSHIP

1. This Commission will have a two-fold function: (a) to design and execute a year-round program of Stewardship in all areas of the parish life, and (b) conduct the annual Every Member Canvass.

2. STEWARDSHIP EDUCATION. "Stewardship" should be understood as the Christian's giving of his whole life to God, as understood in the Baptismal service and in the vows taken at Confirmation. Education in this area is the leading of every Christian to see that every aspect of his life is held in trust from God, and rightfully must be used in God's service. Each Christian must be led to examine the gifts within himself that can be used in this service, and helped to offer these and use them creatively. A serious understanding of the Ministry of the Laity underlies this concept, so that "stewardship" is not confined to merely doing stereotyped "church work," but covers every person's sense of vocation in whatever he is doing as a human being in God's world. Within the life of the Church as a functioning community, each member has a Stewardship responsibility also: to see that what he is and has entrusted to him in this world is offered freely and Sacramentally so that the Christian community can make a strong witness to the world.

This Commission would explore all the facets of the concept of "Stewardship," and keep this view before every parishioner at all times. Service through the "tasks" of the parish—teaching, worship, organizational responsibilities, evangelism—must be clearly shown as a concrete part of one's giving, as well as the way he gives his money through the Offering. This view is based upon the premise that the money gift a person makes takes on meaning only within the context of the way he views his whole life as being dedicated to God.

This Commission is to develop detailed plans to present aspects of this teaching through each week's bulletin, each issue of the parish paper, through the conscious teaching of same in the Church School, the Adult Education Program, Youth Ministry, and any other area of the parish's life. Such a program should be specific, concrete, and worked out in writing.

3. THE EVERY MEMBER CANVASS. This is the operation which happens annually in the parish during which members are to make their pledges for the following year. It is the present policy of the parish to base its budget upon the giving of the people, rather than asking them to respond to a budgetary request. There is a common objection to this view which generally says that people should respond to stated needs, and that anything less is risky business from a fiscal point of view. The Every Member Canvass CAN be creatively operated from a strictly Stewardship point of view if the following procedures are followed:

1. The parish clearly states its expectations of its members to give of themselves in all aspects of its life—membership standards built on stewardship lines;
2. The year-round teaching is done as outlined above;
3. The canvass must be extremely thorough. This means much more than making a contract with each person for a pledge, but the making certain each person has "heard" the message.
4. The parish should be kept continually informed about the status of their Stewardship, by receiving information about its giving of both service and money.
5. Members are strongly involved in every aspect of its creative life.
6. This Commission shall, at the May meeting of the vestry each year, bring detailed plans, in writing, regarding its Stewardship Education program for the ensuing year.
7. The Commission shall, at the May meeting of the vestry each year, bring detailed plans, in writing, regarding the Every Member Canvass for the ensuing year.

IMMEDIATE ASSIGNMENT:

Since we are behind the schedule mentioned above, this Commission is to bring a preliminary report, in writing, to the July vestry meeting, and a final report on the Education program and Canvass at the August meeting.

TENTATIVE DESCRIPTION OF THE COMMISSION ON FELLOWSHIP

1. This Commission is to provide opportunity for the entire parish, as well as special groups, to benefit from the fellowship that is necessary for a vital Christian parish.
2. It is to do this by studying needs as reflected in the make-up and character of this parish, and will design a program accordingly.
3. In the course of these studies and recommendations, this Commission is to study facilities, equipment, and other resources necessary for a vital program, including detailed costs and report same to vestry.
4. Whole Parish fellowship activities recommended:
   1. In September, a parish dinner to educate all the members regarding the program for the coming year.
   2. In November, a fellowship event, preferably catered, which will emphasize Stewardship education and be conducted as a major portion of the Every Member Canvass.

3. January or early February, a parish dinner with a pre-Lenten theme.
4. May, a parish dinner which will summarize the events of the regular program year and emphasize plans for the summer.
5. During the summer, an all-parish fellowship event, possibly a picnic.

5. Fellowship Program for individual groups:
   1. For Youth. This program has been in operation for some time in reference to the Episcopal Young Churchmen, and should be augmented and studied for its effectiveness.
   2. Episcopal Church Women. This program has also been in operation for some time and should be continued as it continues to meet the needs of the group involved.
   3. Young Couples. This group of persons in our parish has recommended that a special group be created which will emphasize fellowship among them. Someone representing this group should be on the overall Commission and be able to turn to the Commission for help as needed.
   4. Newcomers. In conjunction with the Commission on Outreach, the Commission on Fellowship should provide opportunities throughout the year for newcomers to meet members of the parish and become more involved in the parish life.
   5. Sunday morning fellowship. There should be a way determined whereby we can offer opportunities for people to meet each other in a casual manner during a fellowship hour every Sunday morning.

6. This Commission is to seek out and utilize talent throughout the parish in developing its program, operating upon the assumption that all the parish is actually responsible for supporting such a program and will benefit therefrom. Among talents that can be utilized are those which are able to provide for artistic settings, entertainment, as well as the usual activities of preparing some kind of fellowship event.

TENTATIVE DESCRIPTION OF COMMISSION ON OUTREACH

1. This Commission shall determine an overall philosophy of evangelism for St. Philip's Parish, by serious study and consultation on the subject. This consultation can be with any persons or materials it considers useful.
2. This Commission shall establish and implement a program seeking the non-Christian, the unchurched Episcopalian, and lapsed members of the parish.
3. This Commission shall establish and implement a program to integrate new members into the functioning life of the parish on a creative level.
4. This Commission shall determine the appropriate stance of the parish regarding public relations—use of news media, advertising, printed materials, etc., and will make specific recommendations regarding same to the rector and vestry.
5. This Commission shall keep a close check on the membership picture of the parish, and determine areas of weakness, along with recommended programs to meet these needs.
6. This Commission shall further define its concerns and recommendations in terms of facilities, equipment and financing necessary to do the job well.
7. This Commission shall report to the vestry quarterly regarding its activities, as well as the membership picture of the parish.
8. This Commission shall work with the Commission on Personnel and Training to train and select any personnel needed to carry out its task.

IMMEDIATE ASSIGNMENT:
1. To carry out at least one training event for its members.
2. Give the vestry, stated specifically in writing, recommendations regarding a suitable public relations program as outlined in #4, at the vestry's July meeting.

TENTATIVE DESCRIPTION OF THE COMMISSION ON CHRISTIAN SOCIAL ACTION

1. This Commission shall determine the areas of social concern which properly confront St. Philip's Parish, and recommend to the Vestry the most appropriate response in each area.
2. This Commission shall be responsible for being knowledgeable regarding the program of the national Church and Diocese in this area, and for seeing that the Parish is educated in the same.
3. In the event of the organization of any joint effort among the Episcopal churches of Durham, or among all the churches of Durham in the area of Urban Work, etc., this Commission shall represent this parish in same.
4. In the event an outside agency requests support or involvement of the parish in some social concern, this Commission shall be the agency to whom the request should come, and they make appropriate recommendations regarding same to the vestry.
5. This Commission is encouraged to realistically work toward helping this parish take a stance in this Community which will clearly indicate our concern for all its people and their needs.
6. This Commission is to determine facilities, equipment, etc., which would be needed to carry out an excellent program, and report same to the Commission on parish future.

IMMEDIATE ASSIGNMENT:
To survey the alternatives open to St. Philip's at the present time, and report to the vestry with appropriate recommendations by the July meeting.

TENTATIVE DESCRIPTION OF COMMISSION ON PERSONNEL AND TRAINING

1. This commission is to develop an overall philosophy of training as related to the needs of a Christian congregation in the modern era. This is to be done in terms of the ministry of the laity, the terms of program action and leadership.
2. It is to identify personnel needs, and assist various groups needing persons to serve in finding same. This area includes the obvious leadership needs of today, and projections of leadership needs for the future.
3. Design training programs to meet these needs, in conjunction with the groups involved.
4. In designing programs, this Commission will be specific about financing, equipment, and facilities needed.
5. Become well informed in the field of leadership training as promoted in the Episcopal Church, with people and training resources available, and with literature, etc. available.
6. This Commission is to report, in writing, to the vestry, with specific and detailed recommendations, at the various points it desires to implement aspects of its responsibilities.

7. This Commission will, at least annually, survey the training picture in the parish, evaluate it by previously established standards, and revise or augment its program accordingly.

IMMEDIATE ASSIGNMENT:

To design and implement leadership training programs for the following:
1. Church School teachers,
2. Adult Education leaders,
3. Youth Ministry workers,
4. General Organizational leaders.

The [Diocesan] Department of Program is willing to assist St. Philip's Parish in becoming a "pilot" congregation in the field of leadership, both by making available its trained personnel, and by aiding St. Philip's locate trained professionals and resources from outside the Diocese.

This Commission is to present a preliminary report, in writing, to the July meeting of the vestry.

TENTATIVE DESCRIPTION OF COMMISSION ON PARISH FUTURE

1. This Commission shall be responsible for surveying the alternatives available to the parish, projected for a period of at *least five years*, the committing of same in writing, and listing of recommendations to the vestry.
2. This is to be accomplished in three ways:
   a. By gathering information from the various agencies and commissions of the parish which have been given, as a part of their duties, the detailed study of needs, both in facilities and personnel, to carry out an excellent program. For example: the group responsible for Christian Education will make specific recommendations regarding space needs, equipment needs, etc., which can be a basic part of any study regarding a projected building program.
   b. By the study of the programs of other parishes, Episcopal and other, which are in similar circumstances.
   c. By consultation with knowledgeable persons in the field of church planning.

Recommended timetable:

By July Meeting—to have clearly established guidelines for its work, stating areas of concern, and listing concrete steps for accomplishing same.

By October Meeting—to have gathered information enough for preliminary recommendations to the vestry regarding needs and ways to meet them.

APPENDIX L. THE GENERAL CONVENTION SPECIAL PROGRAM'S GUIDELINES FOR APPLICANTS

I. Purposes:

The applications shall fall into one or more of these three categories.

A. Community self-determination on national, metropolitan and neighborhood levels (urban, suburban and rural) for social, political or economic power, including basic research and planning to these ends.

B. Programs of service to the poor, designed and controlled by those to be served; including training and skills necessary to assure effective conduct of such programs.

C. Community leadership training and experience in areas of need identified by the applicants.

II. Criteria:

A. In conformity to the provisions of Resolution #6, General Convention:

1. The purposes and ends sought to be obtained by the proposed program falls within one or more of the Purposes enumerated above.

2. The proposed program is based upon the fundamental principle of assisting the poor to organize themselves so that they may stand on their own two feet and have a full share in determining their own destiny.

3. The proposed program, by its terms, provides that none of the funds received by the proposed grant recipient will be utilized for the benefit of, or in connection with, the activities of any individual or group, including the recipient, which advocates the use of violence as a part of its program.

4. The proposed program, by its terms, provides that neither the Episcopal Church, nor its Executive Council nor any officer or agency thereof, shall exercise any supervision or control whatsoever over:

   a. The proposed grant, once it has been made, or

   b. the administration and execution thereof by the recipient, or

   c. ends and purposes sought to be obtained thereby.

5. The proposed program, by its terms, provides for at least semi-annual financial accounting and reporting by the proposed grant recipient in accordance with customary accounting procedures.

6. The proposed program, by its terms, provides for at least annual evaluation of:

   a. the administration and execution of the proposed program, and

   b. the progress of such program towards the attainment of the purposes and ends sought thereby.

7. The Screening and Review Committee of the Executive Council shall determine, as a part of its initial appraisal of the proposed program, that the proposed grant recipient is reasonably able to attain the purpose and ends sought thereby.

B. Need:

1. Is there a critical local, metropolitan, or national need for this project?

2. How is this need demonstrated: Statistics, personal testimony, other?

C. Feasibility:

1. Do the stated purposes, objectives and timetable represent a coherent, reasonable plan?

2. Will this project have a wide range of impact on society?

3. Is there a high degree of readiness for the project? (Actors, sponsor, system)

4. Can the project accomplish its goals without an unhealthy dependence on other agencies?

5. Is the project non-paternalistic?

6. Will the project stimulate new self-understanding of and visions for the people?

7. Does the proposal promise increased self-determination for the poor people?

D. Use of Resources:

1. Is the budget realistic?
2. Are there budget projections for eventual self-support?
3. Will this project generate other sources of funding if the G.C.S.P. supports it?
4. Are the required trained personnel available and ready?
5. Is there a reasonable plan for human resource development? On-the-job-training of indigenous leadership, etc.?
6. Is there maximum utilization of local resources, human and financial?

E. Local Support:

1. Who wants this project?
2. Can the proponents demonstrate a significant base of support for initiating or continuing this project?
3. Have the constituency participated in the planning and designing of this application or is it just the work of professionals?
4. What is the overall relationship between this project and the members of the neighborhood or community?

APPENDIX M. LETTERS OF WALTER MASON TO THE CONGREGATION

SAINT PHILIP'S EPISCOPAL CHURCH

403 East Main Street
P. O. Box 218
Durham, North Carolina 27702

September 19, 1970

(Reading Time: Approx. 3 minutes)
Dear St. Philippian:

Please won't you take 3 minutes of your time to learn more about the self-study program which is underway at St. Philip's?

Although the program was described in the *Epistle to the Philippians* of August 9, and further details were explained by the Reverend David Covell from the Division of Strategic Services, Executive Council, New York in the Adult Class on Sunday, September 13, quite reasonably many questions must exist in the minds of our parishioners.

As the success of this study will be entirely dependent upon the sympathetic understanding, assistance, and cooperation of the entire parish, certainly the answer to each of these questions should be communicated to every St. Philippian:

Who authorized the study? Why?
What will it cost?
What is its purpose?
How will it proceed?

1. *Authorization*:

The Vestry, as our elected representatives and trustees of the parish, is charged with the conduct of all secular affairs, just as the Rector is charged with the conduct of all spiritual affairs. In the exercise of their duties and responsibilities the Vestry and the Rector need guidance, guidance which can only come from the members of the parish. St. Philip's is ninety years old this year. What is the mission and the future of a downtown church in a rapidly changing neighborhood? Will it be here ninety years from now? Dependent upon the assessment of the future, should continuous Urban Renewal land now available be purchased before someone else buys it? Are our services to the congregation and our services to the community adequate? If not, would additional physical plant provide the means to make them adequate?

These are tough questions requiring rigorous answers. To be sure, the Rector and each member of the Vestry has carefully considered opinions based on observations, judgments, and conversations with members of the parish, but can any one of these dedicated people be absolutely certain that what he believes does represent the views of the congregation? The Vestry concluded that guidance must come from the congregation. To learn how we can obtain and compile information about the parish and from the congregation in a meaningful, structured and cohesive manner which will lend itself to evaluation, the Vestry turned to the Division of Strategic Services of the Executive Council. After becoming familiar with the services of the Division and convinced of their value, the Vestry authorized the self-study program.

2. *Cost*:

The Division of Strategic Services is a consulting service available to any parish or diocese in the church. It is staffed by competent personnel who teach and supply tried techniques for self-study. The emphasis is on the *"self"* as the study will be conducted by the parish committee, but the information will come from you, the congregation. When all of the data has been gathered, the Division of Strategic Services will offer its written evaluation of the data.

The basic charge for the self-study is $500 of which $150 is paid by the National Church. Charge for the Division's statisticians to construct and analyze a tailor-made questionnaire pertinent to the issues at St. Philip's will be approximately $250 to $375. We will also be responsible for the travel expenses of Division personnel for five or six trips to Durham. The total expenditure will be somewhere between $1,000 and $1,500. Unlike the several opinion surveys and questionnaires over the last several years, this effort has a price in dollars aside from the time that members of the congregation will contribute. If your Self-Study Committee did not believe, as the Rector and Vestry do believe, that commensurate value will be received for this expenditure, we would not be involved in this undertaking.

3. *Purpose*:

The study is a serious attempt to learn about ourselves as a congregation, about our parish organizations, about what the community thinks of us, and, above all, what each parishioner thinks about our parish's mission, future, and needs. It is truly your chance to influence the future! There are no tricks to the study, no gimmicks. It is not an attempt to con anyone into anything, but an honest effort to obtain the views of the congregation to provide guidance to the Rector and Vestry in tough decisions regarding our mission, our future, and our needs. *Neither the Vestry nor Rector will in any way attempt to influence the results of the study.*

4. *Procedure*:

There will be five phases to the study which will be completed in the sequence mentioned although work on more than one phase will be performed concurrently.

a) Preparation of a parish residence map.

b) Completion of self-study booklets by leaders of parish organizations reflecting the views of their members. Much of the work on this phase has already been accomplished in the meetings conducted by Dr. James E. Davis' Committee on Parish Evaluation last April. Information will be gathered also from external organizations in the community.

c) Visitation in the congregation and the community by a team from the Division office. They will talk to a cross-section of the congregation—the elderly, the middle-aged, the young married, youth, traditionalists, modernists—in a "no holds barred" meeting to which *the Vestry and the Rector are not invited.* The team will remove their clerical collars and go out into the community as well.

d) Completion by every adult parishioner, and possibly children down to age 12, of an Attitude Survey in which each person's *anonymity* will be strictly preserved. You will be asked to sign a card that you have participated in the survey, *but there will be absolutely no way to match your card with your anonymous survey.* The survey will be processed in a completely impersonal manner by a computer.

e) The study will conclude with an evaluation by the Self-Study Committee of all of the data gathered and an independent evaluation by the Division of Strategic Services.

The committee will keep you fully informed of the progress of the study and will solicit your assistance and cooperation as appropriate. Many members of the congregation will be contacted personally to assist in some aspect of the study. The committee has the following membership:

> Mrs. Ed Hodges (Betty)
> Mrs. Isaac Manning (Dorothy)
> Dr. Harold Parker
> Mrs. Richard Watson (Ruth)
> Walter P. Mason, Chairman

If you have any questions concerning the study, any of us would be pleased to try to answer them.

> For the Committee,
> Faithfully yours,
>
> Walter R. Mason

SAINT PHILIP'S EPISCOPAL CHURCH

> 403 East Main Street
> P. O. Box 218
> Durham, North Carolina 27702
>
> November 5, 1970

IMPORTANT INFORMATION: PARISH SELF-STUDY
(Reading Time: Approx. 2 minutes)

Dear St. Philippian:

Two extremely important events in the self-study process are about to take place!

1. *Attitudinal Survey*:

At the conclusion of the 7:45 service and the 10:00 o'clock service on this coming Sunday, November 8, those in attendance will be asked to adjourn to the parish hall to participate in the Attitudinal Survey. THIS IS YOUR OPPORTUNITY TO INFLUENCE THE FUTURE OF ST. PHILIP'S.

As has been mentioned in earlier letters, your answers to the survey questions will be strictly anonymous. You will be asked to sign a card that you have participated in the survey, but there will be absolutely no way to match your card with your answers. The cards will be deposited in one box, the surveys in another. The entire process will require no more than *15 or 20 minutes* of your time. Between now and Sunday, please consider your views on the following issues and points:

 a) Mission of St. Philip's
 b) Use of St. Philip's facilities
 c) Laity's expectations of clergy
 d) Laity's expectations of vestry
 e) Role of the laity
 f) Parish leadership
 g) Favorability/feasibility of capital funds drive
 h) Adult education
 i) Sunday School program
 j) Parish profile
 k) Financial expectations

While the adults are completing the survey in the parish hall, young people who are confirmed will be completing the survey in their classrooms.

If for any reason you will not be attending services next Sunday, please stop in at the Parish House anytime during the week of November 8, to complete your survey. A first-floor room will be set aside all week for this purpose.

Your participation is most important as the Division of Strategic Services advises that we must have at least 70% participation to obtain valued results. Can't we please count on you?

2. *Visitation*:

On Monday and Tuesday, November 9 and 10, the Reverend David Covell will visit in the parish and in the community. External to the parish, he is particularly interested in talking to the city planners and to clergymen of other denominations.

On Monday evening, November 9, he will meet with a representative group of St. Philippians, not exceeding 20 in number, to gain an insight into the climate and the image of St. Philip's. This group has been kept small at Mr. Covell's request to allow a free exchange of ideas and opinions.

As no one member of the Self-Study Committee, or the committee collectively, is personally acquainted with every St. Philippian, it was a difficult task to select parishioners for this meeting. We hope you understand that not every parishioner could be asked, but realizing that many of you may wish to speak to Mr. Covell, he will maintain office hours in the Parish House on Tuesday, November 10 from 3 P.M. to 6 P.M. *ANY MEMBER OF ST. PHILIP'S IS WELCOME TO SPEAK TO HIM IN PRIVATE DURING THESE HOURS.*

Again, we ask your continued understanding, assistance and cooperation.

For the Committee,
Faithfully yours,

Walter R. Mason

APPENDIX N. SOME NOTES REGARDING POSSIBLE RE-ORGANIZATION
OF ADMINISTRATIVE AND PROGRAM AREAS OF ST. PHILIP'S PARISH

1. It is suggested that we organize into a departmental structure, under general headings. The choice of headings can vary, since, in a sense, most categories, if extended to their fullest implications, could encompass all the others. Therefore, whatever headings are chosen should be accompanied by precise definitions.

2. This procedure envisions the following relationship with the Vestry and the working program structure of the parish at large:

Rector-Vestry

Responsibilities basically legislative—this means all ultimate authority, by Canon, lies here, and that final policy decisions rest with this body alone. The Vestry is to be responsible for keeping a representative relationship with the parish at large, in a lay ministry.

Executive Committee

Would consist of the Rector, Wardens, Secretary and Treasurer of the Vestry. The Committee would be responsible for administrative implementation of all Vestry policies, and would have broad powers, within the limits of those predetermined policies, to execute. This Committee would be the communications link between departments, and between the departments and the Vestry.

3. Suggested Departmental structure, with tentative definitions and job descriptions:

Departments

Responsibilities basically program planning and action. Departments relate to the parish at large through consistent involvement of a broad spectrum of the membership in the program. They are accountable to the Vestry.

A. *ADMINISTRATIVE*

Property Committee—It is appropriate that this committee be considered a part of the Administrative Department, since it is responsible for day-to-day maintenance of the property, and this is tied in so closely with the budget and general policy matters. The Property Committee would operate under a detailed plan for inspection, maintenance, and repair.

Phase I and Phase II Committees—Until the period of renovation and land acquisition is completed, it seems best that these committees be included under administration.

Insurance Committee—This has long been a standing committee of the Vestry. Its sole purpose is to make annual review and recommendations regarding insurance coverage and needs, and to process claims, if any.

Evaluation Committee—To develop standards by which the effectiveness of program and personnel may be evaluated, and will be responsible for a detailed evaluation of same annually, which will be presented to the Vestry, with recommendations.

Stewardship and Canvass—To be responsible for Stewardship Education throughout the year, and the conducting of the Every Member Canvass.

Nominating Committee—Recently adopted Vestry procedure spells out this committee's duties with some precision. It is to be appointed at the September Vestry meeting each year to plan for the January Elections.

Fine Arts and Memorials Committee—It is recommended that this Committee be re-established in the parish, and serve, in addition to its study of liturgical arts, as a Memorials Committee. As a Memorials Committee it would screen all needs for memorials in St. Philip's, and make appropriate suggestions to the Rector and Vestry.

B. *LAY MINISTRY*

Assuming that the special report approved by the February Vestry meeting is implemented, the following areas could be formed into working groups:

Outreach Committee—To be responsible for developing and implementing a viable program for reaching newcomers, unchurched, inactives, and integrating them into parish life.

Committee on Recruitment—This would be a "volunteer personnel" committee. Its purpose would be to match people to program needs, and to recommend programs to match people's needs. This is one of the major needs in our parish program structure.

Episcopal Church Women, Laymen's Group, & EYC—All auxiliary groups should have a connection with the total picture and activities in Lay Ministry.

C. *CHRISTIAN EDUCATION*

Training Division—This should be a special section, which would devote its time to developing skills to aid other people in doing their program tasks, and then offering a consistent program of training.

Church School—The committee would be composed of the divisional chairman of the Church School.

Adult Education—This is a weak area at the present time, and needs a special group to study needs, methods and programs for recommendation to the total program of the parish.

Library Committee—This committee is responsible for the operation and publicity of the parish library.

D. *COMMUNITY ACTION*

Assuming that the special report which will be submitted to the March Vestry meeting will be approved, the following areas perhaps might fit the need.

Center City Church Council—This group would be made up of the five parish representatives on the Council, and would be responsible for keeping St. Philip's concerns before the Council, and the Council's concerns before St. Philip's.

Neighborhood Direct Involvement—While working with and through the Center City Church Council, St. Philip's needs to have a direct action group which will relate to the Oldham Towers residents, the Coordinating Council for Senior Citizens, residents of the Liberty Street Project, youth and recreation, food needs (we have an infant food program), and day care. It is possible that we will need to establish separate groups under some or all of these headings—such as a Youth Action or Coffee House Ministry Committee.

E. *WORSHIP*

Since the issue of worship has become one of great interest and concern during the recent years, it is necessary that serious coordination be made between all groups in the parish connected with it.

Liturgical Committee—Since the Episcopal Church will no doubt be dealing with the issue of Trial Use for some years to come, it is important that we maintain this group which was established to evaluate and recommend regarding these liturgical concerns.

Music Department.—The expansion of this program promises an impact of broad proportions, and should be included in the Worship Department.

Altar Guild—Though operating with a set program, the involvement of the Guild in the planning of worship and education regarding same is vital.

Lay Readers and Acolytes—These programs are not highly structured but should be included in all planning.

Ushers—The hopes we have for the expansion of this program to include young people calls for their involvement in planning.

Operation of above outlined structure:

1. Department Executive Committees, made up of a general chairman, and chairmen of the various sub-groups, would meet monthly, and make a written report to the Vestry.
2. Sub-Groups, since they vary greatly in amount of activity needed, would meet as needed.
3. Department Chairmen would meet Quarterly for planning and review.
4. All members of all departments and sub-groups would meet twice yearly.
5. The Executive Committee would serve as the communications link between departments and between the departments and the Vestry.
6. All departments would share in over-all parish planning, including purposes, goals, budget planning, calendar planning, etc. . . .

APPENDIX O. REPORT OF THE EPISCOPAL CHURCH WOMEN

(Annual Congregational Meeting, January 23, 1972)

It is a pleasure to report on the activities of the Episcopal Church Women of St. Philip's for the year 1971. Working together the members have sought to make a Christian witness within the church and within the community both locally and abroad.

There are five chapters—one night chapter, one for mothers of pre-school children and three others. Every woman of St. Philip's is a member of ECW and those who desire to belong to a chapter are so assigned.

The book of Acts was the subject of our Educational Program for the year. The presentations and discussions have been very meaningful. Our worship led by the Devotional Chairmen have been the source of our inspiration and strength.

The Committees of Material Aid, Missions and Christian Social Relations work together in the fall and spring ingatherings of household items and clothes which are distributed to Church World Service, Migrant Project, Gravely Sanatorium, Thompson Children's Home and local organizations. The ingatherings this year totaled 2,485 pounds. Some adult clothes which were unsuitable for our recipients were sold at the Nearly New Shoppe for $57.00. This money helped buy material used for the layettes and children's clothes which we made. The film presented at the fall joint chapter meeting, the display on the bulletin board were all great incentives to the fulfillment of this project.

The Christian Social Relations Committee has established a Baby Food Closet at St. Philip's. The Durham Social Service Department and the Community Action Committee will be the channels through   which this food will be dispensed. All church women are asked to contribute to the closet. A designated barrel has been placed in the parish house to receive the food. Also 52 ditty bags were made and filled to be sent to overseas servicemen.

The Missions Committee has presented excellent reports at chapter meetings on missionaries and missionary projects. A box was also compiled to send to Mrs Rachel Wolf. The Missions and Social Relations Committees have also given monetary help to many other causes.

The Spring and Fall ingatherings of the United Thank Offerings totaled $903.54. It is important that each church women realize the value of her participation in this gift of gratitude which has such a great role in the life of the church.

The profit of the Christmas Bazaar to date is $3,689.71. We all enjoyed the marvelous feeling of fellowship and co-operation as we worked together on this wonderful project.

A profit of $765.12 was realized from the Pansy Sale. St. Margaret's Guild representatives sell books, note cards, recipe cards and knives. Coupons and stamps have been sent to Thompson Orphanage to be redeemed for either cash or necessary items.

Volunteers have assisted the coordinating Council for Senior Citizens by helping provide rides for Senior Citizens to hospitals, doctors' offices, social agencies and grocery shopping. Prizes have been furnished for Bingo games.

Magazines have been taken monthly to local hospitals and rehabilitation homes. We have visited newcomers, remembered with prayers and cards those members who were bereaved, sick or shut-in. A card file was compiled on church members away at school and the Epistle is being sent to them. We assisted with the Christmas Party for Duke students at the Episcopal student center. The Hospitality and Social Period Committees handled arrangements for the following events: Youth Day, Feb. 14; Lenten Suppers: March 10, 17, 24, 31; Dinner and reception following combined church service at St. Philip's and Parish dinners. Every Sunday they have a social period between the 9:30 and 11:00 A.M. services. The Parish Housekeeping Committee has seen that everything is clean and in readiness for the fall activities and the Bazaar. Through our Memorial Book Fund books are purchased for the Parish Library in memory of women communicants of St. Philip's.

Members of the Episcopal Church Women attended and participated in these other events.

Diocesan Convention
World Day of Prayer
Annual ECW Diocesan Convention
Kanuga
Liturgical Conference
Woman's Day St. Augustine College
Consultation on Church Union (three Sunday Conferences)
ECW Convocation Executive Board meeting
Center City Council meetings and services

We have a representative on the board of the Center City Church Council and we are looking forward to working with this organization in its endeavor to co-ordinate the ministries of the churches of Durham. The council meets monthly and has held several joint worship services throughout the year.

A copy of the budget follows. We finance a nursery attendant for St. Hilda's Chapter meetings, a male attendant for St. Cecilia's night chapter meetings and the services of the maid who has special weekly cleaning duties in the Parish House. Along with the Parish we pay the attendants for the nursery on Sunday. Volunteers from ECW and Junior High School girls assist these paid attendants.

The sincere dedication, whole hearted co-operation of the Committee chairmen, their committees and the members of the staff of St. Philip's have made this a wonderful year. My thanks to each of them.

Respectfully submitted,

Julia Royall (Mrs. Kenneth)
President

EXECUTIVE BOARD

President	Mrs. Kenneth C. Royall, Jr.
Vice-President	Mrs. W. L. D. Townsend
Past President	Mrs. George C. Pyne, Jr.
Secretary	Mrs. John Cahoon
Treasurer	Mrs. Victor Moore, Jr.
Secretary Devotional Life	Mrs. Clarence Cobb
Secretary Christian Education	Mrs. Blaine Nashold
Secretary Christian Social Relations	Mrs. James E. Davis
Secretary of Missions	Mrs. B. W. C. Roberts
Secretary Material Aid	Mrs. Norman Ross
United Thank Offering	Mrs. Kenneth Podger
St. Margaret's Guild	Mrs. Robert Cowan
Pansy Sale	Mrs. Warren B. Watkins, Jr.
Christmas Bazaar Chairman	Mrs. Alexander Barnes
Christmas Bazaar Vice-Chairman and Chairman Elect	Mrs. Will London

CHAPTER CHAIRMEN

St. Agnes	Mrs. John E. Markham
St. Anne	Mrs. T. C. Cooke
St. Cecilia	Mrs. Robert Bailey
St. Elizabeth	Mrs. George Watts Carr, Jr.
St. Hilda	Mrs. C. Franklin Knott, Jr.

STANDING COMMITTEE CHAIRMEN

Christian Ministries and College Work	Mrs. Ernest Elsevier
Special Correspondent	Mrs. Frank Webb
Parish Hospitality	Mrs. Grover Hunter
Sunday Social Periods	Mrs. Edwin B. Hamshar
	Mrs. J. Norman Black
	Mrs. C. L. May
Parish Housekeeping	Mrs. Alton Jernigan
Church Periodicals	Mrs. Frank K. Borden
Coupons	Mrs. E. L. Embree
Nursery	Mrs. B. W. C. Roberts
Membership	Mrs. George Pyne
Promotion	Mrs. Edward Hodges

BUDGET 1971–1972

CONTRIBUTIONS

OUTSIDE PARISH

Children's Work in Durham	$50.00
Children's Work Overseas	50.00
Church World Service Clothing Appeal	30.00
College Work	20.00
Convocation Missions Christmas Gifts	25.00
Convocation Dues	25.00
Diocesan Church Periodical Club	25.00
Diocesan Pledge	925.00
Discretionary Funds	
Diocesan Bishop	50.00
Hospital Chaplain	75.00
Ministry to Deaf	50.00
St. Philip's Mission Chm.	100.00
St. Philip's Christian Social Rel.	100.00
Episcopal Child Care Service of N.C.	100.00
Kanuga	50.00
Migrant Work	50.00
Missionary Assigned St. Philip's	25.00
Presiding Bishop's Fund	50.00
St. Augustine's College	100.00
St. Mary's Junior College	100.00
World Mission Project	50.00
TOTAL OUTSIDE	$2,050.00

INSIDE PARISH

Capital Improvements (Aux. Rm. Acct.)	200.00
Church Hour Nursery	300.00
Discretionary Fund—Rector	200.00
EYC Conference Fund	20.00
Gifts to Church Staff	110.00
Choirs (Appreciation)	50.00
Parish House Upkeep (Lottie $467.00)	625.00
Memorial Book Fund	30.00
Contingency	100.00
TOTAL INSIDE	$1,635.00

EXPENSES

ADMINISTRATION

Audit	40.00
Chapter Expenses	
St. Cecilia's Male Attendant	45.00
St. Hilda's Nursery	45.00

Conference Fund	200.00
Postage and Supplies	
Christian Education Chm.	75.00
Devotional Chm.	25.00
Material Aid	35.00
Officers	45.00
Special Correspondent	20.00
United Thank Offering Chm.	25.00
Year Book	250.00
Contingency	100.00
Total Expenses	$ 905.00
TOTAL BUDGET	$4,590.00

APPENDIX P. REPORT OF PAT ROBINSON ON THE FAITH ALIVE WEEKEND AT ST. PHILIP'S CHURCH

Since the Church is not a commercial or industrial enterprise, nor are people a commodity, it is impossible to give you a report that would be acceptable to you as business men and women. However, if we can see the Church for what it is and what it tries to be, I can give you, what I believe is, a comprehensive report on the results of the Faith Alive Weekend.

The Church is unlike any other group of people who come together. Much of the time, we have nothing in common with one another, except the fact that we believe in the same God. Even in that fact, we have found that we all see God differently, and often cannot agree on just how His Church should function in the world.

The Holy Scripture offers us directions and guidelines that we could follow, but often do not. Christ Himself taught us truths about His Church that we have neglected and ignored. The power and the influence of the early Church, I think, can be traced to the Christ-centeredness of those early believers, who prayed often and had much fellowship with one another—because their need was so great. In this time of affluence and wealth our material need has diminished, but our need for Christian fellowship has greatly increased, because of the crush of the secular world that is all around us.

We have little impact on our society as individuals. Nevertheless, our Christian commitment must come from us as individuals. Also, since the unit of our society is the family, we must strengthen the position of the Christian family. So we must begin by being real Christians at home—we must begin to pray together, if we are not already doing so. We must begin to understand and love one another—as Jesus commanded us. You think that I am talking, now, of your individual homes—which I am. But, I am also including the larger "family" of the Church. If we are to survive, more than that, if we are truly to find joy in this life, then we must come together in an atmosphere of love and understanding, which God, in His wisdom, provided in the structure of the Church.

The Faith Alive Weekend provided us with an opportunity to hear what other people were experiencing in Christianity. We heard from representatives of all age groups, that Jesus Christ was a reality, and that the power of the Holy Spirit was visibly at work in their lives and in their Churches. We heard, not that they didn't have any problems, but that because they were now aware of the presence of their Lord, no problem was impossible—because with God, anything is possible! We heard them praying for one another as they stood to bear witness to Jesus Christ. Even if the personal witness is "not your thing," I saw positive effects in the lives of fellow St. Philippians, as a result of this. If only one person's life has been changed as a result of this weekend, I think God would have considered it a success—since He is the same God who would seek after one sheep, even if the 99 were already safe. But there was more than one life changed—there were many lives changed. You ask me, "How many?", and I say "Look around you!" Look into the faces of our people and listen to what they say. You will know, unless, you have eyes that do not see and ears that cannot hear! If you could have seen the assembly room, Saturday night, crowded with our people, who were hugging one another and sharing with one another their thoughts, fears, doubts, joys, sorrows, and faith, you wouldn't need this report. Anyone who now walks closer to his Lord, will now be a better St. Philippian.

In the love of Jesus Christ,

APPENDIX Q. VESTRY RESOLUTIONS REGARDING THE BUILDING OF AN URBAN MINISTRIES CENTER, 1982

To: Durham Congregations in Action Board
    From: St. Philip's Episcopal Church
    Re: Urban Ministries Center
          A. St. Philip's Resolutions

On February 20, 1982 the Vestry of St. Philip's approved the following resolutions unanimously:

1. The Vestry approves a fund raising campaign to build the Urban Ministries Center if Meals on Wheels and the Community Kitchen initially agree to become tenants upon completion of the building. Construction may not commence until $375,000 is committed. The Vestry wishes to explore all possible sources of funds to make this a reality.

2. The Vestry of St. Philip's approves the Urban Ministries Building Project as outlined with fund raising to be chaired by William M. Harrison, Jr.

3. An organizational committee for Urban Ministries, Inc. (the manager, operator, and absolutely net lessee of the premises) be formed, consisting of three (3) members of the Vestry and the Rector to explore the organizational structure of Urban Ministries, Inc. in cooperation with Durham Congregations in Action and other interested parties.

4. The Vestry of St. Philip's shall cause to be formed Urban Ministries, Inc., a nonprofit corporation: Charles L. Steel, IV, our attorney, is empowered to form this corporation; the specific purpose of this corporation shall be defined as the net operating lessee of the Urban Ministries Building, and the net rental of said building shall be mutually satisfactory to lessor and lessee.

5. The Vestry of St. Philip's Church authorizes the negotiation of and entering into a long-term net lease by and between St. Philip's Church as landlord and Urban Ministries, Inc. as tenant providing for the use and occupancy of the Urban Ministries Building to be located at the corner of Queen and Liberty Streets, as follows:

    1. Meals on Wheels
    2. Community Kitchen
    3. Church League Basketball Program

4. DCIA office space
5. Other uses approved by the Rector of St. Philip's requested by Urban Ministries, Inc.
   The net lease shall be subject to the final approval of the Vestry.

APPENDIX R. STATISTICAL ACCOUNTING OF FINANCIAL REALITIES, 1978–1993

	Communicants	Average Attendance	Pledging Units	Pledges Budgeted	Total Budget
1978	502	257	212	$92,900	$95,350
1979	541	199	208	110,000	117,000
1980	603	230	188	117,000	129,000
1981	610	292	205	139,000	
1982	635	293	220	141,935	156,082
1983	682	301	235	149,000	162,900
1984	706	330	241	157,500	173,300
1985	737	357	247	187,230	210,500
1986	791	424	254	195,000	238,500
1987	801	454	261	226,000	244,000
1988	828	449	265	234,000	269,170
1989	816	429	221	240,000	264,000
1990	821	381	223	268,000	302,294
1991	921	327	219	274,130	321,372
1992	925	350	228	293,000	308,835
1993				295,000	325,100

Number of communicants is drawn from the *North Carolina Diocesan Journal*; average attendance and number of pledging units were compiled by Thomas Rightmyer; total pledges budgeted (not always paid) and the total budget were drawn from the annual treasurer's reports. Since these reports did not always follow the same form, the amounts over the years were not always consistent or strictly comparable with each other. Nevertheless, the major trends are visible.

Notes

PROLOGUE — THE WALK

1. Joseph Blount Cheshire, Jr., "Preliminary Statement of My Connection with This Mission," St. Philip's Episcopal Church (Durham, N.C.), *Parish Register* I, 6.

2. On North Carolina and the Episcopal Church in the Diocese of North Carolina at that time, see Bishop Thomas Atkinson, "Bishop's Address," *NCDJ* (1876), 38–39; "Report of Bishop Theodore B. Lyman," *North Carolina Diocesan Journal* (*NCDJ*) (1881), 89–90, and (1882), 83–84; Buxton, "Missionary and Educational Enterprise," 312–16, 343, 346.

3. Lyman, "Report of Assistant Bishop T. B. Lyman," *NCDJ* (1878), 51.

4. Atkinson, "Report of Bishop's Acts, 1877–1878," *NCDJ* (1878), 43.

5. London, *Cheshire*, pp. 19–20.

6. Report of J. B. Cheshire, Jr., Deacon Officiating, Chapel of the Cross, Chapel Hill, *NCDJ* (1879), 117–19.

7. Cheshire, "Preliminary Statement," *Parish Register* I, 6.

8. *The Book of Common Prayer* (1856).

9. Ibid., p. 102.

10. Cheshire, "Preliminary Statement," *Parish Register* I, 7; Lyman, "Episcopal Acts, 1879–1880," *NCDJ* (1880), 89. ·

11. *The Book of Common Prayer* (1856), p. 61.

12. The high regard with which the Book of Common Prayer was held by Episcopal communicants surfaces time and again, every decade. For example, when the Diocesan Committee on the Ratification of the Book of Common Prayer was protesting in 1882 the proposed shortening of weekday services, it wrote: "Our daily Morning or Evening Prayer is regarded by the great authorities on ritual, and by the general sense of the Church of Christ, as a most happy fruit of the divinely guided wisdom of the Church. It is rich in matter, complete in its comprehension of all the parts of public prayer, and it is very beautiful in its structure and symmetry. Any shortened service should preserve, as far as may be, these features of our Morning and Evening Prayer, and should be services which will not by their mutilation, and want of harmony with the Sunday services, shock the feelings of our devout people." *NCDJ* (1882), 43.

CHAPTER I. IN SEARCH OF A RECTOR WHO WOULD STAY, 1878–1898

1. See table 11, "Salaries of Clergy of White Congregations of Four Major Denominations in Durham, by Decades, 1880–1930," in Watson, "A Religious Profile," 211–13.

2. Many gifts were not in money: for example, a beautiful marble font from the Sunday School of Calvary Church, Tarboro, and a Bible and prayer books for the chancel.

3. London, *Cheshire*, 19–20.

4. Evidence as to the Cheshire years is found in Cheshire, "Preliminary Statement," *Parish Register* I, 6–8; reports by Cheshire, *NCDJ* (1879), 118–19; (1880), 127; and (1881), 118–19; re-

ports of Assistant Bishop Lyman, *NCDJ* (1880), 89; report of Bishop Lyman, *NCDJ* (1881), 78; London, *Cheshire*, 23–25.

5. For C. J. Curtis and his stay at St. Philip's, see Cheshire, "Preliminary Statement," *Parish Register* I, 7–8; *NCDJ* (1882), 117, 171, and (1883), 157.

6. Bishop Lyman, in reporting the consecration of the Church of the Ascension at Hickory, complimented "the zealous young Rector and his earnest co-workers," *NCDJ* (1882), 79.

7. On John Huske and his ministry, see *NCDJ* (1883), 60, 111–12, 157; (1884), 84; (1885), 24, 34, 68; (1886), 24, 92–93.

8. *NCDJ* (1887), 28, 85.

9. *The Tobacco Plant*, June 9, 1888, January 5, July 20 and 27, 1881.

10. *NCDJ* (1887), 86; (1890), 125.

11. *NCDJ* (1882), 86.

12. Ibid., 85–86.

13. *NCDJ* (1883), 35.

14. *NCDJ* (1887), 86. Tense of quotations changed to fit the context.

15. *NCDJ* (1888), 91. This paragraph is largely a modified quotation from George's report.

16. *NCDJ* (1890), 21.

17. *NCDJ* (1890), 126; (1895), 59.

18. *NCDJ* (1895), 58, 60.

19. Ibid., 83.

20. *NCDJ* (1890), 125; (1891), 96–97, 140; (1892), 91; (1893), 103–4; (1894), 106–7; (1895), 83.

21. Watson, "A Religious Profile," 25–26.

22. *NCDJ* (1893), 104. See also (1891), 77, 140; (1894), 107, 145.

23. Watson, "A Religious Profile," 26.

24. St. Philip's, *Parish Register* I.

25. *NCDJ* (1890), 126.

26. Watson, "A Religious Profile," 194.

27. *Durham Daily Sun*, August 2, 1895.

28. Watson, "A Religious Profile," 24.

29. Ibid., 52.

30. *Durham Daily Sun*, March 12, 1898.

31. Ibid., March 15, 1898.

32. Watson, "A Religious Profile," 45.

33. *NCDJ* (1895), 83; (1898), 80.

34. Durden, *The Dukes of Durham*, 128–29.

35. Gant, *The Episcopal Church in Burlington*, 2, 5, 7.

36. *NCDJ* (1895), 13. Erwin was a delegate and Powe was an alternate. The other lay delegates from St. Philip's were J. M. Manning, T. H. Martin, and W. L. Wall; the other alternates were W. B. LaFar, Charles McGary, and L. W. Wise.

37. Watson, "A Religious Profile," 45.

CHAPTER II. THE BOST YEARS: EXPANSION, CONSOLIDATION, AND HESITATION, 1898–1935

1. Anderson, *Durham County*, 305–6.

2. Ibid., 257.

3. Ibid., 222.

4. W. F. Carr, Chair, Board of Directors, Interracial Committee for the County of Durham, to K. P. Lewis, October 26, 1925; Lewis to Carr, November 2, 1925; Lewis to W. D. Carmichael, March 1, 1926, Kemp Plummer Lewis Papers; *Durham Morning Herald*, March 4, 5, 1926. Photocopies contributed by David Ross, research associate for this history of St. Philip's.

5. McBryde, "Cheshire," 33.

6. London, "The Diocese in the First Decades of the Twentieth Century," 310–11.

7. Brawley, "The Episcopal Church in North Carolina, 1883–1900," 305.

8. Ibid., 279.

9. London, "The Diocese in the First Decades of the Twentieth Century," 330–31. He continues: "It should be noted that the (national) Triennial Meeting of the Woman's Auxiliary in 1919 expanded its work 'to include religious education and social service as well as missions.' It also changed the name of the organization from the 'Woman's Auxiliary to the Board of Missions' to the 'Woman's Auxiliary to the Presiding Bishop and Council.'"

10. London, "The Diocese in the First Decades of the Twentieth Century," 332.

11. Brawley, "The Episcopal Church in North Carolina, 1883–1900," 302–3.

12. *NCDJ* (1899), 80.

13. Anderson, *Durham County*, 243–44, 316.

14. Burcham, "History of St. Andrew's," 1.

15. *NCDJ* (1913), "Bishop's Address."

16. Bowman, "Bost," 42.

17. "Minutes of Annual Congregational Meeting, December 4, 1916," Vestry minutes, St. Philip's Parish. Because the figure in the minutes for the number of communicants in 1916 is somewhat inflated, we have substituted the figure given in the Diocesan *Journal* for 1916. The figures for St. Joseph's and St. Andrew's are not separated from those of St. Philip's Church until 1925. Until then we do not know the size of the congregation of the mother church but only the totals for the St. Philip's *Parish*.

18. Vestry minutes, June 4, 1919.

19. As a reminder of what sitting in a hot, non-airconditioned church was like, consider this tidbit from the Vestry minutes for June 4, 1919: "Mr. K. P. Lewis offered a motion that no fans bearing advertisements be allowed in the church, that fans now in the church bearing advertisements be removed and other fans be purchased in their stead at the expense of Mr. Lewis. Motion adopted."

20. *Durham Morning Herald*, May 4, 1924. Clipping contributed by Ben Roberts.

21. Burcham, "History of St. Andrew's," 2.

22. Anderson, *Durham County*, 264.

23. These men comprised the continuing core group. Other parishioners who served for a time and then left included (in order of appearance): F. S. Westbrook, Lawrence Cowan, G. E. Masters, J. A. Robinson, H. W. Knorr, W. M. Woodlief, J. J. Blacknall, H. B. Lindsey, W. B.

Miller, T. T. Dawson, G. B. Darracott, and Bailey Hobgood. At. St. Joseph's another chapter of the Brotherhood flourished, with J. Harper Erwin one of its leaders.

24. The moderate reform provided that after serving a three-year term a vestryman had to wait a year before standing for election again.

25. *The Christian Nurture Series* (edition of 1923).

26. Interview with Hugh White.

27. Bowman, "Bost," 43.

28. Brotherhood of St. Andrew, Chapter 225, Minutes, September 13, 1920.

29. Esser, "Rapid Growth and Financial Crisis, 1923–1941," 352–53.

30. Ibid., 356.

31. Vestry minutes, September 9, 1930.

32. Bost to K. P. Lewis, September 11, 1928, Kemp Plummer Lewis Papers.

33. Details with regard to the purchase of the Guthrie property are found in a circular letter of Kemp Lewis to "Dear Fellow Members of St. Philip's Parish, December 6, 1923" (Kemp Plummer Lewis Papers) about the Every Member Canvass and the proposed budget for 1924. The puzzle is this: why, in the prosperous 1920s, did the Vestry make no attempt to amortize the debt incurred by the purchase of the Guthrie property?

34. Kemp P. Lewis to Murray Jones, Secretary of the Vestry, September 5, 1932.

35. Esther Cowles Bost to Murray Jones, September 30, 1932 (tenses have been edited to fit our narrative).

36. Minutes of Annual Congregational Meeting, December 1, 1930.

37. *NCDJ* (1932), 53.

38. *NCDJ* (1934), 48.

39. Minutes of Annual Congregational Meeting, December 10, 1934.

40. Esser, "Rapid Growth and Financial Crisis, 1923–1941," 374.

41. L. F. Butler to the Vestry, St. Philip's Church, October 4, 1932.

42. St. Philip's YPSL to St. Philip's Vestry, October 30, 1932.

43. Resolution of Committee on the Parish Council to the Vestry of St. Philip's Parish, December 21, 1932; Vestry minutes, January 4, 1933; Bailey W. Hobgood, Acting Secretary of the Vestry, to J. H. Erwin, Jr., January 7, 1933.

44. Vestry minutes, February 8, 1933.

CHAPTER III. MISSION TO THE DEAF

Sources Consulted

Diocese of North Carolina, *Journal of the Annual Convention*
Durham Herald
Durham Morning Herald
Durham Sun
Interview with the Reverend James R. Fortune, 1977
Interview with Juanita Fortune, April 1995
Interview with James R. Fortune, Jr., June 1995
Kemp Plummer Lewis Papers, North Carolina Collection, University of North Carolina
    at Chapel Hill

Lawrence Foushee London and Sarah McCulloh Lemmon, eds., *The Episcopal Church in North Carolina 1701–1959*. Raleigh: Episcopal Diocese of North Carolina, 1987.
North Carolina Churchman

CHAPTER IV. THE RECTORSHIP OF DAVID YATES, 1935–1945

1. Reminiscence of Sibyl G. Powe and Louise Newton.

2. Holloway, *Unfinished Heaven*, 127–33; Vestry minutes, March 10, August 30, September 8, October 5, November 9, 1937.

3. Minutes of Congregational Meeting, January 29, 1936.

4. Minutes of meeting of Church School Faculty, January 29, 1936.

5. A. Stratton Lawrence to the Vestry, April 1937, in Vestry minutes.

6. Vestry minutes, December 30, 1937. The quality of the minutes of Vestry meetings depend on how the secretary to the Vestry conceived his function. Most secretaries thought a record of Vestry decisions was sufficient. To be sure, this record is useful to the historian but it is not always illuminating. However, during the Bost years Lester F. Butler and during Yates's rectorship Nat Gregory also recorded the discussions that preceded votes. They thus earned the gratitude of every historian of St. Philip's and offered a model for later secretaries.

7. Vestry minutes, February 10, 1938.

8. The euphoria over the success of the campaign was also dampened by news that the property adjoining the east side of the church building had been leased for construction of a bus station. Despite negotiations to moderate the noise, the sounds of buses roaring in, discharging their passengers, and "revving up" and departing continued to disturb Sunday morning worship services for nearly half a century. For the negotiations, see Vestry minutes, April 2, 3, 17, 30, 1941, and Minutes of Special Congregation Meetings, April 27, May 1, 1941.

9. Vestry minutes, September 9, 1939.

10. Annual Report of St. Andrew's Episcopal Church, Durham, N.C., for the year 1942, submitted by Josiah T. Carter, Priest in Charge, attached to the Minutes of the Annual Congregational Meeting, January 11, 1943, filed with Vestry minutes. On the action taken, see Burcham, "History of St. Andrew's," 2.

11. Minutes of meeting of Church School faculty, January 6, 1937.

12. Ibid., February 22, 1937.

13. Reminiscence of Sibyl G. Powe and Louise Newton.

14. Interview with J. Harper Erwin, Jr.

15. Annual Report of the Altar Guild, 1944, submitted by Elizabeth Felts Lyon, President, on January 29, 1945, attached to the Minutes of the Annual Congregational Meeting, January 29, 1945, filed with Vestry minutes.

16. The "Woman's Auxiliary," Scrapbook of Woman's Auxiliary, St. Philip's Church, 1952.

17. Interview with Angus and Priscilla McBryde.

CHAPTER V. THE RECTORSHIP OF CLARENCE R. HADEN, JR., 1945–1951

1. Unidentified newspaper article pasted in the "Scrapbook" of the Woman's Auxiliary of St. Philip's, 1952.

2. Interview with Allan Bone; Bone's reports to the Annual Congregational Meeting, January 12, 1948 and January 1949.

3. The exact figures are these. At the end of September 1945 the Parish House Building Fund stood at $19,741.50. Pledges totaled $25,804.10, but only $19,571.80 had been paid. (Additional funds came from rent on the corner service station.) The Vestry authorized Ben Roberts, the treasurer of the fund, to make one last appeal to the delinquents. The appeal was not without effect, for on January 14, 1946 the fund totaled $20,990.54. However, at the end of September 1945 the fund's loan to St. Philip's for the purchase of the Rectory amounted to $9,006.78. See the treasurer's reports filed with Vestry minutes, December 11, 1945 and February 11, 1946.

4. As of March 11, 1946 the drive secured in pledges $56,718.00. From that was deducted $935.93 for a concurrent "Reconstruction and Finance Fund" drive and $65.60 for a dinner in connection with the Building Fund Drive. See Vestry minutes, March 11, 1946.

5. Minutes of the Annual Congregational Meeting, January 12, 1948, filed with Vestry minutes.

6. Address of Bishop Edwin A Penick, May 10, 1949, *NCDJ* (1949).

7. Reports of Mrs. B. W. Roberts, January 12, 1948, and Mrs. J. M. M. Gregory, January 1949, both presidents of the Altar Guild; filed with minutes of the Annual Congregational Meeting in the Vestry minutes.

8. Reports of N. A. Gregory, Superintendent of the Sunday School, January 1948, 1949, and 1951, ibid.

9. Report of Mrs. A. W. Kennon, Director of the Pre-School Department, January 1949, ibid.

10. Reports of the Sunday School Choir for January 12, 1948 by Mrs. Charles A. Moore, Director, and for January 1949 by Mrs. J. M. Ruffin, Choir Mother; ibid.

11. Reports of John W. Harris, Warden and Secretary of the Order of St. Vincent, January 2, 1948 and January 1949, ibid.

12. Reports of Grant Hurst, January 12, 1948, and George L. Lyon, Jr., January 1949, both presidents of the YPSL; ibid.

13. Unidentified newspaper article in "Scrapbook" of the Woman's Auxiliary of St. Philip's, 1952.

14. Reports of Mrs. R. G. Hurst, President of the Woman's Auxiliary for both 1948 and 1949; ibid.

15. Reports of R. H. Leigh, January 12, 1948, and Frank H. Kenan, January 1949, both presidents of the Laymen's League; ibid.

16. On September 14, 1950, at a Special Diocesan Convention called to elect a Bishop Coadjutor, Haden led on the first two ballots in the lay order and was only two votes shy of leading in the clerical order. Richard H. Baker of Baltimore, Maryland, was ultimately elected on the seventh ballot. *NCDJ* (1951), last page.

CHAPTER VI. THE RECTORSHIP OF TOM TURNEY EDWARDS, 1951–1956

1. Minutes of called meeting of Search Committee, July 13, 1951, with the Vestry minutes.

2. Minutes of called Vestry meeting, August 19, 1951.

3. Memorandum, August 20, 1951, of William H. Ruffin, Senior Warden, on the Vestry

meeting of August 19, 1951. Roberts may have had in hand a newspaper clipping (now in the St. Philip's Archives) from the *Statesville Daily Record* giving a rave review of Edwards's activity there:

THE REV. MR. EDWARDS IN STATESVILLE FOR THE SUMMER

Another Boom—Speaking of booms—as we've been doing here lately—Trinity Episcopal church is experiencing something of a spiritual mushroom growth since the advent of Rev. Tom T. Edwards to the parish.

When Mr. Edwards was assigned this summer to the local church by Bishop Edwin A. Penick, the bishop told the church vestry that the new minister would "pack the church" even on the hottest summer days.

And he's been doing exactly that. Old faces that hadn't been seen in church in years and new ones not seen before are now in regular attendance.

The vestry (board of directors) would be planning a new church building were it not for one simple catch: Mr. Edwards goes back to Harvard this winter to continue his studies.

Speaking about the church and Statesville, the minister said he believed both have a great future. Under the proper leadership, the local Episcopal Church—now one of the smallest denominations here—could become one of the largest, he thinks.

It's too bad Mr. Edwards isn't twins, so one of them could go back to school and the other could stay here and continue to revitalize an old, old church which is showing signs of becoming younger by the day.

4. *Epistle to the Philippians*, June 29–July 5, 1952. The *Epistle to the Philippians* for the years 1952 to 1967 were contributed by Libby Roberts. The history of that period could not have been written without them.

5. Vestry minutes, November 1, December 11, 1951.

6. Interview with Mattie West.

7. Minutes of the monthly meeting of the Sunday School Faculty, December 10, 1951.

8. Ibid., January 14, 1952; also March 31, 1952.

9. Vestry minutes, February 11, 1952.

10. Anderson, *Durham County*, 397. Italics are mine.

11. Kenneth Podger, Chair, Every Member Canvass, to Members and Friends of St. Philip's Parish, November 14, 1952, filed with Vestry minutes.

12. "History of the Daughters of the King of St. Philip's Church, Durham, North Carolina" by Mrs. B. W. Roberts (Libby), Historian of the chapter, St. Philip's Archives.

13. Interviews with Dorothy Manning, Nancy Mason, and Elizabeth (Libby) Roberts.

14. *Epistle to the Philippians*, May 9–15, 1954.

15. "Trial Balloon" (ca. June 8, 1952), filed with *Epistle to the Philippians*. Edwards went ahead with the *Epistle* without Vestry authorization or budget. He requested an annual subscription fee of two dollars from every household. Later the *Epistle* was budgeted at $800.

16. *Epistle to the Philippians*, July 13–19, 1952.

17. Vestry minutes, April 9, 19, June 8, 1953; Bishop Edwin A. Penick to R. L. Fortune, Clerk of the Vestry of St. Philip's, June 28, 1953.

18. Watson enrolled in a graduate course taught by Harold T. Parker, the author of this chapter, and wrote his Master's thesis, "A Religious Profile of Durham, North Carolina 1880–

1930," under the supervision of Richard L. Watson, also of St. Philip's. Both mentors testify to his intellectual ability and to his promise as a research scholar and professor, if he had chosen that route.

19. Vestry minutes, November 1, December 11, 1951 and February 11, March 3, 1952; Treasurer's Report of Current Fund for 1951, filed with minutes of Annual Congregational Meeting, January 20, 1952, filed with Vestry minutes, January 1952.

20. Minutes of the Sunday School Faculty Meeting, May 31, 1952.

21. The *Epistle to the Philippians*, September 7–13, 1952; January 11–17, 1953. The scheduled program of the Men's Bible Class for the second semester reads:

January

11	Prof. John Hallowell
18	Prof. John Hallowell
25	Prof. Urban T. Holmes, Dept. of Romance Languages, U.N.C. "Concepts of Society and Religion in the Middle Ages."

February

1	Prof. Ray Petry, Dept. of Church History, Duke. "St. Francis."
8	Continued
15	Prof. John Hallowell
22	Prof. John Hallowell

March

1	Prof. Wallace Caldwell, Dept. of History, U.N.C. "Christianity and the Roman Empire—How and Why the Religion Survived."
8	Continued.
15	Prof. John Hallowell.
22	Prof. William Poteat, Dept. of Philosophy, U.N.C. Subject to be announced.
29	Continued

April

5	Prof. John Hallowell and
12	Prof. Claiborne S. Jones, Dept. of Zoology, U.N.C.
19	speaking on Science and Religion.
26	Exact dates to be set.

May

3	Prof. John Hallowell, alternating with
10	Prof. Robert Cushman, Dept. of Theology
17	Duke Divinity School, and
24	Prof. Preston H. Epps, Classics Dept., U.N.C.
31	Exact dates and topics to be announced.

22. Ibid., September 13–19, 1953.

23. Ibid., September 20–26, 1953.

24. "Excerpts from a Study of the Episcopal Church in the City of Durham, North Carolina by the Rev. Joseph G. Moore, Director," filed with Vestry minutes, September 14, 1953.

25. Sherman, "The Revival of Religion, 1941–1959," 404.

26. *NCDJ* (1951), 52.

27. Edwards contributed his personal wake-up call to the Diocese of North Carolina in his report as chair of the annual Diocesan Convention Committee on the State of the Church (1953). Appointed each year by Bishop Penick, previous committees had submitted reports sugary bland in tone and self-congratulatory in substance. Typical was the report of the preceding year, written by Rev. Edwin B. Jeffress, director of Christian Education for the Diocese. It opened: "The Committee on the State of the Church, having before it statistics for the years 1949, 1950, and 1951, notes steady and health growth to the Diocese of North Carolina" (*NCDJ* [1952], 135). In contrast, Edwards's report scintillated with epigram and bristled with statements that seemed to many listeners outrageous or even perverse. "The growth of enrollment in the church schools," it said, "was no more impressive than in the overall membership. . . . It should be plain from the above figures that there is no great cause for self-congratulation or complacency. . . . The Committee was unable to avoid the conclusion that in no way, by no stretch of the imagination, could the Diocese of North Carolina be considered as keeping pace with the progress of the State as a whole. . . . The state of the church is not good, or at least not as good as might reasonably be expected, all things considered" (*NCDJ* [1953], 140–45).

Basing its critical remarks on the falling off of the number of confirmations and the only slight gain in the number of communicants from 1951 to 1952, the report searched for areas of expansion. It recommended formation of parochial schools, stronger support of missions within the Diocese, and entry into such institutions of service as nursing home, homes for the aged, and hospitals (*NCDJ* [1953], 140–45).

Although reports of later years chided Edwards for basing his conclusions on slim statistics, they granted the substance of his charge: the Diocese of North Carolina was not doing very well. The report for 1954, for example, declared: "We cannot tell if the Diocese is running hard to stay in the same place or sitting quietly in the same place. We are forced to say it is not going forward" (*NCDJ* [1954], 141). Edwards had thus altered the tone and terms of the discussion.

28. "Address of the Bishop Coadjutor," *NCDJ* (1953), 93.

29. Vestry minutes, November 1, 1951.

30. "Address of the Bishop Coadjutor," *NCDJ* (1953), 99.

31. The calculated percentages of growth for St. Philip's *Church* were distorted by the failure of the editors of the Diocesan Survey to notice that the figures for 1920 (the base line) were for St. Philip's *Parish*, which then included St. Joseph's and St. Andrew's. Hence, we have started our tabulation with 1925, after those missions were dropped from the figures for St. Philip's Church.

32. "Excerpts from a Study of the Episcopal Church in the City of Durham, North Carolina." The order of the quoted sentences has been rearranged.

33. Ibid.

34. Ibid.

35. Ibid.; *Epistle to the Philippians*, March 27–April 2, 1955.

36. Sherman, "The Revival of Religion, 1941–1959," 415; interview with Albert Nelius.

37. *NCDJ* (1953), 56–57.

38. Ibid., 31.

39. *Epistle to the Philippians*, May 24–30, 1953.

40. Ibid., April 11–17, 1954.

41. Ibid., December 19–25, 1954.

42. Ibid.

43. Here is an outline of what was covered in the Lenten music course (1955).

On March 1: some basic considerations concerning Music, Worship, and their combination in Church Music.

On March 8: a detailed Study of the Service of Holy Communion, with explanation and examples of the musical portions, and how they relate to the whole service.

On March 15: a study of the services of Morning and Evening Prayer, with similar explanations and examples.

On March 22: brief remarks about the occasional services: The Litany, Holy Baptism, Marriages, and Funerals. Also a short description of the Canons and Rubrics concerning music which guide us in this field.

On March 29: hymns and anthems; A look at the Hymnal with some suggestions about a fuller use and appreciation of its many riches, together with a short discussion of the anthems we hear sung by our choir.

On April 5: the final session. A short talk about the use of the organ in Church Music, the use of other instruments, special musical performances, and the theory behind our Junior Choir program.

44. *Epistle to the Philippians*, April 17–23, 1955.

Answers to Music Quiz

1. b	8. b; d
2. c	9. b
3. b	10. a
4. c	11. c
5. Kyrie Eleison, a	12. b
Sanctus, d	13. c
Agnus Dei, b	14. a
Gloria in Excelsis, c	15. c
6. c	16. b
7. a	

45. *Epistle to the Philippians*, March 1–7, 1953.

46. *Durham Morning Herald.*

47. *Epistle to the Philippians*, March 13–19, 1955. See also, ibid., February 6–12, February 27–March 5, March 6–23, 20–26, and 27–April 2, 3–9, 1955; also February 12–18, 19–25, March 11–17, 1956.

48. Ibid., October 12–18, 1952; February 14–20, February 18–March 6, March 21–27, April 4–10, May 16–22, October 10–16, 1954; February 13–19, 20–26, October 16–22, November 27–December 3, 1955; September 9–15, 1956.

49. At Wilson (*NCDJ* [1955], 87); at Raleigh (Ibid., [1956], 78); at Chapel Hill (*Durham Morning Herald*).

50. In the *Epistle to the Philippians*, December 26, 1954–January 1, 1955. Edwards also quoted passages from the sermon Bishop Penick had preached at the recent Synod of the Prov-

ince of Sewanee, held at New Orleans on November 16 and 17. It was radical in its theological statement, "Proclaim the living Christ," but gradualist in its approach to reform: "It requires flexibility, time and room for the exercise of genuine enlightened—not darkened—public conscience. Millions of people cannot be forced at once." We shall review the stance taken by the clergy in a later chapter, when crisis seized St. Philip's and the Diocese of North Carolina.

51. Edwards to the Vestrymen of St. Philip's Church, April 29, 1955, filed with Vestry minutes. See also *Epistle to the Philippians*, March 27–April 2, 1955.

52. On the formation of St. Luke's, see *Epistle to the Philippians*, September 11–17, October 2–8, 23–29, November 6–12, November 27–December 3, 1955; January 8–14, June 3–9, September 16–23, 23–29, 1956; also Hollingsworth, *St. Luke's*, 2–14.

53. Facts and several phrases from Margo Wilson, "Have You Met?"; *Epistle to the Philippians*, September 9–15, 1956.

54. Material on the budget and the canvass can be found in the Vestry minutes, November 10, 1952, February 9, May 11, October 12, 1953, June 27, November 8, December 13, 1954; in the *Epistle to the Philippians*, January 4–10, November 1–7, 8–14, December 6–12, 1953, February 21–27, 1954, March 6–13, 1955, February 26–March 3, March 11–17, 1956; and in a letter of Edwards to E. K. Powe, September 10, 1954, in which the Rector expressed his exasperation: "Personally, I am tired of living all year in the suspense of wondering whether we are going to have adequate funds to meet our obligations, and I am sure the other members of the Vestry are too. I would like to see an intensive all-out [door-to-door] drive conducted over a period of a week—and then forget about it." The Vestry minutes for 1955 and 1956 have been lost.

55. *Epistle to the Philippians*, September 9–15, October 21–27, 1956.

56. Ibid., October 14–20, 1956.

57. Ibid., November 4–10, 1956.

CHAPTER VII. THE RECTORSHIP OF LEVERING BARTINE SHERMAN, 1957–1967

1. "A Message from Your Senior Warden," *Epistle to the Philippians*, October 21, 1956.

2. Bulletin of St. Philip's Church, March 24, 1957.

3. "Official Acts of the Bishop," *NCDJ* (1952), 63; (1953), 65–66; (1954), 63.

4. *NCDJ* (1951), 5; (1954), 40.

5. Interview with Sherman.

6. Penick to Sherman, February 15, 1957, Sherman's personal archive.

7. Denham to Sherman, undated but February 5, 1957 or soon after, Sherman's personal archive. The long quotation is abridged from a much longer letter.

8. Interview with Sherman.

9. *Epistle to the Philippians*, March 16, 1958.

10. Ibid., September 14, 1958.

11. Interview with Sherman. He has donated to the St. Philip's Archives a nearly complete collection of his sermons.

12. Sherman to London, February 13, 1957, Sherman's personal archive.

13. *Epistle to the Philippians*, September 18, 1960.

14. Ibid., October 5, 1958.

15. Memo of the Rector of St. Philip's Church to All Members of the Parish, December 16, 1958. For Sherman's account of the negotiations leading to the formation of St. Stephen's, see Appendix G.

16. Register of Communicants, St. Stephen's Episcopal Church (Durham); photocopy courtesy of St. Stephen's

17. *NCDJ* (1957), 214, 222; (1958), 216, 224; (1959), 202, 210; (1960), 212, 220.

18. *Epistle to the Philippians*, September 6, 1959.

19. Ibid., September 29, 1963.

20. Ibid., May 10, 1959. The complete text of Pizarro's essay on "Wedding Music" is reproduced in Appendix H.

21. Interview with Susan Rose.

22. *Epistle to the Philippians*, December 18, 1960.

23. Nicholson was junior warden in 1960–62 and 1965–66.

24. Cloister Garden Committee to Fellow Parishioners, October 18, 1961; plan submitted by Richard C. Bell, landscape architect; Hodges, "A Spot to Which One May Withdraw for Quiet, Prayer."

25. Dedication Service Litany.

26. The entire passage about the statuary is quoted from Hodges, "Impressive Sculpture Is Memorial Garden Addition."

27. Contemporary flyer entitled "The Burton Craige Ruffin Memorial."

28. *Epistle to the Philippians*, March 6, 1960.

29. Interview with Nelius. The spirituality of the group and of many other women of St. Philip's was expressed in the meditation of Mrs. Watts Carr, Jr., reproduced in Appendix I.

30. *Epistle to the Philippians*, November 12, and *The Three Musicians*, 1961.

31. Some of the other paintings displayed were Matthias Grunewald, *Angel Choir*, from the Isenheim Altarpiece; Hieronymus Bosch, *The Adoration of the Magi*; Rembrandt, *Moses*; William Blake, *The Ancient of Days*; Honoré Daumier, *Crispin and Scapin*; Vincent Van Gogh, *Crows in a Corn Field*; Henri Rousseau, *War*; Diego Rivera, *Man and Machine*; Pablo Picasso, *Lady with Artichoke, The Three Musicians*, and *Guernica*; Jose Clemente Orozco, *Struggling Mankind*.

32. *Epistle to the Philippians*, April 24, 1966.

33. Charles Greene, Director of Program, Episcopal Diocese of North Carolina, to Albert Nelius, December 12, 1966.

34. Bulletin of the eleven o'clock service, May 29, 1966. During the rectorship of Sidney Stuart Bost, J. A. Robinson, founder of the *Durham Sun* and outstanding civic leader and churchworker, had started a Bell Fund. But the money was invested for growth in the Hosiery Mill, which failed during the Great Depression. When Nelius revived the idea, it was first thought that a foundry in County Durham, England, would do the job, but that idea, too, collapsed because of expense. See *Citizens Press: Durham's Newest and Most Complete Weekly Newspaper*, December 14, 1939; Hodges, "Sister Cities in Joint Effort on Church Bell."

35. *Epistle to the Philippians*, no date (early June 1966).

36. Information for these four paragraphs is taken from the early pages of the *North Carolina Diocesan Journal (NCDJ)* for the eleven Conventions from 1957 through 1967.

37. "Address of the Bishop," *NCDJ* (1956), 64.

38. Interestingly, Thomas J. Pearsall, chair of the legislative committee that authored the

bill, was a leading layman of the Church of the Good Shepherd (Rocky Mount) and from 1955 to 1958 a member of the Diocesan Executive Council. See *NCDJ* (1956), 6. It may be noted also that on July 24, 1956 at 9:30 A.M. Bishop Coadjutor Baker, as president of the North Carolina Council of Churches, appeared before the General Assembly in Raleigh regarding the Pearsall Plan and presented the resolution adopted by the most recent annual meeting of the North Carolina Council of Churches as "the position of that body in the matter." See "Official Acts of the Bishop Coadjutor, 1956," *NCDJ* (1957), 132.

39. Anderson, *Durham County*, 432–35.

40. The story is told in Sherman, "The Revival of Religion, 1941–1959," 420–23. He uses the term "tragicomedy."

41. "Address of the Bishop," *NCDJ* (1960), 61.

42. "Journal of Proceedings," *NCDJ* (1960), 47–50.

43. "Report of Vade Mecum by the Reverend Edwin B. Jeffress, Jr.," *NCDJ* (1961), 159.

44. "Journal of Proceedings," *NCDJ* (1964), 55.

45. "Report of the Commission on Race," *NCDJ* (1965), 134, 143–44. At some point the title of the commission was changed from "Racial Subjects" to "Race."

46. Anderson, *Durham County*, 439–40; *Durham Morning Herald*, May 19, 20, 21; *Raleigh News and Observer*, May 20, 21, 22, 1963.

47. L. Bartine Sherman, "The Holy City," sermon preached on Sunday after Ascension, May 26, 1963, St. Philip's Archives. Two or three sentences in the sermon have been condensed; otherwise the excerpts have been printed intact.

48. "Report on the State of the Church," *NCDJ* (1960), 183.

49. "Report on the State of the Church: Diocesan Convention: Statistical Analysis," *NCDJ* (1959), 153.

50. Ibid., 154

51. "Address of the Bishop Coadjutor [Thomas Fraser]," May 14, 1963, *NCDJ* (1963), 83.

52. Two charters certifying to the organization of St. Philip's Parish (1880) and to the consecration of its church edifice (1912) might be cited as equally important. Sherman described his life as Fellow in a series of glowing letters to the congregation that were printed in the *Epistle to the Philippians* (April 12, 26, and May 24, 1964).

53. L. Bartine Sherman to "My dear friend," August 13, 1963; my précis of his paper is based on this summary and "reprint," St. Philip's Archives.

54. "Report of the Deputation to the 61st General Convention," *NCDJ* (1965), 107.

55. "Report of the Committee on the State of the Church," *NCDJ* (1965), 115.

56. Ibid.

57. Robinson, *Honest to God*, 114, 112, 132, 134. See also *Time*, December 25, 1964.

58. Ogletree, *The Death of God Controversy*, 75–108.

59. "Sharing Christ's Sufferings," a sermon preached by Sherman on Passion Sunday, April 4, 1965. The urban and ethical revolutions are mentioned in other sermons.

60. "The Letter and the Spirit," a sermon preached by Sherman on Trinity 12, September 5, 1965. For other references to Bishop Robinson, see "The Will to Serve," a sermon preached on Trinity 18, September 27, 1964; "I Know that God Is," Easter 2, April 24, 1966; "Which Way Shall I Pray?" 12th Sunday after Trinity," August 28, 1966.

61. "I Know That God Is," Easter 2, April 24, 1966; "God and the Saints," St. Philip and Saint James' Day, May 1, 1966; "The Name of God," Trinity 16, September 25, 1966; "The

Light of the World," Epiphany 1, January 8, 1967; "Right Judgement and Holy Comfort," May 14, 1967; "The Lordship of Christ," Easter 3, April 16, 1967; "What We Know and Don't Know about Eternal Life," Easter 4, April 23, 1967; "Worship and Love," Trinity 2, June 4, 1967. See also the parallel comments of Bishop Thomas A. Fraser on the "God Is Dead" theologians in a talk to teenagers in Charlotte, reported in *The Churchman*, June 1966.

62. Walker, *History*, 540.

63. Ibid., 541–42.

64. Cavert, *On the Road to Christian Unity*, 38.

65. "Official Acts of the Bishop Coadjutor, 1954," *NCDJ* (1955), 110.

66. "Official Acts of the Bishop Coadjutor, 1955," *NCDJ* (1956), 115; "Annual Report of the Woman's Auxiliary, 1957," *NCDJ* (1957), 187; "Official Acts of the Bishop Coadjutor, 1957," *NCDJ* (1958), 120.

67. "Address of the Bishop Coadjutor," *NCDJ* (1957), 117.

68. "Official Acts of Bishop Baker, 1960," *NCDJ* (1961), 70; "Official Acts of Bishop Baker, 1961," *NCDJ* (1963), 76. Bishop Baker also served on the Joint Commission on Ecumenical Relations, College of Preachers, Washington, D.C. ("Official Acts of Bishop Baker, 1963," *NCDJ* [1965], 72)

69. Cushman, "The Lund Conference: The Dilemma of the Ecumenist," in Cushman, *Faith Seeking Understanding*, 260.

70. Cavert, *On the Road to Christian Unity*, 54.

71. "Address of the Bishop Coadjutor," *NCDJ* (1957), 117–18.

72. "All One Body We," a sermon preached by Sherman on Epiphany 3, January 24, 1965, Consultation on Church Union Pulpit Exchange, Trinity Methodist Church, Durham. We have only an outline of the sermon preached at St. Philip's, entitled "Church Unity" and delivered on October 2, 1966.

73. *Epistle to the Philippians*, March 8, 1964.

74. Ibid., October 25, 1964. Italics are mine.

75. Ibid., October 31, 1965.

76. Transfers "In" and "Out" of St. Philip's were published in the *Epistle to the Philippians*, October 25, 1965.

77. Ibid., October 22, 1961.

78. Ibid., October 6, 1963.

79. Interviews with George Watts Carr, Jr., John Chatham, Dorothy Manning, Albert Nelius, and Susan Rose.

80. The Vestry paid tribute to Susan Rose in a resolution adopted unanimously at its meeting on December 8, 1964: WHEREAS Mrs. Susan Rose, although not a member of the Parish, served as a member of the Choir of St. Philip's for over fifteen years, and WHEREAS her conscientious performance of her duties, her unfailing regular attendance at rehearsals and services, and her ready spirit of cooperation, have provided an outstanding example to other members of the Choir; therefore BE IT RESOLVED that the Rector, Wardens, and Vestry of St. Philip's Church, on behalf of the entire congregation, note with deep regret Mrs. Rose's resignation from the Choir; do express to her our great and abiding gratitude for her long and faithful service; and do assure her of our continued friendship and very best wishes. *Epistle to the Philippians*, December 13, 1964.

81. "Stop and Look Both Ways," a sermon preached by Sherman on the Feast of the Dedi-

cation (Epiphany 4), January 31, 1965, outlining the list of commissions that had been already adopted.

82. Vestry minutes, January 13, 1965.

83. "Report of the Senior Warden," Annual Congregational Meeting, January 9, 1966.

84. Vestry minutes, December 9, 1965, and January 13, February 10, March 13, April 14, May 12, June 23, September 8, October 13, November 10, December 8, 1966; report of Buildings and Grounds Commission entitled "Some Immediate and Long-Range Needs," filed with Vestry minutes, March 13, 1966.

85. "Report for the Commission on Worship and the Liturgical Arts by George C. Pyne, Jr., Chairman," Annual Congregational Meeting, January 9, 1966. The *Epistle to the Philippians*, (May 30, 1965) reported: "Mr. Capen is currently holding the position of Organist-Choirmaster at the First Parish Church of Beverly, Massachusetts. He was born in Augusta, Georgia, in 1943, but grew up in New York State. He graduated from Boston University with the degree of Bachelor of Music in 1964, with a Major in Organ. A fairly new Episcopalian, he has served as summer Organist at All Saints' Cathedral in Albany for two years; while still in high school he was Organist-Choirmaster at St. Andrew's Episcopal Church in Scotia, New York. Since 1961 he has been Organist-Choirmaster in Beverly, directing both the adult choir and two children's choirs, as well as acting as coordinator of the First Parish Church Music series."

86. Report for the Commission on Worship and the Liturgical Arts, Annual Congregational Meeting, January 9, 1966.

87. *Epistle to the Philippians*, April 11, 1965, Palm Sunday.

88. On one occasion the Commission on Finance and Administration stepped beyond its financial duties: on the suggestion of George Williams and Richard L. Watson, both professors at Duke University, the commission recommended the immediate appointment of a parish archivist to collect and preserve the records of St. Philip's and the ultimate appointment of a historiographer to write its history. Although the commission, chaired at that time by Dr. Angus McBryde, strongly endorsed the two ideas, the Vestry did nothing. Vestry minutes, May 13, 1965.

89. "Report to Chairman of Vestry of St. Philip's Church from Chairman of Long-Range Planning Commission of St. Philip's Church," September 9, 1965, filed with Vestry minutes of that date.

90. Ibid.

91. Vestry minutes, June 23, 1966.

92. On the financial recommendations of the Finance Commission and the Vestry decision, see Vestry minutes, May 13, September 9, December 9, 1965; March 13, May 12, September 8, and December 8, 1966, as well as the minutes of the Annual Congregational Meeting, January 9, 1966. The actions of the Stewardship Commission are found in the Vestry minutes for April 14, May 12, June 23, November 10, and December 8, 1966.

93. "Report of the Commission on Social Action," Annual Congregational Meeting, January 9, 1966; Vestry minutes, January 13, February 10, March 13, April 14, May 12, October 13, November 10, December 8, 1966; "Compassion and Love," a sermon preached by Sherman on Trinity 11, June 4, 1967.

94. Four other commissions were operative. The Commission on Outreach and Public Relations, chaired by Dr. J. Caulie Gunnells, met once (April 22, 1965) and suggested a variety

of measures at the annual congregational meeting on January 9, 1966: (1) to call the attention of the Durham community to the activities of St. Philip's Parish, (2) to increase the personal contact of parishioners with each other, and (3) to welcome newcomers. Except for the purchase and installation of the Bell, which was already in the works, there is no record to show that these measures were ever implemented. The Youth Commission, chaired by Charles Steel, sponsored a very successful basketball program with several teams in the various age groups but failed to find a scoutmaster for a proposed St. Philip's Boy Scout Troop. The Commission on Christian Education (Adult) was apparently inactive, except to sponsor in title a very successful Lenten program organized in 1966 and 1967 by Sherman: it consisted of a School of Religion, jointly presented by all Durham Episcopal churches but meeting at St. Philip's and consisting of four mini-courses running concurrently on a weekday night in Lent. The Commission on Missions (or Mutual Responsibility and Interdependence), chaired by Dorothy Manning, was just getting under way. It persuaded the Vestry to appropriate $63, as half the cost of a trip by Randy Embree as EYC representative, to the Companion Diocese of Panama; the Episcopal Church Women donated the other half. It also persuaded the Vestry to authorize Sherman's appointment of Mr. and Mrs. Clarence Cobb as St. Philip's delegates on the Bishop's Pilgrimage to the Diocese of Panama. In addition, the commission sponsored two successful covered-dish suppers in the fall of 1966.

95. "Results of Interviews with Approximately 150 Communicants of St. Philip's," December 6, 1966, filed with Vestry minutes, December 8, 1966.

96. *Epistle to the Philippians*, December 4, 11, 1966.

97. *The Churchman*, February 1967, 5, 7–8.

98. Sherman to the Vestry, August 10, 1967; Sherman to the Parish, August 13; Senior Warden, E. K. Powe, to the Parish, August 15; *Epistle to the Philippians*, September 3, 17.

CHAPTER VIII. THE RECTORSHIP OF THOMAS EUGENE BOLLINGER, 1967–1978

1. E. K. Powe to the members of St. Philip's Episcopal Church, August 15, 1967.

2. Interview with James E. Davis.

3. *Epistle to the Philippians*, mid-November 1967.

4. *NCDJ* (1959), Parochial Statistics.

5. Obituary of Thomas Eugene Bollinger (1932–83), *NCDJ* (1984).

6. *NCDJ* (1961, 1968), Parochial Statistics.

7. *NCDJ* (1960), 8; (1961), 8, 46, 139–40.

8. *NCDJ* (1962), 189.

9. Ibid., 5, 7.

10. *NCDJ* (1963), 9; (1964), 9.

11. *The Churchman*, January 1966.

12. Ibid., May, September 1966. Clarence and Mary Lucy Cobb from St. Philip's were also members of the group.

13. *NCDJ* (1965), 5; (1968), 6. See photograph of the council in *The Churchman*, September 1967.

14. *NCDJ* (1961), 139–40.

15. *The Churchman*, January 1963.

16. Ella Harper, "Parish Has Campus Ministry: Holy Comforter Reaches out with College Student Center," *The Churchman*, January 1965.

17. "N.C. Diocese Opens New Frontier in Shopping Center at Burlington," *The Churchman*, January 1965. See also the account in *NCDJ* (1966), 122.

18. *Epistle to the Philippians*, September 3, 1967.

19. This interpretation of the situation is based on the footnoted narrative that follows, on interviews with several persons who worked closely with Bollinger (Richard and Anne Berkley, George Watts Carr, Jr., John and Hilda Chatham, James E. Davis, Harding Hughes, Dorothy Manning, Walter and Nancy Mason, Angus and Priscilla McBryde, Victor and Anne Moore, and E. K. Powe), and on personal reminiscence of Harold Parker.

20. *Epistle to the Philippians*, November 26, December 3, 1967.

21. Ibid., November 12, 26, 1967.

22. Ibid., January 21, 1968.

23. Ibid., February 18, March 3, 17, 1968.

24. Ibid., September 8, 29, 1968.

25. Ibid., March 31, 1968.

26. Ibid., April 28, 1968.

27. Ibid., March 3, 1968.

28. Ibid., March 3, 17, June 30, 1968.

29. Ibid., March 3, 1968.

30. Ibid., March 3, 31, 1968.

31. Ibid., March 31, August 11, 1968.

32. Vestry minutes, September 12, 1968.

33. Report of Ralph N. Strayhorn, Chair, Commission on Stewardship, Annual Congregational Meeting, January 19, 1969.

34. Report of C. L. May, Jr., Superintendent of the Church School, Annual Congregational Meeting, January 19, 1969.

35. Vestry minutes of St. Luke's Episcopal Church, December 4, 1968, recorded by the Vestry's Secretary, Seth Warner, professor of mathematics at Duke University, quoted in Hollingsworth, *St. Luke's*, 49.

36. *Epistle to the Philippians*, April 28, 1968; Vestry minutes, April 21, 1968.

37. Vestry minutes, April 21, 1968. In both lists the items varied in their order from time to time.

38. Gene Bollinger to the Vestry and Associate Vestry, May 6, 1968.

39. Vestry minutes, August 8, September 12, October 10, November 14, 1968; *Epistle to the Philippians*, August 11, September 29, October 27, 1968; Report of Commission on Stewardship, Annual Congregational Meeting, January 19, 1969, filed with Vestry minutes; interview with James E. Davis.

40. *Epistle to the Philippians*, November 10, 1968.

41. Vestry minutes, December 12, 1968.

42. Report of Commission on Stewardship, Annual Congregational Meeting, January 19, 1969, filed with Vestry minutes.

43. Report of Richard L. Watson, Chair, Commission on Worship, Annual Congregational Meeting, January 19, 1969. Watson had already reported these figures to the Vestry. Vestry minutes, August 8, 1968.

44. Report of Lawson Moore, Advisor to the Acolytes, Annual Congregational Meeting, January 19, 1969.

45. *Epistle to the Philippians*, June 30, 1968.

46. Ibid., October 13, 1968; Report of William K. Miller, Choirmaster, Annual Congregational meeting, January 19, 1969; Vestry minutes, October 1968, September 11, 1969.

47. William K. Miller to the Rector, Wardens, Vestrymen, and Members of the Parish, August 8, 1972, filed with Vestry minutes.

48. Bollinger's "Especially for Vestrymen . . . and Those Who Elect Them," Appendix J.

49. Interviews with Walter and Nancy Mason and Victor and Anne Moore; personal reminiscence of Harold Parker.

50. Report of C. L. May, Jr., Superintendent of the Church School, Annual Congregational Meeting, January 19, 1969; *Epistle to the Philippians*, September 8, 1968; Vestry minutes, September 12, 1968.

51. Report of Mark Featherston, President of EYC, Annual Congregational Meeting, January 19, 1969. At the folk mass the lessons were read by Harold Parker, Jane Elsevier, and Dick Featherston; the Meditation was by William Wells. *Epistle to the Philippians*, September 29, 1968.

52. *Epistle to the Philippians*, October 13, 1968.

53. Ibid., October 27, December 15, 1968; January 19, 1969.

54. Ibid., October 13, 1968.

55. Vestry minutes, February 13, May 9, 1969, January 8, April 9, June 8, 1970; Report of Senior Warden, Annual Congregational Meeting, January 18, 1970. Richard Parker reported the results of a questionnaire the diocesan Youth Commission had distributed "to as many young people as possible":

> One of the questions on our questionnaire was: "What do you think adults want most to say to young people?" Some of the answers from the Central Convocation were: "Be quiet." "Think what we think." And "Spend more time on useful things." Answers from the Northwest Convocation were: "Follow orders blindly." "Get down to earth and accept responsibility instead of protesting everything." Other significant answers from the Sandhills Convocation were: "You are too young to understand the problems of today." And "Finish what we have begun."
>
> The youth of today ironically do understand problems of the present, and many wouldn't consider finishing what their parents and others have begun. All eighteen-year-old boys are certainly aware of the draft, the war, and the bomb. Newspapers, magazines, and news reports are more abundant today than ever before. Oh yes, we are aware of the problems in the world, and they seem pretty dirty. The protesters around our country are simply people saying that they will not finish what their parents and others have begun because who wants to finish dirty jobs.
>
> We asked the young people what they most wanted to say to adults. From the Central Convocation we got answers like: "Please understand us and accept us for what we are. We need someone to understand us." "Please don't belittle our ideas." "Let me be myself. Let me run my own life." And "Don't treat us like yesterday's teen-agers." One guy from that same convocation said, "Most youth don't know how to talk to adults because the majority of adults don't know how to listen." Someone from the Northwest

Convocation said, "Try to regard us as people who are great now, not just people with great potential." . . . Trying to sum up all of these remarks into a sort of general trend or general thought turns out something like this: "The Church is a group of people who meet in a warm building on Sunday mornings who think they're saving the world by repeating worn-out prayers. Religion is my life with God and the way I feel about Him and the way I react to Him." This last remark from the Northwest Convocation and all of the other remarks will let you know what most of your young people really feel about Churches and religion. You see, the youth of today sometimes feels that singing sentimental hymns in a draggy musical style or sitting listening to a sermon that they don't agree with is pleasing to their parents. But they are not pleasing themselves, and they don't think that they are pleasing God.

Speakers like Father Malcolm Boyd are able to attract huge audiences on college campuses from coast to coast because the youth feel that such people are not selling "pie in the sky" but a faith related to such realities as the draft, the war, and problems of poverty. You know—real stuff. Tangible things that determine realistic life and death. Phrases like the "Fatherhood of God" and the "Brotherhood of Man" are no longer enough. We need more religious leaders to speak to us on a real tangible level. "Report of Richard Parker, President of Episcopal Young Churchmen, Diocese of North Carolina," *NCDJ* (1969), 148–50.

56. Interview with William Wells, Jr.; Vestry minutes, February 13, March 13, December 4, 1969. Wells was ordained priest during his stay at St. Philip's on June 24, 1969.

57. Vestry minutes, October 10, November 14, 1968.

58. Hollingsworth, *St. Luke's*, 46–55, gives an excellent detailed account of the ensuing negotiations. The sources for the St. Philip's side of the story are found in its Vestry minutes (November 25, December 12, 22, 1968, January 9, 19, February 13, March 13, April 10, 1969) and in interviews with George Watts Carr, Jr., James E. Davis, and Harding Hughes. Hughes later remembered: "When Bollinger asked me to serve on the liaison committee he was aware of my preliminary doubt about the desirability of merger. I explained to him that I had been very much involved in the organization and building of a new church in Winston-Salem (St. Timothy's) and that my perspective was that increasing, not decreasing, the number of churches in town represented progress. Bollinger somehow believed that it would be helpful to have on the committee a person initially dubious yet willing to examine advantages and disadvantages with an open mind." Hughes to Harold Parker, April 26, 1995.

59. St. Philip's Vestry minutes, January 19, 1969. Bollinger was summarizing a "white paper" he had prepared for a meeting of the "Liaison Committee" on December 31, 1968 and distributed to St. Philip's Vestry at its meeting of January 9, 1969.

60. Thomas A. Fraser, "Bishop Views Parish of the Future," *The Churchman*, November 1967.

61. Hollingsworth, *St. Luke's*, 48–49.

62. Vestry minutes, January 19, 1969.

63. Ibid., December 22, 1968.

64. Rev. J. E. C. Harris, Chair, Ecumenical Commission, Diocese of North Carolina, "Diocese Favors Grass Roots Ecumenism," *The Churchman*, February 1969.

65. Vestry minutes, March 13, 1969.

66. Ibid., March 12, May 24, 1970.

67. Ibid., May 24, June 11, 1971.

68. Ibid., May 14, 1970.

69. Ibid., May 14, 1970.

70. Yannella, "Race Relations at Duke University," passim. The following account is also based on interviews with Charles McKinney and Kara Miles Turner, two history graduate students at Duke University; on Miles, "Malcolm X University," and on Mrs. Turner to Harold Parker, August 17, 1995.

71. Anderson, *Durham County*, 425–26.

72. Miles, "Malcolm X University, "7–8.

73. Ibid., 9.

74. Ibid., 9–14.

75. Ibid., 14–15.

76. Ibid., 15–16. The development of the school was followed in a series of articles in the *Durham Morning Herald*, May 22, July 23, August 31, September 21, October 10, 19, 25, 26, 28, and in the *Raleigh News and Observer*, October 5, 10, 1969. Articles also appeared in the *Duke Chronicle*, October 28, November 3, 1969.

77. *NCDJ* (1968), 141.

78. *NCDJ* (1970), 154.

79. Vestry minutes, July 10, August 14, October 9, 1969.

80. Figures given were the quotas for 1969, *NCDJ* (1970), Disbursements.

81. Vestry minutes, December 4, 1969.

82. Ibid., May 14, 1970. "At this point, the Rector [Bollinger] introduced the Reverend William Spong and Mr. Robert Merritt, both of the Diocesan Council, who had been asked by Bishop Fraser to discuss the Diocesan program with the Vestry. . . . In the discussion that followed, it was emphasized that the purpose of the visit was a frank exchange of views. Mr. Spong and Mr. Merritt stated that they not only had come to inform but to gain an understanding of the views of the Vestry, and that the Council had adopted a policy of 'visitation.' Mr. [Harding] Hughes stated that, so far as the Malcolm X grant was concerned, there had been a strong disagreement on the part of many with the general principle [of the program] as well as with the specific grant to Malcolm X, and that in addition there had been a strong feeling that the wishes of the local clergy and parishioners had been disregarded (in much the same way apparently as the diocesan leaders felt that they had been over-ruled by the National Church). At the end of the discussion, Mr. Spong and Mr. Merritt withdrew with the thanks of the Vestry for the visit."

83. Interview with Harding Hughes, then senior warden.

84. Vestry minutes, November 13, 1969. The Vestry minutes of the decisive October meeting are missing.

85. Vestry minutes, November 13, December 4, 29, 1969, February 23, March 12, 1970; Annual Congregational Meeting minutes, January 18, 1970.

86. Report of Arch Bass, Chair, Every Member Canvass, December 19, 1969. In the next few days, an additional $1,000 was pledged.

87. *NCDJ* (1970), (1971), Disbursements.

88. *NCDJ* (1970), 188; (1971), 141.

89. *NCDJ* (1970), 74–75.

90. Communication of the Self-Study Committee with the Vestry was assured by Harold Parker. A member of both the Associate Vestry and the Self-Study Committee, he was the liaison between them. His reports to the Vestry of the work of the Self-Study Committee were summarized in the Vestry minutes for September 17, October 8, and December 10, 1970. They serve as a basis for this account. Communication of the Self-Study Committee with members of the congregation was achieved by long letters by Walter Mason. Two of these letters are reproduced in Appendix M.

91. Bollinger, "Rector's Report," Annual Congregational Meeting, January 24, 1971.

92. David R. Covell, Jr., and Sheila M. Kelly, "A Special Study of St. Philip's Church, Durham, North Carolina, Diocese of North Carolina" (January 11, 1971), 8. Later quotations within our summary are from this report.

93. Watts Carr, Jr., to the Vestry of St. Philip's Episcopal Church, January 20, 1971.

94. Bollinger, "Rector's Report," Annual Congregational Meeting, January 24, 1971.

95. Richard L. Watson, "Minutes of the Annual Congregational Meeting, January 24, 1971": "Mr. Bollinger, in addition to the [printed] rector's report, contrasted the pessimism of a year ago with the optimism of the present; he credited this to the leadership of the vestry and the work and enthusiasm of the self-study and called for vigorous participation by the parishioners in the work of the Church. Mr. [Watts] Carr, Jr., commenting on his report, emphasized that the self-study, important though it was, would be virtually worthless unless something were done about it, and he called for action."

96. Papers of the Annual Congregational Meeting, January 24, 1971.

97. Vestry minutes, February 4, 11, 1971.

98. Ibid., March 11, 1971.

99. Ibid., March 21, 1971.

100. Ibid., July 8, 1971.

101. Administrative Committee minutes, December 7, 1971.

102. In an extreme case—a caricature, to be sure, of the Vestry's operation (but then a caricature is only an exaggeration of the truth)—one of Bart Sherman's Vestries had spent eight months debating where to place a children's water fountain on the basement level of the parish house. The issue was finally resolved by referring it to a committee of Sherman, his wife, and one other person, who settled it within a week. See Vestry minutes, November 9, 1972.

103. Vestry minutes, October 5, 1971. The members of the Lay Ministry Subcommittee were Lillian Cahoon, Beth Caudle, Susan Chatham, Thomas Hampton, Abbott Lloyd, Angus McBryde (chair), Mary (Mrs. George C.) Pyne, B. W. C. Roberts, David Robinson, Norman Ross, George Sylvester, and W. L. D. Townsend. The members of the Community Action Subcommittee were Arch Bass, Jr., Ruth Bollinger, John Chatham, Margaret Davis, James E. Davis (chair), Glynn Fox, Lillian Lee, Carolyn London, Anne Moore, Sibyl Powe, and Julia Royall. They were all able church workers, chosen because they would broadly represent the experience and viewpoints of many segments of the parish. The Lay Ministry report is filed with the Vestry minutes of February 1972; the Community Action report was supposedly filed with the Vestry minutes of March 1972 but has been lost.

104. Vestry minutes, May 7, 1972.

105. Ibid.

106. Ibid., August 10, 1972; Bollinger to All Program Departments, August 1972. Daughters of the King was a special lay religious order and reported directly to the Rector. Episcopal

Church Women (ECW) was an excellent auxiliary organization that did its own in-house planning.

107. Vestry minutes, May 10, 1973; Bollinger to the Vestry, between June 1 and June 10, enclosing a thick packet of departmental reports, filed with Vestry minutes for that month.

108. Vestry minutes, December 10, 1970.

109. Bollinger, "Orientation Statement to Worship Committee," December 13, 1970.

110. "Recommendations of Rector to Vestry in Response to Liturgical Committee's Recommendations of 2/6/72," filed with Vestry minutes, February 10, 1972.

111. The situation was discussed at length in the Vestry. See Vestry minutes, February 10, 1972 and attached papers.

112. Administrative Committee minutes, June 6, 1972.

113. Executive Committee minutes, July 6, 1972; interview with Kent Otto.

114. Vestry minutes, December 12, 1973; Kent Otto, Choirmaster's Report, Annual Congregational Meeting, January 27, 1974.

115. Report of Lay Readers, Annual Congregational Meeting, January 27, 1974.

116. This account of the Education Department and EYC is based on their reports to the congregation in January 1973 and 1974 and on the personal reminiscences of Mina Hampton, Harold Parker, and David Ross.

117. The objectives were grouped under five headings: (a) Life and Its Setting: The Meaning and Experience of Existence; (b) Revelation: The Meaning and Experience of God's Self-Disclosure; (c) Sonship: The Meaning and Experience of Redemption; (d) Vocation: The Meaning and Experience of Discipleship; (e) The Church: The Meaning and Experience of Christian Community.

118. Report of Mina Hampton, Chair, Youth Action Committee, to the Annual Congregational Meeting, January 16, 1975. See also Vestry minutes of July 12, 1973 and May 4, 1974, as well as the reports of Charlotte Hampton and Kathy Moore, presidents of EYC, to the congregational meetings of, respectively, January 28, 1973 and January 25, 1976.

119. Report of the Lay Ministry Department, Annual Planning Session, June 10, 1973. Tense changed to fit the narrative.

120. Report of the Committee on Recruiting and Classification of Lay Talent, Annual Congregational Meeting, January 27, 1974.

121. "History of the Center City Church Council," Report of Lay Ministry Department, Annual Congregational Meeting, January 27, 1974.

122. Request to the Rector and Vestry, St. Philip's Episcopal Church, from the Board of Directors, Durham Nursery School Association, September 11, 1972, signed by Anne Moore, President, with Vestry minutes, September 14, 1972. See also Executive Committee minutes, September 5, October 24, 1972; Vestry minutes, September 14, November 9, 1972, February 8, May 10, 1973.

123. Vestry minutes, November 8, December 13, 1973, January 10, 1974; interview with Victor and Anne Moore.

124. Vestry minutes, December 14, 1972, January 11, February 8, 1973; conversation with Rita Bollinger.

125. Vestry minutes, April 12, 1973, with attached Pat Robinson's report, which is reprinted as Appendix P; interview with Victor and Anne Moore. The Moores were an example of where an entire family—Victor, Anne, and their two daughters—were affected by the weekend. In

later months Vic took his testimonial witness to other Faith Alive Weekends in other Episcopal churches.

126. Vestry minutes, April 7, June 10, 17, 1971; interviews with George Watts Carr, Jr., and Dorothy Manning.

127. Rothange, *Sizing Up a Congregation for New Member Ministry*, passim. It is possible that under Bollinger's successor, the Reverend C. Thomas Midyette III, St. Philip's entered the fourth stage of a *corporate* church.

128. Bollinger, Report of the Rector, Annual Congregational Meeting, January 26, 1975.

129. Vestry minutes, March 14, 1974: Bollinger to St. Philip's Finance Committee, no date.

130. The entire series is present in the St. Philip's Archives.

131. The transition was noted in the Vestry minutes.

132. Departmental self-evaluations, dated July 11, 1974, are filed with Vestry minutes of that date.

133. Report of the Senior EYC, Annual Congregational Meeting, January 26, 1975 and January 25, 1976.

134. Vestry minutes, September 12, 1974; Edward F. Glusman, Jr., Report of the Assistant Rector, and Harold Parker, Report of the Department of Education, Annual Congregational Meeting, January 26, 1975.

135. Report of the Department of Christian Education, Annual Congregational Meeting, January 26, 1975.

136. Vestry minutes, January 9, 1975; Harold Parker, "Brief Informational Report on St. Philip's Episcopal Church," November 1975, filed with Vestry minutes.

137. Vestry minutes, January 9, March 13, 1975.

138. Ted Glusman, Jr., Report of the Assistant Rector, Annual Congregational Meeting, January 26, 1975. There is no way to measure the increase in the number of *active* communicants, but the evidence points in that direction.

139. After a year of experimentation, the Youth Division dropped the program of the Educational Center of St. Louis. It did not seem theologically or psychologically suitable for St. Philip's. However, use of the program enabled St. Philip's to discover teachers who could communicate with teenagers: for the junior high schoolers Sam Simmons, a chemical engineer at Burroughs Wellcome who had been a football player at Auburn University, and his wife Yvette; and for the senior high schoolers, Mrs. Ann Zener, widow of the founder of the Duke University Psychology Department. She lured the senior high schoolers to study the Greek language and a Platonized version of Christian theology, and after class wisely counseled individual members of the class about their dating problems.

140. Dorothy Manning, Report of the Adult Education Division, Annual Congregational Meeting, January 25, 1976.

141. Joan Troy, Report of the Second-Hour Division, Annual Congregational Meeting, January 25, 1976.

142. Richard L. Watson, Report of the Senior Warden, Annual Congregational Meeting, January 25, 1976.

143. Victor Moore, Report of the Christian Social Action Department, Annual Congregational Meeting, January 25, 1976.

144. James R. Turner, "Report of the Episcopal Laymen's Association 1976," *NCDJ* (1977), 183.

145. Note of Bollinger to Richard L. Watson in Vestry archives; personal reminiscence of Harold Parker.

146. Vestry minutes, March 10, September 8, 1977; interviews with Richard and Anne Berkley and Katherine Bradley Johnson; personal reminiscence of Harold Parker. The early *cursillistas* from St. Philip's included Richard and Anne Berkley, Dwight and Pam Emory, Ruie and Ann Eubanks, Barney Hawkins, Katherine Bradley Johnson, Harold Parker, Ethel Reade, Jane Sharpe, and William Townsend.

147. Minutes of Vestry retreat, Governor's Inn, February 13, 1977.

148. Richard L. Watson, Report of Senior Warden, Annual Congregational Meeting, January 25, 1976.

149. Vestry to Members of St. Philip's Parish, November 23, 1976, filed with Vestry minutes.

150. Vestry minutes, June 9, September 8, November 10, December 18, 1977. Even after the Every Member Canvass in the fall of 1977, references to financial stringency appeared.

151. The figures, compiled by Thomas Rightmyer, read as follows:

	Communicants	Average Attendance
1967	521	360
1968	489	390
1969	559	461
1970	561	477
1971	572	390
1972	569	444
1973	572	407
1974	580	443
1975	589	421
1976	573	428
1977	563	379

152. Vestry minutes, August 11, September 8, 1977.

153. Ibid., December 8, 1977.

154. Ibid., December 18, 1977.

155. Ibid., February 9, 1978.

CHAPTER IX. SOME THOUGHTS ON THE RECTORSHIP OF C. THOMAS MIDYETTE III, 1978–1994

1. Members of the Vestries of 1977–78 who participated in the search included James David Barber, Robert W. Carr, Dwight Emory, Thomas Hampton, Priscilla McBryde, Anne Moore, Irene Nashold, Francis Newton, Harold Parker, Daniel Pearson, Charles Peete, Clifford Sanderson, Ralph Strayhorn, and Richard L. Watson.

2. "A Resolution of Thanksgiving for the Ministry of C. Thomas Midyette III at St. Philip's Church, unanimously adopted by the Vestry of St. Philip's Church in Durham, North Carolina, on January 24, 1994 and presented to the Reverend C. Thomas Midyette III in the presence of the congregation on the 30th day of January 1994."

3. Midyette, Report on the State of the Parish, 1993, Annual Meeting of St. Philip's Church, January 16, 1994. Profile and goals are quoted from Midyette's summary of them.

4. E. K. Powe, Senior Warden's Report, Annual Meeting of St. Philip's Church, January 16, 1994.

5. Jacqueline Harris to Harold Parker, May 13, 1995.

6. Clifford Wesley Sanderson, Report of the Associate for Street Ministry–Alcohol Counselor, Annual Parish Meeting, January 27, 1980. The counselors included David Ross, research associate of this history of St. Philip's.

7. Reports of William M. Harrison, Jr., Chair, Community Kitchen Committee, and Richard L. Watson, Chair, Program Area of Social Action, Annual Parish Meeting, January 1981; Report of Richard L. Watson, Chair, Community Kitchen Committee, Annual Parish Meeting, September 25, 1983, December 16, 1984; C. Thomas Midyette III, Annual Report to Parish Meeting, December 6, 1987; Memorandum of John Bowman to Gert Embree, December 3, 1990.

8. Vestry minutes, January 21, February 11, 1982.

9. The Vestry minutes for the Emerald Isle retreat are missing; the Resolutions of February 20, 1982 are with the Vestry minutes of March 11, 1982. The account of the retreat is based on information contributed by Midyette and Steel.

10. Reports of the campaign are found in Vestry minutes, March 11, April 22, May 20, July 8, August 12, September 9, October 14, November 11, and December 9, 1982; Midyette, Report on the State of the Parish, December 11, 1983.

11. Midyette, Report on the State of the Parish, December 11, 1983.

12. Minutes of the Annual Parish Meeting, December 16, 1984, December 8, 1985, January 15, 1989; Reports of Richard L. Watson, December 8, 1985, January 15, November 19, 1989; Watson to Ms. Lynn Bradley of the Grants Committee, October 28, 1985, and to Rev. William E. Smyth, Chair, Parish Grants Commission, 1987, of the Diocese of North Carolina. The facts and even their phrasing in this paragraph are drawn for the most part from Watson's reports and letters.

13. Minutes of Special Parish Meeting, November 14, 1982.

14. Minutes of Parish Meeting, September 23, 1983.

15. Minutes of Annual Parish Meeting, December 16, 1983; Report of Harold Parker, Chair, Christian Education Commission, to Annual Parish Meeting, December 16, 1984; Mina Hampton, Report of Preschool and Grade School Sunday School, December 16, 1984; Midyette, State of Parish Report, December 8, 1985, December 7, 1986, December 16, 1987; Mina Hampton, Report on Christian Education, January 15, 1989, November 25, 1990; Elizabeth Steel, Chair, Christian Education Commission, and Mina Hampton, Christian Education Director, Annual Report of the Christian Education Commission, January 17, 1993.

16. These brief remarks on the Journey to Adulthood program are largely based on interviews with Tom Midyette and Amanda J. Smith, on her reminiscent printed article "The Genesis of the 'Journey to Adulthood' Program: Stories Behind the Journey," and on a flyer advertising the published curriculum. For confirming evidence see Midyette, Report to the Parish, December 6, 1987, December 16, 1993; Mina Hampton, Report to the Parish on Christian Education, January 15, 1989, November 25, 1990; Richard Dideriksen, Report of the Youth Commission, November 19, 1989; Elizabeth Steel, Report of the Christian Education Commission, January 12, 1992.

17. Midyette, Report to the Parish, December 6, 1987.

18. Testimony to the influence of the program in the Diocese of North Carolina appeared in an article in the diocesan *Communicant* (April 1995) written by Cathy Bouggy, youth director at Christ Church, Raleigh. Entitled "Middlers: Made in the Image of God," the article read:

Brown Summit—Over the weekend of March 3–5, nearly 125 young people gathered at the Summit for the Winter Middlers' Conference and—although our theme was "Sexuality: God's Gift to Us" and our motto was "Celebrate Your Self"—believe it or not, we didn't talk about sex all weekend. However, this wonderful group of young people began to answer the following questions: What does it mean to be made in the image of God? Why do you not have to prove your gender? Why is it safe to be yourself? What does it mean to be comfortable in your own body? How can we celebrate being ourselves? Here are some of their answers. "I learned that everybody is beautiful in his or her own way because we are all made in the image of God. I learned that, no matter what, I belong, I am someone. I learned that I don't have to be perfect, but I do have to be myself . . . and I am pretty cool. God strengthens me to be able to do and be all things I want to do and be. I am beautifully made in the image of God and that can't be taken away. I have learned that I am beautiful in God's eyes, and those are the ones that matter." Amanda Hughes and David Crean [both of St. Philip's] and their incredible staff of young people and adults guided the Middlers through a weekend of dialogue in small group and large group, intermingled with beautiful music, spiritually uplifting worship, funny games, crazy dancing, moving meditation, and dramatic improvisation. Music leadership for the weekend was a wonderful gift from Chris Goers of Atlanta. It was quite obvious that this group came away with a better sense of who they are as young men and young women made in the image of God. I know that I did!

19. Midyette, Report on the State of the Parish, November 25, 1990; John Bowman, Report of Social Ministries Committee, December 3, 1990, January 8, 1992; Neil Boothby and Ed Embree, Report of Social Ministries Committee, January 16, 1994.

20. Bowman, Report of Social Ministries Committee, December 3, 1990, January 8, 1992; Boothby and Embree, Report of Social Ministries Committee, January 16, 1994.

21. Boothby and Embree, Report of the Social Ministries Committee, January 17, 1993, January 16, 1994.

22. Midyette, Report on the State of the Parish, January 16, 1994.

23. Board of Directors, The Liberian Refugee Tutorial Program, Abidjan, Ivory Coast, to James David Barber, December 28, 1992; Barber to St. Philip's Committee on Liberia, April 20, 1993; Mrs. Christine Norman, President, Liberian Refugee Tutorial Program, Abidjan, Ivory Coast, to Barber, May 17, October 6, 1993; Barber to Christians in St. Philip's who sent funds for the rescue of children from Liberia, December 4, 1993; Neil Boothby and Ed Embree, Report of the Social Ministries Committee, January 16, 1994; *Raleigh News and Observer*, February 25, 1994; *The Tutorial Bell*, June 26, 1994.

24. Midyette, Parish Report, January 1981.

25. Thomas Rightmyer, Report of Chair of Priest Associates, January 12, 1992.

26. Barney Hawkins, Report of Lay Pastoral Assistant, January 28, 1979.

27. Jess Gaither, Report of Assistant Rector, January 27, 1980; Midyette, Parish Report, January 1981.

28. Midyette, Report on the State of the Parish, December 11, 1983.

29. Midyette, Report on the State of the Parish, December 8, 1985, January 15, 1989.

30. Midyette, State of the Parish Report, December 8, 1985; Rightmyer, Report of Priest Associates, January 12, 1992.

31. Midyette, Report on the State of the Parish, November 19, 1989; Richard Dideriksen, Report of the Youth Commission, November 19, 1989.

32. Katherine B. Johnson, Report of Coordinator of Ministries, January 12, 1992; Midyette, Report on the State of the Parish, January 16, 1994.

33. Praise of staff appears in every one of Midyette's annual reports.

34. Treasurer's Report, December 31, 1978, December 31, 1980.

35. Minutes of Annual Parish Meeting, January 27, 1980.

36. Minutes of Annual Parish Meeting, January 16, 1983; Treasurer's Report; Statement of Cash Receipts and Disbursements for the Year Ended December 31, 1982.

37. Midyette, Report on the State of the Parish, December 7, 1986, January 15, November 19, 1989.

38. Midyette, Report on the State of the Parish, January 16, 1994.

39. Rhodes Craver, December 1991 Treasurer's Report, January 1, 1992.

40. Midyette, Report on the State of the Parish, January 17, 1993; David Shumate, Report of the Treasurer, January 13, 1993.

41. Dorothy Smith, Report of the Junior Warden, January 10, 1993; the estimate was made informally in conversation with the author. Another casualty of the budget crunch was the proposed renovation of the multipurpose meeting room that housed the parish library. From 1982 to 1993 the parish librarians were Drs. Harold and Louise Parker. They were aided by the counsel and work of an excellent committee which also included Charlotte Abbate, Helen Dorward, Mina Hampton, George Pyne, and Frances Thackston. Building on the select collection that had been started by David Yates, they more than doubled the number of books until the collection formed what Tom Rightmyer termed "the best parish library he had ever seen." The library's collection was built totally by donations, selectively accepted. Each year ECW gave a sum of money to purchase a book apiece as a memorial of each ECW member who had died the preceding year. ECW authorized the librarians to purchase those books that were appropriate both to the deceased and to the needs of the library. Clarence and Mary Lucy Cobb, Harold and Louise Parker, George and Mary Pyne, and David and Dorothy Smith together gave several hundred books. The estate of Thomas Eugene Bollinger donated his scholarly library of eight hundred volumes, especially rich in theology; the librarians accepted five hundred and distributed the rest to other churches and to seminaries that needed them. Louise Parker, as a founder and third president of the North Carolina chapter of the national Church and Synagogue Association, reviewed books for the association's bi-monthly bulletin and donated them to the parish library. Frances Thackston, who had been librarian at Duke University and the Library of Congress, personally typed a shelflist of the 1,500 books, and Harold Parker reconstructed the author and subject catalogues. What was then needed was new bookshelves, displays, furniture, and drapes, so arranged as to invite readers to come in and browse. George Pyne, with his usual genius, both drew up an attractive architectural plan and by a personal presentation persuaded the Vestry to place the sum of $8,000 in the estimated budget for 1989. However, when the Every Member Canvass failed to raise sufficient pledges for this and other enterprises, the library item was the first to be cut. Aided by

the ingenuity of Mina Hampton in finding and arranging old pews and hand-me-down book-shelves, the librarians continued to make do with what they had. Harold Parker, Report of the Christian Education Commission, December 16, 1984; Mina Hampton, Report of Christian Education, January 15, 1989.

42. Tom Metzloff, Report of the Stewardship Committee, November 19, 1989.

43. Midyette, Report on the State of the Parish, January 17, 1993.

44. E. K. Powe, Report of the Stewardship Commission, January 12, 1992.

45. Minutes of Annual Parish Meeting, January 17, 1993; Neil Boothby and Ed Embree, Report of the Social Ministries Committee on Transitional Housing, January 17, 1993.

46. Homily Given by the Reverend C. Thomas Midyette III, August 1, 1993, for Thomas Hamlin Hampton, Sr.

Bibliography

PRIMARY SOURCES

Oral Interviews
Richard and Anne Berkley
Sarah Lindsay Boettke
Allan H. Bone
Mrs. A. E. Burcham
Lester C. Butler
George Watts Carr, Jr.
John and Hilda Chatham
James E. Davis
J. Harper Erwin, Jr.
The Reverend James R. Fortune
The Reverend James R. Fortune, Jr.
Juanita Fortune
Nathaniel Gregory
Mina Hampton
Jacqueline Harris (by telephone)
Kate Herndon
Harding Hughes
Katherine Bradley Johnson
Florrie Jones
Richard and Kitty Leigh
Angus and Priscilla McBryde
Nelson McGary
Charles McKinney
Dorothy Manning
Walter and Nancy Mason
The Reverend Charles Thomas Midyette III
Victor and Anne Moore
The Reverend Albert A. Nelius
Kitty Nelson
Kent Otto (by telephone)
E. K. Powe
The Reverend Thomas N. Rightmyer
Elizabeth (Libby) Roberts
Susan Rose
David Ross
The Reverend Levering Bartine Sherman
Amanda Smith

Charles L. Steel IV (by telephone)
Kara Miles Turner
Claudia Powe Watkins
William Wells, Jr. (by telephone)
Mattie West
Hugh White

Manuscript Evidence
William A. Erwin Papers, Division of Manuscripts, Duke University Library
Kemp Plummer Lewis Papers, North Carolina Collection, University of North Carolina at
　Chapel Hill
St. Philip's Episcopal Church, Durham, North Carolina, Archives (referred to throughout as
　St. Philip's Archives). Except for records currently in use, they are housed in the Division
　of Manuscripts, Duke University Library. They include:

(a) *Epistle to the Philippians*, 1952–1994
(b) Minutes of the meetings of the Church School Faculty, 1935–1956
(c) *Parish Register*
(d) Roberts, Mrs. B. W. "History of the Daughters of the King of St. Philip's Church,
　　Durham, North Carolina" (typewritten).
(e) Scrapbook of Episcopal Church Women, 1952
(f) Sermons and instructional essays by (in order of delivery) David Yates, Tom Turney
　　Edwards, Robert M. Watson, Levering Bartine Sherman, Albert Nelius, Thomas
　　Eugene Bollinger, and Charles Thomas Midyette III
(g) Vestry minutes and associated papers, comprising the treasurers' reports and the
　　reports presented to the annual congregational meeting, 1914–1920, 1930–1955,
　　1958–1994

Printed Evidence
The Book of Common Prayer and Administration of the Sacraments and Other Rites and Cere-
　monies of the Church, According to the Use of the Protestant Episcopal Church in the United
　States of America: Together with the Psalter, or Psalms of David. New York: Thomas N.
　Stanford, 1856. Certified as conforming to the Standard Book by Jona. M. Wainwright,
　Provisional Bishop of the Diocese of New York, Easter, 1854.
The Churchman, 1963–1969
Diocese of North Carolina, *Journal of the Annual Convention* (referred to throughout as
　NCDJ), 1876–1978
Durham Daily Sun
Durham Morning Herald
Durham Sun
Hodges, Betty. "Impressive Sculpture Is Memorial Garden Addition." *Durham Morning*
　Herald, February 2, 1964.
———. "Sister Cities in Joint Effort on Church Bell." *Durham Morning Herald*, ca. 1965.
　(Clipping in St. Philip's files.)

―――. "A Spot to Which One May Withdraw for Quiet Prayer." *Durham Sun*, May 17, 1963.

Pike, James A., and W. Norman Pittenger. *The Faith of the Church*. New York: Seabury Press, 1964.

Raleigh News and Observer

Robinson, John A. T. *Honest to God*. Philadelphia: Westminster Press, 1963.

Smith, Amanda. "The Genesis of the 'Journey to Adulthood' Program." 1995.

The Tobacco Plant

The Tutorial Bell: Quarterly Newsletter of the Liberian Tutorial Program

Wilson, Margo. "Have You Met?" *Durham Sun*, October 5, 1956.

SECONDARY ACCOUNTS

Anderson, Jean Bradley. *Durham County: A History of Durham County, North Carolina*. Durham: Duke University Press, 1990.

Bowman, Phyllis. "Sidney Stuart Bost." Paper presented to the General Meeting of the Episcopal Church Women of St. Philip's Church, Durham, January 1977.

Brawley, James S. "The Episcopal Church in North Carolina, 1883–1900." In London and Lemmon, *The Episcopal Church in North Carolina*, 276–305.

Burcham, A. E. "History of St. Andrew's Church, Durham, N.C." 1944. Revised in 1961 for the First Homecoming Day, July 16, 1961. (Photocopy of typed manuscript contributed by Mrs. Matthew West.)

Buxton, Jarvis. "Missionary and Educational Enterprise." In *Sketches of Church History in North Carolina: Addresses and Papers by Clergymen and Laymen of the Dioceses of North and East Carolina*. Wilmington: Wm. L. De Rosset, Jr., 1892.

Cavert, Samuel McCrea. *On the Road to Christian Unity: An Appraisal of the Ecumenical Movement*. New York: Harper and Brothers, 1961.

Cushman, Robert E. *Faith Seeking Understanding: Essays Theological and Critical*. Durham: Duke University Press, 1981.

Durden, Robert F. *The Dukes of Durham*. Durham: Duke University Press, 1975.

Esser, George H. "Rapid Growth and Financial Crisis, 1923–1941." In London and Lemmon, *The Episcopal Church in North Carolina*, 346–85.

Gant, Margaret Elizabeth. *The Episcopal Church in Burlington, 1879–1979: One Hundred Years in History*. Undated.

Hollingsworth, Harry D. *St. Luke's Episcopal Church, Durham North Carolina, with Supplements for 1982–1986 and 1987–1991*. Durham: St. Luke's, 1992.

Holloway, Betsy. *Unfinished Heaven. Durham, North Carolina: A Story of Two Schools*. Orlando, Fla.: Persimmon Press, 1994.

Lloyd, Roger. *The Ferment in the Church*. New York: Morehouse-Barlow, 1964.

London, Lawrence Foushee. *Bishop Joseph Blount Cheshire: His Life and Work*. Chapel Hill: University of North Carolina Press, 1941.

―――. "The Diocese in the First Decades of the Twentieth Century, 1901–1922." In London and Lemmon, *The Episcopal Church in North Carolina*, 308–45.

London, Lawrence Foushee, and Sarah McCulloh Lemmon, eds. *The Episcopal Church in North Carolina, 1701–1959*. Raleigh: Episcopal Diocese of North Carolina, 1987.

McBryde, Priscilla. "Bishop Joseph Blount Cheshire, D.D. (1850–1932)." Paper presented to the four chapters of the Episcopal Church Women of St. Philip's Church, Durham, 1977.

Miles, Kara. "Malcolm X University: Institution Building during the Black Power Era." Seminar paper written for History 310S, Professor Raymond Gavins, Graduate School of Duke University, May 3, 1993.

Ogletree, Thomas W. *The Death of God Controversy*. Nashville, Tenn.: Abingdon Press, 1966.

Rothange, Arlin J. *Sizing Up a Congregation for New Member Ministry*. N.p.: Seabury Press, n.d.

Sherman, L. Bartine. "The Revival of Religion, 1941–1959." In London and Lemmon, *The Episcopal Church in North Carolina*, 388–425.

Walker, Williston. *History of the Christian Church*. Revised by Cyril C. Richardson, Wilhelm Pauck, and Ed Robert T. Handy. New York: Charles Scribner & Sons, 1959.

Watson, Robert M., Jr. "A Religious Profile of Durham, North Carolina, 1880–1930." M.A. thesis, Duke University, 1964.

Yannella, Don. "Race Relations at Duke University and the Allen Building Takeover." M.A. thesis, Duke University, Oral History Program, 1985.

Index

An index looks backward, to what has been said in the book. A thoughtful index also looks forward, as an invitation to further inquiry, study, and reflection. It raises questions. For example, consider the item Diocese of North Carolina and its subheads and its bishops. What were the interrelationships of the Diocese and its bishops to St. Philip's and its parishioners and rectors? What happened and why? What does the book say? What information does this history offer? What else would we like to know? Similarly, with regard to items entitled Woman's Auxiliary/Episcopal Church Women, or Youth, or many others: what happened over time and why? What else would we like to know? Such questions, open-ended in perspective, lead us far afield and deepen our understanding.